Women, Crime, and Justice

Women, Crime, and Justice

Balancing the Scales

Elaine Gunnison, Frances P. Bernat,
and Lynne Goodstein

WILEY Blackwell

Registered Office
John Wiley & Sons Ltd, The Atrium, Southern Gate, Chichester, West Sussex, PO19 8SQ, UK

Editorial Offices
350 Main Street, Malden, MA 02148-5020, USA
9600 Garsington Road, Oxford, OX4 2DQ, UK
The Atrium, Southern Gate, Chichester, West Sussex, PO19 8SQ, UK

For details of our global editorial offices, for customer services, and for information about how to apply for permission to reuse the copyright material in this book please see our website at www.wiley.com/wiley-blackwell.

Library of Congress Cataloging-in-Publication Data

Names: Gunnison, Elaine, author. | Bernat, Frances P., author. | Goodstein,
   Lynne, author.
Title: Women, crime, and justice: balancing the scales / Elaine Gunnison,
   Frances P. Bernat and Lynne Goodstein.
Description: Chichester, West Sussex, UK: John Wiley & Sons, [2017]
Identifiers: LCCN 2016004472 | ISBN 9781118793466 (pbk.)
Subjects: LCSH: Female offenders—United States. | Women—Crimes
   against—United States. | Sex discrimination in criminal justice
   administration—United States.
Classification: LCC HV6046 .G86 2017 | DDC 364.082/0973—dc23 LC record available at http://lccn.loc.
gov/2016004472

A catalogue record for this book is available from the British Library.

Cover image: GettyImages/©Darrin Klimek

Set in 9/12pt Meridien LT Std by Aptara

Printed in Singapore by C.O.S. Printers Pte Ltd

1 2017

For the wonderful boys in my life who make each day special:
Daniel, Zachary, and Evan

For my parents: Walter and Jane

—E. G.

To Nick and Emily, may your days be as filled with love and joy
as mine have been with you in my life.

—F. B.

To Grace, whose love of reading will be a source of great joy
throughout your lifetime.

—L. G.

Contents

Acknowledgments

This book would not have been possible without the support of many individuals. First, and foremost, we must thank Wiley Blackwell for providing us with an opportunity to write this important book. A special thanks to Julia Teweles, our original Acquisitions Editor, who helped us with our proposal and the initial stages of this work. We also are greatly appreciative of our Editors, Julia Kirk and Haze Humbert. They continued our project through the several internal and external reviews of our chapters and have provided us with much needed support and guidance for the past two years. We also would like to thank Project Editor Allison Kostka for her assistance, Copy Editor Joanna Pyke for her insightful revisions, and our several anonymous reviewers who provided substantive recommendations for improving this academic work. A great big thank you to Jane Poore at Seattle University and Erick Martinez at Texas A&M International University. We owe particular thanks to these two graduate students, Jane and Erick, who were instrumental in helping us edit our chapters and compile the ancillary materials that accompany this book. Jane worked tirelessly on obtaining recent materials for the chapters, editing the chapters, and completing significant portions of the ancillary materials, producing great work on short timelines. She was a pleasure to work with, and she truly was an asset to this project. Erick brought charm and attention to the needs of having a male voice in editing the chapters, finding ancillary materials that provide a gender and ethnic/racial balance to the completed project. He was also a pleasure to work with and Fran valued his help and contributions to this book.

Elaine would like to thank the Dean's Office of the College of Arts and Sciences at Seattle University for their support. Additionally, Elaine would like to thank her Criminal Justice Department colleagues and staff who have been so supportive throughout this project: Jackie Helfgott, Matthew Hickman, Stephen Rice, Peter Collins, William Parkin, David Connor, Kate Reynolds, and Devin MacKrell. Finally, Elaine would like to thank her family, friends, and loved ones who cheered her along the way. Since Elaine arrived at Seattle University in 2004, Jackie Helfgott has been an incredible mentor and friend. Thanks, Jackie, for all the lunches, coffee breaks, advice, and attempts to get Elaine to de-stress or get her from a Type A to a Type A-. Your friendship means the world to Elaine. Elaine is also thankful to her husband, Daniel, who has yet again stood by her side and offered his support. Thanks, Daniel, for always being there, cheering her on, and being the best friend ever. Elaine is also so thankful for her wonderful little boys, Zachary and Evan. Both boys are smart, kind, loving, caring, talented, and hardworking, and Elaine is so proud to be their Mom. She will always cherish their Summer bike rides, the "whale pool," and all of their silly moments. Elaine must also thank her miniature dachshund, Snaps, who slept next to her almost the entire time when she worked on this book. Elaine waited her whole life for Snaps, and she was well worth the wait. Elaine would also like to thank her many friends from graduate school (Lo Presser, Julie Kiernan-Coon, Lisa McCartan-Kim, Randy and Kati Pagulayan) and beyond (Katie and Paul Windle, the Collins family) for their encouragement. Last, but not least, Elaine would like to thank her parents, Walter and Jane, for all their support. Thanks for all your phone calls, visits, and words of wisdom.

Fran would like to thank the Dean's Office of the College of Arts and Sciences at Texas A&M International University for their support. The college's executive assistant, Hilda Dennis, provided much needed office staff support for which Fran is very grateful. In addition, TAMIU library provided additional support with legal and academic research. In particular, we want to thank Jeanette Hacker for her diligence and help in finding difficult literary materials. Fran would also like to extend a thank you to her wonderful colleagues who have provided her with stimulating academic conversations and fun over the years. Of particular note she wishes to thank the friendship and colleagueship of: Faith Lutze, Jacqueline Helfgott, Mary Stohr, Daniel Georges-Abeyie, Marie Griffin, Tom Winfree, Larry Mays, Otwin Marenin, Allen Brawley, Sara Aléman, Emilia Martinez Brawley, Jean Hong, Candace McCoy, Rich Gitelson, Joy Pollock, Lynette Lee, and Paz Zorita. Fran wishes to thank the academic colleagueship from members of the Academy of Criminal Justice Sciences and the American Society of Criminology: Alida Merlo, Meda Chesney-Lind, Rosemary Gido, Loraine Gelsthorpe, Merry Morash, Angela Gover, Delores Jones-Brown, Sesha Kethineni, Leanne Alarid, Christine Sellers, Brenda Blackwell, Frankie Bailey, Joanne Belknap, Kimberly Dodson, and many others who have devoted their time and much needed attention to the study of women and criminal justice. Fran also warmly thanks her family and friends who make life a joy every day. She is proud of her children and knows that they help to make the world safe with their kind attention to the needs of others. As adults, her children continue to espouse the best of what individuals can and should be: intelligent, loving, thoughtful, responsive, and fun to be around. The world is a better place with each of the aforementioned persons in it. Fran thanks you from the bottom of her heart.

Lynne is grateful to the many colleagues who chose to invest their careers in studying and writing about women and crime. Many of you are featured in this book; you know who you are. Also to be thanked are colleagues at Penn State and the University of Connecticut who have supported her throughout her career. Thanks go also to the undergraduates who helped make this book better by reading early chapter drafts and providing useful feedback. Finally, Lynne sends a special thank you to her family, mother Elaine, husband Peter, sons Zach and Aaron, daughter-in-law Susan and granddaughter Grace, for their abundance of love and caring.

About the website

www.wiley.com/go/gunnison

The *Women, Crime, and Justice: Balancing the Scales* companion website features resources created by the authors to help you use this book in university courses, whether you're an instructor or a student.

For Instructors
- **PowerPoint slides**
- **Essay questions**
- **Quiz questions with answer key**
- **Chapter outlines**
- **Media suggestions**

For Students
- **Chapter outlines**
- **Media suggestions**
- **Student engagement activities**
- **Further reading suggestions**
- **Glossary**

CHAPTER 1

Foundations for understanding women and crime

Student learning outcomes

After reading this chapter, you should be able to:
- Explain why a text on women and crime issues is important.
- Describe the difference between the terms "sex" and "gender."
- Identify core dimensions affecting our understanding of women and crime.
- Summarize the feminist movement in the United States and globally incorporate the role of feminist theory and feminist criminology.

Introduction

Each day, all elements of the criminal justice system (i.e., police, courts, corrections) are allied in a battle to reduce crime and obtain justice for victims. As citizens, we understand that there are both offenders and victims, and we also know that offenders and victims can be of any gender, race/ethnicity, or sexual orientation. However, the acceptance and acknowledgment of women as being both offenders and victims by society has not always been the case. One of the first infamous cases that put women in the limelight and captured the attention of the American public was the case of Lizzie Borden. In 1892, Borden's father and step-mother were killed in their home in Massachusetts with a hatchet. Due to the brutality and shocking circumstances surrounding the crime, it soon garnered national attention when Borden was arrested and charged with the murders (Unknown 1892). After all, it was certainly shocking that a woman could be the perpetrator of such a horrific crime. Following an intense trial and media circus, Borden was found not guilty of the murders in 1893 (Howard 1893). Despite her acquittal, she was still ostracized from society and speculation has continued for over 100 years regarding her innocence. While Borden's case highlighted the fact that women could indeed be criminals, criminologists of the time were neither interested nor inspired to begin examining women offenders and the crimes they committed.

Women, Crime, and Justice, First Edition. By Elaine Gunnison, Frances P. Bernat, and Lynne Goodstein.
© 2017 John Wiley & Sons, Ltd. Published 2017 by John Wiley & Sons, Ltd.

The plight of women as victims of domestic abuse seemed to go unnoticed by the American public or researchers until the case of Francine Hughes. Hughes had experienced 13 years of domestic violence by her ex-husband and had finally reached her breaking point in the late 1970s (McNulty 1980). In 1977, Hughes gathered her children into her car and then went back into the house and set her ex-husband's bedroom on fire, which killed him in his sleep (McNulty 1980). While Hughes certainly was not the first woman to experience domestic abuse, her case garnered national attention and prompted a greater awareness of domestic violence – particularly when actress Farrah Fawcett portrayed Hughes in a television movie called *The Burning Bed.* Since Hughes' case, other victims of domestic violence have further fueled the awareness that domestic violence exists and it can occur to any woman regardless of her status. For instance, the murder of Nicole Brown Simpson by O.J. Simpson, her ex-husband, in 1994 created a media sensation at the time (Rimer 1994). Nicole had a history of experiencing domestic abuse at the hands of Simpson. More recently, South African Olympic athlete Oscar Pistorius shot and killed his girlfriend, Reeva Steenkamp, in 2013 (Alter 2014). While Pistorius claims the shooting was accidental, many believe Steenkamp was a victim of domestic abuse.

The aforementioned cases highlight the fact that women are an integral part of the criminal justice system as offenders or victims. Yet, these cases are reminders that the media picks and chooses which cases to highlight and report on, creating an incomplete portrait of the modern-day female offender and victim. This text provides a detailed investigation into the role of women in the criminal justice system as offenders, victims, and working professionals. Specifically, in this chapter, we explore the reasons why a text and courses on the subject matter are so critical. Next, we define concepts to enable a better understanding of women and crime issues. Finally, we describe the importance of gender in criminology and criminal justice.

Reasons for the focus on women and crime

While you may be able to quickly recount examples of women as offenders, victims, and working professionals in the criminal justice system, you might be surprised to learn that most of what we know about women in these realms has emerged from researchers only in the past several decades. Wait, how can that be? To fully grasp why our knowledge of women in these areas is rather sparse, we first have to examine why our understanding of women as offenders, victims, and professionals has been historically limited. Within the field of **criminology**, the study of the causes of crime and criminal behavior, women were largely overlooked. Throughout the 1800s and most of the 1900s, criminologists were primarily interested in understanding why men committed crime (Chesney-Lind 1989; Heidensohn 1985). This was due, in part, to the fact that men were exhibiting more criminal behavior and committing more serious crimes. Thus, it was argued by many that understanding male offending was the logical place to start in order to understand offending and subsequently reduce crime. Unfortunately, this line of thinking resulted in the examination of female offending being brushed aside. Also, it should be noted that many of the early criminologists were male. Thus, their gender may have played a role in their approach to examine male criminal behavior first. Whatever the true underpinnings of the historical failure to try to understand female offending, the result of this initial oversight has carried over into other areas of research regarding women. For instance, historically, women were left out of the discussion and analysis of crime in many criminology and criminal justice texts as offenders, victims, or even as workers within the criminal justice system. Although textbooks in the field have evolved over time to integrate gender into topics of discussion, many researchers argue that the inclusion of such discussions is still limited. For example, in some cases, the inclusion of women in a topic on criminal justice may be biased. One of the authors of this book can recall using an Introduction to Criminal Justice text within the past decade that featured a section within one chapter entitled "Do women make good police officers?" Besides the obvious problem of the aforementioned section title, the book failed to include another section asking the same question regarding male police officers. Given the oversight of women in the many criminology or criminal justice texts or biased presentations of women presented in these texts, this book is devoted to a detailed examination of women as offenders, victims, and professionals.

Along with books specific to women and crime, courses on women and crime are critical. Reflect on your career goals. Do they include working at all with offenders or victims? If so, it is critical that you understand the population that you likely will be working with. By acquiring knowledge of women and crime issues, it will greatly improve your preparation for professions in law and in the criminal justice system. Besides the acquisition of knowledge of various problems and how they impact women and men, you will be able to articulate the steps that you and others may need to take in order to ameliorate or eliminate these problems through the use of **policy implications**. Policy implications refer to policies that can be implemented to combat a social problem. In the future, you may find yourself working in the criminal justice profession and will need to suggest policies to help the population you may be working with. Today, it is not enough to recognize that a problem exists in the criminal justice system, and think that the problem is unfortunate or that you are powerless to make a difference. Rather, there are many ways in which you can get involved in some form of activism on the topic, whether it is through knowledge dissemination to the public or more formal types of activism such as establishing a grassroots campaign to change a law or institute a policy.

 CASE STUDY: Chibok kidnappings

In mid-April 2014, over 200 female students were kidnapped from their school in the town of Chibok in Nigeria (McCoy 2014). The kidnappers broke into their school with brute force and shot at guards. The female students that were captured were loaded into trucks to either be later killed, or required to work as domestic servants or sex slaves. Some female students were able to escape but many students are still missing. The Islamic terrorist group that claimed responsibility for this atrocity is known as Boko Haram. Apparently, the rationale for their actions was their quest to stop Westernization, which includes the education of women (McCoy 2014). These kidnappings have gained international attention, with the slogan "#BringBackOurGirls" being placed all over the Internet, including social media sites, and mentioned by celebrities and political officials (Dixon 2014). Additionally, the kidnappings have captured the attention of US government officials, who are now planning to send in troops to assist in the search of the missing girls (Londoño 2014).

Concepts of importance

To obtain a better grasp on women and crime issues presented in this book, it is important to understand the critical concepts – not only their definitions but also how these concepts are interwoven throughout the text. In the 1970s and 1980s, feminist scholars began to articulate the difference between the concepts **sex** and **gender** (Daly 1997). Today, the distinction between these two terms is still relevant and very important. One reason that scholars were beginning to make distinctions between the concepts was due to concerns that the term "sex" was being utilized to not only reinforce stereotypes about women in society, but even as a justification for discrimination against women in society.

Let's examine the stereotypes circulating about women during these decades. Before Sarah Palin became a household name in 2008, when she was selected as John McCain's running mate for the presidential election, another woman had already blazed the trail – Geraldine Ferraro. Ferraro, in 1984, was selected as the vice-presidential running mate for Walter Mondale. When Ferraro was selected as the vice-presidential running mate, concerns arose about whether she had gone through menopause yet – yes menopause! The reasoning behind the "concern" was that if she had yet to undergo this biological transformation and if she underwent it as a vice-president and even became president, she might be more likely to exert power and perhaps even be compelled to start a war (Goodman 1992). West and Zimmerman (1987, 127) define sex as "a determination made through the application of socially agreed-upon biological criteria for classifying males and females." Using this definition, you can consider the biological differences such as genitalia, chromosomes, or other physical features as the main distinguishers between males and females. However, examining women and crime issues in the context of only their sex, or biological differences, was considered too simplistic by many feminist scholars, who expressed concern that the role of biology was too intertwined with the term "sex" (Daly 1997). Due to the limited scope of the sex definition, more scholars began to utilize the term "gender" as a better method of distinguishing between males and females. As described by West and Zimmerman (1987, 129), gender is "not a set of traits, nor a variable, nor a role" but rather a product of social interactions. In other words, gender depends on social factors and interactions such as the role or position that an individual has in society, as well as the identity that he/she has formed. Hence, the gender definition helped remove the biological connotation associated with the term "sex." In popular culture, you can find limitless examples of social interactions that are meant to shape a gender identity. Take the "reality" television show *The Bachelor*, in which a single man looks for love while countless young and attractive women compete against one another each episode in hopes of being chosen and proposed to in the end, as a prime example of the shaping of gender identities. When reflecting on women in society, as offenders, or even as victims, think about how their power in society and how social interactions with others might shape their gender. Today, feminist scholars more commonly utilize the term "gender," and in this book, the term "gender" is utilized as opposed to the term "sex."

Another concept of importance to understand as you read this book is the law – particularly the impact it has on women. Without a clear comprehension of the role of law and how it impacts women, your ability to understand women and crime issues would be limited. Whether you agree or disagree with the **Roe v. Wade (1973)** decision, the historic Supreme Court ruling permitting abortion, you likely understand the impact this legal decision has had on women across the United States. **Laws** that define particular acts as illegal, known as **criminal law**, are not intentionally created to harm women but sometimes do. In the 1980s, policymakers re-ignited a "war on drugs" campaign. While regulating the distribution of drugs had already been a concern in the United States in the early 1900s, during the 1980s renewed attention on outlawing drugs became the new national concern for policymakers. As a result of this campaign, drug penalties increased for those in possession of drugs whether for personal use or distribution. Although the new penalties were theoretically intended to be applied equally across race, class, and gender, this, unfortunately, was not the case. Ultimately, from arrest to incarceration, women of color were swept up in the drug war – more so than other groups in society (Bush-Baskette 2000). Other laws that are not criminal also impact women and may even be established to prevent women from being victimized. For example, you may have noticed that the media and news outlets do not report the names of rape victims. However, this was not always the case. Prior to the adoption of **rape shield laws**, not only were rape victims identified in the media, but they also often underwent a form of sexual interrogation when testifying in court during questioning by the defendant's attorney. That is, defense attorneys would ask the victim about the number of sexual partners that she had had before the victimization and would typically try to paint a picture that the victim was promiscuous or was a spurned lover – particularly if the victim and offender were acquaintances. By the late 1970s and early 1980s, most states had adopted rape shield laws, prohibiting rape victims from being identified in the media as well as rape victims being questioned about their prior sexual history when testifying in court (Haddad 2004). Additionally, laws impact women even outside of crime and victimization. Women working in the United States have benefited from laws that have allowed them to have greater access to predominately male-dominated professions as well as equal pay – although despite these laws women are still trying to break barriers into professions and receive equal pay.

 SPECIAL LEGAL ISSUES: Legal considerations for the burqa and niqab

Due to cultural and religious beliefs, many Muslim women wear an Islamic veil such as a hijab, a headscarf, or a burqa or niqab that covers their entire head, face, and body (Chesler 2010). The difference between the burqa and the niqab is that the niqab has a small space cut out for the eyes, allowing the woman's eyes to be seen. Women who wear burqas for their entire lives may experience adverse health outcomes such as eye damage, osteoporosis, heart disease, hypertension, and depression (Chesler 2010). Apart from the physical and mental health concerns, some view the wearing of a burqa by women not as freedom of choice but rather as a symbol of the oppression of women and misogyny (Chesler 2010). Lévy (2010) argues, "The burqa is not a dress, it's a message, one that clearly communicates the subjugation, the subservience, the crushing and the defeat of women." Because of such viewpoints, many countries have implemented legal reforms in regard to the wearing of burqas or niqabs.

Several countries in the Middle East, as well as Tunisia, Malaysia, and Morocco, have legally banned the wearing of Islamic dress. In 2010, Syria became the latest Middle East country to ban the burqa and niqab in public spaces (Chesler 2010). The first European country to tackle the issue of religious dress was France. In 2004, France outlawed the wearing of any religious clothing in public schools, including the hijab, veils, and even Christian crosses (Chesler 2010). Several years later, in 2010, Belgium outlawed the wearing of burqas and niqabs in public. By 2011, France had also banned the wearing of burqas or niqabs in public spaces. Unfortunately, this has resulted in an increase of attacks on Muslim women who reside in France and still wear their burqas or niqabs (Chrisafis 2011). More recently, in 2013, the Netherlands outlawed the wearing of burqas and niqabs in public (Nikolas 2012).

When exploring women and crime topics, it is important to recognize that these topics cannot be merely examined from a lens only focused on gender. Race/ethnicity, social class, sexual identity, and even nationality/immigration status play a significant role in our understanding of women and crime issues. It is imperative to recognize the **intersectionality** of gender with other core status dimensions when examining the relationship between women and offending, victimization, and professional employment (Crenshaw 1991; Daly 1993; Daly and Stephens 1995). Daly and Stephens (1995, 193) explain that utilizing an intersectional approach to examining crime allows for explorations into "how class, gender, and race (and age and sexuality) construct the normal and deviant … how these inequalities put some societal members at risk to be rendered deviant or to engage in law-breaking, and … how law and state institutions both challenge and reproduce these inequalities." For instance, examining crime and victimization issues for African-American women in terms of how they relate only to gender or race provides for a conceptually incomplete understanding of these issues. As explained by Crenshaw (1991, 1244),

> the experiences Black women face are not subsumed within the traditional boundaries of race or gender discrimination as these boundaries are currently understood, and … the intersection of racism and sexism factors into Black women's lives in ways that cannot be captured wholly by looking at the race or gender dimensions of those experiences separately.

Richie (1996), in a classic study of 37 African-American women incarcerated at Rikers Island Correctional Facility in New York, lends support to Crenshaw's (1991) assertions that crime and victimization issues must be examined through the intersectionality of race, class, and gender. In her study, she discovered that approximately one-half of her offender sample were also victims of domestic violence and that intertwinement of race, class, and gender can propel battered African-American women to engage in criminal offending. As Richie (1996, 133) explains, "some women are forced or coerced into crime by their culturally expected gender roles, the violence in their intimate relationships, and their social position in the broader society." When Richie (1996) further explored the link between victimization and offending, and the impact of domestic violence on African-American women, it became clear that race, class, and gender were critically intertwined. Similarly, in order to understand hate crime victimization, it is also necessary to examine the intersectionality of various status dimensions. While there have been many instances of hate crimes in our society, especially against African-Americans, one particular case brought renewed attention to hate crime victimization as it related to gender and sexuality, and even resulted in a Hollywood film entitled *Boys Don't Cry* (Fairyington 2013). In 1993, Brandon Teena, born a female but self-identified as a male, was targeted for victimization and raped in Nebraska due to his sexual status. When Brandon reported the rape to the police, this infuriated the perpetrators, which subsequently resulted in them murdering him (Fairyington 2013). This case is a key example of why it is crucial for scholars to avoid examining hate crime victimization only through the lens of gender or sexuality, so that they are able to obtain a more comprehensive understanding of the issue.

Along with the need to examine women and crime issues with an intersectionality focus, there is also a need to recognize that victimization and criminality cannot be examined separately from each other. Research has consistently supported prior sexual abuse as a moderate to strong predictor of female offending (Siegel and Williams 2003). For example, numerous researchers have explored female offending and have linked prior sexual abuse to the onset and persistence of criminal offending patterns (Bailey and McCloskey 2005; Chesney-Lind and Pasko 2004; Comack 2005; Goodkind, Ng, and Sarri 2006; Gunnison and McCartan 2005; Widom 1995). The link between victimization and offending has been found for female offenders in the United States and across the world. Stathopoulos and colleagues (2012) report that incarcerated women in Australia have high rates of sexual victimization histories. For some women, there is a direct link between victimization (i.e., sexual and physical) and criminal involvement, but for other offenders the link between victimization and offending is indirect (DeHart 2005). In a study of 60 incarcerated women, DeHart (2005) discovered that for some of the incarcerated women the abuse contributed to their further marginalization in society, resulting in blocked access to legitimate institutions. For example, some abused women used drugs and/or alcohol as a coping tool for the abuse, and this use led them to become addicted. The addiction then blocked them from participating fully in society, such as derailing their ability to obtain legal employment. Thus, they became involved in crime to support themselves and their addiction.

Gender in criminology and criminal justice

When one of the authors of this text was in graduate school, a faculty member told her that researching women was just not that important. Imagine the shock the author had upon hearing that statement. Unfortunately, many in society, including academics, politicians, and even citizens, adhere to this same idea – that somehow women are unworthy of our attention. Why does this happen? It could be a reflection of society in general. If women are not valued in society, which was the situation during Borden's case, then it should not be surprising that concerns regarding their plights as offenders, victims, or working professionals in the criminal justice system may also be dismissed. On the other hand, oftentimes such statements are made due to a lack of knowledge about the importance of researching women in society in roles such as offenders, victims, or professionals. Some scholars have asserted that because women offenders are a smaller percentage of the offending population, it is not a priority to study this group. However, the smaller percentage of women in the offending population does not justify lack of research, especially when considering that women offenders are living among us right now. They are driving on the same roads you and I drive on and perhaps are sipping coffee near you at your local coffee shop. If they are not already among us, they will likely be released from prison back into society. Thus, what happens to them before, during, or after incarceration may impact you in small or large ways – or perhaps ways you will never know. Women who experience victimization are also worthy of our attention. Only by understanding the nature of the victimization that they experience, can we work towards policies and laws to assist victims, such as Hughes, and also help prevent future victimizations. Further, women have had to break down barriers to work not only in society in general but also to obtain employment in various areas of the criminal justice system. Thus, the question today should not be "why is it important to examine women in the criminal justice system?" but rather "why would it *not* be important to examine women in the criminal justice system today?"

Women's roles – past and current

When you think of the role women had in society in the past, what images pop into your mind? In the 1950s, a popular television show called *Leave it to Beaver* dominated airwaves. The show depicted a contemporary family, in which the mother of the children stayed home, took care of the children, baked cookies, and did not work outside the home – after all, that was the expectation at the time. This portrayal of mothers was a bit of a throwback, though, because when World War II broke out, a dramatic shift in women's roles began to occur, with many women entering the workforce during that time. After the war was over, many women continued to work in their jobs. However, it seems that despite these trends, many in the entertainment industry could not relinquish their tendency to portray women in stereotypical roles. Despite such portrayals, the trend of women entering the workforce continued steadily thereafter. Today, what roles pop into your mind for women today? The new mantra for women today seems to be that "you can have it all." That is, you can work, be married if you choose, and also raise your children – it is no longer a choice between work and family. Stronger images of women in television and film now appear more frequently. That is, women are being portrayed less as damsels in distress. Perhaps the movies *Kill Bill* or *The Hunger Games* come to mind. In the *Kill Bill* movie, a strong female character played by Uma Thurman exacts justice on her terms through killing with impressive martial arts maneuvers. Women have made great strides in society, and their greater representation as a focus of study in regard to their offending and victimization is due to the feminist movement.

The feminist movement in Western countries

In the United States, the feminist movement can be viewed as unfolding in three distinct waves over a 100-year time span (Burgess-Proctor 2006). During the mid- to late 1800s, the first wave of feminism began in the United States (Burgess-Proctor 2006). At this time, women began to reflect on their roles in society as well as the inequalities they were experiencing, such as the inability to work outside the home and attend school – all because of their gender. Women of this era became disillusioned by not having the same constitutional rights as men, such as the right to vote. This disillusionment with their position in society culminated in the first women's rights convention known as the **Seneca Falls Convention** held in New York in 1848 (Wellman 2004). Following the convention, a document called the **Declaration of Sentiments** was drafted, signed by both women and men, and released to the public. The Declaration of Sentiments outlined the disenfranchisement of women in society by men through the articulation of 18 points, or sentiments. Wellman (2004, 192) describes the Declaration of Sentiments as a "second Declaration of Independence" due to its importance and impact on society. According to Wellman (2004, 192), the document captured both the imagination and spirit of women of the time and was "the single most important factor in spreading the news of the women's rights movement around the country in 1848 and into the future." The document and convention sparked the **suffrage movement**, the organized movement established to advocate the right for women to vote, some 20 years later (DuBois 1998). However, it was not until 1920 and the creation of the Nineteenth Amendment that women would be permitted to vote (DuBois 1998) (Figure 1.1).

Figure 1.1 Women suffragists picketing in front of the White House, 1917. *Source*: National Woman's Party Records, Manuscript Division, Library of Congress, LC-USZ62-31799.

The second wave of feminism, occurring in the 1960s, 1970s, and ending in the 1980s, was a continuation of the earlier feminist movement (Whelehan 1995). The spark that created the examination of gender issues during this period can be attributed to the social context of the time. With the Civil Rights movement underway in the 1950s and 1960s, a greater social awareness emerged as many in society began to examine other marginalized groups, such as prisoners and women. During this second wave, feminists recognized that there was a wide range of issues to tackle that impacted women, including family, employment, education, reproductive rights, and inequalities not only in society but also in laws (Whelehan 1995). Employment opportunities, for example, were limited for women in that most options available to them were for positions predominately female dominated such as nursing, teaching, or secretarial work. Women also found themselves discriminated against when pursuing post-baccalaureate education. Supreme Court Justice Ruth Bader Ginsburg recalled entering Harvard Law School in the 1950s and being asked by the dean why she was in law school and "occupying a seat that could be held by a man" (Ginsburg 2010).

Feminists of this era were divided as to how to tackle the aforementioned issues. On the one hand, some feminists argued that women are the same as men and should be treated equally (Burgess-Proctor 2006). However, on the other hand, some feminists disagreed with the "sameness" approach and believed that women are distinct from men and, thus, should be treated differently and argued for a "difference" approach (Burgess-Proctor 2006). Regardless of which approach feminists favored to ameliorate inequities facing women, scholars noted that both perspectives recognized the subordinate role that women had in society and that whatever differences women had they were by no means equal to male differences (Burgess-Proctor 2006; MacKinnon 1991). Despite the tension in the perspectives, significant changes materialized for women, such as the passage of the **Equal Pay Act of 1963** which established equal pay for equal work for women and men, **Title VII of the Civil Rights Acts of 1964** which prohibited employment discrimination, and **Title IX of the Education Amendments of 1972** which prohibited educational discrimination by gender for those institutions receiving federal aid (Mezey 2011). Other significant changes impacting women during this time were the establishment of **battered women's shelters**, safe housing for women who were victims of domestic violence, the removal of **marital rape exemption** laws that had permitted a man to rape his wife, and the establishment of **correctional programming**, or treatment programs, in prisons for women (Dobash and Dobash 1992; Ryan 1995). While improvements had been gained for women offenders, victims, and professionals, many feminists did not view these gains as impacting all women in the same ways. This concern led to the third wave of feminism in the United States.

The third wave of feminism began in the 1990s and continues to the present time (Burgess-Proctor 2006). At the onset of this third wave, feminist scholars were largely concerned that individuals who were spearheading the fight for issues impacting women were Caucasian and heterosexual women who came from a higher socioeconomic background. Essentially, the group of women who were championing for changes lacked perspectives from women of color, women of different ethnicities, women of lower socioeconomic backgrounds, and lesbian women (Burgess-Proctor 2006; Sokoloff, Price, and Flavin 2004). The oversight of not examining additional perspectives from women led feminist scholars to encourage researchers to examine the intersectionality of gender, race, social class, and sexuality when either discussing issues impacting women or rallying for any change that might impact women offenders, victims, or professionals. Research soon emerged on the intersecting inequalities of gender, race, social class, and sexuality in regard to women's experiences as criminal offenders, victims, and workers in the criminal justice system (Renzetti 2013). For example, researchers have found that women of color who live in impoverished neighborhoods may engage in violent offending, but they also may be victims of violent victimization (Renzetti 2013). Hence, researchers examining women engaging in violent offending without also inspecting their victimization experience and socioeconomic status will not obtain a conceptually complete understanding of violent female offenders. Additionally, researchers have found that women of color who are victims of intimate partner violence are less likely to seek out help from family, friends, social service agencies, or report the abuse to police (Kaukinen 2004; Potter 2006). Such findings reveal that not all victims of domestic violence reach out for help in the same manner and policymakers must consider race and ethnicity when developing programs to assist victims. Further, research has emerged that lesbian and gay police officers encounter employment barriers on the job that are similar to barriers experienced by minority officers (Colvin 2009). Hence, the role of sexuality is also an important one to consider in relation to gender and race. Besides research that emerged on intersectionality of various criminal justice topics, significant legal reforms were made during the third wave of feminism that impacted all women. These included the **Family and Medical Leave Act of 1993**, which required employers to provide leave and job security to employees who needed a period of absence from work for medical and family reasons. In 1994, the **Violence Against Women Act (VAWA)** was passed. This allocated federal funding to the investigation and prosecution of violence crimes against women (Renzetti 2013). At the time of the passage of this act, the focus was on domestic violence and sexual assault crimes against women. Since its initial passage, the act has been re-authorized and additional forms of victimization experienced by women besides domestic violence and sexual assault are also now a focus, such as violence experienced in dating relationships and stalking. Moreover, feminists are rallying against the **glass ceiling**, the invisible barrier that blocks working women from advancing into senior positions in the workplace (Morrison, White, and Van Velsor 1992). Today's third-wave feminist scholars are continuing to explore female offending, victimization, and workplace issues impacting females using an intersectional lens and working to implement policies that will benefit all women – not just Caucasian women.

The feminist movement worldwide

Some feminist movements worldwide were already underway in some form or fashion before the feminist movement in the United States emerged. However, the feminist movement in the United States is still considered to be officially the first feminist movement and the one that helped spark feminist movements across the globe (Evans 1977). The feminist movement in Britain can be characterized as the second feminist movement in the world (Evans 1977). In the 1860s and 1870s, the female suffrage movement was underway in the United Kingdom and some women were permitted to vote in 1918 (e.g., women over age 30, property owners) but not until the passage of the **Representation of the People Act** in 1928 were all women permitted the right to vote (Johnston 2013). The **Eligibility of Women Act**, passed in 1918, permitted women to be elected to Parliament. Like the second wave of feminism in the United States, feminist scholarship emerged in the United Kingdom in the 1960s and 1970s and centered on issues impacting women, such as discrimination. Their efforts led to the passage of the **Sex Discrimination Act** in 1975, which prohibited sex discrimination in employment and education (Russell 2000). Such legislation paved the way for the first female prime minister of the United Kingdom, Margaret Thatcher. Feminism in the United Kingdom today is still underway with feminists pushing for the elimination of sexual discrimination, such as the gender gap in pay, and male sexual violence against women (Mackay 2011).

Influenced by the feminist movement in the United States, women began to organize for the right to vote in the mid-1800s in Australia (Evans 1977). During this time, Australia was not the country that we think of today but rather was comprised of several colonies with each colony establishing its own laws. As a result of this structure, women landowners were given the right to vote in 1860 (Evans 1977). In 1895 and 1900 women were permitted to vote in South Australia and Western Australia respectively (Evans 1977). In 1901 colonies became united into the country of Australia, paving the way for the passage of the **Commonwealth Franchise Act** in 1902, which provided all women in Australia (except for some Aboriginal women) with the right to vote (Norberry 2003).

In European countries such as Germany, France, Belgium, the Netherlands, and Italy, the feminist movement had difficulties getting a foothold due to government structures (e.g., communism or dictatorships) as well as resistance from religious institutions such as the Roman Catholic Church (Evans 1977). Women in France, for example, began to organize during the French revolution in 1789, but they did not gain the right to vote until 1945 (Evans 1977). During the 1970s, French feminist scholarship emerged and feminists achieved several victories for women, including the passage of **Projet de loi du 15 mars 1983** which prohibited discrimination based on sex, and the **Manifeste des 10** in 1996 which required equal representation of women in politics (Burr 2003; Federico and Moore 1997). Feminists in European countries, such as France, continue to fight for causes impacting women today including legal discrimination, sexual harassment, and sexual assault.

In Asian countries, such as India, the feminist movement developed much later than it did in the United States or in European countries. For example, women in India were not granted the right to vote until 1947 (Basu 2008). Like the feminist revolution in the United States in the 1960s and 1970s, India's feminist campaigns during this time were rallying against dowry murders, or "deaths of young brides who were being harassed by their in-laws for more dowry," and rape of women by police (Kumar 1989, 22). Feminists were also organizing the unionization of women workers (Kumar 1989). Today, a "Womanifesto" feminist movement is underway to help curb male sexual violence against women – a pervasive problem in India (Nallu 2014). Feminists in the Middle East, in countries such as Egypt, are striving to increase access to education, employment, health care, and political participation for women (Al-Ali 1997). Within the past decade, feminists in Egypt have been attempting to further expand their agendas by rallying for reproductive rights for women and addressing the violence against women in society (Al-Ali 1997).

Regardless of where women reside, many are united in their cause to help improve conditions for women as offenders, victims, and professionals. Given the importance of issues impacting women across the globe, it is necessary that feminist scholars consider global perspectives when researching topics. It is only through having a deeper understanding of gender issues that they will have the tools to effectively help women regardless of where the women may reside.

GLOBAL PERSPECTIVES: An example of feminism in Saudi Arabia

Most of the time when you get into a vehicle to drive, you don't think much about it. You certainly don't worry about being detained by law enforcement officials for driving. For women in Saudi Arabia, the ability to drive is a right that they yearn for. While the Saudi Arabian government does not have a law forbidding women to drive, the government does not issue driver's licenses for Saudi Arabian women (Abdullah al-Shihri and Aya Batrawy 2013). Because a woman cannot obtain a license, she is not supposed to drive. If she does drive, then she will be punished by officials. In 1995, 50 Saudi women drove their cars in defiance of the ban, which resulted in them being jailed for one day, having their passports confiscated, and some losing their jobs (Abdullah al-Shihri and Aya Batrawy 2013). Some officials argue that the ban is a necessity as driving could damage a woman's ovaries and result in her being unable to have children (Winter 2013). Despite the pushback, in 2013 Saudi women again protested their right to drive and garnered international attention (Winter 2013) (Figure 1.2). Slowly, women in Saudi Arabia are gaining some rights. According to Winter (2013) sex equality reforms have been introduced that permit women to vote in municipal elections. While some gains have been made, clearly more reforms are needed.

Figure 1.2 Saudi activist Manal Al Sharif, who now lives in Dubai, drives her car in the Gulf Emirate city on October 22, 2013, as she campaigns in solidarity with Saudi women preparing to take to the wheel on October 26, defying the Saudi authorities, fight for women's right to drive in Saudi Arabia. Under the slogan "driving is a choice," activists have called on social networks for women to gather in vehicles on October 26, the culmination of the campaign launched in September, in the only country in the world where women do not have the right drive. *Source*: MARWAN NAAMANI/AFP/Getty Images.

Feminist criminology and feminist theory

The feminist movement in the United States and worldwide gave rise to a proliferation of scholarship on women as offenders, victims, and professionals. Feminist scholars, in the United States and abroad, have carved a new place in the literature for issues impacting women to be examined. In fact, within the discipline of criminology, a new field of criminology emerged in the 1970s during the second wave of feminism known as **feminist criminology**. Feminist criminology is a branch of study within the field of criminology that seeks to understand women who offend, victimization that impacts women, and women who work in the criminal justice system. The ambition by feminists to establish their distinct field of inquiry to examine issues impacting women stemmed from the desire to separate themselves from an androcentric bias in the discipline where the focus was on understanding male criminality by theorists who were most often male (Britton 2000; Chesney-Lind 1989). Additionally, many of the explanations that had been put forth to explain female offending centered on identifying their sexuality as the root cause of their involvement in crime (Klein 1973). However, this changed in the mid-1970s. Freda Adler, in her publication *Sisters in Crime* in 1975, suggested that the liberation of women in US society allowed for more women to enter the workforce in greater numbers and, hence, these women now had more opportunities to engage in crime. Her **liberation hypothesis** inspired scholars to begin thinking differently about female criminality and her work contributed to the future feminist criminological theories. Britton (2000, 58) explains:

> The founding of feminist criminology can be somewhat arbitrarily fixed at 1976, with the publication of Carol Smart's *Women, Crime and Criminology: A Feminist Critique*. Though a handful of earlier works had addressed some of the general themes she raised, Smart's book brought them together in a systematic critique of the treatment (or lack thereof) of women offenders in mainstream criminology and the neglect of women's experiences as victims in an attempt to set out some directions for the new field of feminist inquiry.

Feminists wanted to bring attention to female offenders, who were often overlooked, and escape the stereotypes applied to female offenders; and feminists achieved this by carving out their own niche in the field. With critiques put forth by Smart and other feminist scholars during this time, feminists were inspired to challenge the assumptions about women and crime, resulting in a wide range of feminist theories and perspectives emerging thereafter. The ways in which female offenders are ignored in mainstream criminological theories will be covered in Chapter 2.

Feminist theory refers to specific theories or perspectives that offer explanations for female offending, victimization, or gender inequality. Within the field of feminist criminology, there is not a single feminist theory that has been put forth to explain the issues impacting women, but rather several feminist theories and perspectives. For instance, some feminist theories examined the role of capitalism and how differences in power between women and men may explain the types of crimes that they commit, while other feminist perspectives explored the relationship between victimization and offending. Other feminist theories posited that crime is an expression of "doing gender" in which males commit crimes that assert their masculinity while females commit crime that asserts their femininity. A further exploration of these various perspectives will be presented in Chapter 2. Today, feminist theorists and researchers recognize that to understand issues impacting women, one must adopt a perspective that incorporates an intersectional approach whereby social class, gender, race, and sexuality are examined in tandem with the issue at hand (Barak 1998). In other words, feminist theories and perspectives should be more integrated if they are to be effective in explaining issues relevant to women.

The impact of feminism and feminist criminology for women cannot be overstated. Besides a firestorm of research on topics of female offending, victimization, and workers in the criminal justice field, the feminist movement has created new avenues for scholars and students. Both the American Society of Criminology and the Academy of Criminal Justice have established specific divisions that allow scholars to share research, discuss issues impacting women, and problem-solve together to ameliorate these issues. More universities are offering courses specific to women and crime (Britton 2000). If you are in a "Women and Crime" course right now, it is likely the result of your department recognizing the importance of the course to your curriculum of study. Further, more women than ever are being hired in the criminal justice field. In fact, one of the authors of this text knows that her first job in academia out of graduate school was due to the fact that the department she was being hired into wanted to hire more female scholars. This era may be one of the best moments in time for you to become engaged in the discipline if you choose, due to the burgeoning research in the field and the support of faculty who not only are more willing than ever to accept the importance of scholarship of issues impacting women but also would enjoy working with you on projects.

Conclusion

The foundation has been established for your comprehension of why women as offenders, victims, and professionals have historically been overlooked in the literature, the importance of examining women and crime issues, and critical key terms. As you move through the remainder of the text, keep in mind the terms and discussions from the chapters. Today, you are no longer a passive participant in the understanding of women's issues – you can play a pivotal role in the changes impacting women in the United States and at an international level.

Suggested readings

Alarid, Leanne Fiftal, and Paul Cromwell. 2005. "In Her Own Words: Women Offenders' Views on Crime and Victimization: An Anthology." New York, NY: Oxford University Press.
Erez, Edna, and Anat Berko 2010. "Pathways of Arab/Palestinian Women in Israel to Crime and Imprisonment: An Intersectional Approach." *Feminist Criminology*, 5(2): 156–1 94. DOI: 10.1177/1557085110367742
Steffensmeier, Darrell J., Jennifer Schwartz, and Michael Roche. 2013. "Gender and Twenty-First-Century Corporate Crime: Female Involvement and the Gender Gap in Enron-Era Corporate Frauds." *American Sociological Review*, 78(3): 448–476. DOI: 10.1177/0003122413484150

Student engagement activities

1 Research the history of the roles of women and the portrayal of women in society from the 1900s to today. Be sure to collect information from scholars and newspapers, and gather photographic and/or video images of how women are being portrayed in society. Write a three-page summary of the history of women's role in society and the images used to portray women in society. Be sure to include a few images or video links to illustrate your examples.
2 It is sometimes assumed that all women, regardless of race/ethnicity or social class, were "on board" and working towards the same goal during the feminist movement in the United States in the 1970s. However, this was not the case. Research some of the tensions within the feminist movement and uncover why *not all* women may have felt their thoughts and opinions were being represented in the movement. Write a one-page summary of these tensions during the feminist

movement and include examples as to how some women felt that their voices were still not being heard.

3 Research the feminist movement in a country besides the United States. Write a five-page essay covering the history of the feminist movement in your selected country. Be sure to cover the struggles that women faced before, during, and after the movement. Also, make sure you highlight important laws or changes in society as a result of the feminist movement. Finally, be sure to note what issues and reforms feminists are pushing for today.

Discussion questions

1 How have women's roles changed over the past 100 years? How has the response by the criminal justice system changed for women as offenders, victims, and professionals over the past 100 years?
2 Compare and contrast the feminist movement in the United States and worldwide.
3 Given what you may know at this point about women as offenders, victims, and professionals, what policies do you think are needed *right now* to assist them?

Key terms

Battered women's shelters
Commonwealth Franchise Act
Correctional programming
Criminal law
Criminology
Declaration of Sentiments
Eligibility of Women Act
Equal Pay Act of 1963
Family and Medical Leave Act of 1993
Feminist criminology
Feminist theory
Gender
Glass ceiling
Intersectionality
Laws

Liberation hypothesis
Manifeste des 10
Marital rape exemption
Policy implications
Projet de loi du 15 mars 1983
Rape shield laws
Representation of the People Act
Roe v. Wade (1973)
Seneca Falls Convention
Sex
Sex Discrimination Act
Suffrage movement
Title VII of the Civil Rights Acts of 1964
Title IX of the Education Amendments of 1972
Violence Against Women Act (VAWA)

References

Abdullah al-Shihri and Aya Batrawy. October 26, 2013. "Saudi Arabia: Women's Protest Over Driving Ban Kicks Off." *The Independent.* Accessed May 23, 2014, http://www.independent.co.uk/news/world/middle-east/saudi-arabia-womens-protest-over-driving-ban-kicks-off-8905976.html

Adler, Freda. 1975. *Sisters in Crime*. New York, NY: McGraw-Hill.

Al-Ali, Nadje. 1997. *Women's Movements in the Middle East: Case Studies of Egypt and Turkey.* Centre for Gender Studies: University of London, 1–40. https://eprints.soas.ac.uk/4889/2/UNRISD_Report_final.pdf

Alter, Charlotte. April 10, 2014. "Pistorius' Tears Aren't Necessarily a Sign of Innocence." *Time*. Accessed May 5, 2014, http://time.com/56043/oscar-pistorius-reeva-steenkamp-courtroom-theatrics/

Bailey, Jennifer A., and Laura A. McCloskey. 2005. "Pathways to Adolescent Substance Use Among Sexually Abused Girls." *Journal of Abnormal Child Psychology*, 33: 39–53. DOI: 10.1007/s10802-005-0933-0

Barak, Gregg. 1998. *Integrating Criminologies*. Boston: Allyn & Bacon.

Basu, Aparna. 2008. "Women's Struggle for the Vote: 1917–1937." *Indian Historical Review*, 35(1): 128–143.

Britton, Dana M. 2000. "Feminism in Criminology: Engendering the Outlaw." *Annals of the American Academy of Political and Social Science*, 571: 57–76.

Burgess-Proctor, Amanda. 2006. "Intersections of Race, Class, Gender, and Crime: Future Directions for Feminist Criminology." *Feminist Criminology*, 1: 27–4 7 DOI: 10.1177/1557085105282899

Burr, Elisabeth. 2003. "French, Gender and Language Politics in France." In *Gender Across Languages: The Linguistic Representation of Women and Men, Volume 3*, edited by Marlis Hellinger and Hadumod Bußmann, 119–139. Amsterdam: John Benjamins Publishing Company.

Bush-Baskette, Stephanie R. 2000. "The War on Drugs and the Incarceration of Mothers." *Journal of Drug Issues*, 30(4): 919–928.

Chesler, Phyllis. 2010. "Ban the Burqa? The Argument in Favor." *Middle East Quarterly*, 17(4): 33–45.

Chesney-Lind, Meda. 1989. "Girl's Crime and Woman's Place: Toward a Feminist Model of Female Delinquency." *Crime and Delinquency*, 35(1): 8–10. DOI: 10.1177/0011128789035001002

Chesney-Lind, M., and Linda Pasko. 2004. *The Female Offender: Girls, Women, and Crime*. Thousand Oaks, CA: Sage.

Chrisafis, Angelique. (September 19, 2011). "France's Burqa Ban: Women are 'Effectively Under House Arrest.'" *The Guardian*. Accessed May 27, 2014, http://www.theguardian.com/world/2011/sep/19/battle-for-the-burqa

Colvin, Roddrick. 2009. "Shared Perceptions Among Lesbian and Gay Police Officers Barriers and Opportunities in the Law Enforcement Work Environment." *Police Quarterly*, 12(1): 86–101. DOI: 10.1177/1098611108327308

Comack, Eileen. 2005. "Coping, Resisting, and Surviving: Connecting Women's Law Violations to Their Histories of Abuse." In *In Her Own Words: Women Offenders' Views on Crime and Victimization*, edited by Leanne Alaraid and Paul Cromwell, 33–43. Los Angeles, CA: Roxbury.

Crenshaw, Kimberle. 1991. "Mapping the Margins: Intersectionality, Identity Politics, and Violence Against Women of Color." *Stanford Law Review*, 43(6): 1241–1299.

Daly, Kathleen. 1993. "Class-Race-Gender: Sloganeering in Search of Meaning." *Social Justice*, 20, 56–71.

Daly, Kathleen. 1997. "Different Ways of Conceptualizing Sex/Gender in Feminist Theory and Their Implications for Criminology." *Theoretical Criminology*, 1(1): 25–51.

Daly, Kathleen, and Deborah J. Stephens. 1995. "The 'Dark Figure' of Criminology: Towards a Black and Multi-Ethnic Feminist Agenda for Theory and Research." In *International Feminist Perspectives in Criminology: Engendering a Discipline*, edited by Nicole Hahn Rafter and Frances Heidensohn, 189–215. Philadelphia, PA: Open University Press.

DeHart, Dana D. 2005. "Pathways to Prison: Impact of Victimization in the Lives of Incarcerated Women." Washington, DC: US Department of Justice. https://www.ncjrs.gov/pdffiles1/nij/grants/208383.pdf

Dixon, Robyn. (May 22, 2014). "Fear and Determination for Nigerians at Heart of #BringBack-OurGirls." *Los Angeles Times*. Accessed May 22, 2014, http://www.latimes.com/world/africa/la-fg-nigeria-girls-20140522-story.html

Dobash, R. Emerson, and Russell P. Dobash. 1992. *Women, Violence and Social Change*. New York, NY: Routledge.

DuBois, Ellen Carol. 1998. *Woman Suffrage and Women's Rights*. New York, NY: New York University Press.

Evans, Richard J. 1977. *The Feminists: Women's Emancipation Movements in Europe, America and Australasia 1840–1920*. Sydney: Croom Helm.

Fairyington, Stephanie. December 31, 2013. "Two Decades After Brandon Teena's Murder, a Look Back at Falls City." *The Atlantic*. Accessed May 20, 2014, http://www.theatlantic.com/national/archive/2013/12/two-decades-after-brandon-teenas-murder-a-look-back-at-falls-city/282738/

Federico, Salvatore, and Catherine Moore. 1997. "French Women in the Corporate World." *Global Business Languages*, Vol. 2, Art. 12. Available at: http://docs.lib.purdue.edu/gbl/vol2/iss1/12

Ginsburg, Ruth Bader. August 17, 2010. "Interview: Ruth Bader Ginsburg, Justice of the U.S. Supreme Court." *Academy of Achievement*. Accessed May 14, 2014, http://www.achievement.org/autodoc/printmember/gin0int-1

Goodkind, Sara, Ng, Irene, and Rosemary C. Sarri. 2006. "The Impact of Sexual Abuse in the Lives of Young Women Involved or at Risk of Involvement with the Juvenile Justice System." *Violence Against Women*, 12: 456–477. DOI: 10.1177/1077801206288142

Goodman, Ellen. December 22, 1992. "Year of the Woman Ends with Bad Omens." *Seattle Times*. Accessed May 14, 2014, http://community.seattletimes.nwsource.com/archive/?date=19921222&slug=1531459

Gunnison, Elaine, and Lisa M. McCartan. 2005. "Female Persisters in Criminal Offending: A Theoretical Examination of Predictors." *Women and Criminal Justice*, 16: 43–65. DOI: 10.1300/J012v16n03_03

Haddad, Richard I. 2004. "Shield or Sieve? People v. Bryant and the Rape Shield Law in High-Profile Cases." *Columbia Journal of Law and Social Problems*, 39: 185–221.

Heidensohn, Frances. 1985. *Women and Crime*. London: Macmillan Press.

Howard, Joe. June 20, 1893. "Not Guilty! Miss Lizzie A. Borden is Acquitted." *Boston Globe*. Accessed May 5, 2014, http://law2.umkc.edu/faculty/projects/ftrials/LizzieBorden/news16.html

Johnston, Neil. 2013. "The History of the Parliamentary Franchise." Research Paper, 131/14. Accessed May 22, 2014, http://www.parliament.uk/business/publications/research/briefing-papers/RP13-14/the-history-of-the-parliamentary-franchise

Kaukinen, Catherine. 2004. "The Help-Seeking Strategies of Female Violent-Crime Victims: The Direct and Conditional Effects of Race and the Victim-Offender Relationship." *Journal of Interpersonal Violence*, 19(9): 967–990. DOI: 10.1177/0886260504268000

Klein, Dorie. 1973. "The Etiology of Female Crime: A Review of the Literature." *Issues in Criminology*, 8(2): 3–30.

Kumar, Radha. 1989. "Contemporary Indian Feminism." *Feminist Review*, 33: 20–29. DOI: 10.2307/1395212

Lévy, Bernard-Henri. February 15, 2010 . "Why I Support a Ban on Burqas." *The World Post*. Accessed May 27, 2017, http://www.huffingtonpost.com/bernardhenri-levy/why-i-support-a-ban-on-bu_b_463192.html

Londoño, Ernesto. May 22, 2014. "U.S. Deploys 80 Troops to Chad to Help Find Kidnapped Nigerian Schoolgirls." *Washington Post*. Accessed May 22, 2014, http://www.washingtonpost.com/world/national-security/us-deploys-80-military-personnel-to-chad/2014/05/21/edd7d21a-e11d-11e3-810f-764fe508b82d_story.html

Mackay, Finn. 2011. "A Movement of Their Own: Voices of Young Feminist Activists in the London Feminist Network." *Interface: A Journal for and about Social Movements*, 3(2): 152–179.

MacKinnon, Catherine A. 1991. "Difference and Dominance: Onsex Discrimination." In *Feminist Legal Theory*, edited by Katharine T. Bartlett and Rosanne Kennedy, 81–94. Boulder, CO: Westview.

McCoy, Terrence. April 28, 2014. "The Group that Kidnapped 234 Nigerian School Girls and Its Murderous Campaign Against Education." *Washington Post*. Accessed May 22, 2014, http://www.washingtonpost.com/news/morning-mix/wp/2014/04/28/the-group-that-kidnapped-234-nigerian-school-girls-and-its-murderous-campaign-against-education/

McNulty, Faith 1980. *The Burning Bed*. San Diego, CA: Harcourt.

Mezey, Susan G. 2011. *Elusive Equality: Women's Rights, Public Policy, and the Law*. Boulder, CO: Lynne Rienner.

Morrison, Ann M., White, Randall P., and Ellen Van Velsor. 1992. *Breaking the Glass Ceiling: Can Women Reach the Top of America's Largest Corporations?* New York, NY: Perseus Publishing.

Nallu, Preethi. April 14, 2014. "Gender Issues Could Be a Game Changer in India's Elections." *Time*. Accessed May 20, 2014, http://time.com/61122/india-womanifesto-election-women-voting/

Nikolas, Katerina. January 30, 2012. "Netherlands to Ban the Burqa in 2013." *Digital Journal*. Accessed May 27, 2014, http://digitaljournal.com/article/318703

Norberry, Jennifer. 2003. "The Evolution of the Commonwealth Franchise: Tales of Inclusion and Exclusion." In *Realising Democracy: Electoral law in Australia*, edited by GraemeOrr, BryanMercurio, and GeorgeWilliams, 80–99. Sydney: Federation Press.

Potter, Hillary. 2006. "An Argument for Black Feminist Criminology Understanding African American Women's Experiences with Intimate Partner Abuse Using an Integrated Approach." *Feminist Criminology*, 1(2): 106–124. DOI: 10.1177/1557085106286547

Renzetti, Claire M. 2013. *Feminist Criminology*. New York, NY: Routledge.

Richie, Beth. 1996. *Compelled to Crime: The Gender Entrapment of Black Battered Women*. New York, NY: Routledge.

Rimer, Sara. June 23, 1994. "The Simpson Case: The Victim; Nicole Brown Simpson: Slain At the Dawn of a Better Life." *New York Times*. Accessed May 5, 2014, http://www.nytimes.com/1994/06/23/us/simpson-case-victim-nicole-brown-simpson-slain-dawn-better-life.html

Roe v. Wade, 410 U.S. 113 (1973).

Russell, Meg. 2000. "Women's Representation in UK Politics: What Can Be Done Within the Law?" Accessed May 20, 2014, http://www.ucl.ac.uk/constitution-unit/publications/tabs/unit-publications/60.pdf

Ryan, Rebecca M. 1995. "The Sex Right: A Legal History of the Marital Rape Exemption." *Law and Social Inquiry*, 20(4): 941–1001. DOI: 10.1111/j.1747-4469.1995.tb00697.x

Siegel, Jane A., and Linda M. Williams. 2003. "The Relationship Between Childhood Sexual Abuse and Female Delinquency and Crime: A Prospective Study." *Journal of Research in Crime and Delinquency*, 40(1): 71–94. DOI: 10.1177/0022427802239254

Smart, Carol. 1976. *Women, Crime and Criminology*. London: Routledge

Sokoloff, Natalie, Price, Barbara R., and Jennifer Flavin. 2004. "The Criminal Law and Women." In *The Criminal Justice System and Women, 3rd edition*, edited by Barbara R. Price and Natalie Sokoloff, 11–29. New York, NY: McGraw-Hill.

Stathopoulos, Mary, Quadara, Antonia, Fileborn, Bianca, and Haley Clark. 2012. *Addressing Women's Victimization Histories in Custodial Settings*. Australian Institute of Family Studies. Australian Centre for the Study of Sexual Assault, Melbourne, Australia.

Unknown. August 11, 1892. "Miss Borden Arrested: Charged with Murdering Her Father and His Wife." *New York Times*. Accessed May 5, 2014, http://law2.umkc.edu/faculty/projects/ftrials/LizzieBorden/news5.html

Wellman, Judith. 2004. *The Road to Seneca Falls: Elizabeth Cady Stanton and the First Women's Rights Convention*. Illinois: University of Illinois Press.

West, Candace, and Don H. Zimmerman. 1987. "Doing Gender." *Gender & Society*, 1(2): 125–151.

Whelehan, Imelda. 1995. *Modern Feminist Thought: From the Second Wave to Post Feminism*. Edinburgh: Edinburgh University Press.

Widom, Cathy S. 1995. *Victims of Childhood Sexual Abuse – Later Criminal Consequences*. National Institute of Justice, US Department of Justice.

Winter, Stuart. October 27, 2013. "The Women Driven to a Desperate Act over Saudi Arabia Ban." *Sunday Express*. Accessed May 24, 2014, http://www.express.co.uk/news/world/439396/The-women-driven-to-a-desperate-act-over-Saudi-Arabia-ban

CHAPTER 2

Women and the crimes that they commit

Student learning outcomes

After reading this chapter, you should be able to:
- Describe the characteristics of the modernday female offender.
- Summarize the types of crimes that women commit and how their involvement in crime may be similar to or different from males.
- Identify and describe criminological theories that may explain why women commit crime.

Introduction

The zip code 90210 may elicit immediate thoughts of Hollywood, excess behaviors such as the use of drugs or alcohol, wild late night parties involving sexual escapades, and perhaps even images from Aaron Spelling's television show by the same name, which launched many young actors' careers. You may also think of prostitution on Hollywood Boulevard, which Julia Roberts portrayed almost as a fairytale life in her 1990 movie *Pretty Woman*. More recently, the Lifetime television show called *The Client List*, starring Jennifer Love Hewitt, perhaps might add to your perceptions that prostitution is not always occurring on the streets but that it occurs in other establishments such as massage parlors. You may not immediately think of Heidi Fleiss, a young Caucasian woman in her twenties, born and raised in Los Angeles, and the daughter of a pediatrician, as fitting into the female offender role. However, Fleiss became a household name in the 1990s when her role in the illegal sex industry became public. In fact, she still surfaces in the media: her most recent appearance was in 2009 on the VH-1 television show *Celebrity Rehab with Dr. Drew.* The path that would later pave her involvement in criminal activity began in the late 1980s, when Fleiss had a chance meeting with Madam Alex, the owner of an exclusive prostitution ring in Los Angeles. Fleiss began managing Madam Alex's prostitution ring in the late 1980s and, by the early 1990s, she broke away from managing for Madame Alex and started her own business. Under her management, the business flourished immediately and Fleiss earned millions with her elite call girl service, serving rich and powerful men from Hollywood and around the world. By 1993, however, Fleiss' luck ran out and she was arrested for pandering (i.e., a person who solicits another for prostitution; also referred to as a pimp). Her arrest catapulted her into the spotlight of the media, which dubbed her the "Hollywood Madam." She was

Women, Crime, and Justice, First Edition. By Elaine Gunnison, Frances P. Bernat, and Lynne Goodstein.
© 2017 John Wiley & Sons, Ltd. Published 2017 by John Wiley & Sons, Ltd.

Figure 2.1 Accused "Hollywood Madam" Heidi Fleiss sits in court during closing arguments in her pandering trial, November 28, 1994. *Source:* © STR New/Reuters.

eventually convicted of pandering, but the charge was later overturned on an appeal. Charged by the federal government with tax evasion and money laundering, she was convicted and sentenced to a seven-year prison term (Hubler 1997) (Figure 2.1). Fleiss only served approximately three years of her sentence and spent the remainder of her sentence on supervised release. While on release, she violated one of her supervising conditions by using methamphetamine and was later sent to a drug rehabilitation center.

While Fleiss' involvement in crime was rather transparent, other criminal acts committed by women offenders may not be. It appeared to be a typical summer Sunday in July of 2009 in New York as 36-year-old mom, Diane Schuler, made her way home from a campground with her children and three nieces in her minivan. While Schuler was driving, one of her nieces called her mother to say, "There is something wrong with Aunt Diane." Schuler spoke to her brother and told him she was disoriented. He told her to pull over, but she didn't. She had been driving in the wrong direction on the freeway for almost 2 miles. Shortly after that phone call, she crashed into oncoming traffic, killing herself, her daughter, her three nieces, and three passengers in another car (Figures 2.2a and 2.2b). Only her son survived (Baker and Kovaleski 2009). Due to the shocking and horrific circumstances, the crash made the national headlines. How did this happen? What *was* wrong with Aunt Diane?

At first, there was speculation that possible medical conditions, such as diabetes or a tooth abscess that was bothering her earlier in the day, may have somehow incapacitated her while she was driving. However, as the investigation began to unfold, it was found that Schuler was in fact a criminal. She, like Fleiss, was not the typical criminal you may see portrayed on the news or in the movies. Typically, in the major news outlets, criminals have been portrayed as women of color or women that have committed violent attacks. But Schuler was Caucasian, considered a loving wife and mother, and had not committed any violent assault. Then, how does she "fit" into this pre-described role of the "typical" female criminal? While Schuler was not formally defined as a criminal by the criminal justice system prior to the accident, she had engaged in criminal behavior. When officers arrived at the scene, they found a broken Absolut vodka bottle in her vehicle, raising their suspicions

Figures 2.2a and 2.2b Diane Schuler's charred minivan after a head-on collision, July 26, 2009, on the Taconic State Parkway in Briarcliff Manor, NY. Eight people – Schuler, her daughter, three nieces and three men – died in the crash. *Source:* © Alan Zale/The New York Times/Redux/eyevine; (b) Daniel Schuler held a press conference at his lawyer Dominic Barbara's office. He spoke out about the toxicology reports that revealed that his wife, Diane Schuler, was drunk and high when she crashed her car on the Taconic Parkway, killing herself and her daughter, Erin Schuler, along with her three nieces, Alyson Hance, Kate Hance, and Emma Hance. She had a blood alcohol count of .19, more than twice the legal limit, as well as THC, indicating that she had smoked marijuana as recently as an hour before the crash. Schuler drove her minivan down the wrong way on the Taconic Parkway and crashed into a SUV. Also killed were father and son Michael Bastardi, 81, and Guy Bastardi, 49, of Yonkers, and a family friend, Daniel Longo. Schuler's son, 5-year-old Brian Schuler, was hospitalized but survived. *Source:* © Polaris/eyevine.

that Shuler was driving under the influence. Toxicology reports later revealed that not only was her blood alcohol level .19, well above the .08 legal limit, but she had high levels of THC, the key ingredient of marijuana, in her body as well (Baker and Kovaleski 2009).

Understanding the true nature of female criminality and crime trends can be obfuscated by the role of the media, which often distorts and embellishes women's criminal involvement and the types of crime they may commit. On the surface, both Heidi Fleiss and Diane Schuler did not appear to be the type of criminal we might expect a female offender to be. Over the past few decades and even more recently media coverage of cases has provided countless reports on female offenders alleged to have committed homicide, such as Susan Smith, Andrea Yates, Amanda Knox, Casey Anthony, and Jodi Arias. In some cases, the media has used these females' sexuality to garner public interest in their cases. For example, Amanda Knox, a University of Washington student, was convicted in 2009 of killing her roommate while studying abroad in Italy – although her conviction was overturned in 2015. Throughout her Italian trial and subsequent appeals, Amanda has been referred to as "Foxy Knoxy" by the press in the United States and Europe (Johnson 2009). Hollywood films are equally guilty in misguiding the public about portrayals of female offenders. Movies such as *Fatal Attraction, Basic Instinct, Kill Bill, Jennifer's Body,* and *American Mary* characterize the female perpetrator as a beautiful white woman who is also murderous, again distorting the picture of female criminality.

In this chapter, we break down the stereotypical images of female offenders and provide a detailed account of the modern-day female offender. Specifically, we begin with an explanation of law and how it is defined in the United States. Next, we will provide a description of female offenders in regard to their race, class, and age, and will review the predominant types of crimes that female offenders commit. Finally, we will focus on the reasons why women commit crime, by presenting several theoretical perspectives, including feminist perspectives, on the nature of female criminality.

 CASE STUDY: Rosemary West

One of the most famous female offenders in the United Kingdom is Rosemary West. Rosemary, along with her husband, Fred, raped and sexually assaulted dozens of young girls and women throughout the 1970s until the late 1980s. West also participated in the killings of many of these young women – including her own daughter and step-daughter (Wright 2014). The authorities did not catch wind of the atrocities occurring at the West home until five children were removed from their home by Child Protective Services in the early 1990s due to sexual abuse allegations (Hunt 2013). Once removed from the home, the children recounted a "family joke" about the whereabouts of their missing sister, Heather. The children kept mentioning that the missing girl was "under the patio" (Hunt 2013). This "joke" blew the case wide open and authorities began to investigate the married couple. Through their investigation, the authorities learned that the Wests had sexually abused, tortured, and mutilated perhaps 30 young women. Some of the dismembered remains of their victims were found buried on their property. Fred West committed suicide before his trial, but Rosemary was tried and convicted for 10 murders in 1995. She is currently serving a life sentence for the murders (Wright 2014).

Defining crime

Before delving into the modern-day portrait of the female offender, it is first necessary to define **crime** and examine the role of Western law in determining what behaviors and actions constitute crime – an illegal act. One of the most frequent definitions of crime that is utilized in the literature was put forth by Tappan (1947). Tappan (1947, 100) has defined crime as "an intentional act in violation of the criminal law committed without defense or excuse, and penalized by the state." Thus, for a particular act to be defined as criminal, it must first be defined as such. How do actions become defined as criminal in the first place? Who is making the decisions in defining what acts are criminal? Historically and even today, those who hold the power define what is criminal in Western law. Who are these powerful individuals? Within US society, those who hold the power are non-minority males from upper socioeconomic backgrounds. From a historical perspective, the **Jim Crow laws** prevented African-Americans from participating in activities afforded to male Caucasians, such as voting. Similarly, women were unable to vote until 1920. These laws clearly demonstrate those with power exerting their influence over the powerless. Denying African-Americans and women the right to vote ensured that those who held powerful positions within the state and federal government would remain in power. Additionally, because definitions of crimes sometimes encompass the sexuality of women, they can adversely impact them. For example, prostitution can still be defined as a criminal act by those in power (i.e., men). The only exception occurs in Nevada where select counties license brothels such as The Moonlite Bunny Ranch. Because men predominately own and operate these brothels, there are jurisdictional variations as to what acts may be defined as crimes. In the case of sexual exchanges in Nevada, men define prostitution and where it is criminal (e.g., streets of Las Vegas) and where sex can be paid for legally (i.e., licensed brothels). In the case of Fleiss, her brothel/call girl service was defined as illegal in California, but had she been running her operation in Nevada, she would have been immune from prosecution. Besides the actual definitions of crimes, those in power also set the penalties for acts defined as criminal. Women are much more likely to engage in prostitution as compared to men, and their clients are more likely to be men. While solicitation of prostitution may be illegal too, the punishments for both are not necessarily similar. These offenses (prostitution, solicitation) are **misdemeanors**, or less serious crimes, meaning that they carry lower levels of punishment. However, in various states, penalties for these offenses which are also set by those in power (i.e., men) have distinct differences. In the state of California, for instance, if a person is convicted of prostitution, he/she has to register as a sex offender but those convicted of solicitation do not.

Besides the differences in power due to gender, race, and even social class in the United States, as well as in other countries, culture, religion, sexual orientation, and nationality also affect definitions of crime as well as punishment. In 2007, a 19–year-old gang rape victim in Saudi Arabia was sentenced to 200 lashes and six months in jail. While she was the victim of a horrific gang rape, she violated a law requiring segregation of the sexes (Clarion Project 2013). Religion and the Old Testament of the Bible in particular have often set the foundation for definitions of **crime** and criminal acts. In the United States, for example, **sodomy laws**, laws that prohibit deviant sexual acts such as anal intercourse, stem from a religious foundation. Since sodomy inhibits procreation, many religious faiths encouraged the formation of such laws in the United States as well as in approximately 80 other countries across the globe (Hepple 2012). These laws, while not specific to homosexuals, were often enforced *against* homosexuals. Further, laws prohibiting abortion were rooted in religious traditions and have impacted women across race and social class. However, legal and social definitions of crime can change over time. As mentioned earlier, Jim Crow laws ended in the 1960s and the US Supreme Court ruling, *Roe v. Wade* **(1973)**, lifted many state and federal restrictions on abortions. Moreover, the US Supreme Court ruled in *Lawrence v. Texas* **(2003)** that state statutes criminalizing sodomy were unconstitutional. Despite this ruling, the Uniform Code of Military Justice – Article 125, a federal law, still prohibits consensual sex between gay/lesbian enlisted service members (Serwer 2013). Additionally, federal legislation passed in 1969 banning **hate crimes**, crimes directed at another based on their race, color, religion, or national origin, was recently expanded in the Matthew Shepard and James Byrd, Jr. Hate Crimes Prevention Act in 2009 to include gender, sexual orientation, gender orientation (i.e., transgendered), and those with disabilities.

Currently defined laws do impact women and cut across race, ethnic, and social class lines. A more detailed examination of laws and how they impact women differentially will be presented in Chapter 4. The next section examines how crime is measured in the United States, with a specific focus on the nature and extent of crimes that women commit.

⚖️ SPECIAL LEGAL ISSUES: Differences in the definitions of crime

While there are global similarities in the types of criminal offenses that females may commit (e.g., property crimes, prostitution), there are distinct differences in the types of crimes that are defined as criminal for females. This is due to the fact that the types of crimes defined as criminal for females are often intertwined with cultural and religious values and controls on the sexuality of women. For instance, in many Middle Eastern countries, such as Iran and Afghanistan, female offenders are defined as criminal for committing moral crimes. Examples of moral crimes include:

adultery; lesbianism; or running away to escape domestic violence or an impending marriage (Human Rights Watch 2012). Like the sodomy laws in the United States, while not directly written to inhibit lesbian and gay relationships, laws covering moral crimes were written, in part, to prohibit lesbianism.

In other instances, females are defined as criminal after reporting that they have been raped. It is not uncommon for the victim to be charged with the crime of zina – voluntary sexual intercourse between a man and a woman as extramarital sex or premarital sex (Human Rights Watch 2012). Over 400 girls and women are currently imprisoned in Afghanistan for moral crimes such as zina, lesbianism, or leaving their husbands (Human Rights Watch 2012). Thus, the legal definitions of crime can vary across the world and often are infused with social and cultural values that may influence the types of crimes females are officially reported to engage in most often. The roles of cultural traditions and the sexuality of women cannot be ignored when reflecting on how criminal definitions may impact females across the world.

Measuring crime

Because assumptions about female criminality are often influenced by the media, they may not be accurate when actual statistics are considered. Media portrayals of women who commit crime starkly contrast with the reality of the types of crimes that women commit. Additionally, the media can distort the race/ethnicity of the violent or dangerous female offender. Perhaps you can recall a recent homicide case reported on in the media where the perpetrator was a female. Did race/ethnicity or sexual orientation play a role in the case? Research has revealed that media depictions of lesbian female offenders often portray these offenders as demons or try to masculinize these offenders in some way (Brennan and Vandenberg 2009; Cecil 2007; Farr 1997; Farr 2000). Media portrayals of female offenders in Hollywood films exemplify this practice well. For instance, in 2003, the movie *Monster* was released, starring Charlize Theron, which depicted the serial killer Aileen Wuornos. While the crimes Wuornos committed were serious, the film was more entertainment at face value, and, in fact, the actress who played Aileen Wuornos, Charlize Theron, won an Academy Award for her performance. The movie did depict some of the abuse Aileen experienced as a child, but it failed to peel back the complex layers of abuse and trauma that she experienced during her childhood and how these experiences contributed to her commission of crimes. Rather, the movie centered on Wuornos' physical appearance, the crimes she committed, and her lesbian relationship – this was much of what the news media was focused on when reporting her case at the time. How lesbian offenders are portrayed in the media is of concern. Martin (2010) suggests that social media can be the hidden force at jury trials. If the women are portrayed as evil, how might potential jurors consuming the reports be affected?

Some scholars have suggested that since women were liberated in the 1970s from their subservience to men and the role of domestic engineer in their homes, they have embraced this new-found "equality" and entered both legal and illegal forms of employment. In fact, some scholars would suggest that the liberation movement resulted in a significant increase of female involvement in crime (Adler 1975). Perhaps another result of the movement is that the media began to pay closer attention to the crimes that women were committing and reports began to suggest that women were now committing crimes at an alarming rate. Yet, is that the case? To ascertain an accurate answer to that question, it is necessary to inspect crime statistics. There are two crime statistics tools that researchers use to understand female and male criminality: (1) official statistics, such as the **Uniform Crime Reports**, and (2) **self-report surveys**. The Uniform Crime Reports are published each year by the FBI and report on the number of arrests, as reported to police, for **Index I crimes** (i.e., murder, sexual assault, robbery, burglary, aggravated assault, larceny-theft, arson, and motor vehicle theft). Self-report surveys, administered by researchers, ask respondents about the number of crimes that they committed over a specific time period. Inspection of crime statistics for female offenders demonstrate that there are inaccuracies in media reporting on female crime trends as well as some similarities and differences between female and male offenders.

Offender characteristics

Who is the modern-day female offender? Let's first examine official statistics in order to help understand this. Overwhelmingly, women are not only less likely to be arrested than males but they are also less likely to commit serious offenses (FBI 2014). Specifically, females were arrested for approximately 27% of Index I crimes, with males being arrested for approximately 73% of index crimes (FBI 2014). One might argue that official crime statistics which rely on arrest data may not reflect the reality of female offending. However, researchers have also discovered that females self-report less criminal involvement than males and are more likely to self-report criminal behavior that is non-violent (Chesney-Lind 1989). Steffensmeier and Haynie (2000) state that males offend at a rate of approximately five to ten times higher than females. This finding was supported regardless of whether the researchers were inspecting official or self-report data. Thus, the finding by the FBI (2014) that women commit fewer serious crimes should quickly dispel the myth put forth by the media in news reports and on truTV trial coverage that women are cold and calculating killers. The fact is that women are more likely to be arrested for committing property crimes, or the Index crimes of larceny-theft, robbery, and burglary (FBI 2014). Their involvement in less serious crimes is what sets women offenders apart from their male counterparts. The idea that women are out of control and committing crime in record numbers has not been substantiated with official data. According to the Uniform Crime Reports (FBI 2014) the overall arrest trends for both adult females (i.e., 9.6%) and juvenile females (i.e., 49.8%) have decreased since 2005. Upon closer examination of the data for adult females arrested in 2014 compared to adult females arrested in 2005, adult females were arrested at a higher rate for burglary, robbery, and larceny-theft (FBI 2014). Advances in technology (i.e., internet fraud; printers to create bad checks; small, expensive, lightweight, portable items that are easy to steal) may account for the increase in arrests for adult women. Technology can make it easier, or more tempting, for adult women to commit crime. Law enforcement officers may also arrest women for crimes they might have committed in an effort to make enforcement of laws more equal across the genders.

With the news showing Caucasian women (e.g., Casey Anthony) to be the likely perpetrators of homicides, and fictional crime television shows, movies, and video games often portraying persons of color as being responsible for other **serious crimes** such as robbery or assault (e.g., *Grand Theft Auto: San Andreas*), let's consider how race fits into the description of the modern-day female offender. The FBI (2014) indicates that 69% of women and men arrested were White, 27% were Black, and the remaining percentages were other races (i.e., American Indian/Alaskan Native, or Asian/Pacific Islander). Additionally, African-Americans had a higher percentage of arrests for serious crimes such as homicide and robbery than Caucasians. While Caucasian offenders were arrested more for Index I offenses, there were disproportionate numbers of African-Americans arrested given their population numbers in the United States. According to the US Census Bureau (2010), African-Americans represent approximately 12% of the total US population. Thus, with 27% of all arrests being attributed to African-Americans in 2014, their arrest rate is not proportionate with their population numbers. Unfortunately, the official crime reports in 2014 do not further break down the percentage of arrests by both gender and race. Self-report surveys can help shed some light on how gender and race intersect, thereby aiding our understanding of crime. Historically, findings from self-report criminal surveys do not support the official statistics that African-Americans are consistently committing more crimes and at higher rates than Caucasians. Results of self-report criminal surveys reveal that Caucasians and African-Americans report similar levels of involvement in criminality regardless of gender – particularly for less serious offenses (Chambliss and Nagasawa 1969; Gould 1969; Piquero and Brame 2008; Tracy 1987; Walker, Spohn, and DeLone 2011). That is, women offenders, regardless of their race, commit similar types of crimes and at the same rates. The disproportionality of arrests for persons of color may stem from bias in the US culture towards minorities or the fact that there are poorer minority women and men residing in urban areas where more law enforcement officers are hired to patrol. Thus, in urban areas, both men and women of color may be more likely to be captured for offenses than those living in rural areas who are not subjected to as much surveillance.

In regard to examining social class as it relates to female offending, there are no official statistics that report on the social class that female offenders belong to. Thus, researchers have relied on self-report data to uncover the relationship between social class and offending. Results from studies using self-report data have generally found that criminal involvement for females and males is similar across the classes (i.e., upper, middle, and lower) and that no one social class is responsible for crimes committed (violent or property) (Dunaway et al. 2000; Hirschi 1969; Jensen and Thompson 1990). However, when examining women in the criminal justice system, women who are poor end up serving sentences in prison more than women from upper socioeconomic backgrounds.

Finally, in regard to age, the majority of those arrested in 2013 were over the age of 18 (FBI 2014). Specifically, arrests in 2014 for those over age 18 were approximately 7.9 million versus 804,000 for those under the age of 18. This finding is consistent with previous research. Researchers have long identified an **age–crime curve**, where those who commit crimes are more likely to be between the ages of 16 and 24, with criminal involvement tapering off thereafter over the life course (Hirschi and Gottfredson 1983). The relationship between age and crime is consistent for both genders, demonstrating that women and men are more likely to commit crime in early adulthood.

Gender differences in type and extent of criminal behaviors

Apart from the differences in the actual crime trends for women and men gleaned from official and self-report data, there are some distinctions in the crimes the two groups may commit.

Homicide

While females commit less serious offenses, they are certainly capable of committing serious crimes. According to the most recent Uniform Crime Reports (FBI 2014), less than 10% of all homicides committed in the United States are committed by women. When females commit a violent crime, such as homicide, it is typically directed at a relative or intimate, such as a child or spouse, and the female acts alone in the commission of the crime (Browne and Williams 1989; Gauthier and Bankston 1997; Gauthier, Chaudoir, and Forsyth 2003). Thus, for the commission of homicide, there is a distinct difference between women and male offenders. For instance, men are more likely to commit homicide with a weapon, and their victims of homicide may be intimates, acquaintances, or strangers. On the other hand, when women kill a child, it is more likely their own and they do so more often with their own hands than with the use of a weapon. One infamous case was that of Susan Smith, who in 1994 allowed her car to roll into a lake in South Carolina with her two young boys strapped in their car seats. Her two sons died (Bragg 1995). Rather than admit to the murders, she fabricated a story that an African-American man had carjacked her and stolen her children and asserted her pleas for the boys' safe return across national media outlets. She was later sentenced to life in prison (Bragg 1995).

In another infamous case, which occurred in 2001, Andrea Yates, a housewife in Texas, methodi-cally drowned each of her five children in a bathtub one by one with her bare hands (Denno 2003). Yates had a history of suicide attempts, and, had a history of postpartum depression and postpartum psychosis. Her final pregnancy exacerbated her psychological problems. On that fateful day, her hus-band left for work and figured that the hour gap between his departure and Yates' mother's arrival at the home would not result in any catastrophic event. Yates was later found not guilty by reason of insanity (Denno 2003).

Much of the violent crime perpetrated by females is directed at intimate males, as opposed to strangers or other females. In many cases, the male victim had been previously victimizing them (e.g., physically and/or sexually). Women who kill their abuser tend to do so after suffering and enduring long periods of abuse, often over years, and will engage in lethal force in an effort to defend their own lives. Unlike women who kill their children using their hands, women who kill their abuser may resort to the use of a gun or knife. In 2008, Barbara Sheehan shot and killed her husband, a former police sergeant, due to years of physical and emotional abuse at the hands of her husband. Sheehan claimed it was self-defense, and she was later acquitted of his murder in 2011 (Bilefsky 2011). When examining female intimate partner homicides where males are the victims, **situational factors**, factors surrounding the event, have emerged that may explain their use of lethal force. Research has indicated that the presence of a history of violence, the location of the incident (e.g., the home), time of day (e.g., evening), and the presence of a weapon (e.g., a gun) are associated with female intimate partner homicide (Campbell et al. 2007; Jurik and Winn 1990; Mann 1998; Riedel and Best 1998; Swatt and He 2006).

Robbery

Although women are less likely than men to commit robbery, they are certainly not incapable of committing this offense. Women express the same motivations as men for committing the act (e.g., money, material possessions) and are also likely to select women as victims. However, the selection of a weapon is a chief difference between the groups. Men who commit robbery almost always use a gun regardless of the gender of the victim, while women are less likely to use a weapon – although women will use force when necessary (Rennison and Melde 2014). Women who use a weapon tend to use a knife either to complete the commission of the robbery act or out of fear that a male victim might overpower them. Women who rob female victims may work with other females, but when they rob male victims, women most often work with other men (Miller 1998). One female robber recalls her act of robbery:

> This was at a little basketball game. Coming from the basketball game. It was over and we were check-ing her out and everything and she was walking to her car. I was, shit fuck that, let's get her moth-erfucking purse. Said let's get that purse. *So* I walked up to her and I pulled out the knife. I said "up that purse." And she looked at me. I said "shit, do you think I'm playing? Up that purse." She was like "shit, you ain't getting my purse. Do what you got to do." I was like "shit, you must be thinking I'm playing." So I took the knife, stabbed her a couple of times on the shoulder, stabbed her on the arm and snatched the purse. Cut her arm and snatched the purse. She just ran, "help, help." We were gone. (Miller 1998, 52)

While male robbers do not discriminate in their selection of robbery victims, female robbers tend to be a bit more selective and are much more likely to rob a female (Rennison & Melde 2014).

Situational factors such as the neighborhood context, peers, and addictions contribute to female commission of crimes such as robbery or assault, and these factors are identical to factors influ-encing male offenders of such crimes (Bennett and Brookman 2009; Rennison and Melde 2014; Sommers and Baskin 1993). Committing a robbery may be a method for earning respect in one's neighborhood. Laura, an offender in the United Kingdom, explains: "I think that's why I've got respect, because I've been in and out of jail, survived. If you're a survivor, stupid things like fighting. I got respect when I did that street robbery and then when I got charged with Section 18, stabbing" (Bennett and Brookman 2009, 628). Besides neighborhood conditions oriented towards crime that may foster a propensity towards crime by its residents, a neighborhood can contribute to criminality in other ways. If men and women are situated in poor, urban areas of a city where education is not valued and there are no legal employment opportunities, then the environment creates a catalyst for crime. If there are no legal means of gaining income, individuals will resort to crime to obtain the necessary resources for survival (e.g., food) and perhaps the "extras" we are told that we need by the greater US culture (e.g., jewelry, nice clothes). Further, if the woman robber associates with other robbers, then she is more likely to engage in robbery. In the female robber's account above, she might not have engaged in robbery had she not been with another female who was also entrenched in the female robbery lifestyle.

Gangs

Another serious type of crime that women are involved in is gangs. Generally a **gang** is defined as a group of three or more individuals that share an identity and often engage in criminal activity. The *National Gang Threat Assessment* (FBI 2011) reports that female entry into male-dominated gangs has burgeoned in the United States, with members coming from all different racial, ethnic, and socioeconomic backgrounds. For the most part, female gangs are racially and ethnically exclusive. Additionally, there exists a mixture of female-exclusive gangs as well as male-dominated gangs with female members. Some female gangs are highly organized in the United States and engage in crimes that generate a profit (e.g., property crimes, drug selling), or engage in violence for **turf protection** or to establish neighborhood boundaries, or for **ethnocentric** reasons (i.e., pride in their race/ethnicity) (Miller, 2001). However, female gang members are more likely to engage in property offenses as part of a gang as opposed to violent crimes (Joe and Chesney-Lind 1995).

Overall, gangs in the United States are predominately male. In those gangs where women are permitted to be members alongside males, women take on subservient roles to the males or perhaps as a means to fit in. In a comparative study of female gang members in St Louis and Columbus, Miller (2001) found that female gang members who were members of a predominately male gang would try to distinguish themselves from the other female gang members and would try to fit in as "one of the guys." More often than not, a female member of a male gang is exploited, as her role is to support male gang members at any cost; and this often results in the female becoming a victim. This may be perhaps why Miller (2001) found that female gang members yearned to fit in – to avoid being victimized. For instance, many male gang members rape female gang members or use female gang members for prostitution or sex trafficking (Miller 2001). One former female gang member of a male gang recalls the sexual exploitation of the female gang members by the males: "They [male gang members] used to tell me, 'I don't have any homegirls – just ho-girls'" (Vigil 2008, 61). Thus, if the male gang member is not exploiting the female gang member for his own sexual interests or to demonstrate his power over her, he exploits her to others outside the gang to earn money for the gang. Despite the risks of victimization or violence inflicted on them, female gang members may view their role with a sense of empowerment – as a method to attain gender equality or gain some form of control of their lives (Miller 2001).

Female gangs are not exclusive to the United States and examples of female participation in gangs can be found throughout the world (see Covey 2010). A common characteristic among most international female gangs is that many members are impoverished, marginalized, less educated, come from broken families, experienced inequality, and are of a minority status (Covey 2010). Like their US counterparts, international female gang members may engage in profit crimes or violence to defend their reputation or turf. Female gang members in the United Kingdom called the Peckham Girls, for example, will engage in aggression or violence to defend their reputation or territory (see Archer 1995). In some countries, such as Guatemala or New Zealand, female gang membership is small and they do not run their own gang enterprise (Covey 2010; Eggleston 2007). Moreover, like female gang members in the United States, many international female gang members experience physical and sexual victimization from their male gang associates (Eggleston 1997).

Property crimes

When inspecting the types of property crimes that female offenders were arrested for most often in 2014, both larceny-theft and fraud were the most common offenses (FBI 2014). In fact, women were more likely to be arrested for these types of crimes than male offenders. Women have become increasingly involved in **white-collar crime** offenses such as insider trading, medical fraud, and embezzlement (Dodge 2008). White-collar crimes refer to crimes committed in the course of white-collar occupations (e.g., banking, corporate offices) within the workplace. Historically, white-collar crimes have been predominately committed by males; however, more recently, women have been increasingly engaging in these crimes. **Embezzlement**, one type of white-collar crime that women are more likely than males to commit, is described as the stealing of funds from an account that a person has been entrusted to oversee, such as a financial account for a school, business, or the government. In 2013, Rita Crundwell, a former city comptroller in the town of Dixon, Illinois, was sentenced to over 19 years in prison for embezzling approximately $54 million from the city over a 22-year period to fund a horse-breeding operation. This is the largest case of embezzlement in the history of the United States (Jeneco 2013).

There are some differences between male and female white-collar crime criminals. One difference is that male offenders tend to commit their crimes in higher positions within an organization (e.g., CEO) whereas female offenders may commit these crimes in clerical positions such as clerks or administrative assistants. Male and female offenders also differ in motives for the crime. Male white-collar criminals may commit these crimes more out of "greed" while female white-collar criminals may commit these crimes more out of "need" (Daly 1989). More recently, Klenowski, Copes, and Mullins (2011) interviewed 20 men and 20 women convicted of a federal white-collar crime and found that both genders reported that support of their families or others was their chief motivation. There may be a few explanations for why women are more likely to commit white-collar crimes. Some scholars have argued that the feminist movement resulted in more women joining the workforce and, hence, increased opportunities for women to engage in crimes at the workplace (Simon 1975). Other scholars have argued that economic marginality has propelled women to dip into the coffers (Daly 1989). Because women are working to support their families but make less money on average than males, they may steal from their employer to compensate for their financial shortfall.

Sex crimes

While not captured in official statistics, it has been estimated that approximately two million women in the United States are currently working as prostitutes; and nearly 50–80% of those involved in prostitution have never been arrested (Murphy 2010). The majority of those involved in prostitution, or other **sex crimes**, do not end up in power positions, or madams, as we saw with the Heidi Fleiss case. More commonly, we hear about cases such as Ashley Wright who worked as a prostitute from her Zumba studio in Maine. Wright's Zumba business partner and alleged pimp, Mark Strong, was her co-partner in the prostitution ring. According to Wright, Strong manipulated her into working as a prostitute by explaining that her role was not as a prostitute but as a state spy that was trying to uncover and expose "sexual deviants" (Metzler 2013). In 2013, Wright was sentenced to a 10-month incarceration term (Metzler 2013). Strong, on the other hand, received a 20-day incarceration term (Sharp 2013).

Historically, prostitution has been a female-dominated profession and women are indeed more likely than males to be arrested for prostitution (Vandiver and Krienert, 2007). However, over the past several decades, with the advancement in technology, males have become increasingly involved in the sex trade. The advancement of technology has also enabled prostitutes, male or female, to seek out clients on Craigslist, dating websites, and Backpage.com, making it more difficult for law enforcement to detect their crimes. For instance, in a study of 23 male sex workers in Melbourne, Australia, McLean (2013) states that the men reported that the Internet is convenient and accessible to so many potential clients. Both male and female prostitutes may work on the streets, in bars, or as part of an escort service. You may have caught some televisions shows featuring male and female escorts. *Blue* is a YouTube Wig series, starring Julia Stiles, who works as an escort. The series launched in 2012 and is still airing online. *Gigolos*, a Showtime reality television series that debuted in 2011 and is still airing today, chronicles male sex escorts working in Las Vegas. There are more similarities than differences between male and female prostitutes – particularly in their journey to the profession. Both males and females may become involved in prostitution due to a lack of income, family conflict, prior abuse, or to support a drug addiction (Matthews 2008; McLean 2013). For female prostitutes, more so than for males, their entry into the profession is often guided by a pimp or other male. In the case of Wright, she claimed that prior sexual abuse by her father was a contributory cause of her involvement in prostitution, and that her involvement was also due to a male accomplice (Metzler 2013).

Drug/alcohol offenses

The FBI (2014) reports that 130,000 arrests were made for females driving under the influence. This number is substantially lower than arrests made for male offenders in the same year. Drug abuse violations also account for a significant proportion of arrests for women (Chesney-Lind and Pasko 2004). In 2014, females were arrested for approximately 169,000 drug abuse violations (i.e., production, distribution, or use of illegal substances), less than the rate of arrests for male offenders. Recall that both Fleiss and Schuler had histories of alcohol and drug use. This finding may not be surprising given the "get tough on crime" policies, particularly for drug use and/or possession. The "war on drugs" campaign re-ignited in the 1980s, resulting in an increasing number of women being arrested for drug violations – particularly African-American women (Bush-Baskette 2010). Harsh drug laws in Latin American countries have also resulted in women being arrested and incarcerated at alarming rates. Youngers (2014) reports that of those incarcerated for drug-related offenses in specific countries, women comprised 30% in Mexico, 60% in Brazil, 75% in Ecuador, and 90% in Argentina.

For female offenders, drug use may be a means of numbing past traumatic experiences (e.g., childhood physical and/or sexual abuse), escaping current problems (e.g., poverty, violence), or coping with any illegal activity they may be a part of (e.g., prostitution) (Chesney-Lind and Pasko 2004). For female offenders involved in the drug-selling business, more often than not, females are not the sellers of drugs but rather the **mules** or carrier of drugs for a boyfriend or spouse (Acoca and Raeder 1999). In spite of the image of a woman dominating the drug-growing and -selling business on a national and international level, as portrayed by actress Mary-Louise Parker in the popular Showtime television series *Weeds*, it is men who dominate the drug-trafficking business, leaving women to serve as the couriers of drugs. Because drug traffickers believe that women will not arouse suspicion, they employ them to transport drugs across states and borders. However, many women become mules because they are poor and are tempted to smuggle the drugs out of necessity to feed their families.

Clearly, female offenders are not a carbon copy of their male counterparts and there are distinct differences in the crimes committed by males and females. The differences in the types of crimes that women and men commit beg the following questions: How do female offenders like Fleiss and Schuler become offenders in the first place? Why is there such a huge gender imbalance in the commission of most crimes? For women who do commit crime, *why* do they do it? One approach is to examine both historical and contemporary theoretical explanations of crime.

 GLOBAL PERSPECTIVES: Female offenders across the globe

Reflecting the findings in the United States, the Ministry of Justice (2011) reported that, in England and Wales, females were less likely to be arrested for committing crimes than males (16% vs 84%). Those arrested in England and Wales were more likely to be members of a minority group. Results from a longitudinal self-report survey in the United Kingdom found that females are less likely to self-report involvement in crime than males (Hales et al. 2009). When females did commit crimes, they self-reported far fewer serious offenses than males. Additionally, results from the survey revealed that the average peak age of offending for females was 14–17 and that minorities did not self-report more criminal involvement than their Caucasian counterparts. In a recent study of men and women in the United Kingdom which asked subjects to self-report criminal involvement, Thorton, Graham-Kevan, and Archer (2012) found that women self-reported involvement in a wide range of crimes including robbery, drug offenses, sex offenses, and fraud/forgery. While women in the United Kingdom self-reported involvement in some violent crimes, like US women they predominately self-reported participation in non-violent crimes.

The Australian Institute of Criminology (2010) reported that males were responsible for most criminal activity, with females constituting approximately 23% of all offenders in 2007–2008. For those females committing crime, they were more likely to commit theft crimes as opposed to violent crimes such as homicide. Additionally, females had the most involvement in crime in the age range of 15–19. Thus, female offenders in Australia are similar in nature to their US counterparts.

Research on female offenders in the Netherlands has also revealed that women commit fewer criminal offenses than men and are more likely to engage in non-violent offenses. Female offenders in this country often are involved in the human trafficking of women. In some instances, females are supporters of existing sex trafficking operations run by men. However, it was also found that females partner with males or run their own sex trafficking operations (Siegel and de Blank 2010).

It is difficult to determine if the characteristics of female offenders are similar for all female offenders across the world. In Russia, for instance, it is known that females are less likely to commit violent crimes such as homicide (Eckhardt and Pridemore 2009). One reason for the difficulty is the inconsistent crime statistic data collection, particularly in Third World countries, which has resulted in researchers providing estimates of female offending (see Adler 1975). For example, while the Ministry of Home Affairs (2014–2015) publishes data on crime statistics in India, it does not report these offenses by gender or race for all crime categories. Despite the limitations in crime data collection, it appears that female offenders in the United States are similar to other female offenders across the world in that they tend to engage in less serious crimes.

Explanations for crime

Gender imbalance of crime

With men committing more crime than women, let's investigate the gender gap. The answer to the question of why men commit more crime than women is not simple. Historically, criminologists developed a theory to explain male offending and then declared that the theory would explain female offending too. However, we can draw from several theoretical perspectives to better understand both male and female criminal involvement. First, let's explore the theories that could explain why a gender gap has existed in crime patterns over the past 100 years and pay specific attention to understanding what theoretical perspectives may shed light on why men commit more crime than women.

Biology/biosocial

Throughout the nineteenth and twentieth centuries, the primary focus of theorists and researchers was on explaining male offending behavior (Chesney-Lind 1989). The early theorists' ideas about offending were consistent with the **positivist school of crime** where crime was thought to be due to some individual difference (e.g., biological or psychological) as opposed to the **classical school of crime** whereby crime is deemed to be a rational choice. Lombroso (1876) stated that male offending was due to atavistic traits, or denigration in evolutionary human development. For instance, criminals exhibited traits such as high cheek bones, long arms, and excessive hair. Essentially, males were involved in crime due to their biology and they were born as criminals. The environment played no role in shaping their criminal tendencies. These early views were referred to as belonging to the **biology theoretical perspective**. Since the 1900s, biological perspectives have been further refined and replaced with biosocial criminological perspectives. **Biosocial criminology**, in fact, is an emerging perspective in the field of criminology. Unlike earlier biological theories posited in the late 1800s and early 1900s, which viewed biology as directly contributing to criminal behavior, biosocial criminologists seek to understand the role of both biology and environmental factors together in terms of how they contribute to criminal behaviors (Walsh 2002; Walsh 2009; Walsh and Beaver 2009). Today, the view of biology in explaining male offending has shifted. Rafter (2008, 244) explains that "responsible researchers no longer claim that biology alone causes behavior problems, for they recognize that behavior results from interactions between nature and nurture, biology and environment. Similarly, responsible biocriminologists today reject biological determinism."

Within the realm of biosocial criminology, scholars have pointed to hormones to explain gender differences in violent behavior. For instance, Wilson (1993) posits that exposure to male sex hormones (androgens), such as testosterone, explains why men are inherently more violent than females. That is, those with higher levels of testosterone are more likely to engage in crime – particularly violent crime. More recently, Kingston et al. (2012) examined the relationship between hormones, including testosterone, and sexual and violent recidivism for 771 male sex offenders. The researchers found a link between hormones and sexual aggression. Research has found that men incarcerated for violent offenses have higher testosterone levels than men incarcerated for property offenses (Anderson 2007). Additionally, some biosocial researchers have argued that the environment can influence biology, specifically that observing violent behavior can increase testosterone levels (Book, Starzyk, and Quinsey 2001). Thus, biology and the environment together can make the perfect mix to explain the predominance of violent male offending behavior.

One of the more prominent biosocial theories in the field was proposed by Moffitt in 1993. Moffitt maintains that there are two distinct groups of offenders: (1) life-course persisters and (2) adolescent-limiteds. She states that predictors of life-course persistence in offending can be seen very early on in the life course. In developing her theory, Moffitt (1993) examined the deleterious effect of biological factors on healthy development and highlighted premature birth as being particularly detrimental. Children born prior to full-term are subject to a number of health risks such as ADHD (Karr-Morse and Wiley 1999; Singh et al. 2013) and low birth weight. Beyond the deleterious health effects, neuropsychological vulnerabilities set children up for a host of cognitive and behavioral deficits. In turn, these deficits can lead to a restricted behavioral repertoire, poor academic performance, difficulty in personal relationships, and life-course-persistent offending. These deficits, accompanied with a difficult temperament, may make parental bonding and socialization more difficult, which can lead to engagement in antisocial behavior. In sum, Moffitt's theory posits that children with neuropsychological injuries will exhibit the early onset of offending, commit crimes over their life course, commit more serious crimes, and are at risk for developing into life-course-persistent offenders. Drawing from the existing literature finding that males are more likely to be chronic offenders, she states that life-course persisters will be predominately male. On the other hand, adolescent-limited offenders begin engaging in criminality later than their life-course-persister peers, mimic life–course-persistent antisocial behavior, engage in less serious crime, are comprised of males and females, and are more likely to demonstrate discontinuity, or desistance, in offending. Empirical investigations of Moffitt's theory have demonstrated links between male delinquent or criminal behavior and low birth weight (McGloin and Pratt 2003; Tibbetts and Piquero 1999), neuropsychological deficits (Moffitt, Lynam, and Silva 1994; Morgan and Lilienfield 2000; Veneziano et al. 2004), birth complications (Arseneault et al. 2002; Raine, Brennan and Mednick 1997), and conduct problems (Moffitt et al. 1996; Moffitt et al. 2001). She believes that early biological disruptions in conjunction with the environment contribute to the development of pervasive male criminal offending patterns.

Evolutionary biosocial theories also arose in the 1990s and posit that biology may play a role in male criminal behavior (Fishbein 2001). Theorists utilizing an evolutionary framework argue that criminal behavior is merely an adaptation to the innate drive to reproduce in order to ensure the continuation of genetic material. These theories have been utilized to explain both criminal and deviant behaviors. This has left some scholars to assert that evolution explains aggression and violence. In the context of explaining male offending, evolutionary theorists would argue that violent offending, including rape, in men is a reproductive strategy whereby aggression allows the male to display physical strength to females and deter genetic competition (Helfgott 2008).

Power-control

One of the most useful theories in explaining the gender gap is **Power-control Theory**, introduced in 1985 by Hagan, Gillis, and Simpson. This theory, which explicitly focuses on the criminality of women, can help us better understand why men commit more crime than women. These criminologists assert that positions held by parents in the workplace (e.g., power positions that males hold in the workplace) affect patriarchal attitudes in the home. The patriarchal attitudes result in different levels of control (e.g., supervision and punishment) and socialization that are placed on boys and girls. Fathers carry their power position from society into the home and expect mothers to socialize children in a manner consistent with traditional gender roles. For instance, both historically and in the modern era, boys are socialized to be dominant and to take risks while girls are socialized to be passive and submissive (Witt 2000). Hagan and colleagues (1985) argue that the differing levels of control play a role in whether the children within the home engage in deviance. Since greater levels of control are placed on girls in patriarchal homes, boys are more likely than girls to be delinquent. On the other hand, in egalitarian families, equitable parental positions in the workplace, or in greater society, translate into more equitable treatment (i.e., control and socialization) of children at home. The theorists posit that in egalitarian families the socialization of boys and girls is similar, which results in comparable involvement in delinquent behavior for both groups. While Hagan and colleagues suggest that the difference in family structure results in differential delinquency rates between males and females, other researchers have found that girls are less delinquent than boys in any type of family, including single-parent families (Morash and Chesney-Lind 1991). If males are socialized from a young age to fit gender stereotypic roles, qualities such as aggression and risk taking may not be expressed in pro-social activities (i.e., sports) but rather in antisocial activities (i.e., crime).

Self-control

You have probably had countless opportunities to commit a crime during your lifetime but you have chosen not to. Perhaps you noticed a tablet unattended in the library but walked on by. According to Gottfredson and Hirschi (1990) in their formulation of the **General Theory of Crime (GTC)**, the reason that you did not was due to your levels of **self-control**. The researchers explain that individuals with low self-control are impulsive, risk takers, short-sighted, and want immediate gratification. GTC maintains that crime will occur when an individual with low self-control is exposed to a criminal opportunity. Low self-control, according to Gottfredson and Hirschi, results from ineffective parenting involving an absence of supervision, nurturance, and discipline. Gottfredson and Hirschi (1990) assert that low self-control is established by age 8 and is a time-stable criminogenic trait – an internal trait geared towards crime that does not change after age 8 over the life course. The researchers dismiss gender, race, or social class as playing a role in offending as they posit that the theory can explain all types of crime for all people. Drawing on the principle of control from Power-control Theory, Gottfredson and Hirschi (1990) would explain gender differences in offending as being due to differences in self-control. Since males have lower levels of self-control, they argue, they are more likely to commit crimes compared to their female counterparts. This higher level of self-control may stem from the differences in socialization (i.e., monitoring of behavior and punishment) of girls and boys as first posited by Hagan and colleagues. Several researchers have in fact found that girls exhibit higher levels of self-control than boys (LaGrange and Silverman 1999; De Li 2004).

Why do women commit crime?

With women committing a smaller percentage of crimes and less serious crimes, the question becomes, why do these select women commit crime? When reflecting on the cases of Fleiss or Schuler or others that may have caught your attention in the news, such as Casey Anthony or Lindsay Lohan, you may have some ideas as to why these women engaged in criminality. Surprisingly, over the past 100 years, attention to the *why* aspect of female offending has been largely overlooked. In fact, female offenders are sometimes referred to as the forgotten or "invisible" offenders because the root causes of their criminal behavior were not examined by early criminologists (Belknap 2007; Chesney-Lind 1989; Heidensohn 1985). Some feminists claim that one likely reason females were overlooked is due to androcentric bias – a focus on male criminality by theorists who were most often male. Perhaps another reason attention was not given to examining female offending is due to their lower levels of offending compared to males. Since males commit more crimes, many early researchers focused their attention on understanding and assisting this group first. Whatever the true reasons for the failure to examine and explain the underpinnings of female offending by criminologists, subsequent theories have evolved to aid our understanding of why a small number of women do indeed engage in crime.

Associations

Lindsay Lohan, a Hollywood actress, and Paris Hilton, a Hollywood socialite, are famous across the globe, and they also were friends at one point in the past. Given their close friendship at one time and the Hollywood scene, it is not surprising that they shared common interests and experiences such as partying and using drugs and alcohol. Additionally, they each found themselves in some trouble with the law. Hilton was convicted of a drug offense while Lohan has convictions for driving under the influence (DUI) and theft (McCartney 2011; Silva 2010). Their friendship, or association, with one another clearly influenced their behaviors – non-criminal and criminal.

It was Edwin Sutherland who, in 1924, first posited this idea that one's social environment can influence behavior – particularly criminal behavior. Sutherland (1939; 1947) claimed that criminal behavior is learned from intimate personal groups – **differential associations** – and you are unlikely to learn crime from watching crime television shows. Do you think that you could be influenced to become a drug smuggler by watching others on television smuggle drugs? Most likely you would not; however, if your best friend was a drug smuggler, you might be more apt to try it and even feel confident at your ability to smuggle drugs successfully. Female offenders are indeed influenced by their peer associations, male or female. In fact, peer associations have consistently been linked to female involvement in *both* violent and property crimes (for exceptions, see Leonard 1982). Recall that female robbers tend to commit robberies with other women, and, in some cases, with men. Heidi Fleiss created her own call girl enterprise through her association with Madam Alex; it's doubtful whether she would have done so independently. As for Diane Schuler, her alcohol use may have been influenced by her husband, who had a previous DUI conviction. Besides the association with other criminals that can influence behavior, Sutherland asserts that there is a tipping point at which an individual may engage in criminal behavior – when the individual has more definitions favorable, rather than unfavorable, to the violation of the law. The tipping point can cause an individual to cross the line from conforming to criminal behavior. In the case of Fleiss, while she knew she was participating in illegal acts, she may have justified the business in that the sexual acts were between two consenting adults and that the women she supervised were well compensated.

Strain

Stress causes some people to smoke or drink. For others, stress may cause them to be a bit feistier than their normal self. Perhaps strain or stress would not propel you to commit a crime, but many women do commit crimes that are influenced by the different strains they experience. Several strain theorists (i.e., Merton; Cloward and Ohlin; Agnew), who put forth **strain theoretical perspectives**, may help us understand why women may commit crime, or commit less crime than men.

In 1938, Merton proclaimed that within the US culture there is much pressure to obtain pecuniary, or monetary, success, a strain that continues to exist in society today. However, not all individuals are able to achieve monetary success through legitimate channels (e.g., legal employment, education), which causes strain. When individuals become strained, Merton (1938) explains that they may resort to illegitimate means (i.e., crime) to achieve their goals. Females, thus, may resort to crime when strained. This may have been the motivation for Fleiss, as she yearned to have a luxurious lifestyle, yet she dropped out of high school in tenth grade. Her lack of education undoubtedly would not afford Fleiss access to high-paying jobs that would allow her to reside in the exclusive Beverly Hills. Perhaps for Lohan, the strains of a dwindling acting career resulting in a loss of income and an alcohol/drug addiction motivated her to steal a gold necklace. She was subsequently convicted for the offense (Winton 2011). One problem with Merton's theory is his belief that all citizens within the United States share the same goals (i.e., monetary success) regardless of social class or gender. Subsequent strain theorists have attempted to refine Merton's original theoretical formulation. In

1960, Cloward and Ohlin further refined Strain Theory, stating that just because one cannot achieve the American dream through legitimate means doesn't necessarily mean one has access to illegitimate means. This is an important point to consider in the context of crime. Even in the "criminal world," men have more power as they are often the ones holding the reins in major criminal operations (e.g., prostitution, organized crime). In the same way that opportunities are limited for women in the US employment market, their opportunity to lead criminal enterprises is also limited. Cloward and Ohlin (1960) further explain that when individuals become strained due to goal blockage, they may resort to gang involvement in order to cope. This may explain female involvement in gangs. More often than not, female gangs are not organized for economic gain; instead, their involvement in gangs may be a method for them to cope with neighborhood strains, such as crime, violence, and broken homes.

One of the most recent formulations of Strain Theory is referred to as General Strain Theory. Agnew (1985) states that one or more types of strain, such as the failure to achieve positively valued goals (e.g., monetary success), the loss of positively valued stimuli (e.g., loss of a friend or parent), and the presentation of negative stimuli (e.g., family conflict), can lead to anger and frustration. If an individual does not have the proper pro-social coping mechanisms to manage these strains, he/she is more likely to engage in crime. Agnew (2001) further explains that strain is more likely to lead to criminal outcomes when the individual views the strain as unjust. Unjust strains are more likely to induce anger and, coupled with poor coping mechanisms, the chance of invoking criminal responses is increased. Moreover, Agnew recognizes that some strains (e.g., childhood abuse) exhibit long-term effects on individuals. Previous research has indicated that men and women experience different types of strain (Broidy and Agnew, 1997). For instance, men are susceptible to experiencing financial strain which may push them towards both violent and property crime. When female offenders experience strain (e.g., strains in personal relationships), they may also feel anger, but in addition they experience depression, guilt, and blame in tandem with the anger (Sharp et al. 2001). Because of this, female offenders are less likely to engage in crime directed towards others, such as violence; instead, they are more likely to cope with strain internally, such as purging or using drugs (Evans, Forsyth, and Gauthier 2002; Sharp, Brewster, and Love 2005). In the case of Schuler, perhaps she used ineffective coping mechanisms (drugs and alcohol) to deal with the stress she felt in driving five children in her minivan. To cope with the stress of engaging in criminal activity and the subsequent trials she endured following her arrest, Fleiss also turned to drugs.

Labeling

Label theorists believe that labels can impact behavior and even spawn criminal behavior (Lemert 1951; Tannenbaum 1938). Lemert (1951) refined **Labeling Theory** by introducing the concepts of primary and secondary deviance. **Primary deviance** refers to norm violations or crimes that an individual commits that are quickly forgotten and do not affect his/her self-concept. On the other hand, **secondary deviance** refers to when a deviant and/or criminal act comes to the attention of significant others such as friends or family members or formal social control agents, such as police, who then apply a negative label. An individual's self-concept is affected in secondary deviance. That is, the individual may internalize the label of criminal from peers or a court sentence as his/her master status. Thus, the individual views himself/herself as a criminal first before thinking of or defining himself/herself in any other way (i.e., male/female, husband/wife, father/mother, etc.). Fleiss appeared to have accepted her label as a Madam. After completing her prison sentence, she relocated to Pahrump, Nevada, to open a legal brothel there (Hubler 2005). The popularity of Labeling Theory waned in the 1980s , with some researchers finding that Labeling Theory was not appropriate for explaining female criminality. Thus, Labeling Theory pretty much became extinct by 1985 (Leonard 1982; Paternoster and Iovanni 1989). This was due, in part, to the little empirical validity for the theory as a whole. Some argued that it might not be just the label that was spawning criminal involvement but other forces as well (e.g., poverty, criminal associations). However, since the near-extinction of the theory, some scholars have begun to reexamine core components of Labeling Theory and their contribution to explaining male and female offending (Bernburg, Krohn, and Rivera 2006; Chiricos et al. 2007).

In regard to male and females, it could be argued that males are more likely than females to be formally labeled since they commit more crimes than females (Jensen and Eve 1976; Messerschmidt 1993). However, females may be more impacted by labels. Since females tend to be more relationship-oriented than males, when labels are applied by significant others such as family and peers, females may be more likely to internalize negative labels. Further, females may be stigmatized more by others for stepping out of their expected feminine role (Chesney-Lind 1989; Giordano, Cernkovich, and Lowery 2004). Both Fleiss and Schuler have been extensively criticized for their roles in crimes and Schuler, in particular, has been harshly criticized in the media and by the public for not properly taking care of the children in her custody. The internalization of the negative labels and stigmatization may indeed offer some insight into female offending. Chiricos and colleagues (2007) examined the effects that being labeled a convicted felon had on future offending. These researchers examined reconviction data for nearly 100,000 men and women in Florida and found that women who were convicted of a felony were more likely than men to recidivate after a two-year follow-up. This finding suggests that the criminal label applied to women may play a larger role in explaining their offending patterns than previously thought.

Social control

With so much attention by criminologists on determining why individuals commit crime, in 1969 one researcher flipped the thinking in the field by asking, why *aren't* individual's engaging in crime? Hirschi (1969), in his book *Causes of Delinquency*, stated that the reason why individuals do not commit crime is due to their bonds. He described four elements of social bonds: (1) attachment; (2) commitment; (3) involvement; and (4) belief. If individuals are attached to someone else, committed to pursuing goals, involved in pro-social activities, and believe laws are to be followed, then they are not apt to engage in crime. However, Hirschi (1969), in this **social control theoretical perspective**, states that if there is a breakdown in one or more of these bonds for an individual, then he/she is likely to engage in crime. While he purports that his theory explains both why males and females do not commit crime, he failed to prove this when he analyzed his female sample data. In a footnote in his book, he states that the "girls disappear" from his analysis and "since girls have been neglected for too long by students of delinquency, the exclusion of them is difficult to justify. I hope I return to them soon" (Hirschi 1969, 35–36). However, he never did. Given the question he was trying to answer, his failure to include females in his analyses was perplexing to many scholars (Chesney-Lind 1989; Naffine 1987). Since females are less likely to offend, it would have made more sense to start his empirical investigation with that sample. While Hirschi did not empirically examine his theory for females, his theory can certainly explain *why* women are not committing crime – for example, because of the bond of attachment. He explains that individuals become attached via **direct** and **indirect controls**. Direct controls refer to the parental supervision and punishment of their children when in their immediate presence. Indirect control refers to the control that parents can have on their children when they are not in their immediate presence. If you ever refrained from doing something either as a child or as an adult because you thought that your parent would "kill" you if you did, then you were successfully controlled by and attached to your parent. Hagan and colleagues' (1985) assertions about the socialization of boys and girls may demonstrate that girls experience more direct controls of their behavior and have a greater internalization of indirect controls than boys. Thus, girls may be more attached to a parent than boys, and, therefore, less likely to commit crime. For those women who commit crime, it is due to a breakdown in bonds and perhaps lack of attachment to a parent or significant other. In the case of Fleiss, she did not have attachments to other pro-social individuals or institutions, which might have made it easier for her to engage in criminality. Without a parent or partner to indirectly control her behavior and her belief that criminal wrongdoing was acceptable, these breakdown in bonds opened the door for Fleiss to engage in crime. For Lindsay Lohan, her estrangement from her father and her strong attachment to her mother, who often partied with Lindsay, may have contributed to some of her entanglements with the law for DUI and theft.

Life course

Some question whether it is possible for behavior to change over time. **Life-course** criminologists examine patterns of offending behavior over time and believe that change may be possible. Specifically, life-course criminologists examine the transitions and turning points in individuals' criminal offending pathways to explain various facets such as onset, desistance, and persistence in criminality. One of the most salient life-course theories, **Age-graded Theory of Crime**, was proposed by Sampson and Laub in 1993. While not a feminist theory, it has been called a "pro-feminist" theory by many scholars. Sampson and Laub's (1990; 1992; 1993) theory argues two points: (1) childhood antisocial behaviors are linked to a host of adult problems, and (2) changes in adult social bonds can change offending trajectories. These changing bonds can increase an individual's chances of persisting with or desisting from crime. That is, if individuals are able to develop quality and pro-social bonds, they are more likely to transition out of prior criminal offending patterns. In empirical examinations of Age-graded Theory, factors such as marriage, association with criminal friends, employment, and military involvement have been linked to changes in offending trajectories (Horney, Osgood, and Marshall; Sampson and Laub 1993; 1996). For example, in an examination of 236 young adults, Simons et al. (2002) found that women involved with a non-criminal romantic partner, who maintain a strong job attachment and who fail to associate with non-criminal friends, significantly reduce the chances of the offending persisting into adult offending. Other researchers have found that being married does not alone lead to desistance from criminality for female offenders, but rather that the marriage needs to be of quality and her spouse also must be pro-social in order for desistance to be fostered (Giordano, Cernkovich, and Holland 2003; Giordano, Cernkovich, and Rudolph 2002). The Schuler case most clearly reflects this point. It is unknown whether Schuler's marriage was of quality, as some reports indicated the marriage was not on a solid footing (Sullivan 2009). More recently, in interviews with 43 female ex-offenders who had recently been released from prison, Opsal (2012) indicated that some females reported employment as the chief avenue to their breaking away from crime and reentering their communities successfully. One subject, Freesia, reported on the transformative role of employment in her life: "I've never been a self-sufficient adult in my life. I've never done stuff for myself … it's my goal to grow up … I want to survive, you know what I'm saying? On my own" (Opsal 2012, 389). Thus, women who engage in crime and continue to do so over the life course tend to be unable to establish quality bonds to pro-social people in their lives or with pro-social institutions (i.e., employment, education).

Feminist perspectives

Feminist perspectives on offending recognize that traditional criminological theories may not be suitable for explaining female criminality. Traditional criminological theories have been criticized by feminists as they often do not account for distinct differences between males and females in their theoretical tenets. The feminist movement in the 1970s brought a renewed interest in issues impacting females in society, including female offenders, causing feminist theories and perspectives on offending to flourish.

Social Feminist Theory

The Socialist Feminist Theory examines the gendered social organization of men and women within the context of capitalism in the United States. Drawing from Marx, a capitalist society creates two distinct classes of individuals: (1) those with power; and (2) those who are powerless. In US society, in terms of gender, the individuals who hold the power are males and those who are powerless are women. Additionally, those who are powerless include other marginalized groups in society such as minorities and those from lower socioeconomic classes. Men, particularly powerless men (i.e., minority, lower class), are more likely to commit violent crime in an effort to reclaim power. On the other hand, crimes committed by women reflect their social organization in society. Even in the criminal world, women lack access to many opportunities that men have, such as the ability to join an organized crime enterprise (e.g., car theft ring). Thus, women are essentially left to commit non-violent crimes such as prostitution or white-collar crimes.

Pathways

One of the most prominent feminist perspectives contends that the **pathways** to offending for women are distinct and, thus, are different from male pathways into offending (Chesney-Lind and Shelden 2004; Daly 1992). From the extant literature, it is clear that prior sexual abuse and physical abuse are catalysts for the onset and persistence of offending patterns for women (Belknap 2007; Chesney-Lind and Pasko 2004; Gunnison and McCartan 2005). In fact, prior victimization of women sets them distinctly apart from male offenders. It is glaringly apparent that sexual abuse figures prominently within the life histories of female offenders. Research into offending has also indicated that women in prison have a higher level of sexual victimization than the general population (Blackburn, Mullings, and Marquart 2008; Siegel and Williams 2003). Blackburn and colleagues (2008) reported that incarcerated female offenders had high rates of childhood and adult sexual victimization over their lifetime. The research further suggests that sexual abuse increases a female's chances of engaging in delinquent and criminal behavior and is also related to running away, instigation of a criminal career, prostitution , aggression, and both onset and persistence in offending (Baskin and Sommers 1998; Belknap 2007; Belknap, Holsinger, and Dunn 1997; Chesney-Lind 1989; Chesney-Lind and Pasko 2004; Gunnison and McCartan 2005). Several researchers have also linked prior sexual abuse to the use of drugs and/or alcohol for women (Bailey and McCloskey 2005; Chesney-Lind and Pasko 2004; Comack 2005; Gilfus 1992; Goodkind, Ng, and Sarri 2006; Widom 1989). For instance, Bailey and McCloskey (2005) examined the link between childhood sexual abuse and later substance abuse (i.e., alcohol and drug use) and found that there is indeed a relationship between the variables. The researchers found that the relationship between childhood sexual abuse and substance abuse held even when they controlled for other factors such as family, alcohol/drug patterns, and early deviant behavior. Oftentimes, the offenders are sexually victimized by a male family member (e.g., father, step-father, uncle, or brother) causing the women to run away from home and turn to the streets for survival. In order to survive, women may turn to prostitution to gain income. Given their involvement in prostitution, women will often use drugs and/or alcohol in tandem as a way to numb previous abuse and their feelings about being involved in prostitution. Women may also become involved in the drug trade as a method of gaining income. Their entry into the drug trade often leads to drug addiction – or further addiction if they were involved in drug use previously. For instance, Kelly, Blacksin, and Mason (2001), who examined 70 women who were receiving substance abuse treatment either as inpatients or outpatients, found that over half of the women had experienced childhood sexual victimization.

Physical abuse experienced by women has been linked to the onset of involvement in criminal activity (Acoca 1998; Belknap et al. 1997; Chesney-Lind and Shelden 2004). As with prior sexual abuse, women are more likely to be victims of physical abuse by intimates. Acoca (1998), who examined abuse histories of young female offenders, reported that physical abuse was related to the onset of drug abuse and gang membership for young women. Lansford and colleagues (2002) found that early physical abuse was related to aggression at age 16 more often for girls than for boys. In 2007, Lansford and colleagues, in a prospective longitudinal study of 574 children, examined the relationship between early physical abuse and later violent offending. The researchers found that men and women who were physically abused at an early age were more at risk as juveniles of being arrested for both violent and non-violent offenses. Further, the researchers also found that the impact of early physical abuse on women and other life experiences was more pronounced for this group than for their male counterparts. Specifically, "females who had been physically abused were approximately 3 times more likely to have been fired and to have been a teen parent" (Lansford et al. 2007, 241). More recently, Teague and colleagues (2008), who examined male and female offenders in Queensland, Australia, found that offenders in their sample who were physically abused engaged in more violent and property crimes than offenders who had not experienced such abuse. As with sexual abuse, the experience of physical abuse by women has a profound and enduring impact on their offending trajectories and may impact their lives in differing ways than male offenders who have experienced such abuse.

Masculinities and crime

Other feminist perspectives do not necessarily view crime as a pathway model but rather as an expression of gender. Messerschmidt (1993), in his masculinities and crime hypothesis, explores the influence of gender, in tandem with race and class, on *both* male and female offending. He asserts that crime is an expression of "doing gender." First, let's briefly examine males. According to Messerschmidt, men and women engage in crime to assert their masculinity. Because males are socialized to prove their masculinity, they may be more likely to commit crime when legitimate means of demonstrating masculinity are thwarted due to inequities in society. For instance, if traditional opportunities to express masculinity (e.g., education, employment) for men are blocked due to their race or socioeconomic status, then they will engage in crime as a means to express their masculinity and secure resources (i.e., money, property). Further, he accounts for gender differences in crime as a matter of the increased need for males to express their masculinity and power more than females. On the other hand, women often engage in crime that is an expression of their femininity. Prostitution, for example, is a crime committed predominately by women as a reflection of their sexuality and femininity. However, women can also engage in crime to demonstrate their masculinity. Given the inequity in power of women when compared to men in the United States, women may engage in crime to assert masculinity. Perhaps Fleiss in her role as a Madam was asserting masculinity in an effort to obtain power and success, something that she was unable to do in the general society. Can we expect female gang members to be passive in male gangs? Probably not. Female gang members would need to demonstrate aggression and violence, masculine characteristics, in order to remain a member of the gang and to survive. Hunt and Joe-Laidler (2001), in a study of 141 female gang members in San Francisco, report that female gang members will indeed resort to violence. The researchers explain, "Within this context of honor, respect, and a fear of achieving a bad reputation, the homegirls often referred to others 'talking shit.' When 'talking shit' occurs, homegirls confront each other, demand a recantation or an explanation, and if it is not forthcoming, then violence can and does occur" (Hunt and Joe-Laidler 2001, 373).

A thorough understanding of how and why Fleiss and Schuler engaged in criminal activity may never emerge. However, these cases illustrate that female offending pathways are complex. It is important to understand that one perspective may not adequately explain offending, but rather a combination of theoretical perspectives may be needed to untangle the pathway to offending for women.

Conclusion

The face of crime is often painted in the media as a White woman who commits violent offenses against men and children, resulting in a portrait of the modern-day female offender that is distorted. The female offender in the twenty-first century is comprised of all races, ethnicities, social classes, and sexual orientations. While she is not incapable of committing violent offenses, the modern female offender will predominately commit non-violent property offenses. Despite the growth in knowledge about female offending over the past several decades, scholars still have much to learn. Although several theoretical perspectives can explain why men may commit more crime and why women do engage in crime, there is knowledge yet to be gained. If we do not have a full comprehension of the multifaceted reasons why women commit crime, then correctional administrators, practitioners, and policymakers may not implement policies that are needed to help women. Assistance is needed to help girls who may be on a troubled path and to help women who are already involved in offending to stop. Without such knowledge-acquisition fueling meaningful policies for girls and women, the revolving door of justice will remain in motion.

Suggested readings

Irwin, Katherine, and Corey Adler. 2012. "Fighting for Her Honor: Girls' Violence in Distressed Communities." *Feminist Criminology*, 7(4): 350–380. DOI: 10.1177/1557085112436837

Jones, Nikki. 2009. *Between Good and Ghetto: African American Girls and Inner City Violence*. New Jersey: Rutgers University Press.

Piper, Kerman. 2011. *Orange Is the New Black: My Year in a Women's Prison*. New York: Random House.

Pizarro, Jesenia M., Christina DeJong, and Edmund F. McGarrel. 2010. "An Examination of the Covariates of Female Homicide Victimization and Offending." *Feminist Criminology*, 5(1): 51–72. DOI: 10.1177/1557085109354044

Student engagement activities

1 Research how both newspapers and the media are depicting suspected female offenders over a specific time period (e.g., one week to one month). Be sure to research local, regional, and national coverage. Record how women are being portrayed in terms of race, class, gender, and sexual orientation. What trends do you notice?

2 There is often a disconnect between the media and criminal justice academics and practitioners. Randomly select a country from a box provided by your instructor before you leave class. Once a country is selected, research a social justice issue pertaining to women in that country. Write a short paper on the social justice issue or issues you found and briefly present your findings in class. Include how the media has, or has not, portrayed the social justice issue(s).

3   Given that women in this country, as well as other countries, often have no voice due to their status, how might you be better able to provide these marginalized groups, specifically female offenders, with a voice? Think about ways in which you could reach out in your community to help offenders have a greater voice and educate your community about their plights. You could immerse yourself in research or conduct case studies about women of various races/ethnicities and social classes involved in crime to better understand their unique journeys into crime. With this knowledge, you could write an editorial in a newspaper, or prepare a presentation on female criminality and give it to your community and/or members of the media.

Discussion questions

1   What is the role of the media in shaping our perceptions of the modern-day female offender? Provide some examples of how the media can shape our perceptions from outside this text.
2   How are women offenders distinct from male offenders?
3   What theory/theories resonate most with you to explain why women engage in crime? Why? Can you think of policies and/or programs to help assist women who engage in crime?

Key terms

Age–crime curve
Age-graded Theory of Crime
Biology theoretical perspective
Biosocial criminology
Classical school of crime
Crime
Differential associations
Direct controls
Embezzlement
Ethnocentric
Gang
General Theory of Crime (GTC)
Hate crimes
Index 1 crimes
Indirect controls
Jim Crow laws
Labeling Theory
Lawrence v. Texas (2003)
Life course
Misdemeanors

Mules
Pathways
Positivist school of crime
Power-control Theory
Primary deviance
Roe v. Wade (1973)
Secondary deviance
Self-control
Self-report surveys
Serious crimes
Sex crimes
Situational factors
Social control theoretical perspective
Social feminist theory
Sodomy laws
Strain theoretical perspectives
Turf protection
Uniform Crime Reports
White-collar crimes

References

Acoca, Leslie. 1998. "Outside/Inside: The Violation of American Girls at Home, on the Streets, and in the Juvenile Justice System." *Crime and Delinquency*, 44(4): 561–589. DOI: 10.1177/0011128798044004006

Acoca, Leslie, and Myrna S. Raeder. 1999. "Severing Family Ties: The Plight of Nonviolent Female Offenders and Their Children." *Stanford Law & Policy Review*, 11: 133–151.

Adler, Freda. 1975. *Sisters in Crime*. New York: McGraw-Hill.

Agnew, Robert. (1985. "A Revised Strain Theory of Delinquency." *Social Forces*, 64(1), 151–167.

Agnew, Robert. 2001. "Building on the Foundation of General Strain Theory: Specifying the Types of Strain Most Likely to Lead to Crime and Delinquency." *Journal of Research in Crime and Delinquency*, 38: 319–361. DOI: 10.1177/0022427801038004001

Anderson, Gail S. 2007. *Biological Influences on Criminal Behavior*. Boca Raton, FL: Simon Frasier University Press.

Archer, Debbie. 1995. "Riot Grrrl and Raisin Girl: Femininity Within the Female Gang: The Power of the Popular." *The British Criminology Conferences: Selected Proceedings. Volume 1: Emerging Themes in Criminology*: 18–21.

Arseneault, Louise, Tremblay, Richard E., Boulerice, B., and Jean-François Saucier. 2002. "Obstetrical Complications and Violent Delinquency: Testing Two Developmental Pathways." *Child Development*, 73(2): 496–508 DOI: 10.1111/1467-8624.00420

Australian Institute of Criminology. 2010. *Australian Crime: Facts and Figures, 2009*. Canberra.

Bailey, Jennifer A., and Laura A. McCloskey. 2005. "Pathways to Adolescent Substance Use Among Sexually Abused Girls." *Journal of Abnormal Child Psychology*, 33: 39–53. DOI: 10.1007/s10802-005-0933-0

Baker, Al, and Serge F. Kovaleski. August 7, 2009. "Details About Alcohol and Phone Calls Emerge in Wrong-Way Crash." *New York Times*. Accessed March 11, 2013, http://www.nytimes.com/2009/08/08/nyregion/08crash.html

Baskin, Deborah R., and Ira Sommers. 1998. *Casualties of Community Disorder: Women's Careers in Violent Crime*. Boulder, CO: Westview Press.

Belknap, Joanne. 2007. *The Invisible Woman: Gender, Crime, and Justice*. Belmont, CA: Thomson/Wadsworth.

Belknap, Joanne, Holsinger, Kristi, and Melisasa Dunn. 1997. "Understanding Incarcerated Girls: The Results of a Focus Group Study." *Prison Journal*, 77(4): 381–404. DOI: 10.1177/0032855597077004003

Bennett, Trevor, and Fiona Brookman. 2009. "The Role of Violence in Street Crime: A Qualitative Study of Violent Offenders." *International Journal of Offender Therapy and Comparative Criminology*, 53(6): 617–633.

Bernburg, Jon G., Krohn, Marvin D., and Craig J. Rivera. 2006. "Official Labeling, Criminal Embeddedness, and Subsequent Delinquency: A Longitudinal Test of Labeling Theory." *Journal of Research in Crime and Delinquency*, 43: 67–88. DOI: 10.1177/0022427805280068

Bilefsky, Dan. October 6, 2011. "Wife Who Fired 11 Shots Is Acquitted of Murder." *New York Times*. Accessed March 24, 2014, http://www.nytimes.com/2011/10/07/nyregion/barbara-sheehan-who-killed-husband-is-found-not-guilty-of-murder.html?pagewanted=all

Blackburn, Ashley G., Mullings, Janet L., and James W. Marquart. 2008. "Sexual Assault in Prisons and Beyond: Toward an Understanding of Lifetime Sexual Assault Among Incarcerated Women." *The Prison Journal*, 88(32): 351–377. DOI: 10.1177/0032885508322443

Book, Angela, Starzyk, Katherine, and Vernon Quinsey. 2001. "The Relationship Between Testosterone and Aggression: A Meta-Analysis." *Aggression and Violent Behaviour*, 6: 579–599.

Bragg, Rick. 1995. July 29, 1995. "Carolina Jury Rejects Execution for Woman Who Drowned Sons." *New York Times*. Accessed March 18, 2015, http://www.nytimes.com/1995/07/29/us/carolina-jury-rejects-execution-for-woman-who-drowned-sons.html

Brennan, Pauline K., and Abby L. Vandenberg, 2009. "Depictions of Female Offenders in Front-Page Newspaper Stories: The Importance of Race/Ethnicity." *International Journal of Social Inquiry*, 2(2): 141–175.

Broidy, Lisa, and Robert Agnew. 1997. "Gender and Crime: A General Strain Theory Perspective." *Journal of Research in Crime and Delinquency*, 34: 275–306. DOI: 10.1177/0022427897034003001

Browne, Angela, and Kirk R. Williams. 1989. "Exploring the Effect of Resource Availability and the Likelihood of Female-Perpetrated Homicides." *Law and Society Review*, 23: 63–73.

Bush-Baskette, Stephanie. 2010. *Misguided Justice: The War on Drugs and the Incarceration of Black Women*. Bloomington, IN: iUniverse.

Campbell, Jacquelyn, Glass, Nancy, Sharps, Phyllis W., Laughon, K., and Tina Bloom. 2007. "Intimate Partner Homicide: Review and Implications of Research and Policy." *Trauma, Violence, and Abuse*, 8(3): 246–269. DOI: 10.1177/1524838007303505

Cecil, Dawn K. 2007. "Dramatic Portrayals of Violent Women: Female Offenders on Prime Time Crime Dramas." *Journal of Criminal Justice and Popular Culture*, 14(3): 243–258.

Chambliss, William J., and Richard H. Nagasawa. 1969. "On the Validity of Official Statistics: A Comparative Study of White, Black and Japanese High-School Boys." *Journal of Research in Crime and Delinquency*, 6(1): 71–77.DOI: 10.1177/002242786900600108

Chesney-Lind, Meda. 1989. "Girl's Crime and Woman's Place: Toward a Feminist Model of Female Delinquency." *Crime and Delinquency*, 35(1): 8–10. DOI: 10.1177/0011128789035001002

Chesney-Lind, M., and Linda Pasko. 2004. *The Female Offender: Girls, Women, and Crime*. Thousand Oaks, CA: Sage.

Chesney-Lind, Meda, and Randall Shelden. 2004. *Girls, Delinquency, and Juvenile Justice*. Belmont, CA: Thompson/Wadsworth.

Chiricos, Ted, Barrick, Kelle, Bales, William, and Stephanie Bontrager. 2007. "The Labeling of Convicted Felons and Its Consequences for Recidivism." *Criminology*, 45(3): 547–581. DOI: 10.1111/j.1745-9125.2007.00089.x

Clarion Project. 2013. "Saudi Arabia Defends Barbaric Sentence Given to Rape Victim." Accessed March 18, 2014, http://www.clarionproject.org/news/saudi-arabia-defends-barabric-sentence-given-rape-victim#

Cloward, Richard A., and Lloyd E. Ohlin. 1960. *Delinquency and Opportunity: A Theory of Delinquent Gangs*. New York: Free Press.

Comack, Eileen. 2005. "Coping, Resisting, and Surviving: Connecting Women's Law Violations to Their Histories of Abuse." In *In Her Own Words: Women Offenders' Views on Crime and Victimization*, edited by Leanne Alaraid and Paul Cromwell, 33–43. Los Angeles, CA: Roxbury.

Covey, Herbert C. 2010. *Street Gangs Throughout the World*. Springfield, IL: Charles C. Thomas Publisher.

Daly, Kathleen. 1989. "Gender and Varieties of White-collar Crime." *Criminology*, 27(4), 769–794.

Daly, Kathleen.1992. "Women's Pathways to Felony Court: Feminist Theories of Lawbreaking and Problems of Representation." *Southern California Review of Law and Women's Studies*, 2: 11–52.

De Li, Spencer. 2004. "The Impacts of Self-Control and Social Bond on Juvenile Delinquency in a National Sample of Mid-Adolescents." *Deviant Behavior*, 25: 351–373. DOI: 10.1080/01639620490441236

Denno, Deborah W. 2003. "Who Is Andrea Yates? A Short Story About Insanity." *Duke Journal of Gender Law & Policy*, 10(1): 1–60.

Dodge, Mary. 2008. *Women and White-Collar Crime*. Upper Saddle River, NJ: Prentice Hall.

Dunaway, Gregory, Cullen, Francis T., Burton, Velmer S., and T. David Evans. 2000. "Myth of Social Class and Crime Revisited: An Examination of Class and Adult Criminality." *Criminology*, 38(2): 589–632. DOI: 10.1111/j.1745-9125.2000.tb00900.x

Eckhardt, Krista, and William A. Pridemore. 2009. "Differences in Male and Female Involvement in Lethal Violence in Russia." *Journal of Criminal Justice*, 37: 55–64. DOI: 10.1016/j.jcrimjus.2008.12.009

Eggleston, Elaine. 1997. *An Ethnography of Youth Texts on Gangs, Trouble and Rehabilitation*. Doctoral Dissertation, New Zealand

Evans, Rhonda, Forsyth, Craig J., and DeAnn K. Gauthier. 2002. "Gendered Pathways Into and Experiences Within Crack Cultures Outside of the Inner City." *Deviant Behavior*, 23(6): 483–510. DOI: 10.1080/01639620290086468

Farr, Kathryn. A. 1997. "Aggravating and Differentiating Factors in the Cases of White and Minority Women on Death Row." *Crime and Delinquency*, 43(3): 260–278. DOI: 10.1177/0011128797043003002

Farr, Kathryn. A. 2000. Defeminizing and Dehumanizing Female Murderers: Depictions of Lesbians on Death Row." *Women and Criminal Justice*, 11(1): 49–66. DOI: 10.1300/J012v11n01_03

FBI (Federal Bureau of Investigation). 2011. *National Gang Threat Assessment: Emerging Trends*. Washington, DC.

FBI (Federal Bureau of Investigation). 2014. *Uniform Crime Report*. Washington, DC.

Fishbein, Diane. H. 2001. *Biobehavioral Perspectives on Criminology*. Belmont, CA: Thomson/Wadsworth.

Gauthier, Deann K., and William B. Bankston. 1997. "Gender Equality and the Sex Ratio of Intimate Killing." *Criminology*, 35: 577–600. DOI: 10.1111/j.1745-9125.1997.tb01231.x

Gauthier, Deanne K., Chaudoir, Nancy K., and Craig J. Forsyth. 2003. "A Sociological Analysis of Maternal Infanticide in the United States, 1984–1996." *Deviant Behavior*, 24(4): 393–404. DOI: 10.1080/713840226

Gilfus, Mary E. 1992. "From Victims to Survivors to Offenders: Women's Routes of Entry and Immersion into Street Crime." *Women and Criminal Justice*, 4: 63–89. DOI: 10.1300/J012v04n01_04

Giordano, Peggy C., Cernkovich, Stephen A., and Allen R. Lowery. 2004. "A Long-Term Follow-Up of Serious Adolescent Female Offenders." In *Aggression, Antisocial Behavior and Violence Among Girls*, edited by MarthaPutallaz and Karen L.Bierman, 186–202. New York, NY: Guilford Press.

Giordano, Peggy C., Cernkovich, Stephen A., and Jennifer L. Rudolph. 2002. "Gender, Crime, and Desistance: Toward a Theory of Cognitive Transformation." *American Journal of Sociology*, 107(4): 990–1064. DOI: 10.1086/343191

Giordano, Peggy C., Cernkovich, Stephen A., and Donna D. Holland. 2003. "Changes in Friendship Relations Over the Life Course: Implications for Desistance from Crime." *Criminology*, 41(2): 293–327. DOI: 10.1111/j.1745-9125.2003.tb00989.x

Goodkind, Sara, Ng, Irene, and Rosemary C. Sarri. 2006. "The Impact of Sexual Abuse in the Lives of Young Women Involved or at Risk of Involvement with the Juvenile Justice System." *Violence Against Women*, 12: 456–477. DOI: 10.1177/1077801206288142

Gottfredson, Michael R., and Travis Hirschi.1990. *A General Theory of Crime*. Stanford, CA: Stanford University Press.

Gould, Leroy C. 1969. "Who Defines Delinquency: A Comparison of Self-Reported and Officially Reported Indices of Delinquency for Three Racial Groups." *Social Problems*, 16(3): 325–336. DOI: 10.1525/sp.1969.16.3.03a00060

Gunnison, Elaine, and Lisa M. McCartan. 2005. "Female Persisters in Criminal Offending: A Theoretical Examination of Predictors." *Women and Criminal Justice*, 16: 43–65.DOI: 10.1300/J012v16n03_03

Hagan, John, Gillis, A. R., and John Simpson. 1985. "The Class Structure of Gender and Delinquency: Toward a Power-Control Theory of Common Delinquent Behavior." *American Journal of Sociology*, 90: 1151–1178.

Hales, Jon, Nevill, Camilla, Pudney, Steve, and Sarah Tipping. 2009. *Longitudinal Analysis of the Offending, Crime and Justice Survey 2003–2006*. London: Home Office.

Heidensohn, Francis. 1985. *Women and Crime*. Basingstoke: Macmillan.

Helfgott, Jacqueline B. 2008. *Criminal Behavior: Theories, Typologies, and Criminal Justice*. Los Angeles, CA: Sage.

Hepple, Joshua. 2012. "Will Sexual Minorities Ever Be Equal? The Repercussions of British Colonial 'Sodomy' Laws." *Equal Rights Review*, 8: 50–64.

Hirschi, Travis. 1969. *Causes of Delinquency*. Berkeley: University of California Press.

Hirschi, Travis, and Michael Gottfredson. 1983. "Age and the Explanation of Crime." *American Journal of Sociology*, 89: 552–584.

Horney, Julie, Osgood, D. Wayne, and Ineke Marshal. 1995. "Criminal Careers in the Short-Term: Intra-Individual Variability in Crime and Its Relation to Local Life Circumstances." *American Sociological Review*, 60: 655–673.

Hubler, Shawn. January 8, 1997. "Fleiss Sentenced to 37 Months for Tax Evasion." *Los Angeles Times*. Accessed March 12, 2013, http://articles.latimes.com/1997-01-08/local/me-16452_1_heidi-fleiss

Hubler, Shawn. November 17, 2005. "Fleiss Plans a Brothel to Serve Women. The Former Hollywood Madam and a Partner Hope to Open 'Heidi's Stud Farm' in Nevada." *Los Angeles Times*. Accessed March 12, 2013, http://articles.latimes.com/2005/nov/17/local/me-fleiss17

Human Rights Watch. 2012. *"I Had to Run Away." The Imprisonment of Women and Girls for "Moral Crimes" in Afghanistan*. Accessed March 15, 2013, http://www.hrw.org/sites/default/files/reports/afghanistan0312webwcover_0.pdf

Hunt, Elisa. May 12, 2013. "British Mum Rosemary West Is a Shocking Serial Killer Among Our Female Felons in True Crime Scene." *Herald Sun*. Accessed March 24, 2014, http://www.heraldsun.com.au/news/law-order/british-mum-rosemary-west-is-a-shocking-serial-killer-among-our-female-felons-in-true-crime-scene/story-fnat7jnn-1226639619598

Hunt, Geoffrey, and Karen Joe-Laidler. 2001. "Situations of Violence in the Lives of Girl Gang Members." *Health Care for Women International*, 22: 363–384. DOI: 10.1080/07399330152398909

Jeneco, Melissa. Febuary 13, 2013. "Ex-Dixon Comptroller Gets 19 1/2 Years for $54 million Fraud." *Chicago Tribune*. Accessed March 21, 2013, http://articles.chicagotribune.com/2013-02-14/news/chi-rita-crundwell-sentencing-20130214_1_rita-crundwell-dixon-coffers-paul-gaziano

Jensen, Gary F., and Raymond Eve. 1976. "Sex Differences in Delinquency." *Criminology*, 13: 427–448. DOI: 10.1111/j.1745-9125.1976.tb00679.x

Jensen, Gary F., and Kevin Thompson. 1990. "What's Class Got to Do With It? A Further Examination of Power-Control Theory." *American Journal of Sociology*, 95: 1009–1023.

Joe, Karen A., and Meda Chesney-Lind. 1995. "Just Every Mother's Angel: An Analysis of Gender and Ethnic Variations in Youth Gang Membership." *Gender and Society*, 9(4): 408–431. DOI: 10.1177/089124395009004002

Johnson, Gene. December 4, 2009. "Family of Amanda Knox Vows to Continue the Fight." *The Seattle Times*. Accessed March 17, 2013, http://seattletimes.nwsource.com/html/localnews/2010428614_apwastudentslainknoxfamily2ndldwritethru.html

Jurik, Nancy C., and Russ Winn. 1990. "Gender and Homicide: A Comparison of Men and Women Who Kill." *Violence and Victims*, 5: 227–242.

Karr-Morse, Robin, and Meredith S. Wiley. 1999. *Ghosts from the Nursery: Tracing the Roots of Violence*. New York, NY: Atlantic Monthly Press.

Kelly, Patricia, Blacksin, Beth, and Ellen Mason, 2001. "Factors Affecting Substance Abuse Treatment Completion for Women." *Issues in Mental Health Nursing*, 2: 287–304. DOI: 10.1080/01612840121344

Kingston, Drew A., Seto, Michael C., Ahmed, Adekunle G., Fedoroff, Paul, Firestone, Philip, and John M. Bradford. 2012. "The Role of Central and Peripheral Hormones in Sexual and Violent Recidivism in Sex Offenders." *Journal of the American Academy of Psychiatry and the Law*, 40: 476–485.

Klenowski, Paul M., Copes, Heith, and Christopher W. Mullins. 2011. "Gender, Identity, and Accounts: How White Collar Offenders Do Gender When Making Sense of Their Crimes." *Justice Quarterly*, 28: 46–69.

LaGrange, Teresa C., and Robert A. Silverman. 1999. "Low Self-Control and Opportunity: Testing the General Theory of Crime as an Explanation for Gender Differences in Delinquency." *Criminology*, 37: 41–72. DOI: 10.1111/j.1745-9125.1999.tb00479.x

Lansford, Jennifer E., Dodge, Kenneth A., Pettit, Gregory S., Bates, John E., Crozier, Joseph, and Julie Kaplow. 2002. "A 12-year Prospective Study of the Long-Term Effects of Early Child Physical Maltreatment on Psychological, Behavioral, and Academic Problems in Adolescence." *Archives of Pediatrics and Adolescent Medicine*, 156: 824–830.

Lansford, Jennifer E., Miller-Johnson, Shari, Berlin, Lisa J., Dodge, Kenneth A., Bates, John E., and Gregory S. Pettit. 2007. "Early Physical Abuse and Later Violent Delinquency: A Prospective Longitudinal Study." *Child Maltreatment*, 12(3): 233–245. DOI: 10.1177/1077559507301841

Lawrence v. Texas, 539 U.S. 558. 2003.

Lemert, Edwin M. 1951. *Social Pathology: Systematic Approaches to the Study of Sociopathic Behavior.* New York, NY: McGraw-Hill.

Leonard, Eileen B. 1982. *Women, Crime and Society: A Critique of Theoretical Criminology.* New York, NY: Longman.

Lombroso, Cesare. 1876. *The Criminal Man.* New York, NY: Knickerbocker Press.

Mann, Coramae R. 1998. "Getting Even? Women Who Kill in Domestic Encounters." *Justice Quarterly*, 5: 33–51. DOI: 10.1080/07418828800089601

Martin, Christine. 2010. "Social Media: The Hidden Force at Jury Trials." *Westlaw Journal*, 17(15), 1–3.

The Matthew Shepard and James Byrd, Jr., Hate Crimes Prevention Act of 2009, 18 U.S.C. § 249.

Matthews, Roger. 2008. *Prostitution, Politics & Policy.* New York, NY: Routledge.

McCartney, Anthony. July 21, 2011. "Judge: Lohan Needs to Speed up Community Service." *Seattle Times.* Accessed March 19, 2014, http://www.seattletimes.nwsource.com

McGloin, Jean M., and Travis C. Pratt 2003. "Cognitive Ability and Delinquent Behavior Among Inner-City Youth: A Life-Course Analysis of Main, Mediating, and Interaction Effects." *International Journal of Offender Therapy and Comparative Criminology*, 47: 253–271.

McLean, Andrew. 2013. "'You Can Do It from Your Sofa': The Increasing Popularity of the Internet as a Working Site Amongst Male Sex Workers in Melbourne." *Journal of Sociology*: 1–16. DOI: 10.1177/1440783313480416

Merton, Robert K. 1938. "Social Structure and Anomie." *American Sociological Review*, 3(5): 672–682.

Messerschmidt, James W. 1993. *Masculinities and Crime.* Langham, MD: Rowman and Littlefield.

Metzler, Rebekah. May 31, 2013. "Maine Zumba Case Ends with 10-month Sentence for Prostitute." *U.S. News and World Report.* Acccessed March 19, 2014, http://www.usnews.com/news/newsgram/articles/2013/05/31/maine-zumba-case-ends-with-10-month-sentence-for-prostitute

Miller, Jody. 1998. "Up It Up: Gender and the Accomplishment of Street Robbery." *Criminology*, 36, 37–66.

Miller, Jody. 2001. *One of the Guys: Girls, Gangs and Gender.* New York, NY: Oxford University Press.

Ministry of Home Affairs. 2014–2015. *Annual Report.* Departments of Internal Security, States, Home, Jammu & Kashmir Affairs and Border Management. Government of India.

Ministry of Justice. 2011. *Statistics on Race and the Criminal Justice System, 2010.* Ministry of Justice Statistical Bulletin. Accessed March 12, 2014, www.justice.gov.uk/statistics/criminal-justice/race

Moffitt, Terrie E. 1993. "Adolescence-Limited and Life-Course-Persistent Antisocial Behaviour: A Developmental Taxonomy." *Psychological Review*, 100(4): 674–701. DOI: 10.1037/0033-295X.100.4.674

Moffitt, Terrie E., Caspi, Avshalom, Dickson, Nigel, Silva, Phil, and Warren Stanton. 1996. "Childhood-Onset Versus Adolescent-Onset Antisocial Conduct Problems in Males: Natural History from Ages 3 to 18 Years." *Development and Psychopathology*, 8: 399–424. DOI: http://dx.doi.org/10.1017/S0954579400007161

Moffitt, Terrie E., Caspi, Avshalom, Rutter, Michasel, and Phil A. Silva. 2001. *Sex Differences in Antisocial Behaviour*. Cambridge: Cambridge University Press.

Moffitt, Terrie E., Lynam, Donald, and Phil Silva. 1994. "Neuropsychological Tests Predicting Persistent Male Delinquency." *Criminology*, 32: 277–300. DOI: 10.1111/j.1745-9125.1994.tb01155.x

Morash, Merry, and Meda Chesney-Lind. 1991. "A Reformulation and Partial Test of the Power-control Theory of Delinquency." *Justice Quarterly*, 8(3), 347–377.

Morgan, Alex B., and Scott O. Lilienfeld. 2000. "A Meta-Analytic Review of the Relation Between Antisocial Behavior and Neuropsychological Measures of Executive Functioning." *Clinical Psychology Review*, 20: 113–136. DOI: 10.1016/S0272-7358(98)00096-8

Murphy, Lyn S. 2010. "Understanding the Social and Economic Contexts Surrounding Women Engaged in Street-level Prostitution." *Issues in Mental Health Nursing*, 31, 775–784.

Naffine, Ngaire. 1987. *Female Crime, the Construction of Women in Criminology*. Sydney: Allen and Unwin.

Opsal, Tara. 2012. "'Livin' on the Straights': Identity, Desistance, and Work Among Women Post-Incarceration." *Sociological Inquiry*, 82: 378–403. DOI: 10.1111/j.1475-682X.2012.00421.x

Paternoster, Raymond, and LeeAnn Iovanni. 1989. "The Labeling Perspective and Delinquency: An Elaboration of the Theory and Assessment of the Evidence." *Justice Quarterly*, 6: 359–394. DOI: 10.1080/07418828900090261

Piquero, Alex, and Robert W. Brame. 2008. "Assessing the Race-Crime and Ethnicity-Crime Relationship in a Sample of Serious Adolescent Delinquents." *Crime and Delinquency*, 54(1): 390–422.

Rafter, Nicole. 2008. *The Criminal Brain: Understanding Biological Theories of Crime*. New York, NY: New York University Press.

Raine, Adrain, Brennan, Patricia, and Sarnoff Mednick. 1997. "Interaction Between Birth Complications and Early Maternal Rejection in Predisposing Individuals to Adult Violence: Specificity to Serious, Early-Onset Violence." *American Journal of Psychiatry*, 154(9): 1265–1271.

Rennison, Callie M., and Chris Melde. 2014. "Gender and Robbery: A National Test." *Deviant Behavior*, 35(4): 275–276. DOI: 10.1080/01639625.2013.848104

Riedel, Marc, and Joel Best. 1998. "Patterns in Intimate Partner Homicide." *Homicide Studies*, 2: 305–320. DOI: 10.1177/1088767998002003010

Roe v. Wade, 410 U.S. 113. 1973.

Sampson, Robert, and John Laub. 1990. "Crime and Deviance over the Life Course: The Salience of Adult Bonds." *American Sociological Review*, 55, 609–627.

Sampson, Robert, and John Laub. 1992. "Crime and Deviance in the Life Course." *Annual Review of Sociology*, 18, 63–84.

Sampson, Robert J., and John H. Laub. 1993. *Crime in the Making: Pathways and Turning Points Through Life*. Cambridge, MA: Harvard University Press.

Sampson, Robert, and John Laub. 1996. "Socioeconomic Achievement in the Life Course of Disadvantaged Men: Military Service as a Turning Point, circa 1940–1965." *American Sociological Review*, 61, 344–367.

Serwer, Adam. 2013. "Why the Military Still Bans Sodomy?" *MSNBC News*. Accessed March 18, 2014, http://www.msnbc.com/msnbc/why-the-military-still-bans-sodomy

Sharp, David. March 21, 2013. "Maine Man Gets 20 Days in Zumba Paid-Sex Case." *USA Today*. Accessed March 19, 2014, http://www.usatoday.com/story/news/nation/2013/03/21/prostitution-sex-maine-zumba/2005533/

Sharp, Susan F., Brewster, Dennis, and Sharon R. Love. 2005. "Disentangling Strain, Personal Attributes, Affective Response and Deviance: A Gendered Analysis." *Deviant Behavior*, 26(2): 133–157. DOI: 10.1080/01639620590522028

Sharp, Susan F., Terling-Watt, Toni L., Atkins, Leslie A., Gilliam, Jay T., and Anna Sanders. 2001. "Purging Behavior in a Sample of College Females: A Research Note on General Strain Theory and Female Deviance." *Deviant Behavior*, 22(2): 171–188. DOI: 10.1080/016396201750065036

Siegel, Dina, and Sylvia de Blank. 2010. "Women Who Traffic Women: The Role of Women in Human Trafficking Networks – Dutch Cases." *Global Crime*, 11(4): 436–447. DOI: 10.1080/17440572.2010.519528

Siegel, Jane A., and Linda M. Williams. 2003. "The Relationship Between Childhood Sexual Abuse and Female Delinquency and Crime: A Prospective Study." *Journal of Research in Crime and Delinquency*, 40(1): 71–94. DOI: 10.1177/0022427802239254

Silva, Cristina. September 17, 2010. "DA: Paris Hilton to Avoid Felony in Vegas Arrest." *Seattle Times*. Accessed March 19, 2014, http://www.seattletimes.nwsource.com

Simon, Rita. 1975. *Women and Crime*. Lexington, MA: Lexington Books.

Singh, Gopal K., Kenney, Mary Kay, Ghandour, Reem M., Kogan, Michael D., and Michael C. Lu. 2013. "Mental Health Outcomes in US Children and Adolescents Born Prematurely or with Low Birthweight." *Depression Research and Treatment*, 2013: 1–13. DOI: 10.1155/2013/570743

Simons, Ronald L., Stewart, Eric A., Gordon, Leslie C., Conger, Rand D., and Glen H. Elder. 2002. "A Test of Life Course Explanations for Stability and Change in Antisocial Behavior from Adolescence to Young Adulthood." *Criminology*, 40: 401–434. DOI: 10.1111/j.1745-9125.2002.tb00961.x

Sommers, Ira, and Deborah R. Baskin. 1993. "The Situational Context of Violent Female Offending." *Journal of Research in Crime and Delinquency*, 30(2): 136–162. DOI: 10.1177/0022427893030002002

Steffensmeier, Darrell J., and Dana Haynie. 2000. "Gender, Structural Disadvantage, and Urban Crime." *Criminology*, 38: 403–438. DOI: 10.1111/j.1745-9125.2000.tb00895.x

Sullivan, C. J. August 6, 2009. "Wed Woes Drove Crash Ma to Drink." *New York Post*. Accessed March 27, 2013, http://www.nypost.com/p/news/regional/item_Mr6vxWRqeoQ7jj0oHM4T5L

Sutherland, Edwin. 1924. *Criminology*. Philadelphia, PA: Chicago, IL: Lippincott Company.

Sutherland, Edwin H. 1939. *Principles of Criminology*, 3rd edn. Chicago, IL: Lippincott Company.

Sutherland, Edwin H. 1947. *Principles of Criminology*, 4th edn. Chicago, IL: Lippincott Company.

Swatt, Marc L., and Ni P. He. 2006. "Exploring the Difference Between Male and Female Intimate Partner Homicides: Revisiting the Concept of Situated Transactions." *Homicide Studies*, 10(4): 279–292. DOI: 10.1177/1088767906290965

Tannenbaum, Frank. 1938. *Crime and the Community*. New York, NY: Columbia University Press.

Tappan, Paul W. 1947. "Who Is the Criminal?" *American Sociological Review*, 12: 96–102.

Teague, Rosie, Mazerolle, Paul, Legosz, Margot, and Jennifer Sanderson. 2008. "Linking Childhood Exposure to Physical Abuse and Adult Offending: Examining Mediating Factors and Gendered Relationships." *Justice Quarterly*, 25(2): 313–348. DOI: 10.1080/07418820802024689

Thorton, Abigail J. V., Graham-Kevan, Nicola, and John Archer. 2012. "A Comparison of Self-Reports, Victims' Reports, and Third-Party Prevalence of Women's Violent and Nonviolent Offending Behavior." *Journal of Interpersonal Violence*, 27(8): 1399–1427. DOI: 10.1177/0886260511425789

Tibbetts, Stephen, and Alex Piquero. 1999. "The Influence of Gender, Low Birth Weight and Disadvantaged Environment on Predicting Early Onset Offending: A Test of Moffitt's Interactional Hypothesis." *Criminology*, 37: 843–878. DOI: 10.1111/j.1745-9125.1999.tb00507.x

Tracy, Paul E. 1987. "Race and Class Differences in Official and Self-Reported Delinquency." In *From Boy to Man, from Delinquency to Crime*, edited by Marvin E. Wolfgang, Terence Thornberry, and Robert M. Figlio, 87–121. Chicago, IL: University of Chicago Press.

US Census Bureau. 2010. *People Quickfacts*. Washington, DC.

Vandiver, Donna M., and Jessie L. Krienert. 2007, "An Assessment of a Cross-National Sample of Men and Women Arrested for Prostitution." *The Southwest Journal of Criminal Justice*, 4(2): 89–105.

Veneziano, Carol, Veneziano, Louis, LeGrand, Scott, and Linda Richards. 2004. "Neuropsychological Executive Functions of Adolescent Sex Offenders and Nonsex Offenders." *Perceptual and Motor Skills*, 98(2) 661–674. DOI: 10.2466/PMS.98.2.661-674

Vigil, James Diego. 2008. "Female Gang Members from East Los Angeles." *International Journal of Social Inquiry*, 1(1), 47–74.

Walker, Samuel, Spohn, Cassia, and Miriam DeLone. 2011. *The Color of Justice: Race, Ethnicity, and Crime in America*. Belmont, CA: Thomson/Wadsworth.

Walsh, Anthony. 2002. *Biosocial Criminology: Introduction and Integration*. Cincinnati, OH: Anderson.

Walsh, Anthony. 2009. *Biology and Criminology: The Biosocial Synthesis*. New York, NY: Routledge.

Walsh, Anthony, and Kevin M. Beaver.2009. *Biosocial Criminology: New Directions in Theory and Research*. New York, NY: Routledge.

Widom, Cathy S. 1989. "The Cycle of Violence." *Science*, 244: 160–166. DOI: 10.1126/science.2704995

Wilson, James Q. 1993. *The Moral Sense*. New York, NY: Free Press.

Winton, Richard. May 12, 2011. "Lindsay Lohan Gets 120 Days in Theft of Necklace." *Los Angeles Times*. Accessed March 19, 2014, http://articles.latimes.com/2011/may/12/local/la-me–lindsaylohan-20110512

Witt, Susan D. 2000. "The Influence of Peers on Children's Socialization to Gender Roles." *Early Child Development and Care*, 162: 1–7. DOI: 10.1080/0300443001620101

Wright, Stephen. February 21, 2014. "Avon, Monopoly and The Archers: Why Rose West Loves Life in Jail So Much She Wants to Die There." *Mail Online*. Accessed March 24, 2014, http://www.dailymail.co.uk/news/article-2565316/Avon-Monopoly-The-Archers-Why-Rose-West-loves-life-jail.html#ixzz2wtwuptOw

Youngers, Coletta. 2014. "Behind the Staggering Rise in Women's Imprisonment in Latin America." *Open Society Foundations*. Accessed March 19, 2014, http://www.opensocietyfoundations.org/voices/behind-staggering-rise-womens-imprisonment-latin-america

CHAPTER 3

Women convicted of crime and their punishments

Student learning outcomes

After reading this chapter, you should be able to:
- Describe the purposes of sanctions and how sentences may differ between men and women.
- Summarize the historical development of corrections for women offenders.
- Identify the types of women who are incarcerated and the issues and challenges they face.
- Identify the legal issues that incarcerated women face as well as the struggles they encounter when reentering society.

Introduction

Martha Stewart is a name that you may recognize from her television shows, her magazines, or perhaps even her merchandise which is sold at K-Mart and Macy's. She has been able to brand herself as the perfect person for knowing how anything domestic, from preparing a turkey to hosting a dinner party, should be done correctly. You may not realize that behind the picture of perfection this iconic woman, who has built a multi-million-dollar empire, is also a formerly incarcerated federal prisoner. In 2001, Stewart had sold shares of ImClone stock which allowed her to avert a loss of approximately $45,000. Apparently, her stock broker had advised her to sell the stock to avoid the financial loss. When questioned about the sale by investigators with the FBI and the US Securities and Exchange Commission, she lied (Hays 2003). As a result, she was charged and later convicted of obstruction of justice in 2004 (Ackman 2004). Stewart served five months in a minimum-level federal prison for women in West Virginia. When she was released, she was placed on two years of parole supervision.

What could be more awe inspiring than watching competitive ice skaters complete complex jumps and maneuvers in the Olympics? As they glide across the ice and twirl at dizzying rates, the farthest thought from your mind may be recollections of criminal acts. However, in 1994 the US Figure Skating Championships became tarnished when ice princess Nancy Kerrigan was struck on the leg by a baton by a male assailant while she practiced for the national championship (Longman 1994). Fortunately for Kerrigan, the injury she sustained did not prevent her from accomplishing

Women, Crime, and Justice, First Edition. By Elaine Gunnison, Frances P. Bernat, and Lynne Goodstein.
© 2017 John Wiley & Sons, Ltd. Published 2017 by John Wiley & Sons, Ltd.

her goal to compete at the 1994 Olympics. As time passed and the investigation moved forward, another female ice skater, Tonya Harding, was named as the mastermind behind the attack. It seems that Harding had wanted to not only ensure she made the US Olympic team, but she had wanted to knock her biggest rival, Kerrigan, out of contention for the coveted Olympic gold medal. Following the Olympic Games, Harding pled guilty to hindering prosecution of those who had carried out the attack and served a three-year probation sentence (Longman 1994). However, troubles for Harding were not over as she later served a short jail sentence in 2000 for domestic violence (Associated Press 2000). As is the case for many other female offenders who serve their punishments in the community (e.g., probation sentences) or those female offenders who serve their punishments in prison, the road to successful reentry into their communities is fraught with difficulties.

In this chapter, we explore the purposes of sanctions for men and women and differences in sentencing for women, including the intersection of race and sexual orientation in criminal sentencing. Next, we provide a historical overview of corrections for women offenders, provide the current statistics of women who are incarcerated, and explore the lives of incarcerated women including those women on death row. Further, we will focus on women serving sentences in the community and their struggles to reenter society successfully. Finally, we review legal issues that are specific to women, their struggles with reuniting with their children, and explore restorative justice practices.

 CASE STUDY: Malala Yousafzai

On October 9, 2012, 15 year-old Malala Yousafzai's life changed forever. It was on this day that the young schoolgirl, who has riding the bus to her school in Pakistan, was shot in the head by Taliban forces (Husain 2013). Yousafzai cared very much about education. As she has stated, "I didn't want my future to be imprisoned in my four walls and just cooking and giving birth" (Husain 2013). Rather, Yousafzai first had aspirations of becoming a medical doctor; however, later she had dreams of becoming a politician. A few years before this fateful shooting, she had begun writing a blog about education under a pseudonym and had even appeared in a *New York Times* documentary, which included a story about her life and her passion for education. Her various media appearances brought her much notoriety and attention, including a nomination for the International Children's Peace Prize in 2011 and Nobel Peace Prize in 2014 (Husain 2013; Toor 2014).

The "crime" Yousafzai committed was speaking out about the importance of education and demanding that education be accessible for all girls (Zeilinger 2013). While her promulgation of education for girls was not illegal under Pakistani law, it was banned by the Taliban. Thus, Yousafzai's actions and the public attention she received infuriated Taliban leaders who wanted to see her and her message about education for girls silenced without any formal court proceedings. Fortunately, Yousafzai survived the attack and has recovered quite well (Husain 2013).

The case of Yousafzai is an example that not all individuals across the world are defined as criminal in the same manner. Girls and women in countries across the world, such as in Middle Eastern countries, may be defined as criminal for actions not defined as such in the United States. Additionally, sentences for breaking formal or informal laws vary across countries. Yousafzai, without any formal justice proceedings, essentially received an automatic death sentence by Taliban leaders for breaking Taliban policies, or informal laws, on education for girls in Pakistan without so much as a trial.

Gender and sentencing

There are many reasons why we punish those who break the law in the United States. One purpose of punishments, or sanctions, for men and women who commit crime is for the offenders to be held accountable for their actions. Some scholars have explored whether gender plays a role in sentencing. From an examination of the existing literature, **gender disparity**, or differences in criminal sentencing due to gender, was first identified by researchers in the 1970s and scholars continue to find gender disparity in sentencing today. Thus, it does appear that gender is considered in sentencing decisions and that women tend to fare better than men in this regard. Specifically, women are less likely to be sentenced to prison and are more likely to receive shorter sentences than men. Even when other extra-legal factors are considered such as race/ethnicity, gender is still considered to be more influential in the disparity in sentencing between men and women (Doerner 2012; Starr 2012; Steffensmeier and Demuth 2006). Steffensmeier and Demuth (2006), who examined sentencing outcomes for female and male offenders convicted of felonies by race and ethnicity, found that gender was significantly related to sentencing outcomes – above and beyond race. Males, in fact, had a 71% higher chance of receiving an incarceration sentence and were 20% more likely to receive a longer sentence than females. In a more recent review of over 100,000 males and females sentenced for federal crimes, Doerner (2012) found that women were less likely to receive incarceration sentences and were more likely to receive shorter sentences than males. There have been several perspectives put forth to explain this phenomenon. According to one perspective, this trend is known as the **chivalry thesis**. That is, female offenders are treated more leniently in the criminal justice system due to the chivalrous attitudes held by law enforcement and court officials. As stated by Rodriguez, Curry, and Lee (2006, 320),

> Sometimes called paternalism, chivalry asserts that women are stereotyped as fickle and childlike, and therefore not fully responsible for their criminal behavior. Women therefore need to be protected by males who, with all due gallantry, are portrayed as wanting to minimize any pain or suffering women might experience. According to the chivalry thesis, when these stereotypes are played out in the arena of the criminal justice system, they will result in preferential treatment for female offenders from predominantly male police officers, prosecutors, and judges.

For instance, those in the criminal justice system may want to spare women from serving lengthy prison sentences, thus shielding them from the harsh confines of prison. Therefore, women may be more likely to be given shorter prison sentences or perhaps no prison sentence whatsoever and serve their sentences in the community. Numerous researchers have found that female drug offenders in the United States receive lesser sentences than male drug offenders (Farrell 2004; Stacey and Spohn 2006; Spohn 2013). Following an examination of approximately 2,000 female and male drug offenders, Stacey and Spohn (2006) state that such sentencing reductions may be due to sympathy on the part of prosecutors or judges. Jeffries and Bond (2010), who examined criminal sentencing by gender in Australia, found that men were more likely to receive incarceration as a sentence. However, recent research by Lu, Liang, and Liu (2013), who examined men and women sentenced for violent crimes in China, did not find any evidence that gender has a significant impact on sentencing decisions. More research is needed on gender and it relationship to sentencing outcomes not only in the United States but across the world as well.

Another perspective put forth by scholars regarding the gender disparity in sentencing is referred to as **Focal Concerns Theory**. This view holds that judges, who are often backlogged with cases, are under pressure to resolve cases as quickly as possible to avoid further delays in the court system. Given the constraints on their time and due to the fact they may not receive complete information on the defendants or their cases, decisions made on these cases might be based on their own generalizations or biases (Rodriguez et al. 2006). Rodriguez and colleagues (2006, 321) explain: "Judges and other court players commonly make contextual attributions about the defendant's culpability, character, and potential recidivism based on three focal concerns: blameworthiness, dangerousness (community protection), and practical constraints." In the context of blameworthiness, women may be viewed by judges to be somehow less culpable for their actions, which could result in lesser sentences for them. That is, if women are committing crimes with male accomplices, women may not be viewed as the mastermind of the criminal acts but rather an accessory to their accomplices and, thus, are less to blame. Additionally, women are indeed less likely to physically harm people and, thus, are less likely to be perceived as dangerous, which could also account for why they receive lesser sentences. Finally, judges may take into consideration constraints that women have when making decisions about sentences. For instance, a judge may mete out a lesser sentence due to the impact that a longer sentence might have, not only on the woman but also on the family of the woman.

Factors, for example, that judges may consider for women include their prior victimization, level of culpability, and even their status as a mother. It may be the case that Harding, for instance, received a probation sentence for her role in the attack of Kerrigan based on her background. At the time of the trial, it became well known and publicized that Harding had come from poverty and a broken home and somehow had been able to beat the odds and rise to the elite level of ice skating. Thus, in her case, her prior victimization and hardships may have contributed to a lesser sentence. Perhaps if the woman is the sole caregiver for her child(ren), then a judge may consider the impact that her incarceration may have on them. A recent case in Minnesota highlights such a consideration for the welfare of children. James and Cynthia Hood were convicted in 2013 of medical assistance fraud, but each received distinct sentences. While James received a prison sentence, the judge sentenced Cynthia to probation, stating that her children were "very, very dependent on [her]" (Furst 2013). The comment made by the judge in this case seems to suggest that a judge may indeed consider the impact that incarceration of a woman may have on her children.

Sentencing disparities based on gender have resulted in fewer women being sent to prison. In regard to the small number of women who do get sentenced to prison, who are they? What are their experiences in prison like? The following sections provide answers to these questions. Not surprisingly, prisons for women as portrayed in Hollywood films, such as the 2002 hit *Chicago*, are not reflective of real prisons for women.

Women in institutional custody

History of corrections for women offenders

Prior to the mid-1800s, the use of prisons and jails in England and in the United States for sentencing women was rare; however, an increasing number of women began being sentenced to prisons thereafter (Freedman 1981). The experiences of incarcerated women in the 1800s can best be described as deplorable. Women were confined in unsanitary, overcrowded, small spaces and served their sentences alongside men as opposed to in separate women's facilities (Freedman 1974). During this time period, incarcerated women experienced severe neglect and abuse (i.e., physical and sexual) at the hands of male inmates and male guards. Thus, it was not uncommon for women to become pregnant while incarcerated. The plight of incarcerated women was first described by Elizabeth Fry, who wrote a book entitled *Observations on the Visiting, Superintendence and Government of Female Prisoners* in 1827 about the confinement of women at the **Newgate Prison** in London. Her unveiling of atrocities experienced by incarcerated women at the Newgate Prison and her ability to organize the women to initiate change inspired future reforms for incarcerated women both in England and in the United States and ignited what is known as the reformatory movement in corrections.

While Fry's (1827) book highlighted the abuse and neglect that incarcerated women were experiencing, she also argued that women were capable of being reformed, or that women could break away from a life of crime if given community support and appropriate moral direction. Her work ignited a shift in the perception of female criminals by the public. Female criminals who were once viewed as evil began to be viewed by those in society as being capable of being "saved" or reformed. This new line of thinking propelled a change in the management and treatment of incarcerated women in jail or prison. The focus, at this time, was on reforming women, not men. It would be another 70 years before the focus on reforming both women and men would be a concern of the American correctional system. Reformers during the early 1800s believed female inmates should be housed in separate facilities from male inmates, be rehabilitated, and that a female warden, other than the traditional male warden, would be best suited to oversee such facilities.

The first breakthrough for incarcerated women in the United States came in 1828 when a separate building for women was erected at the Sing Sing prison in New York (Rafter 1985). With the implementation of a female wing, women no longer had to be incarcerated alongside male inmates. In the following years other states began to accept the idea of opening up separate housing facilities for incarcerated women. However, it was not until 1873 that the first female-only institution, the **Indiana Women's Prison**, finally opened its doors. As prisons opened for women over the next 100 years, primarily in the 1900s, they developed into two distinct categories: (1) **reformatory**; and (2) **custodial** (Rafter 1985). Reformatories and custodial institutions held distinct types of offenders and operated differently. Typically, women who had committed public order offenses such as prostitution, premarital sex, and adultery were sentenced to reformatories – crimes defined as criminal for women but not for men. At reformatories, women would participate in rehabilitation programming and were trained in domestic skills. On the other hand, women who committed felony violent and property crimes were sentenced to custodial institutions. Custodial institutions merely housed offenders, required women to work on prison farms, and offered women inmates little to no rehabilitation programming. There was also a racial bias as to which women were sent to these institutions. Women sentenced to reformatories were predominately Caucasian while African-American were more likely to be sentenced to custodial institutions (Rafter 1985). Do you think this disparity was intentional by those in the criminal justice system? Why do you think there was such a racial disparity in institutions that women were sent to? Reformatories were the prevailing institutions for women until the 1930s when custodial institutions gained traction and became the most utilized type of facility (Rafter 1985). Female institutions today hold some principles of both models. A detailed analysis of correctional institutions for women today will be provided later in this chapter.

Statistics on incarcerated women

When Martha Stewart emerged from serving a five-month federal prison sentence in 2005, she was greeted by a barrage of cameras documenting and analyzing her every move. She was bombarded with questions asking her to recall her experiences and to describe the women she had encountered in prison. Who are the women that are incarcerated today? What are their characteristics? Do they resemble Stewart? The Bureau of Justice Statistics reports that there are currently over 2 million individuals incarcerated in jails and prisons in the United States (Kaeble et al. 2015); 1.5 million individuals are incarcerated in state and federal prisons alone. **State prisons** hold women convicted of crimes that violate state laws such as shoplifting, prostitution, and homicide. On the other hand, **federal prisons** house women convicted of crimes that violate federal laws such as bank fraud, embezzlement, extortion, and drug trafficking. According to the Bureau of Justice Statistics, far more men are incarcerated in state and federal prisons than females (e.g., approximately 1.4 million vs 106,000) (Carson 2015). When examining the racial and ethnic make-up of incarcerated persons, there is an overwhelming overrepresentation of minorities that are incarcerated. The Bureau of Justice Statistics reports that in 2014 for both genders, African-Americans and Hispanic-Americans were disproportionately incarcerated when compared to Caucasians (Carson 2015). Recall from Chapter 2 that individuals self-report similar involvement in less serious crime regardless of race or ethnicity. With this in mind, what could account for the disproportionate numbers of female minorities incarcerated, relative to their numbers in the general population, in state and federal prisons? Perhaps the disparity is due to the nature of the law. Historically, African-Americans had laws specifically applied to just them, referred to as **Jim Crow laws**. Examples of such laws imposed on African-Americans include poll taxes and literacy tests in order to be able to vote. While such laws do not exist today, many scholars have argued that disparity in cocaine versus crack cocaine sentences fueled the increased incarceration for African-American males and females in the 1980s. Sentences for the possession of cocaine, a drug used primarily by upper-class Caucasians, were much less severe than sentences for crack cocaine, a drug used mostly by impoverished African-Americans. Bush-Baskette (1998) reports that the war on drugs campaign in the 1980s resulted in an astonishing 828% increase in the incarceration of female African-Americans. A majority of these women were living in poor urban areas of cities and, in the absence of legal employment, were dealing drugs as a means to survive. Alexander (2012) explains that the war on drugs campaign has contributed to the increased use of incarceration due to federal funding being allocated to law enforcement agencies that resulted in increased arrest rates for drugs offenses. In fact, Alexander (2012) states that as a result of this policy and others, a new Jim Crow – like law system has emerged whereby African-American men and women now face de facto legal discrimination. Ex-felons, who are disproportionately minority, are unable to vote in many states, receive federal assistance, or obtain certain jobs. Thus, the disproportionately in incarceration between the races may stem from laws that continue to discriminate against African-American females or from differences in law enforcement practices.

An inspection of age at incarceration shows there are some similarities between the genders. The Bureau of Justice Statistics reports that in 2014 both male and female offenders were most likely to be incarcerated between the ages of 25 and 34 (Carson 2015). When inspecting the incarceration figures by race and ethnicity, some differences emerge. For males, a higher percentage of African-Americans and Hispanic-Americans were incarcerated than Caucasians in these age categories. However, for females, a higher percentage of Hispanic-Americans and Caucasians were incarcerated than African-Americans in the aforementioned age categories. In regard to educational status, those who are incarcerated in state and federal prisons are undereducated. The majority of those incarcerated have not obtained a high school diploma or GED (Table 3.1).

The Bureau of Justice Statistics reports that in state prisons, males are more likely to be incarcerated for violent offenses whereas females are more likely to be incarcerated for non-violent offenses such as property crimes or drug offenses (Carson 2015). Within the federal system, males and females are more likely to be incarcerated for drug offenses (i.e., specifically drug trafficking) as well as weapons and immigration offenses, as opposed to Index I offenses such as larceny-theft, robbery, or homicide. Finally, the Bureau of Justice Statistics reports that a majority of male and female state (52%) and federal (63%) prisoners had a child under the age of 18 (Glaze and Maruschak 2008). Researchers have indicated that incarcerated persons have approximately 1.7 million minor children, representing about 2.3% of the total US population. For mothers that are incarcerated, they reported having approximately 147,000 minor children. Glaze and Maruschak (2008, 2) state, "The number of children under age 18 with a mother in prison more than doubled since 1991."

Description of women's prisons

As previously mentioned, prisons for women have evolved over the past several hundred years. With the "get tough on crime" movement having gained momentum in the 1970s, as well as claims that rehabilitation does not work (see Martinson 1974), greater emphasis was placed on housing offenders in prisons rather than offering rehabilitation. This trend has continued to the present time

Table 3.1 Estimated percentage of sentenced prisoners under state and federal jurisdiction by sex, race, Hispanic origin, and age, 2011.

Age group	Total[a]	Male					Female				
		All male[a]	White[b]	Black[b]	Hispanic	Other[b]	All female[a]	White[b]	Black[b]	Hispanic	Other[b]
Total[c]	471	890	465	2,724	1,091	968	65	53	109	64	93
18–19	169	317	102	1,072	349	542	14	8	32	17	12
20–24	746	1,365	584	3,868	1,521	1,755	96	72	152	94	109
25–29	1,055	1,912	958	5,434	2,245	2,022	170	150	244	165	208
30–34	1,161	2,129	1,111	6,412	2,457	2,193	185	163	264	174	225
35–39	1,067	1,982	1,029	6,122	2,272	1,878	155	138	229	137	189
40–44	904	1,689	942	5,105	1,933	1,619	132	119	213	107	174
45–49	758	1,417	815	4,352	1,602	1,444	111	90	203	94	161
50–54	567	1,081	633	3,331	1,320	1,112	72	57	128	67	124
55–59	358	698	400	2,178	978	832	37	27	72	42	63
60–64	212	422	252	1,265	680	483	20	15	37	25	37
65 or older	72	158	109	418	299	208	5	4	8	7	12
Number of sentenced prisoners[d]	1,508,636	1,402,404	453,500	516,900	308,700	123,300	106,232	53,100	22,600	17,800	12,800

Note: Counts based on prisoners with sentences of more than 1 year under the jurisdiction of state or federal correctional authorities. Imprisonment rate is the number of prisoners under state or federal jurisdiction with a sentence of more than 1 year per 100,000 U.S. residents of corresponding sex, age, and race or Hispanic origin. Resident population estimates are from the U.S. Census Bureau for January 1, 2015. Alaska did not submit 2014 data to the National Prisoner Statistics (NPS), so totals include imputed counts for this state. See *Methodology*.

[a]Includes American Indians and Alaska Natives; Asians, Native Hawaiians, and other Pacific Islanders; and persons of two or more races.

[b]Excludes persons of Hispanic or Latino origin.

[c]Includes persons age 17 or younger.

[d]Race totals are rounded to the nearest 100 to accommodate differences in data collection techniques between jurisdictions.

Source: Bureau of Justice Statistics, National Prisoner Statistics Program, 2011; Federal Justice Statistics Program, 2011; National Corrections Reporting Program, 2010; and Survey of Inmates in State and Local Correctional Facilities, 2004. US Department of Justice.

(Garland 2001) as prisons today operate under more of the custodial model. Additionally, designs of prisons for women have changed and developed over time (Pollock 2002). Prisons for women follow the common classification of **minimum**, **medium**, and **maximum**. Depending on the classification level, or security level, and whether the prison is state or federally run, the design of prisons can differ. Institutions that are state minimum and medium classified prisons have a very open concept and are considered "campus" style (Clear, Reisig, and Cole 2012). The campus-style institution has buildings that are spread out, with fencing surrounding the perimeter. At these institutions, female inmates may be housed in a traditional cellblock or they may be housed together in cottages. Women housed in the traditional cellblock have separate cells which are often shared with one or two other females. There is one common area for the inmates to congregate outside of their cells. Cottages are smaller units housing anywhere from 25 to 50 women and include their own kitchens and living rooms (O'Connor 2000). These living units were designed to more closely resemble traditional "family life" outside the prison walls. Essentially, the campus style design provides inmates with the ability and freedom to walk outside from one building to another (Clear et al. 2012). This is the type of federal institution where Martha Stewart served her sentence. On the other hand, in a maximum security prison, the campus-style design is less prevalent (Clear et al. 2012). Rather, inmates may be held and receive services (e.g., medical care, programming) all within the same building. Additionally, movement within the facility is achieved through interior corridors rather than outside.

Regardless of classification level, most states have at least one female prison which is **sex segregated**. Like prisons for men, female institutions are oftentimes located in rural areas of the state (Pollock 2002). This geographic isolation, coupled with the fact that there is generally only one prison for women in each state, makes it less likely for female offenders to be housed close to the homes of friends and families, who most likely do not reside near the prison. Therefore, females may have difficulties in coping with prison as they may have experience limited contact with those they care about most, including their children. Another byproduct of the fact that there is generally only one state facility for women is the necessity for these institutions to house a wide range of offenders (i.e., minimum, medium, maximum) within the same facility (Pollock 2002). This has resulted in a mixture of all types of classifications of female offenders being housed together on one property, which sometimes contains a blend of prison designs (e.g., cottages, open campus-style concept).

Women incarcerated in federal institutions face similar constraints. While federal prisons can be found in both urban and rural areas, there are only 28 federal institutions dispersed by region (e.g., Western, North Central) that house females (Federal Bureau of Prisons 2016). Therefore, females serving federal sentences may be housed out of state – even further away from family members and loved ones. Another difference between state and federal facilities is that, unlike state prisons, federal prisons for women are often co-correctional.

Experiments with co-corrections

Co-correctional facilities refer to institutions that house both women and men together in one facility. The shift from sex-segregated prison to co-correctional facilities began in 1971 when the first co-correctional facility for federal inmates opened in Fort Worth (Pollock 2002). By 2011, there were 46 adult state co-correctional facilities and 9 adult federal co-correctional facilities in operation (American Correctional Association 2012). Thus, women are more likely to be incarcerated at a state co-correctional facility than at the federal level. These facilities were viewed as a potential solution to alleviate problems such as prison overcrowding, were thought to be more cost effective, and had the potential to provide more comprehensive services to women prisoners. Contemporary co-correctional facilities do not mirror the earlier co-correctional facilities of the nineteenth century in which women and men were literally housed in the same cells (Pollock 2002). In contemporary co-correctional facilities, women and men are housed separately (i.e., in separate wings, apart from one another)

Figure 3.1 Seatac Federal Detention Center, aerial view. *Source:* Doug Mahugh/Flickr CC BY 2.0 https://creativecommons.org/licenses/by/2.0/.

but have access to the same educational (e.g., high school equivalent courses, vocational opportunities), medical, and social services (e.g., rehabilitation programs such as drug and/or alcohol counseling) (Figure 3.1). The creation of co-correctional facilities was supported by feminists who viewed the "separate but equal" prison facilities for women to have created a legacy of difference (Pollock 2002). That is, women had been housed in sex-segregated prisons, but they were not given the same access to educational, vocational, and rehabilitative programming. Thus, co-correctional facilities were deemed as a viable solution to level the playing field. Females could be housed separately and spared the sexual abuse that they endured by male inmates in previous co-correctional facilities and now they could participate in programming (e.g., vocational programming) that they might not have had access to in sex-segregated prisons (e.g., carpentry).

Whether co-correctional facilities have assisted women as intended remains to be seen. Unfortunately, research on the co-correctional facilities is extremely limited with the latest research on the topic stemming from the 1990s. The few researchers who have examined co-correctional facilities are not optimistic about their success in assisting women. Smykla and Williams (1996), in their review of research on co-correctional facilities from 1973 to 1990, conclude that "co-corrections offer women prisoners few, if any, economic, educational, vocational, and social advantages" (Smykla and Williams 1996, 61). Other researchers have also concluded that co-corrections offer no benefits for women (Rafter 1985). For instance, women may not have been given access to good jobs in the institution or are steered towards traditionally feminine jobs and their access to programming that males are obtaining in the institution may be limited. Further, while women are segregated from male inmates in many institutions in all areas from sleeping units to programming, this is not the case in all co-correctional institutions. Thus, co-correctional facilities have not inhibited sexual relations between the offenders. Smykla (1978), in an ethnography of sex relations in a federal co-correctional facility in California, found that heterosexual sexual relations did occur, thereby leaving open the possibility of female sexual abuse by male inmates. More research on the impacts of co-correctional facilities on women prisoners is needed.

Life of women prison inmates

Prison life for men or women is fraught with obstacles and difficulties. One of the first adjustments that women must make to prison is adhering to prison culture, both formal and informal. Upon entry into prison, the prisoner, or "new fish" in inmate slang, will be institutionalized (Clemmer 1940). **Institutionalization** is the process whereby the prisoner learns the formal rules of the correctional institution. Once admitted into prison, the offender will be strip searched, be stripped of her name and assigned a prison number, given approved prison clothes that she must wear, and assigned to her cell (Pollock 2002). The strip search often evokes emotional stress and trauma – particularly for women with sexual abuse histories (Scranton and McCulloch 2009). Other formal rules are provided to the female inmate in terms of when she should be in her cell, when her meals will be served, when she may interact with visitors, what programs are available to her, and what behavior is expected of her by the correctional guards (Pollock 2002). While the prisoner learns the formal rules of the institution, the prisoner also becomes quickly acquainted with informal rules, put forth by his/her fellow prisoners. This system of norms, values, language, and attitudes that all prisoners are expected to follow is referred to as the **inmate code** (Clemmer 1940). For instance, keeping one's word, not exploiting other inmates, and being tough are common examples of the inmate code adopted by males. Females, on the other hand, adhere to an inmate code that dictates no snitching, no gossiping, refraining from asking other inmates about the crime that landed them in prison, and requires both personal hygiene and room cleanliness (Kerman 2011; Owen 1998). Failure to adhere to the code could result in violence. In a qualitative analysis of the inmate code for females, McGuire (2011, 151) reports on one subject who engaged in violence due to a violation of the inmate code: "Bambi, for example, proudly described an incident where she kicked another inmate 'three times in her liver and she already had cirrhosis and they had to watch her for awhile, 'cuz it caused more swelling.' Bambi justified her actions in part because the other inmate was a 'snitch and a cell burglar.'" Many newly admitted prisoners, male or female, do not readily accept the inmate code at first. Oftentimes, new prisoners will rebel against both the formal rules of the prison and the informal rules put forth by their fellow inmates. Their adjustment to prison and their eventual acceptance of both the formal and informal rules is referred to as **prisonization** (see Clemmer 1940). The prisonization process may take several months to several years for some inmates.

Prisoners often form cliques whereby inmates organize themselves based on their sexual preferences, religious beliefs, ethnicity, personal interests, and the offense they are incarcerated for (Clemmer 1940; Diaz-Cotto 1996). For some inmates, their membership in a clique, such as a gang, stems from their need for protection. In male prisons, it is not uncommon for the inmates to "hook up" or partner up (including sexually) with other inmates in order to receive protection from physical and/or sexual assault from other inmates. On the other hand, female cliques formed in female correctional institutions have been referred to as **pseudo-families** (Foster 1975; Gillombardo 1966; Ward and Kassebaum 1965; Pollock 2002). Unlike in male prisons where membership in a clique, or gang, may be the result of coercion, membership in a female clique is consensual. In pseudo-families, members of the family network adopt roles such as the mother figure or sister figure. The women in the families may or may not engage in sexual relations. Pseudo-families provide female inmates with protection from other inmates, substitution for family relationships broken by imprisonment, financial support, and emotional support. Since female institutions are often located far from family and friends, female inmates may not receive the emotional support they need to adapt to prison life. The pseudo-families assist female inmates in coping with the demands and stresses of prison. For females, relationships are critical to their prison adjustment. However, interviews of incarcerated women in the Midwest conducted by Greer (2000) cast some doubt on the role of pseudo-families for incarcerated females today. Greer (2000) found that women in her sample were somewhat less likely to form pseudo-families, suggesting that a change in the prison subculture for women was afoot. On the other hand, Forsyth and Evans (2003) did find evidence of female pseudo-families in a prison for women in Louisiana, but the female pseudo-family more closely resembled a male prison gang. For example, women grouped with one another for emotional and economic support, for protection, but also as a method to exert aggression and sometimes violence. More research is needed to determine if pseudo-families do indeed still exist for incarcerated women or whether family formations are less centered on support, as they have been historically, than on serving a more violent role. Besides joining pseudo-families, incarcerated females may join a gang, or continue to engage in prior gang activities, for structure and support (Lauderdale and Burman 2009). Unlike male gangs found in prison, female gangs tend to be less violent (Greer 2000). When incarcerated female gang members do engage in violent behavior, it is not to exhibit an allegiance to the gang but rather due to some personal issue that the woman has with another inmate (Lauderdale and Burman 2009).

For both genders, there is a hierarchy in the prison. For example, inmates who have committed crimes against children (i.e., rape) are considered to be at the bottom level of the prison structure (James 2003). These offenders are not welcomed into existing cliques and are often targeted for victimization (i.e., sexual and/or physical). Because of this, these offenders are often segregated from the general inmate population. Sexual victimization is a problem for both genders. Female offenders may experience sexual victimization from other inmates or even guards. In a recent survey of incarcerated men and women in prisons and jails, Beck et al. (2013) found that rates of reported sexual victimization in both prisons and jails were higher for females than for males. Incarcerated women are also at risk of victimization from correctional officers. Susan Smith, a South Carolina woman who drowned her two children in 1994 and was later convicted for their murders, thus far has been sexually involved with two correctional officers during her prison term (Collins 2001; Dorning 1995). The officers have claimed that it was consensual. Regardless of the assertions by the officers, sex between officers and inmates violates correctional policy and professional ethical boundaries. More recently, a prison for women in Alabama has garnered national attention including an investigation by the Department of Justice for rampant sexual abuse of incarcerated women that has spanned over 18 years (Severson 2014). Information has surfaced that over one-third of prison employees have had sex with the incarcerated women (Severson 2014).

Conditions specific to imprisoned women

It is important not to view the incarceration experience for men and women to be identical. While the process of prisonization may be similar for men and women, there are indeed distinct differences between the genders besides how they may adapt to prison. Women experience difficulties ranging from motherhood to **mental health** issues. The next section highlights a few conditions that are specific to imprisoned women.

Women's status as mothers

Both incarcerated men and women are likely to be parents (Glaze and Maruschak 2008). According to Bouchet (2008, 2), "three quarters of incarcerated women are mothers; and two-thirds have children under age 18. There is a disparate impact on minorities, with African-American children nine times more likely and Hispanic children three times more likely than white children to have a parent in prison." Continuing to parent one's child(ren) in prison is extremely difficult for prisoners – especially for females (Coll et al. 1998). In general, incarcerated parents find it difficult to communicate with their children or receive visits from their children due to the complexities of incarceration (La Vigne, Davies, and Brazzell 2008). Prison rules limit the number of phone calls an inmate can make or how often they can receive visits with those on the outside. Recall that visits from family and children may be rare for the female inmate due to the location of the prison. Some prisons for men and women have programs to assist them in maintaining contact with families, such as subsidizing transportation or lodging costs for their visitors, but such programs are not the norm or standard across the Unites States (Hoffman, Byrd, and Kightlinger 2010). For women the deprivation of continued emotional and physical contact with their children can be a hardship (Poehlmann 2005). If the incarcerated parent has a family member taking care of his/her children and the family relationship is strained due to the parent being incarcerated, this may further add to the difficulties for the inmate seeking contact with his/her children. The children of female inmates, in particular, are often placed in the foster care system, as women offenders are more likely to have been the primary caretaker of the child/ren before their arrest and subsequent incarceration (Bouchet 2008; Christian 2009; Travis, McBride, and Solomon 2005). Female offenders with children in the foster care system may find it difficult to establish and maintain contact with those caseworkers who are handling the placement of their children into new residences.

A small number of women enter prison pregnant and subsequently give birth while incarcerated. Maruschak (2008), using data gleaned from a 2004 survey of inmates, reports that an average of 7% of women who had entered state and federal prisons in that year were pregnant. Prisons differ in how they accommodate pregnant women. There are approximately nine correctional facilities in the United States, such as Bedford Hills Correctional Center for Women in New York, that allow incarcerated mothers to keep their child with them in prison for up to two years (Goshin and Byrne 2009; Jbara 2012). These **parenting programs** for incarcerated mothers require mothers to care for their child 24 hours per day in a specialized parent unit under the careful supervision of program administrators. The specialized parenting programs offer activities that increase bonding between the parent and child, teach techniques to make the mother a better parent, and educate the parent on how best to reconnect with her child when she is released (Jbara 2012). The Washington State Corrections Center for Women is another example of a program that offers a unique residential parenting program to pregnant minimum-custody inmates (Fearn and Parker 2004). The Washington State Department of Corrections collaborates with the Puget Sound Educational Service District to offer a residential parenting program with an Early Head Start component. The incorporation of an Early Head Start component into its programming is unique. Currently, no residential parenting programs exist in the United States for incarcerated fathers.

Programming needs of women

Historically, most programming (e.g., counseling, vocational training in cosmetology) found within prison was not gender-responsive. **Gender-responsive programming** refers to programming that meets the specific needs of women. The lack of gender-responsive programming resulted in women not having their needs adequately met. Supreme Court decisions in the 1970s and 1980s forced prisons to provide "equal" treatment for women as current correctional practices at that time violated the equal protection clause of the Fourteenth Amendment. For instance, cases such as *Barefield v. Leach* **(1974)** and *Glover v. Johnson* **(1979)** identified that the lack of programming (e.g., vocational, education, and rehabilitation) that women inmates were receiving was inadequate and required that state prisons provide equal programming opportunities for incarcerated females and males. Further, the decision from the ***Cooper v. Morin* (1980)** case held administrators responsible for providing equal services to both genders and failure to do so was no longer acceptable.

Despite these rulings, adequate rehabilitation programming for women has often fallen short. Some of the rehabilitation programming that was ultimately implemented for women in prisons was not tailored for their specific needs. That is, counseling programs offered to women inmates were often designed and tested only on male inmates. This meant that females were participating in rehabilitation programs that were designed to meet the needs of men. Female offenders are in need of specific programming that will best assist them, as they do indeed have distinct needs that differ from those of male offenders. For instance, women are more likely to suffer from depression and low self-esteem (Bloom et al. 2002; Pollock 2002). Additionally, women are much more likely than men to have suffered prior sexual abuse and many have addiction and physical and mental health problems (Bloom et al. 2002; Kilpatrick et al. 2000; Siegel and Williams 2003). Both male and female inmates bring a multitude of health problems requiring specific and aggressive treatment, including HIV, sexually transmitted diseases, tuberculosis, and hepatitis, into the prison setting (Hammett and Drachman-Jones 2006; Leukefeld et al. 2012; Maruschak 2008). The Centers for Disease Control and Prevention (2012) reported that approximately 1.3% of incarcerated males and 1.7% of incarcerated females were HIV positive, rates significantly higher than among the non-prisoner population. Inmates found to be HIV positive are not able to obtain access to cutting-edge drugs to assist them in warding off the development of AIDS. In addition, women are in need of specialized health care. Access to routine yearly female health screenings such as PAP smears and mammograms is often limited in prisons for women (Springer 2010). For women who are pregnant, access to comprehensive prenatal care, from check-ups to nutrition, is also limited (Hotelling 2008). Much of the reasoning behind the lack of solid health care for incarcerated women surrounds the costs of providing such services. Surprisingly, many states require that women be shackled while giving birth. Some states, such as Maryland, have implemented bans on this practice but it is still rare for prisons to provide opportunities such as those at Bedford Hills and in Washington State, where women inmates can experience humane childbirth and early motherhood (Quinn 2014). In many cases, incarcerated women are forced to give up their babies immediately or within 48 hours and continue serving their sentences as if this major life event never happened (Stern 2004). Relatively few incarcerated women have access to specialized programs that are designed to enhance their parenting skills and bonds with their children (Hotelling 2008). Further, some incarcerated women may receive unwanted medical procedures following the birth of their child. Johnson (2014) reports that the California Department of Corrections and Rehabilitation sterilized 132 women during the years 2006 to 2010 without required state approvals and often without the consent of the women undergoing the tubal ligation procedure (i.e., the closing of the Fallopian tubes which results in sterilization). In some instances, women had no knowledge that the tubal ligation was going to be performed while other women felt pressured or coerced to have this procedure (Johnson 2013). A new bill is being introduced in California, SB1135, to limit the use of this procedure for women (Johnson 2014).

 SPECIAL LEGAL ISSUES: Medical care issues

Oftentimes, medical care access for incarcerated women in the United States is difficult or limited. For incarcerated women in other countries such as the United Kingdom, Argentina, Colombia, or Zambia, access to medical care is also difficult (Kalantry 2013; Martinez 2010; Siva 2010; Todrys and Amon 2011). Todrys and Amon (2011) examined medical care for females incarcerated in four Zambian prisons and found that medical needs were not being met for these women. For instance, pregnant women were not receiving appropriate prenatal care and women were unable to access health care programs that they wanted, such as those that offer screening for HIV. The researchers explain that part of the problem with inmates getting access to medical care is due to the fact that many Zambian prisons lack a health clinic on site. Because of this, women must wait for prison officials to take them to a health facility outside of the prison walls and delays occur due to a lack of transportation options or concerns about security. One inmate reported on the significant delays in obtaining access to medical care services: "There are delays in getting to the clinic. It depends on the officials, if they want to take you there or not. Sometimes you can go as long as a month waiting to go to the clinic."

The deficiencies in health care for women are not only at odds with institutional policies that outline standards of care but also violate the law in many of these countries. For incarcerated women in the United States, the lack of access to medical care violates their **Eighth Amendment** rights, which allow for adequate medical care for medical needs (Columbia Human Rights Law Review 2011). In 2010, the state of Wisconsin settled a federal lawsuit regarding deficient medical care services at its largest prison for women, which culminated in a fine of nearly $1 million. The prison facility was also required to establish new care guidelines (Richmond 2010). Research is scarce as to the legal remedies, if any, available to incarcerated women in other countries who are suffering from inadequate medical care – particularly in third world countries.

In regard to mental health treatment, incarcerated women are in great need and are more likely to suffer from some form of diagnosed mental illness than men in prison (Peters and Hills 1993). James and Glaze (2006) reported that female inmates, in state and federal prisons and jails, had higher rates of mental health issues than male inmates at these same institutions. Estimates of the proportion of women in prison with mental illness range from 19% (Peters and Hills 1993) to as high as 60% (Acoca 1998). Given these percentages, female offenders are in dire need of adequate mental health support (e.g., counseling and access to medications). Inmates' experiences with prior sexual and physical abuse often result in severe depression, posttraumatic stress disorder, and suicidal ideation and attempts (Hegadoren, Lasiuk, and Coupland 2006; Pollock 2002). Further, many women suffer from drug and alcohol abuse, which often stems from early childhood victimization. Failure to address substance abuse problems while women are incarcerated has been linked to recidivism for female offenders. For example, researchers have found substance abuse to be a more significant predictor of recidivism (i.e., technical violations) for female probationers as opposed to their male counterparts (see Olson, Alderden, and Lurigio 2003). Perhaps Harding's continued run-ins with the law while on probation stemmed from her alcohol use.

Finally, many women are in need of job training. However, much of the job programming in women's prisons has been gender stereotypic and focuses on what can be characterized as predominately "women's jobs" (Franklin 2008; Lee 2000). For instance, you would be much more likely to find carpentry programs in men's prisons while cosmetology programs would be more prevalent in women's prisons (Lee 2000). One of the chief problems with providing job training for positions that are low-paying (e.g., telemarketing, data entry, office assistant, food service) is the impact it will have on women upon release. Carpentry, for example, is a rather high-paying occupation while cosmetology is not. In addition, in some states, such as North Carolina, women with a felony conviction can be denied from obtaining a cosmetology license by the state licensing board (Bowes and Rowe 2013). This means that women are being trained in many states in an occupation that may not even be open to them upon release. Aside from the licensing problem, women offenders are often faced with the prospect of not only supporting themselves but also providing care and support for their children, creating additional disadvantages for this group as they attempt to reintegrate into society (Gunnison and Helfgott 2013).

 GLOBAL PERSPECTIVES: Incarcerated female offenders across the globe

As is the case in the United States, the number of women incarcerated in Argentina has risen nearly 200% in the past two decades due to tough drug laws that were implemented and harsh prison sentences that accompanied those offenses (Kalantry 2013). The drug laws were intended to target organized drug traffickers; however, the enforcement of such laws tended to be centered on low-level drug offenders – primarily women (Kalantry 2013). Female drug offenders in Argentina were predominantly involved in the transportation or trafficking of drugs, not the manufacturing or supplying operations of the drug trade.

In 2013, scholars from the United States and Argentina researched and surveyed female federal prisoners incarcerated in Servicio Penitenciaro Federal in Buenos Aires, Argentina. Additionally, the researchers conducted site visits to two other prisons for women in Buenos Aires (Kalantry 2013). The scholars note that many aspects of confinement for women in the institution are in line with aspects of international standards of care for incarcerated persons. However, the researchers did report on some differences between stated institutional policy of care and what might actually occur in the prison based on survey results from female inmates. First, they found that there was no standardization of medical care and that incarcerated Argentinean women, like their female US counterparts, did not always have access to PAP smears or mammograms. Second, the scholars reported that the living conditions were not always hygienic and that the women complained of very slow response times to valid complaints such as cockroach infestations. Third, they found violence to be a problem for these women as the prison policy called for housing the "worst of the worst" female offenders together in a housing unit that was rather unsupervised. Such a housing policy and relative lack of supervision led to pervasive violence problems. Fourth, as is also often the case for women in US prisons, female subjects stated that the federal prison was quite some distance from their family. The researchers reported that over 50% of the incarcerated women lived 60 miles away from family. Finally, the researchers reported that in the two prisons for women in Buenos Aires, there was a co-residence program whereby children were able to reside in the prison with their mothers up to four years of age (Kalantry 2013). Being able to reside with one's child up to the age of four is a bit different from residential parenting programs for women in prisons in the United States whereby women can typically only reside with their child until the child is two years of age.

Transgender inmates

The exact number of **transgendered** individuals – those who identify as a member of the opposite sex – in US society is unknown but some researchers have estimated that it is less than 1% (approximately .3%) (Gates 2011). This small number tells us that the percentage of transgender individuals incarcerated in prisons today is also diminutive, but the challenges posed to prison administrators in dealing with such inmates is anything but small. In the past decade, researchers have begun to examine the experiences of **transgendered inmates** and have reported on many issues that impact this group. One of the first issues that arose for researchers was the use of the word "transgender" to describe individuals who identify as the opposite sex. The term "transgender," or "transman," is not even a term accepted by all females entering prison and identifying as male. One transgender individual explained the sheer complexity of the term "transman":

> Initially when I came out I identified as a lesbian and then a butch lesbian. Today I more identify as genderqueer. I don't identify as a transman … I don't fit either. I don't fit male or female, I'm all and both and none. That's how I look at my gender. They haven't named it because they don't believe in the fluidity of gender and I think there's many genders. (Oparah 2012, 241)

Despite the differences in how female inmates may identify when entering prison, both state and federal prisons have established policies regulating the placement and treatment of transgender inmates. For example, the US Bureau of Prisons (BOP; 2014) examines the case of each transgender inmate entering their facilities and decides where to assign the inmate, taking into consideration management and security concerns as well as the health and safety needs of the inmate. Inmates are assigned to prisons based on their biological sex, regardless of whether there were in the midst of a sex change (i.e., they had begun hormone therapies). However, if the inmate has undergone a full sex change, then the inmate is assigned to a prison based on their new sex. The BOP even goes so far as to reassess placement of the transgender inmate bi-annually to determine if the inmate has experienced any safety issues as a result of their status. Additionally, the BOP does require that transgender inmates have separate shower facilities, but it does not require that these inmates are placed in specialized housing units. Concern for the safety of transgender inmates is critical as they are vulnerable to harassment and even sexual assault by other female inmates.

Jenness and colleagues (2007), in an investigation of transgender male and female inmates in California prisons, found that both male and female transgender inmates were more likely than other non-transgender inmates to report being sexually assaulted. Such evidence that this group is experiencing additional abuse while incarcerated is particularly disturbing as the abuse is likely to compound previous traumas and victimizations that they have experienced in their lives. Further, the prison itself may sequester the inmates' expression of their sexuality by adding yet another layer of victimization. Oparah (2012) reported on the experiences of one inmate, Bakari, whose sexual identity was not accepted by the institution:

> the prison regime attempted to enforce a realignment between Bakari's biological sex and gender expression, by confiscating their boxers as contraband and forcing Bakari to enter the general population wearing panties and what s/he describes as "an old lady housedress." All prisoners experience the temporary loss of items associated with their "free" identities-clothes, jewelry, personal items, and even names-as a part of the privations of imprisonment. However, for Bakari, induction into the prison regime included the psychological violence of being forced to inhabit a gender identity that s/he had rejected as a fundamental part of their sense of selfhood. During their two-year sentence, Bakari witnessed other forms of policing of gender non-conformity. This policing manifested itself in physical violence directed toward prisoners with masculine gender expression-"butch" women, genderqueer prisoners and transmen-as well as the use of institutional sanctions including administrative segregation for transgressive behavior such as growing facial hair. (Oparah 2012, 241)

Girshick (2011) conducted qualitative interviews with 14 prisoners who identified as masculine, in two female prisons. She reported that much of the harassment that these individuals received was perpetrated by male staff as opposed to female staff. As well as suffering victimization, the transgender inmate will not be supported medically in regard to sustaining their gender identity. That is, if a transgender inmate enters prison and was on hormone therapy, they are likely to experience a suspension in this treatment as the prison will not provide it. Likewise, if a transgender inmate wanted to be placed on hormone therapy, this would not be an option. In the case of the BOP, they may consider continuing hormone therapy for a transgender inmate. The decision as to whether this will be granted to the inmate is made by the medical director of the facility. Moreover, if the inmate wanted sex reassignment surgery, this would also not be available to her/him. In 2006, Michelle Kosilek, a transgendered inmate living in an all-male prison, sued the Massachusetts Department of Corrections, citing the cruel and unusual punishment clause of the Eighth Amendment, for refusing to grant her sex reassignment surgery, which she argued was needed to improve her mental health status. A federal judge ruled in 2012 that Kosilek's rights had been violated and ruled that she should receive the surgery (Huus 2012). Research is slowly emerging on transgender individuals but much more research is needed on the transman experiences of females who identify as men in prisons for women.

Women and the death penalty

Historically, women were rarely sentenced to death for committing a homicide and were also less likely than men to be sentenced to death. Since the early 1600s, 571 women have been executed – 2.9% of the total number of executions in the United States (Death Penalty Information Center 2013). Over the past 100 years, over 40 women have been executed, including 12 women since 1976 (Death Penalty Information Center 2013). The first woman known to have been executed (hanged for an unknown offense) in the United States was Jane Champion in 1632 in Virginia. More recently, Kelly Gissendaner was executed by lethal injection in Georgia in 2015 for convincing her boyfriend to murder her husband (Berman 2015).

Approximately 10% of women arrested commit homicide (Cooper and Smith 2011). This figure belies media coverage of cases such as that of Amy Bishop – the University of Alabama biology professor who opened fire on her colleagues at a faculty meeting in 2010, killing three of them. It seems that Bishop was disgruntled as she was not granted tenure. She pled guilty in 2012 and is serving a life sentence without the possibility of parole (Brown 2012). Women rarely commit mass murder as Bishop did. Additionally, a smaller percentage of women who commit homicide are sentenced to death (Cooper and Smith 2011). The Bureau of Justice Statistics reports that those sentenced to death in 2013 were predominantly male, with only 56 of the 2,979 prisoners under the sentence of death – or 2% – being female (Snell 2014). This disparity between men and women being sentenced to death row and executed has not gone unnoticed and has raised a few eyebrows. Streib (2002, 433) refers to the disparity as a sex bias:

> This apparent sex bias has been recognized at the highest levels, including by such extraordinary legal scholars as Justice Thurgood Marshall: "There is also overwhelming evidence that the death penalty is employed against men and not women … It is difficult to understand why women have received such favored treatment since the purposes allegedly served by capital punishment seemingly are applicable to both sexes."

Apart from a sex bias, there are also racial disparities of those women actually sentenced to death. Currently, there are 40 Caucasian and 14 African-American women on death row. Female African-Americans are overrepresented on death row compared to their representation in US society – 12% of the total US population (US Census Bureau 2010). As Greenlee and Greenlee (2008, 330) note from the review of data regarding women on death row since 1973, "the percentage of African American and Native American women receiving death-row sentences greatly exceeded those percentages for women of other races, based on national female population percentages."

Female offenders who are sentenced to capital punishment are more likely to have committed murders intra-racially (i.e., between the same race), and are more likely to have murdered significant others such as family members or close intimates compared to their male counterparts on death row (Death Penalty Information Center 2013). Approximately half of all women on death row have killed significant others such as their husbands, boyfriends, or children (Death Penalty Information Center 2013; Streib 2012). Some researchers have stated that the murdering of close intimates by females is sometimes due to **battered women syndrome** (Browne 1987). Battered women syndrome refers to when a woman is repeatedly physically, sexually, and/or emotionally abused by a spouse and, due to fear for her life, kills her batterer (Walker 1979). In 2008, Barbara Sheehan, a school secretary in New York, shot her husband, a former police sergeant, 11 times with two different guns and killed him while he was shaving in their home (Bilefsky 2011). Sheehan stated that she felt threatened by her husband when she told him that she did not want to go on vacation with him. During the course of her trial, Sheehan claimed that she suffered from battered women syndrome due to the horrific abuse she experienced repeatedly at the hands of her husband over their 24-year marriage. Suspicions about the authenticity of her claims caused some to question whether she was in fact an abused wife or rather an executioner (Bilefsky 2011). Despite such assertions by some members in society, Sheehan was acquitted, or found not guilty, of his murder (Susman 2011). Finally, researchers have reported that approximately half of women on death row committed the crime with another person, typically a male, and the co-defendant received a sentence other than death. The leniency in sentencing for males occurred in cases where the defendants appeared to be equally guilty.

Community corrections and reentry

When Martha Stewart left prison, she was hounded by the media to provide her account of life behind bars, but her reentry into society was rather smooth. Not only did she have a home to return to, but her job that she had left prior to her incarceration was "waiting" for her return. Stewart had the benefit of fame and fortune – her wealth, social class, and race made her transition an aberration, – a far cry from the norm of reentry for most ex-offenders. Tonya Harding, who did not serve a prison sentence for her role in the attack on Nancy Kerrigan, and despite her notoriety as an Olympic-level figure skater, had a tough time transitioning back into society following her probation sentence and has had multiple encounters with the court system. Both Stewart (after her incarceration term) and Harding served **community corrections** sentences – punishments that are served in the community. Research on **offender reentry** over the past 30 years has demonstrated that ex-offenders' ability to reintegrate successfully is hindered by numerous obstacles, such as difficulty in obtaining employment, acquiring housing, being admitted to higher education, obtaining treatment for mental health issues and drug and alcohol addiction, and finding support for serious social and medical problems (Gunnison and Helfgott 2013). Bergseth and colleagues (2011), who examined the needs of female offenders during reentry from the perspective of 24 community service providers, reported that the providers indicated that employment, housing, and family-related needs (e.g., family support, classes on parenting skills, intervention in domestic violence, reunification with children, aid in child-care issues) were the most important needs. Particularly given the abuse that many female offenders endure from family members, reentering offenders may not be able to turn to family for help and support during reentry as they may have severed family ties (Kellett and Willging 2011). Post-conviction restrictions imposed by the criminal justice system regarding housing, employment, legal barriers, and custody may also have a disproportionate impact on women.

Gender-specific housing and employment concerns

Securing housing is a chief concern of women leaving prison and attempting to reintegrate into society. Allen, Flaherty, and Ely (2010) describe one female's struggles with housing concerns and potential homelessness upon release. Veronica, an ex-offender attempting to reenter society while also trying to overcome a drug and alcohol addiction, states,

> That's the serious thing I am dealing with right now – the stress of the unknown or what will happen to me when I get out ... I don't have [an] address to go to. I got no family right now. It's just me, myself, and I. I'll walk out of here hurting with nowhere to go, ... and that's scary. I'm hurtin' bad, and I am crying out for help, and I don't know which way to turn. I am so discombobulated, it's crazy. [Crying] I needed to know how to live without the drink and drugs [and] how to manage my money. It's just like walking all over again, feeding yourself all over again. As an adult, you have to learn everything just like a newborn baby ... I got caught with a five-cent piece of crack cocaine – you get clean and, at the same time, you get clean in jail, [but] you don't know what to do when you get out there ... You're dirty, and the only thing they do is take your kids away from you. They say they're here to help you, [but] they're not. I need help to overcome my drug addiction so I can be with my kids. (Allen et al. 2010, 169)

Housing is an especially stressful endeavor for female ex-offenders due to the fact that in many cases they are not only trying to secure housing for themselves but also for their children. However, female ex-offenders who are mothers soon discover that their children can be a burden in their search for suitable housing because many of the subsidized housing programs do not allow children (Leverentz 2010). Thus, female ex-offenders who are mothers face a difficult choice to either live within subsidized housing by themselves or forgo this housing option to reside with their children. Since women are more prone to have committed drug offenses, their housing options may be limited even more than women who have committed non-drug-related offenses. Status as a convicted drug offender often results in denial of federally assisted housing, impacting thousands of female ex-offenders (US Government Accountability Office 2005). Ex-offenders may discover that the only place they can find housing is in impoverished neighborhoods where they are less likely to find employment – another key obstacle to successful offender reentry.

After long-term imprisonment, many ex-offenders find they lack the skills to search for employment via the internet or newspapers or even to fill out a job application (Kelly and Fader 2012). Many of these released ex-offenders lack the skills to utilize email or even create a resumé. Without the ability to be technologically savvy on a basic level, their efforts to find legitimate employment are even further hampered. If ex-offenders do secure a coveted interview for a job, they are often deficient in life skills such as knowing what to wear to the interview and how to prepare for it, knowledge that would increase the likelihood of success for most job candidates. Richie (2001, 377) reported on one female ex-offender's struggles in regard to employment: "I am 35 years old and have never had a legit [legitimate] job. No one taught me how to do an application, how to get dressed and show up, how to get someone to hire me. Now that I have this X on my back [a criminal record], I'll never find someone to pay me. Not for a legit job anyways." These barriers force many offenders to rely on personal connections to find a job (Visher, La Vigne, and Travis 2004). However, ex-offenders often do not have many appropriate contacts they can rely on for job referrals and they may lack the ability to form social networks that could assist them in their search for employment (Shivy et al. 2007). Even if ex-offenders are successful in landing a job, they have a "limited knowledge of workplace culture and need to develop certain interpersonal and conflict resolution skills to be able to retain a job" (Heinrich 2000, 5). The absence of exhibiting proper social skills in a work environment stems from their lack of an extensive, or in some cases, any past legal work history.

Then there is the stigma of simply being a convicted offender who has served time in prison. Many employers are reluctant to hire ex-offenders (Clear 2007). For employers, especially those in retail or service industries, hiring women convicted of property-related crimes such as theft may be a concern, as would also be the case for women with histories of drug-related crimes. Employers may be concerned that if they hire the woman, she may steal from their business. A final barrier for female ex-offender employment is **gender discrimination**. Women ex-offenders face similar barriers to those experienced by other women without conviction records in securing employment that provides adequate pay in comparison to salary rates for men (Hegewisch, Williams, and Edwards 2013). La Vigne (2010) states that even when female ex-offenders do acquire legal employment, they still struggle more than males with their finances, earning on average $1.50 less per hour than male ex-offenders who obtained legal employment.

Legal issues

In 1996, the federal government overhauled the previous welfare system and replaced it with a new welfare program. The **Federal Welfare Law** of 1996 prohibits states from allowing ex-offenders with drug-related felony convictions to receive any form of welfare benefits, including cash assistance and food stamps, not just for a few years but for a lifetime (Mukamal 2000; Petersilia 2003). The ban on receiving assistance is likely to impact female offenders more than males since women are more likely than men to be incarcerated for drug convictions. In 2002, Allard reported that approximately 92,000 women were impacted by this law and expected that the number of women impacted would grow substantially each year. Further, Allard (2002) states this ban has had an inequitable and disproportionate impact on women of color, who are more likely to be incarcerated for drug offenses because such sentences are often disproportionately applied to this group. More recently, Mauer and McCalmont (2013) explored the impact of one element of this ban, cash assistance, on women. Their findings indicate that women offenders have indeed been severely impacted by this ban. The researchers estimate that between the years 1996–2011 approximately 180,000 women have been impacted by the law banning cash assistance. While the researchers note that the ban was not directed at any one specific race or gender, they found, like Allard (2002), that the ban has had "highly disparate effects on women, children, and communities of color" (Mauer and McCalmont 2013, 4).

Custody and reunification

One significant challenge that female ex-offenders face during reentry is resuming their role as a mother and balancing the role of motherhood with other reentry demands (Robbins et al. 2009). Compared with males released from prison, women offenders are far more likely to have been separated from dependent children during their incarceration (Mumola 2000). The anxiety and concern felt by many mothers for their children's well-being during their incarceration continues, and is often exacerbated, following release (Spjeldnes and Goodkind 2009).

When females are released from prison, they are often very motivated to regain custody of the child/ren. Unfortunately, due to the passage of the **Adoption and Safe Families Act** in 1997, which requires termination of parental rights for children who have been in foster care for at least 15 months, legally regaining custody is likely to be an uphill battle (Mapson 2013; Petersilia 2003). Apart from the legal barriers, mothers face a whole host of stressors as they attempt to resume their role as a parent, ranging from challenges in being reunited with children they may have lost custody of, fear of losing custody, concern for the emotional welfare of their child, and finding housing for the family. Further, many female ex-offenders are faced with overcoming personal problems such as previous domestic violence victimization, an HIV positive diagnosis, coping with depression, earning money, and maintaining sobriety (Arditti and Few 2006; Michalsen 2011).

Correctional programming for women

In light of all the struggles that women face while incarcerated and upon reentry into society, what can assist women to help them succeed? Petersilia (2003, 171) suggests the altering of "the in-prison experience." Specifically, Petersilia suggests that programming experiences (e.g., employment, education, and rehabilitation) should be enhanced for those who are incarcerated. For incarcerated women, employment training must be provided that will allow the women to find gainful employment that is not restricted by licensing requirements and that will provide the necessary means to support them, as well as their child/ren, when they are released back into society. Additionally, a multitude of research has been published on the effectiveness of rehabilitative programs, specifically those that target criminogenic needs and risk factors, in reducing recidivism (Andrews and Bonta 2010). **Cognitive behavioral therapy**, for example, has been identified as an effective treatment at reducing recidivism for offenders. This therapy seeks to change the cognition patterns of offenders, or "thinking errors," and alter negative behavioral patterns.

Addiction issues are a risk factor that increases the likelihood for recidivism and stymies successful reentry. It appears that alcohol was a problem for Harding, as she was sentenced to jail in 2002 for using alcohol while driving and serving a probation sentence which prohibited her from consuming alcohol (Du Bois 2002). Lindsay Lohan has had difficulties in her reentry due to addiction issues (McCartney 2011). Visher, Yahner, and La Vigne (2010) point out that the first few months post-release from prison is the critical time period that ex-offenders are most at risk of relapse and recidivism. Therapeutic communities for drug addicts may be a beneficial program for women (Petersilia 2003). This treatment modality is one of the most widely used for helping drug offenders both within and outside of prison (Zhang, Roberts, and McCollister 2011). Numerous researchers have found support for **therapeutic programming** to assist drug offenders, including those who suffer from co-occurring problems such as mental illness. In particular, therapeutic community programs that assist offenders both within prison and in the community upon release have been linked to lower rates of drug relapse and criminal recidivism (Martin, Butzin, and Inciardi 1995; McCollister et al. 2003). Further, Herrschaft and colleagues (2009) state that reentry programs need to be designed with women specifically in mind, not just modeled after reentry programs that have been designed for men. Thus, programming that addresses the needs of women, such as coming to terms with prior sexual abuse, overcoming addiction, and mental health issues, is critical both within prison and in the community for all races and ethnicities (Chesney-Lind 1989).

Another form of programming that may be beneficial for women is **restorative justice programs**. Such programs recognize that crime is harmful and seek to repair the damage caused by that harm by bringing together offenders, victims, community members, and governmental agencies (Liebmann 2007). A restorative justice approach views community members' participation in coping with the fallout from the criminal acts as critical and stresses the importance of dialogue between offenders and community members about the harm caused by the crime and what can be done to repair the damage. An example of a type of restorative justice program is victim–offender mediation or reconciliation programming (Van Ness and Strong 2010). This program brings together the offender and the victim and provides the offender with the opportunity to express his/her apologies to the victim or the family of the victim. Likewise, the victim, or family members of the victim, is given the opportunity to speak with the offender and express how the crime impacted his/her life.

Regardless of the type of treatment program (e.g., cognitive behavioral or restorative), they must be sensitive to cultural, class, and sex differences. Native American ex-offenders, for example, may not want to seek help for mental health problems, either because of embarrassment or because they do not want to report to a government agency for assistance, due to their distrust of the government (Earle, Bradigan, and Morgenbesser 2001). For Hispanic ex-offenders, programming that is offered to this group must be expansive, given the range of nationalities associated with the term "Hispanic" (see Martinez 2004). That is, one treatment modality applied to all Latinos/as may not be effective in helping this group. Additionally, Asian-American ex-offenders may experience difficulties, such as a loss of family support, as their conviction may have "tarnished" the family name. Treatment providers should strive to design programming that is tailored to specific cultural experiences and traditions. Thus, a one-size-fits-all approach to reforming ex-offenders is not likely to provide the opportunity for all ex-offenders to succeed but rather just a select few (Vigesaa 2013).

Conclusion

The feminist movement brought increased attention to the plight of women in society as well as those held behind prison walls. Researchers have uncovered gender disparity in sentencing decisions, with women of color being more likely to be incarcerated and disproportionately sentenced to death. Additionally, laws such as tough drug sentencing guidelines or restrictions for those receiving welfare are often crafted with the right intentions, but such laws have had a detrimental impact on women offenders. Women offenders struggle to overcome a multitude of personal issues and challenges both inside and outside of prison. Motherhood, mental illness, and drug and/or alcohol addictions are problems faced by women during incarceration and throughout their reentry into society. Rehabilitation programming that addresses the needs of women (e.g., treatment for mental illness, addictions, and prior traumas; reunification with children) are critical to their success during reintegration into society. Additionally, such programming needs to be tailored to specific cultural values and traditions. No longer can treatment providers dispense a program and expect it to stick, or work, for all offenders. Finally, abolishing those laws that inhibit the ability of women to successfully reintegrate into society, such as restrictions on their housing, financial assistance, and employment opportunities, would be the first necessary step to assist them.

Suggested readings

Fedock, Gina, Fries, Lauren, and Sherry P. Kubiak. 2013. "Service Needs for Incarcerated Adults: Exploring Gender Differences." *Journal of Offender Rehabilitation*, 52(7): 493–508. DOI: 10.1080/10509674.2012.759171

McCorkel, Jill A. 2013. *Breaking Women: Gender, Race, and the New Politics of Imprisonment.* New York, NY: New York University Press.

O'Brien, Patricia. 2006. "Maximizing Success for Drug-Affected Women After Release from Prison." *Women & Criminal Justice*, 17(2–3): 95–113. DOI: 10.1300/J012v17n02_07

Stohr, Mary K. 2015. "The Hundred Years War: The Etiology and Status of Transgender Women in Men's Prisons." *Women & Criminal Justice*, 25(1–2): 120–129. DOI: 10.1080/08974454.2015.1026154

Wright, Emily M., DeHart, Dana D., Koons-Witt, Barbara A., and Courtney A. Crittenden. 2013. "'Buffers' Against Crime? Exploring the Roles and Limitations of Positive Relationships Among Women in Prison." *Punishment & Society*, 15(1): 71–95. DOI: 10.1177/1462474512466199

Student engagement activities

1 Conduct research on prisons for women in the state/province/county in which you reside. Write a one-page summary and analysis of the institution, including its location and the type of programming offered to women. Be sure to critically reflect on whether the prison's location will isolate the female offenders in your state/province/county and whether the type of programming offered will allow women the opportunity to establish enough income to support themselves and their children.

2 Does the prison for women in your state/province/county offer any type of residential parenting programs for women? (Hint: Research your state/province/county's corrections website.) If so, what are the strengths and/or weaknesses of the program? Once you have identified

the strengths and have identified further suggestions for improvement in the program, prepare a presentation and/or a paper outlining your recommendations. If a program for incarcerated women does not exist in your state/province/county, investigate why one does not exist. Following your investigation, engage your community and/or legislative leaders in a conversation, with a presentation and/or a paper outlining why such a program is beneficial for incarcerated women. Be mindful in your proposal of sensitivities to budget and how your suggestions would be a cost saving, not only to the institution but also to your state/province/county.

3 What can be done to help women both in prison and on "the other side?" Think about ways in which you can reach out in your community to educate them on their needs. Consider writing an editorial in a local paper, writing a letter for your congress person or officers/officials of Parliament, or find ways to educate the public through the use of media.

Discussion questions

1 What do you think about residential parenting programs? Should women who have committed crimes be allowed to care for their children in prison? What about incarcerated fathers? Should they have such programs?

2 What are the needs of incarcerated women? Can you think of policies and programs to help them?

3 Should prisons offer any additional assistance to those women who identify as transgendered? Should prisons offer hormonal therapy or sex reassignment surgery to transgendered inmates? What are the consequences of not offering such services to transgendered inmates?

Key terms

Adoption and Safe Families Act (1997)
Barefield v. Leach (1974)
Battered women syndrome
Chivalry thesis
Co-correctional facilities
Cognitive behavioral therapy
Community corrections
Cooper v. Morin (1980)
Custodial
Eighth Amendment
Federal prisons
Federal Welfare Law (1996)
Focal Concerns Theory
Gender disparity
Gender-responsive programming
Glover v. Johnson (1979)
Indiana Women's Prison
Inmate code

Institutionalization
Jim Crow laws
Maximum classified prisons
Medium classified prisons
Mental health
Minimum classified prisons
Newgate Prison
Offender reentry
Parenting programs
Prisonization
Pseudo-families
Reformatory
Restorative justice programs
Sex-segregated prisons
State prisons
Therapeutic programming
Transgender inmates
Transgendered

References

Ackman, Dan. March 5, 2004. "Martha Stewart Found Guilty." *Forbes*. Accessed August 9, 2013, http://www.forbes.com/2004/03/05/cx_da_0305marthafinal.html

Acoca, Leslie. 1998. "Outside/Inside: The Violation of American Girls at Home, on the Streets, and in the Juvenile Justice System." *Crime and Delinquency*, 44(4): 561–589. DOI: 10.1177/0011128798044004006

Alexander, Michelle. 2012. *The New Jim Crow: Mass Incarceration in the Age of Colorblindness*. New York, NY: The New Press.

Allard, Patricia. 2002. *Life Sentences: Denying Welfare Benefits to Women Convicted of Drug Offenses*. Washington, DC: The Sentencing Project. Accessed August 15, 2013, http://www.sentencingproject.org/doc/publications/women_lifesentences.pdf

Allen, Suzanne, Flaherty, Chris, and Gretchen Ely. 2010. "Throwaway Mom: Maternal Incarceration and the Criminalization of Female Poverty." *Journal of Women and Social Work*, 25(2): 160–172. DOI: 10.1177/0886109910364345

American Correctional Association. 2012. *Directory of Adult and Juvenile Correctional Departments, Institutions, Agencies, and Probation and Parole Authorities*. Alexandria, VA.

Andrews, D. A., and James Bonta 2010. *The Psychology of Criminal Conduct*. Cincinnati, OH: Anderson.

Arditti, Joyce A., and April L. Few. 2006. "Mothers' Reentry into Family Life Following Incarceration." *Criminal Justice Policy Review*, 17(1): 103–123. DOI: 10.1177/0887403405282450

Associated Press. 2000. "Tonya Harding Sentenced for Attack on Boyfriend." *Seattle Times*. Accessed March 26, 2014, http://community.seattletimes.nwsource.com/archive/?date=20000519&slug=4021850

Barefield v. Leach, 1974.

Beck, Allen J., Berzofsky, Marcus, Casper, Rachel, and Christopher Krebs. 2013. *Sexual Victimization in Prisons and Jails Reported by Inmates, 2011–12: BJS National Inmate Survey, 2011–12*. US Department of Justice: Bureau of Justice Statistics.

Bergseth, Kathleen J., Jens, Katie R., Bergeron-Vigesaa, Lindsey, and Thomas D. McDonald 2011. "Assessing the Needs of Women Recently Released from Prison." *Women and Criminal Justice*, 21: 100–122. DOI: 10.1080/08974454.2011.558799

Berman, Mark. September 30, 2015. "Georgia Executes Kelly Gissendaner after Supreme Court Denies Stay Requests." *Washington Post*. Accessed February 1, 2016, https://www.washingtonpost.com/news/post-nation/wp/2015/09/29/georgia-considering-whether-the-state-will-execute-kelly-gissendaner-the-only-woman-on-its-death-row-as-pope-francis-asks-for-mercy/

Bilefsky, Dan. September 25, 2011. "An Abused Wife? Or an Executioner?" *New York Times*. Accessed August 15, 2013, http://www.nytimes.com/2011/09/26/nyregion/an-abused-wife-or-anexecutioner.html?pagewanted=all

Bloom, Barbara, Owen, Barbara, Covington, Stephanie, and Myrna Raeder. 2002. *Gender-Responsive Strategies: Research, Practice, and Guiding Principles for Women Offenders*. Washington, DC: US Department of Justice. Accessed March 27, 2014, http://static.nicic.gov/Library/018017.pdf

Bouchet, Stacey M. 2008. *Children and Families with Incarcerated Parents. Baltimore*, MD: The Annie E. Casey Foundation. Accessed March 27, 2014, http://www.f2f.ca.gov/res/pdf/ChildrenAndFamilies.pdf

Bowes, Daniel, and Bill Rowe. January 9, 2013. "Facilitating Individualized Assessments of Individuals with Criminal Records in Occupational Licensing Decisions." *North Carolina Bar Association: Administrative Law Section Newsletter*. Accessed March 28, 2014, http://administrativelaw.ncbar.org/newsletters/adminlawjan2013/occupationallicensingdecisions

Brown, Robbie. 2012. "Alabama: Ex-Professor Gets Life Term in Shooting." *New York Times.* Accessed September 12, 2013, http://www.nytimes.com/2012/09/25/us/alabama-ex-professor-gets-life-term-in-shooting.html?ref=amybishop

Browne, Angela. 1987. *When Battered Women Kill.* New York, NY: The Free Press.

Bush-Baskette, Stephanie. 1998. "The War on Drugs as a War Against Black Women." In *Crime Control and Women: Feminist Implications of Criminal Justice Policy,* edited by SusanMiller, 113–129. Thousand Oaks, CA: Sage.

Carson, E. Ann, and William J. Sabol. 2012. *Prisoners in 2011.* Washington, DC: Bureau of Justice Statistics.

Carson, E. Ann. 2015. *Prisoners in 2014.* Washington, DC: Bureau of Justice Statistics.

Centers for Disease Control and Prevention. 2012. "HIV in Prison Settings." Accessed August 25, 2013. http://www.cdc.gov/hiv/resources/factsheets/pdf/correctional.pdf

Chesney-Lind, Meda. 1989. "Girl's Crime and Woman's Place: Toward a Feminist Model of Female Delinquency." *Crime and Delinquency,* 35(1): 8–10.

Christian, S. 2009. *Children of Incarcerated Parents.* National Conference of State Legislatures. Washington, DC. Accessed August 19, 2013, http://www.ncsl.org/documents/cyf/childrenof incarceratedparents.pdf

Clear, Todd. R. 2007. *Imprisoning Communities: How Mass Incarceration Makes Disadvantaged Neighborhoods Worse.* New York, NY: Oxford University Press.

Clear, Todd R., Reisig, Michael D., and George F. Cole. 2012. *American Corrections.* Belmont, CA: Wadsworth/Cengage.

Clemmer, Donald. 1940. *The Prison Community.* Boston, MA: Christopher Publishing.

Coll, Cynthia, Surrey, Janet, Buccio-Notaro, Phyllis, and Barbara Molla. 1998. "Incarcerated Mothers: Crimes and Punishments." In *Mothering Against the Odds: Diverse Voices by Contemporary Mothers,* edited by Cynthia Coll, Janet Surrey, and Kathy Weingarten, 255–274. New York, NY: Guilford Press.

Collins, Jeffrey. September 6, 2001. "Second Former Guard Pleads Guilty to Having Sex in Prison with Child Killer Susan Smith." *Lubbock Avalanche-Journal.* Accessed April 1, 2014, http://lubbockonline.com/stories/090601/upd_075-6441.shtml

Columbia Human Rights Law Review. 2011. "Chapter 41: Special Issue of Women Prisoners." In *A Jailhouse Lawyer's Manual,* 1–22. Accessed April 1, 2014, http://www3.law.columbia.edu/hrlr/jlm/chapter-41.pdf

Cooper v. Morin, 1980.

Cooper, Alexia, and Erica L. Smith. 2011. *Homicide Trends in the United States, 1980–2008. Annual Rates for 2009 and 2010.* Washington, DC: Bureau of Justice Statistics. Accessed August 9, 2013, http://www.bjs.gov/content/pub/pdf/htus8008.pdf

Death Penalty Information Center. 2013. *Facts and Figures.* Accessed September 3, 2013, http://www.deathpenaltyinfo.org/women-and-death-penalty#facts

Diaz-Cotto, Juanita. 1996. *Gender, Ethnicity, and the State: Latina and Latino Prison Politics.* New York, NY: State University of New York Press.

Doerner, Jill K. 2012. "Gender Disparities in Sentencing Departures: An Examination of U.S. Federal Courts." *Women and Criminal Justice,* 22: 176–205. DOI: 10.1080/08974454.2012.687953

Dorning, Mike. July 23, 1995. "Jury Convicts Susan Smith of Murdering Her Two Sons." *Chicago Tribune.* Accessed April 1, 2014, http://articles.chicagotribune.com/1995-07-23/news/9507230215_1_prosecutor-tommy-pope-susan-smith-suicide-attempt

Du Bois, Steven. August 9, 2002. "Harding Sentenced to 10 Days in Jail." *Cincinnati Enquirer.* Accessed August 5, 2013, http://www.enquirer.com/editions/2002/08/09/spt_harding_sentenced_to.html

Earle, Kathleen A., Bradigan, Brace, and Leonard I. Morgenbesser 2001. "Mental Health Care for American Indians in Prison." *Journal of Ethnic and Cultural Diversity in Social Work*, 9(3/4): 111–132. DOI: 10.1300/J051v09n03_06

Farrell, Amy. 2004. "Measuring Judicial and Prosecutorial Discretion: Sex and Race Disparities in Departures from the Federal Sentencing Guidelines." *Justice Research and Policy*, 6(2): 45–78. DOI: 10.3818/JRP.6.2.2004.45

Fearn, Noelle, and Kelly Parker. 2004. "Washington State's Residential Parenting Program: An Integrated Public Health, Education, and Social Service Resource for Pregnant Inmates and Prison Mothers." *California Journal of Health Promotion*, 2(4): 34–48.

Federal Bureau of Prisons. 2016. *Institutions Housing Female Offenders*. Washington, DC: US Department of Justice. Accessed February 1, 2016, http://www.bop.gov/locations/list.jsp

Forsyth, Craig J, and Rhonda D. Evans. 2003. "Reconsidering the Pseudo-Family/Gang Gender Distinction in Prison Research." *Journal of Police and Criminal Psychology*, 18(1): 15–23. DOI: 10.1007/BF02802604

Foster, Thomas W. 1975. "Make Believe Families: A Response of Women and Girls to the Deprivations of Imprisonment." *International Journal of Criminology & Penology*, 3(1): 71–78.

Franklin, Cortney A. 2008. "Women Offenders, Disparate Treatment, and Criminal Justice: A Theoretical, Historical, Contemporary Overview. *Criminal Justice Studies*, 21(4): 341–360. DOI: 10.1080/14786010802554238

Freedman, Estelle. 1974. "Their Sister's Keepers: A Historical Perspective of Female Correctional Institutions in the U.S." *Feminist Studies*, 2: 77–95.

Freedman, Estelle. 1981. *Their Sister's Keepers: Women's Prison Reform in America, 1830–1930*. Ann Arbor, MI: University of Michigan Press.

Fry, Elizabeth. G. 1827. *Observations on the Visiting, Superintendence, and Government of Female Prisoners*. London: John & Arthur Arch.

Furst, Randy. May 6, 2013. "North Oaks Hubby Sent to Prison for Fraud, But Not Mom." *Star Tribune*. Accessed September 15, 2013, http://www.startribune.com/local/east/206279761.html

Garland, David. 2001. *The Culture of Control*. Chicago, IL: University of Chicago Press.

Gates, Gary J. 2011. *How Many People Are Lesbian, Gay, Bisexual, and Transgender?* Los Angeles, CA: The Williams Institute, UCLA School of Law.

Gillombardo, Rose. 1966. *Society of Women: A Study of a Women's Prison*. New York, NY: John Wiley & Sons.

Girshick, Lori. 2011. "Out of Compliance: Masculine-Identified People in Women's Prisons." In *Captive Genders: Trans Embodiment and the Prison Industrial Complex*, edited by Eric A. Stanley and Nat Smith, 189–208. Oakland, CA: AK Press.

Glaze, Laura E., and Lauren M. Maruschak. 2008. *Parents in Prison and Their Minor Children*. Washington, DC: Bureau of Justice Statistics. Accessed September 3, 2013, http://www.bjs.gov/content/pub/pdf/pptmc.pdf

Glover v. Johnson, 1979.

Goshin, Lorie S., and Mary W. Byrne. 2009. "Converging Streams of Opportunity for Prison Nursery Programs in the United States." *Journal of Offender Rehabilitation*, 48(4): 271–295. DOI: 10.1080/10509670902848972

Greenlee, Harry, and Sheila P. Greenlee. 2008. "Women and the Death Penalty: Racial Disparities and Differences." *William & Mary Journal of Women and the Law*, 14(2): 319–335.

Greer, Kimberly R. 2000. "The Changing Nature of Interpersonal Relationships in a Women's Prison." *The Prison Journal*, 80(4): 442–468. DOI: 10.1177/0032885500080004009

Gunnison, Elaine, and Jacqueline B. Helfgott. 2013. *Offender Reentry: Beyond Crime and Punishment*. Boulder, CO: Lynne Rienner.

Hammett, Theodore, and Abigail Drachman-Jones. 2006. "HIV/AIDS, Sexually Transmitted Diseases, and Incarceration Among Women: National and Southern Perspectives." *Sexually Transmitted Diseases*, 33(7): S17–S22. DOI: 10.1097/01.olq.0000218852.83584.7f

Hays, C. L. June 5, 2003. "Prosecuting Martha Stewart: The Overview; Martha Stewart Indicted by U.S. on Obstruction." *New York Times*. Accessed August 19, 2013, http://www.nytimes.com/2003/06/05/business/prosecuting-martha-stewart-overview-martha-stewart-indicted-us-obstruction.html?pagewanted=all&src=pm

Hegadoren, Kathy M., Lasiuk, Gerri C., and Nicholas J. Coupland. 2006. "Posttraumatic Stress Disorder Part III: Health Effects of Interpersonal Violence Among Women." *Perspectives in Psychiatric Care*, 42(3): 163–173. DOI:10.1111/j.1744-6163.2006.00078.x

Hegewisch, Araine, Williams, Claudia, and Angela Edwards. 2013. *The Gender Wage Gap: 2012*. Washington, DC: The Institute for Women's Policy Research. Accessed August 21, 2013, http://www.iwpr.org/publications/pubs/the-gender-wage-gap-2012

Heinrich, Svenja. 2000. *Reducing Recidivism Through Work: Barriers and Opportunities for Employment of Ex-Offenders*. Chicago, IL: Great Cities Institute.

Herrschaft, Bryn A., Veysey, Bonita M., Tubman-Carbone, Heather, and Johnna Christian. 2009. "Gender Differences in the Transformation Narrative: Implications for Revised Reentry Strategies for Female Offenders." *Journal of Offender Rehabilitation*, 48(6): 463–482. DOI: 10.1080/10509670903081250

Hoffman, Heath C., Byrd, Amy L., and Alex M. Kightlinger. 2010. "Prison Programs and Services for Incarcerated Parents and Their Underage Children: Results from a National Survey of Correctional Facilities." *The Prison Journal*, 90(4): 397–416. DOI: 10.1177/0032885510382087

Hotelling, Barbara A. 2008. "Perinatal Needs of Pregnant, Incarcerated Women." *Journal of Perinatal Education*, 17(2): 37–44. DOI: 10.1624/105812408X298372

Husain, Mishal. October 7, 2013. "Malala: The Girl Who Was Shot for Going to School." *BBC News*. Accessed March 26, 2014, http://www.bbc.com/news/magazine-24379018

Huus, K. September 4, 2012. "Sex-Change Surgery for Prison Inmate Granted by Judge." *NBC News*. Accessed September 13, 2013, http://usnews.nbcnews.com/_news/2012/09/04/13660348-sex-change-surgery-for-prison-inmate-granted-by-judge

James, Michael S. August 26, 2003. "Prison is 'Living Hell' for Pedophiles." *ABC News*. Accessed March 27, 2014, http://abcnews.go.com/US/story?id=90004

James, Doris J., and Lauren E. Glaze. 2006. *Mental Health Problems of Prison and Jail Inmates*. Washington, DC: Bureau of Justice Statistics.

Jbara, Anne E. 2012. "The Price They Pay: Protecting the Mother–Child Relationship Through the Use of Prison Nurseries and Residential Parenting Programs." *Indiana Law Journal*, 87(4): 1825–1845.

Jeffries, Samantha, and Christine E. W. Bond. 2010. "Sex and Sentencing Disparity in South Australia's Higher Courts." *Current Issues in Criminal Justice*, 22(1): 81–97.

Jenness, Valerie, Maxson, Cheryl L., Matsuda, Kristy N., and Jennifer Sumner. 2007. *Violence in California Correctional Facilities: An Empirical Examination of Sexual Assault*. Report to the California Department of Corrections and Rehabilitation. Sacramento, CA.

Johnson, Corey G. July 7, 2013. "Female Inmates Sterilized in California Prisons Without Approval." *Center for Investigative Reporting*. Accessed April 1, 2014, http://cironline.org/reports/female-inmates-sterilized-california-prisons-without-approval-4917

Johnson, Corey G. February 20, 2014. "Bill Would Limit Inmate Sterilization for Birth Control." *SF Gate*. Accessed April 1, 2014, http://www.sfgate.com/news/article/Bill-would-limit-inmate-sterilization-for-birth-5253583.php

Kaeble, Danielle, Glaze, Lauren, Tsoutis, Anastasios, and Todd Minton. 2015. *Correctional Populations in the United States, 2014*. Washington, DC: Bureau of Justice Statistics.

Kalantry, Sital. 2013. "Women in Prison in Argentina: Causes, Conditions, and Consequences." *Univeristy of Chicago, Public Law Working Paper 439*. Accessed March 31, 2014, http://papers.ssrn.com/sol3/papers.cfm?abstract_id=2291764

Kellett, Nicole C., and Cathleen E. Willging 2011. "Pedgaogy of Individual Choice and Female Inmate Reentry in the US Southwest." *International Journal of Law and Psychiatry*, 34(4): 256 263. DOI: 10.1016/j.ijlp.2011.07.003

Kelly, Christopher E., and Jamie J. Fader 2012. "Computer-Based Employment Applications: Implications for Offenders and Supervising Officers." *Federal Probation*, 76(1):14–18.

Kerman, Piper. 2011. *Orange s the New Black: My Year in a Women's Prison*. New York, NY: Random House.

Kilpatrick, Dean G., Acierno, Ron, Saunders, Benjamin, Resnick, Heidi S., Best, Connie L., and Paula Schnurr. 2000. "Risk Factors for Adolescent Substance Abuse and Dependence: Data from a National Sample." *Journal of Consulting and Clinical Psychology*, 68: 19–30. DOI: 10.1037/0022-006X.68.1.19

Lauderdale, Michael, and Michelle Burman. 2009. "Contemporary Patterns of Female Gangs in Correctional Settings." *Journal of Human Behavior in the Social Environment*, 19: 258–280. DOI: 10.1080/10911350802694766

La Vigne, Nancy. July 27, 2010. *Female D.C. Code Felons: Unique Challenges in Prison and at Home*. Testimony to the House of Representatives Oversight and Government Reform Subcommittee on Federal Workforce, Postal Service, and the District of Columbia.

La Vigne, Nancy G., Davies, Elizabeth, and Diana Brazzell. 2008. *Broken Bonds: Understanding and Addressing the Needs of Children with Incarcerated Parents*. Washington, DC: The Urban Institute. Accessed March 27, 2014, http://www.urban.org/UploadedPDF/411616_incarcerated_parents.pdf

Lee, Jennifer A. 2000. "Women Prisoners, Penological Interests, and Gender Stereotyping: An Application of Equal Protection Norms to Female Inmates." *Columbia Human Rights Law Review*, 32: 251–288.

Leukefeld, Carl, Havens, Jennifer, Tindall, Michele S., Oser, Carrie B., Mooney, Jennifer, Hall, Martin T., and Hannah K. Knudsen. 2012. "Risky Relationships: Targeting HIV Prevention for Women Offenders." *AIDS Education and Prevention*, 24(4): 339–349. DOI: 10.1521/aeap.2012.24.4.339

Leverentz, Andrea. 2010. "People, Places, and Things: How Female Ex-Prisoners Negotiate Their Neighborhood Context." *Journal of Contemporary Ethnography*, 39(6): 646–681. DOI: 10.1177/0891241610377787

Liebmann, Marian. 2007. *Restorative Justice: How It Works*. London: Jessica Kingsley Publishers.

Longman, Jere. January 6, 1994. "Jealousy on Ice." *New York Times*. Accessed March 26, 2014, http://www.nytimes.com/packages/html/sports/year_in_sports/01.06.html

Lu, Hong, Liang, Bin, and Sivu Liu. 2013. "Serious Violent Offenses and Sentencing Decisions in China – Are There Any Gender Disparities?" *Asian Journal of Criminology*, 8(3): 159–177.

Mapson, Andridia. 2013. "From Prison to Parenting." *Journal of Human Behavior in the Social Environment*, 23(2): 171–177. DOI: 10.1080/10911359.2013.747402

Martin, Steve S., Butzin, Clifford A., and James A. Inciardi 1995. "Assessment of a Multistage Therapeutic Community for Drug-Involved Offenders." *Journal of Psychoactive Drugs*, 27(1): 109–116. DOI: 10.1080/02791072.1995.10471679

Martinez, Damian J. 2004. "Felony Disenfranchisement and Voting Participation: Considerations in Latino Ex-Prisoner Reentry." *Columbia Human Rights Law Review*, 36(1): 217–240.

Martinez, Helda. May 4, 2010. "Women Punished Twice Over in Colombia's Prisons." *Inter Press Service News Agency.* Accessed April 1, 2014, http://www.ipsnews.net/2010/05/women-punished-twice-over-in-colombias-prisons/

Martinson, Robert. 1974. "What Works? Questions and Answers About Prison Reform." *The Public Interest*, 35: 22–54.

Maruschak, Laura M. 2008. *Medical Problems of Prisoners.* Washington, DC: Bureau of Justice Statistics.

Mauer, Marc, and Virginia McCalmont. 2013. "A Lifetime of Punishment: The Impact of the Felony Drug Ban on Welfare Benefits." *The Sentencing Project.* Washington DC. Accessed March 31, 2014, http://sentencingproject.org/doc/publications/cc_A%20Lifetime%20of%20Punishment.pdf

McCartney, Anthony. July 21, 2011. "Judge: Lohan Needs to Speed up Community Service." *Seattle Times.* Accessed March 19, 2014, http://www.seattletimes.nwsource.com

McCollister, Kathryn E., French, Michael T., Prendergast, Michael, Wexler, Harry, Sacks, Stan, and Elizabeth Hall. 2003. "Is In-Prison Treatment Enough? A Cost-Effectiveness Analysis of Prison-Based Treatment and Aftercare Services for Substance Abusing Offenders." *Law and Policy*, 25(1): 62–83. DOI: 10.1111/1467-9930.00140

McGuire, M. Dylan. 2011. "Doing the Life: An Exploration of the Connection Between the Inmate Code and Violence Among Female Inmates." *The Journal of the Institute of Justice & International Studies*, 11: 145–158.

Michalsen, Venezia. 2011. "Mothering as a Life Course Transition: Do Women Go Straight for Their Children?" *Journal of Offender Rehabilitation*, 50: 349–366. DOI: 10.1080/10509674.2011.589887

Minton, Todd D. 2011. *Jail Inmates at Midyear 2010 – Statistical Tables.* Washington, DC: Bureau of Justice Statistics. Accessed August 19, 2013, http://www.bjs.gov/content/pub/pdf/jim10st.pdf

Mukamal, Debbie A. 2000. "Confronting the Employment Barriers of Criminal Records: Effective Legal and Practical Strategies." *Journal of Poverty Law and Policy*, January–February: 597–606.

Mumola, Christopher J. 2000. *Incarcerated Parents and Their Children.* Washington, DC: US Department of Justice.

O'Connor, James V. October 15, 2000. "The Law: The Privileged: Inmates Who Earn Honor Rooms." *New York Times.* Accessed March 26, 2014, http://www.nytimes.com/2000/10/15/nyregion/the-law-the-privileged-inmates-who-earn-honor-rooms.html

Olson, David E., Alderden, Megan, and Arthur J. Lurigio 2003. "Men Are from Mars, Women Are from Venus, but What Role Does Gender Pay in Probation Recidivism?" *Justice Research and Policy*, 5(2): 33–54. DOI:10.3818/JRP.5.2.2003.33

Oparah, Julia C. 2012. "Feminism and the (Trans)Gender Entrapment of Gender Nonconforming Prisoners." *UCLA Women's Law Journal*, 18(2): 239–271.

Owen, Barbara. A. 1998. *In the Mix: Struggle and Survival in a Women's Prison.* Albany, NY: State University of New York Press.

Peters, Roger H., and Holly A. Hills 1993. "Inmates with Co-Occurring Substance Abuse and Mental Health Disorders." In *Providing Services for Offenders with Mental Illness and Related Disorders in Prisons*, edited by Henry J. Steadman and Joseph J. Cocozza, 159–212. Washington, DC: National Coalition for the Mentally Ill in the Criminal Justice System.

Petersilia, Joan. 2003. *When Prisoners Come Home: Parole and Prisoner Reentry.* New York, NY: Oxford University Press.

Poehlmann, Julie. 2005. "Incarcerated Mothers' Contact with Children, Perceived Family Relationships, and Depressive Symptoms." *Journal of Family Psychology*, 19(3): 350–357. DOI: 10.1037/0893-3200.19.3.350

Pollock, Joycelyn M. 2002. *Women, Prison, and Crime.* Belmont, CA: Wadsworth/Thomson Learning.

Quinn, Colleen. March 26, 2014. "Massachusetts House Votes to Restrict Shackling of Pregnant Inmates." State House News Service, *MassLive*. Accessed March 27, 2014, http://www.masslive.com/politics/index.ssf/2014/03/house_votes_to_restrict_shackl.html

Rafter, Nicole. 1985. *Partial Justice: State Prisons and Their Inmates, 1800–1935*. Boston, MA: Northeastern Press.

Richie, Beth E. 2001. "Challenges Incarcerated Women Face as They Return to Their Communities: Findings from Life History Interviews." *Crime and Delinquency*, 47: 368–389. DOI: 10.1177/0011128701047003005

Richmond, Todd. August 18, 2010. "Wisconsin Settles Suit Over Poor Prison Health Care." *Wisconsin State Journal*. Accessed April 1, 2014, http://host.madison.com/news/local/health_med_fit/wisconsin-settles-suit-over-poor-prison-health-care/article_c4a7a44a-ab1d-11df-afc2-001cc4c002e0.html

Robbins, Cynthia. A., Martin, Steven S., and Hilary L. Surratt, H. L. 2009. "Substance Abuse Treatment, Anticipated Maternal Roles and Reentry Success of Drug-Involved Women Prisoners." *Crime & Delinquency*, 55: 388–411. DOI: 10.1177/0011128707306688

Rodriguez, S. Fernando, Curry, Theodore R., and Gang Lee. 2006. "Gender Differences in Criminal Sentencing: Do Effects Vary Across Violent, Property, and Drug Offenses?" *Social Science Quarterly*, 87(2): 318–339. DOI: 10.1111/j.1540-6237.2006.00383.x

Scranton, Phil, and Jude McCulloch. 2009. *The Violence of Incarceration*. New York, NY: Routledge.

Severson, Kim. March 1, 2014. "Troubles at Women's Prison Test Alabama." *New York Times*. Accessed April 1, 2014, http://www.nytimes.com/2014/03/02/us/troubles-at-womens-prison-test-alabama.html

Shivy, Victoria A., Wu, J. Juana, Moon, Anya E., Mann, Shay C., Holland, Jo G., and Christine Eacho. 2007. "Ex-Offenders Reentering the Workforce." *Journal of Counseling Psychology*, 54(4): 466–473. DOI: 10.1037/0022-0167.54.4.466

Siegel, Jane A., and Linda M. Williams. 2003. "The Relationship Between Childhood Sexual Abuse and Female Delinquency and Crime: A Prospective Study." *Journal of Research in Crime and Delinquency*, 40(1): 71–94. DOI:10.1177/0022427802239254

Siva, Navanah. 2010. "New Hope for Prison Health in the UK." *The Lancet*, 375(9713): 447–448.

Smykla, John O. 1978. *Co-Corrections: An Ethnography of Inmate Sex and Violence in a Coed Federal Prison*. Washington, DC: University Press of America.

Smykla, John O., and Jimmy J. Williams. 1996. "Co-Corrections in the United States of America, 1970–1990: Two Decades of Disadvantages for Women Prisoners." *Women and Criminal Justice*, 8(1): 61–76. DOI: 10.1300/J012v08n01_04

Snell, Tracy L. 2014. *Capital Punishment, 2013*. Washington, DC: Bureau of Justice Statistics. Accessed February 1, 2016, http://www.bjs.gov/content/pub/pdf/cp13st.pdf

Spjeldnes, Solveig, and Sara Goodkind. 2009. "Gender Differences and Offender Reentry: A Review of the Literature." *Journal of Offender Rehabilitation*, 48: 314–335. DOI: 10.1080/10509670902850812

Spohn, Cassia. 2013. "The Effects of the Offender's Race, Ethnicity, and Sex on Federal Sentencing Outcomes in the Guidelines Era." *Law & Contemporary Problems*, 76: 75–104.

Springer, Sandra A. 2010. "Improving Healthcare for Incarcerated Women." *Journal of Women's Health*, 19(1): 13–15. DOI: 10.1089=jwh.2009.1786

Stacey, Ann M., and Casia Spohn. 2006. "Gender and the Social Costs of Sentencing: An Analysis of Sentences Imposed on Male and Female Offenders in Three U.S. District Courts." *Berkeley Journal of Criminal Law*, 11: 43–76.

Starr, Sonja B. 2012. "Estimating Gender Disparities in Federal Criminal Cases." University of Michigan Law and Economics Research Paper, No. 12-018, 1–39.

Steffensmeier, Darrell, and Steven Demuth. 2006. "Does Gender Modify the Effects of Race-Ethnicity on Criminal Sentencing? Sentences for Male and Female White, Black, and Hispanic Defendants." *Journal of Quantitative Criminology*, 22: 241–261. DOI 10.1007/s10940-006-9010-2

Stern, Anne H. 2004. *Information Packet: Babies Born to Incarcerated Mothers*. New York, NY: National Resource Center for Foster Care and Permanency Planning.

Streib, Victor L. 2002. "Gendering the Death Penalty: Countering Sex Bias in a Masculine Sanctuary." *Ohio State Law Journal*, 63(1): 433–474.

Streib, Victor L. 2012. *Death Penalty for Female Offenders, January 1, 1973, through December 31, 2011, Issue #66*. Death Penalty Information Center. Accessed August 19, 2013, http://deathpenaltyinfo.org/documents/FemDeathDec2011.pdf

Susman, Tina. October 6, 2011. "Jury Accepts Battered-Wife Defense, Acquits N.Y. Woman of Murder." *Los Angeles Times*. Accessed September 12, 2013, http://latimesblogs.latimes.com/nationnow/2011/10/woman-acquitted-of-murder-jurors-accept-battered-wife-syndrome.html

Todrys, Katherine W., and Joseph J. Amon. 2011. "Health and Human Rights of Women Imprisoned in Zambia." *BMC International Health and Human Rights*, 11: 1–7.

Toor, Omar. Oct. 14, 2014. "At 17, Malala Becomes the Youngest Nobel Peace Prize Winner in History." *The Verge*. Accessed March 24, 2016, http://www.theverge.com/2014/10/10/6956107/nobel-peace-prize-malala-yousafzay-kailash-satyarthi

Travis, Jeremy, McBride, Elizabeth C., and Amy L. Solomon. 2005. *Families Left Behind: The Hidden Costs of Incarceration and Reentry*. Washington, DC: The Urban Institute. Accessed August 19, 2013, http://www.urban.org/UploadedPDF/310882_families_left_behind.pdf

United States Bureau of Prisons. January 6, 2014. *Sexually Abusive Behavior Prevention and Intervention Program*. US Department of Justice. Accessed March 28, 2014, http://www.bop.gov/policy/progstat/5324_011.pdf

US Census Bureau 2010. *People Quickfacts*. Washington, DC.

US Government Accountability Office. 2005. *Drug Offenders: Various Factors May Limit the Impacts of Federal Laws that Provide for Denial of Selected Benefits*. Washington, DC: US Government Accountability Office. Accessed September 13, 2013, http://www.gao.gov/new.items/d05238.pdf

Van Ness, Daniel, and Karen H. Strong. 2010. *Restoring Justice*, 4th edn. Cincinnati, OH: Anderson.

Vigesaa, Lindsey E. 2013. "Abuse as a Form of Strain Among Native American and White Female Prisoners: Predictors of Substance-Related Offenses and Recidivism." *Journal of Ethnicity in Criminal Justice*, 11: 1–21. DOI:10.1080/15377938.2013.739384

Visher, Christy, La Vigne, Nancy G. and Jeremy Travis. 2004. *Returning Home: Understanding the Challenges of Prisoner Reentry. Maryland Pilot Study: Findings from Baltimore*. Washington, DC: Urban Institute.

Visher, Christy, Yahner, Jennifer, and Nancy G. La Vigne. 2010. *Life After Prison: Tracking the Experiences of Male Prisoners Returning to Chicago, Cleveland, and Houston*. Washington, DC: Urban Institute.

Walker, Lenore E. 1979. *The Battered Woman*. New York, NY: Harper and Row.

Ward, David A., and Gene G. Kassebaum.1965. *Women's Prison: Sex and Social Structure*. Chicago, IL: Aldine Publishing Company.

Zeilinger, Julie. July 12, 2013. "On Malala Day, Young Women Sing and Rap in Honor of Malala Yousafzai." *Huffington Post*. Accessed March 26, 2014, http://www.huffingtonpost.com/2013/07/12/malala-day-music-video-yousafzai_n_3586549.html

Zhang, Sheldon X., Roberts, Robert E. L., and Kathryn E. McCollister. 2011. "Therapeutic Community in a California Prison: Treatment Outcomes After 5 Years." *Crime and Delinquency*, 57(1): 82–101. DOI: 10.1177/0011128708327035

CHAPTER 4

Legal control over women's bodies: Pregnancy and crime

Student learning outcomes

After reading this chapter, you should be able to:

- Track the history of involuntary sterilization from the early twentieth century until the present.
- Explain trends in women's access to abortion since the *Roe v. Wade* decision.
- List laws or policies that currently impose restrictions or punishments on pregnant women who use illicit drugs.
- Explain how race and class played a role in demonizing women who used crack cocaine.
- Provide arguments for why physical restraints should not be used on women prisoners during labor and delivery.

Introduction

During the late 1990s and throughout the first decade of the 2000s, The Learning Channel (TLC) aired two popular television shows, *A Baby Story* and *Bringing Home Baby*, which depicted women's experiences with pregnancy, birth, and adjustment to life with a newborn. Typically, the TLC shows featured married women or women in relationships and their journey to motherhood. While the TLC shows did not depict the journey to motherhood as being easy, they failed to provide examples of struggles that some women may face when pregnant (e.g., consideration of abortion, drug dependence, giving birth in shackles). More recently, the VH-1 television shows *Teen Mom* and *16 and Pregnant* have contributed to the expansion of discussions on the topic of pregnancy as it relates to younger women. These VH-1 shows have featured teen mothers: some who decided to keep their babies; some who have considered and obtained abortions; and one who had chosen adoption. Although the VH-1 shows have showcased the hardships that many young women face when pregnant, these shows have also failed to provide examples of the struggles of pregnancy that some women face in the legal and correctional arenas.

Women, Crime, and Justice, First Edition. By Elaine Gunnison, Frances P. Bernat, and Lynne Goodstein.
© 2017 John Wiley & Sons, Ltd. Published 2017 by John Wiley & Sons, Ltd.

In July of 2013, Alicia Beltran, approximately 12 weeks pregnant, went to the West Bend Clinic at St Joseph's Hospital in West Bend, Wisconsin, for a prenatal checkup (Eckholm 2013). In the course of the examination, Beltran volunteered that she had been dependent on the prescription drug Percocet the previous year. She was well aware of the dangers of opiate drugs for newborns and had worked to reduce her dependency by obtaining a drug, called Suboxone (which blocks other opiates) from a friend, because she was unable to afford a prescription for it (Eckholm 2013). Beltran went about reducing the dose over time and stopped using the medication only days before her checkup at St Joseph's. At the time of her appointment, the physician's assistant suggested that she renew her Suboxone prescription, but she declined (Eckholm 2013). Shortly after leaving the clinic that day, Beltran received a phone call from the physician's assistant asking her to return to the clinic for a urine test. Test results confirmed what Beltran had said: she had used Suboxone within the past few days (Eckholm 2013). About a week later Beltran was visited at her home by a social worker who, again, strongly encouraged her to resume taking Suboxone under the supervision of a physician; again she declined (Eckholm 2013). Only two weeks after her clinic appointment and two days following her visit by the social worker, Beltran was met at her home by five police officials who said they had a warrant for her arrest (Eckholm 2013). She was handcuffed and placed in the back of a police car and driven to the hospital, where she was forced to be examined by a doctor. Despite the doctor's finding that her pregnancy was normal, she was then taken to the county jail and, in shackles at the ankles and handcuffs, before the Family Court (Eckholm 2013). The following day she was again placed in handcuffs and shackles and driven two hours away to Casa Clare, a private women's facility for drug treatment (Eckholm 2013). A urine test taken soon after her arrival indicated that she was clear of all drugs, including Suboxone; nevertheless she was kept in the facility, under the threat of jail, until October 4, 2013, when, as a result of a federal habeus corpus filing, she was released from in-patient treatment detention and all charges were dropped (Advocates for Pregnant Women 2014). Meanwhile, Beltran had been detained against her wishes for 70 days and, as a result, lost her job. In the weeks up to the delivery of her baby she said, "I'm scared they can just come back after my baby's born. This is supposed to be the happiest part of my pregnancy, and I'm just terrified" (Eckholm 2013).

In June of 2003, Shawanna Nelson was admitted to the McPherson Unit of the Arkansas Department of Corrections for identity fraud and writing bad checks, both of them nonviolent crimes (Paillé 2012). She was six months pregnant. On September 20 she went into labor and at about 3:00 p.m. went to the prison infirmary (Paillé 2012). By this time she was in considerable pain; and the nurse timed her contractions at about five or six minutes apart, indicating that her labor was progressing quickly. Concerned about an imminent delivery, the infirmary nurses arranged for immediate transport to the civilian hospital (Paillé 2012). A nurse walked the long hallway with her to the control center where she met Officer Patricia Turensky, assigned to accompany Nelson to the hospital. Nelson was experiencing extreme contractions; she had to stop two or three times to lean against the wall until the pain subsided. The nurse shouted to the officers in the sally port, where the van was stationed, that she "wanted [Nelson] out of there," presumably because she was in such advanced stages of labor (Paillé 2012). Regardless of the fact that Nelson was very close to delivering her baby, Officer Turensky put handcuffs on her before she entered the van. When they arrived at 3:50 p.m., Nelson was shackled to the wheelchair and then to the rails of her hospital bed when she was transferred to the hospital room. By then, Nelson was in her final stages of labor. She was in extreme discomfort and asked for an epidural, an anesthetic to dull the pains; but the nurse said she would have to wait until the obstetrician had given approval (Paillé 2012). It was during this last stage of labor that the shackling of Nelson's ankles became especially problematic and hazardous. Each time the nurses came to examine Nelson's progress, Officer Turensky had to unshackle one leg so that her cervical dilation could be measured (Paillé 2012). After each examination, Turensky immediately placed the shackles back on. The doctor arrived at 5:00 p.m. and by 5:13 p.m. Nelson was nine centimeters dilated. The doctor said that it was too late to administer an epidural and gave the patient Tylenol (Paillé 2012). By 6:15 p.m. she was ready to deliver, and the doctor asked that the shackles be removed prior to her being wheeled to the delivery room. Her baby was born at 6:23 p.m. (Paillé 2012). Like many other women who have undergone labor while shackled (Paillé 2012), Nelson was impeded in her efforts to be as comfortable as possible during what is known to be a very uncomfortable time. Moreover, having her legs abnormally constrained may have placed undue stress on her internal organs during the labor process. According to a federal lawsuit that she filed, she claimed, and her doctors corroborated, that in addition to the "extreme mental anguish and pain" she has been left with a permanent hip injury, torn muscles, and damage to her sciatic nerve (Paillé 2012).

In this chapter, we focus on the nexus of women's reproductive lives and legal control by exploring four mechanisms that have been used by the legal, criminal justice, and, in some cases, the social welfare systems to punish, coerce, or restrict the behavior of women during pregnancy and childbirth. Through the process of imposing legal constraints on women simply by virtue of their role as childbearers, certain types of women – minorities, the poor, the incarcerated – have been especially targeted.

The first issue we address in this chapter pertains not to the responsibilities of pregnant women per se, but to the rights of certain women to become pregnant. Early in the twentieth century and continuing to the present time, the US government implemented policies that made it legal for women to be sterilized without their consent or under strong coercion. The groups targeted for this invasive treatment were characteristically powerless, coming from immigrant, Aboriginal, or other stigmatized groups. Thus, race and class, as well as other socially stigmatizing weaknesses such as mental illness, were at play here. The second issue addressed in the chapter is the criminalization of abortion. Increasingly, under certain circumstances women who seek abortions or health care providers who administer abortion procedures and drugs may be criminally charged for their actions. Next, we address a woman's responsibility for the physical environment that the fetus is exposed to during the period of gestation. In recent years, a new legal trend has increasingly held pregnant women accountable for the substances they ingest into their systems, in some cases resulting in arrests for such crimes as delivering controlled substances to minors. Finally, the chapter focuses on an issue that does not exactly criminalize pregnant women but legally restricts and constrains pregnant women who are already criminals. The issue pertains to what is called shackling of inmates who are about to give birth.

 CASE STUDY: Aleksa Lundberg

A popular actress named Aleksa Lundberg in Sweden is not only known for her acting abilities but also because she was sterilized – not by choice, though. In 2000, at age 18, Aleksa, then living as a man, underwent a sex change to become female (Tornkvist 2011). While the Swedish government did permit her to undergo a sex change, the only way that the government would allow Aleksa to be certified as a woman was if she had all of her male sex organs surgically removed (Tornkvist 2011). Since she was young and eager to finally live her life legally as a woman, she did not think about the long-term implications of her "choice." Another condition of her surgery was that she was not given the option to freeze any sperm. Thus, as some have noted, she "has been robbed of a fundamental human ability: procreation" (Tornkvist 2011). Now that she is older, she is very upset about what she was forced to give up – especially because she felt that she did not really have a choice. She states, "It is a violation of human rights to force a person to have surgery that they do not need or want in order to have your gender legally recognized." Fortunately, other transgendered persons in Sweden will not have to undergo such sterilization, as the law requiring sterilization in order for a transgendered person to be recognized as the gender he/she identified with was repealed in December of 2013 (Nelson 2013).

Involuntary sterilization and eugenics

One aspect of the human anatomy and physiology that is unique to the female sex is the ability to conceive and bear children. While not every woman may be able, or chooses, to do so, it is estimated that over 80% of women in the United States ultimately bear children (US Census Bureau 2012). We do not generally think of pregnancy as a crime but rather as a personal and possibly a medical condition. But throughout history instances can be found in which women's reproductive capacity has intersected with legal control.

It may be hard to believe that in the United States, known for its support of freedom and self-determination, there have been thousands of cases in which women and men have been forced to undergo procedures without their consent that would make them unable to conceive children. Yet for about 150 years, beginning in the late 1880s and extending to the present time, **involuntary sterilization** has been practiced on women and men who were viewed by authorities as "unfit" to bear children due to their racial or ethnic status, their mental health capacity, or their involvement in crime (Cepko 1993; Reilly 1991). Both women and men have been affected by such practices, but historically they have used more on women than men. Efforts to use science to improve the characteristics of a population – also known as **eugenics** – became popular around the turn of the last century in the United States. The premise used to justify the practice of forced sterilization is that behavior such as criminality and feeblemindedness is inherited. Hence, if society wishes to reduce the incidence of these behaviors, the most direct means to achieve that end is by preventing individuals who possess certain behavioral traits to reproduce. If a society could prevent those who would produce offspring who would become criminals, mentally retarded, or "dull" from conceiving children, the theory went, society would be better off (Reilly 1991).

In the late 1800s, Cesare Lombroso was one of the first theorists to propose the concept of the **"born criminal,"** the idea that criminals are born, not made (Reilly 1991). Continuing on from his work, other criminologists posed similar theories. For example, Henry Boies observed in his 1893 book *Prisoners and Paupers*, "Everyone who has visited prisons and observed large numbers of prisoners together has undoubtedly been impressed from the appearance of prisoners alone, that a large portion of them were born to be criminals ... Certain recognizable features ... differentiate these from the rest of mankind, and set them apart as a criminal class" (Boies 1893, 267–268). These notions were bolstered by sociologist Richard Dugdale's study of multiple generations of a New York family, the Jukes, whose members were inordinately involved in antisocial activities such as thievery, prostitution, poverty, and the production of illegitimate children (Dugdale 1877). The idea of creating a stronger, smarter, and healthier society appealed not only to scientists but to the wealthy as well. Prominent and influential Americans – such as the Harrimans and Rockefellers – contributed funds to support eugenics studies and established a eugenics institute, the Station for Experimental Evolution at Cold Spring Harbor (Reilly 1991).

It was only a minor logical leap from the premise that criminality and mental retardation are inherited to the argument that society would be better off if persons who possessed these traits were not allowed to reproduce. The first set of laws based on eugenics principles attempted to prevent the production of offspring by making it illegal to marry if one or both members of the couple was "defective." The first law was passed in Connecticut in 1895 prohibiting marriage between "defective persons" – that is, men or women who were "epileptic, imbecile or feeble-minded" (Reilly 1991). The law stipulated that, except when the woman was 45 years or older, parties to a marriage or unmarried persons who had "carnal knowledge" and who possessed the abovementioned characteristics were subject to a three-year prison term (Reilly 1991). By 1913, **marriage restriction laws**, restricting two parties from marrying if they were not "healthy" or "intelligent," had been enacted by 24 states and the District of Columbia (Reilly 1991).

On the heels of marriage restriction laws, another legal approach gained popularity (Figure 4.1). Physicians, penologists, and sociologists argued for **compulsory sterilization** of "defective" individuals – the "surgical solution" (Reilly 1991). These individuals viewed themselves as guided by the most modern science. They believed that involuntary sterilization was a socially responsible – even compassionate – solution to many potential serious societal problems (Largent 2008). They argued that sterilization not only prevented "defective" persons from passing their genes to their offspring but also protected the state from the expense of caring for children whose parents could not care for them themselves. In countries outside of the United States, it was not uncommon to find compulsory sterilization laws and policies for transgendered persons. For instance, France, the Netherlands, Sweden, and Australia had sterilization policies that required transgendered persons to undergo sterilization as part of their sex change operation in order to be legally recognized as the gender of their choice (Tornkvist 2011). However, within the past five years, Italy, Denmark, Germany, and Sweden have repealed such laws (Nelson 2013; Tornkvist 2011).

In the first two decades of the twentieth century, 15 states enacted laws allowing compulsory sterilization of **institutionalized persons**, mostly prison and mental hospital inmates. From about 1930 onward the focus on forced sterilization shifted in two ways. First, advocates became less concerned about genetic defects and more concerned with whether the parent was capable of caring for her child. Poverty, lack of education, and unemployment became more significant factors than mental "feebleness" in determining who would be targeted. Also, about that time the focus shifted primarily to young women. In **Buck v. Bell (1927)**, for example, the Supreme Court upheld the use of sterilization in Virginia. Carrie Buck, a 17-year-old girl, was the first person in Virginia to be sterilized due to her alleged mental deficiencies and parental incapability (Reilly 1991). Writing for the court, Justice Oliver Wendell Holmes stated, "It is better for all the world, if instead of waiting to execute degenerate offspring for crime or to let them starve for their imbecility, society can prevent those who are manifestly unfit from continuing their kind" (Reilly 1991, 87). Sometimes these surgeries were performed immediately following the birth of a child, while the woman was still unconscious. Other times, people were coerced into agreeing to such procedures to avoid the suspension of social services or to avoid imprisonment.

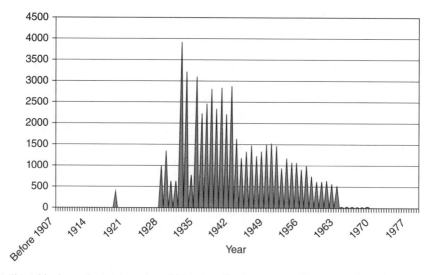

Figure 4.1 This table shows the total number of forced sterilizations per year from 1907 through 1980. The largest number of sterilizations was performed from 1930 through 1944, but a significant number of forced sterilizations continued well into the 1960s (Largent 2008, 77). *Source:* Largent 2008. Reproduced with permission of Rutgers University Press.

An important Supreme Court case challenged a 1935 law in Oklahoma that allowed for the involuntary sterilization of repeat criminals. In *Skinner v. Oklahoma* **(1942)**, the Supreme Court ruled against the compulsory sterilization law (Nourse 2008). The Skinner decision resulted in sterilization laws being repealed in most states (Engs 2003). However, the practice of involuntary sterilization did not end when these laws were deemed unconstitutional.

American society was being destabilized by a number of forces that citizens began to think were out of their control. One was the influx of immigrants and the increased presence of African-Americans and other racial minorities who were needed to support America's increasingly industrialized economy. Another was the adoption of **Jim Crow laws**, which kept African-Americans from social advancement, and the Great Depression's creation of an increasing number of poor and unemployed persons in every racial group. There was a revitalization of interest in eugenics in the 1930s. The American Eugenics Society and the Human Betterment Foundation gained in power and prestige and prompted thinkers to rekindle their interest in eugenics.

Who are the victims of such practices? Involuntary sterilization has historically targeted vulnerable, powerless, and marginalized groups within our society. It has been used on individuals deemed by authorities to possess traits or engage in behaviors associated with criminality, mental defects, or drug use. Race and class played major roles in determining who was likely to be caught in the net. Individuals selected for such treatment have disproportionately come from minority groups and from underprivileged backgrounds characterized by low income, poor education, and underemployment. Native Americans in particular have been targets of this practice, as well as Mexican-Americans and African-Americans.

Public sentiment for coerced sterilization turned negative by the 1960s. By this time, professional groups such as physicians, social scientists, and biologists had developed a more holistic approach to the understanding of the causes of mental illness and criminality. They argued that this practice was too extreme to be used for any physical or social ill. These voices were supported by social activists and feminists who criticized the practice as racist, classist, and sexist. Nevertheless, other forms of coerced sterilization continued well into the last decades of the twentieth century and into the twenty-first.

A particularly painful chapter of US history involves the involuntary sterilization of girls and women of Native American descent who received their health care from the Indian Health Services (IHS) during the 1970s (Carpio 2004). While nationally, involuntary sterilization was winding down, sterilization became increasingly common across Native American reservations. Health care for Native Americans during this period had been notoriously poor, so in 1955 the Department of Health, Education and Welfare (HEW) established the Indian Health Service (IHS), a division of the Public Health Service. The IHS administrators added family planning to its services in 1965, in part to address what were viewed as exceedingly high birth rates among Native Americans. In fact, their birth rate was about 4 children per child-bearing woman compared with a rate of 2.5 for Caucasians (Lawrence 2000). Nevertheless, the IHS ramped up a plan to reduce family sizes of American Indians through sterilization of fertile women. Health care practitioners – doctors, nurses, and medical social workers – began to put pressure on women to consent to sterilization to keep their families small. Most professionals saw this work as socially justifiable. The number of women on welfare, including Native American women, had increased substantially since the mid-1960s. Many White, male doctors viewed sterilization of women from minority groups – African-American and Hispanic as well as Native – as a means to help families to be more financially secure and reduce the welfare rolls. Some paternalistic physicians did not believe that American Indian women had the intelligence to use birth control effectively. Finally, some selfish IHS physicians, working temporarily on Indian reservations to pay off medical school bills, simply viewed sterilization of young women as a means to obtain more surgical practice (Lawrence 2000).

There were no laws authorizing the sterilization of Native American women, as there had been for the "mentally defective" half a century earlier. Indeed, the HEW had passed regulations during this time period emphasizing patients' rights to make informed decisions and mandating that doctors provide full explanations of the purpose of any medical procedure, the risks, and possible alternative treatments. Further, in 1973, a moratorium was instituted on sterilizing women under 21 and women deemed mentally incompetent (Kluchin 2009). Yet, mass sterilizations of Native American women proceeded. In most cases, women did sign consent forms agreeing to sterilization prior to the procedure, although most were not fully informed about the surgeries and many thought the procedure could be reversed. In some cases where women consented, they did so due to coercion or stress. Many women were subject to extreme pressure by health care workers who would visit their homes repeatedly, reassuring them that the surgery was in their and their family's best interests. Others were coerced with threats that they would lose their children or welfare benefits if they did not agree to be sterilized (Lawrence 2000).

Critics have argued that these women were not truly capable of providing informed consent and, in some cases, it is unclear whether the women provided informed consent at all. In one claim, a young woman had gone to an IHS clinic for surgery on an ovarian cyst and left without her uterus, while another who had gone to an IHS hospital for an appendectomy woke up from anesthesia to find that she had been sterilized (Kluchin 2009). Indeed a large number of women woke up from anesthesia associated with childbirth to discover they had been sterilized (Kluchin 2009). A widely known case of forced sterilization among Native American women occurred in 1970 in Western Pennsylvania. A social worker received information that Norma Jean Serena, a Native American, and two of her children were living in "squalid conditions" with a man to whom she was not married. The two children were immediately placed in foster care. At this time, Serena was pregnant. When she went to the hospital to give birth the doctor sterilized her immediately after delivery and without her consent. The doctors were recorded as stating that the patient "was suffering from the following ailment or condition – socioeconomic reasons – and that another pregnancy would, in our opinion, be unadvisable. Therefore, it is medically necessary to perform the sterilization" (Largent 2008, 111). In a subsequent lawsuit, the doctors claimed that they had explained the procedure to the patient and that she had consented – their word against hers. She lost the case.

The numbers of Native American women who were sterilized during this period are staggering (Carpio 2004). One study estimated that between 1970 and 1976, 25–50% of all Native American child-bearing women were sterilized (Lawrence 2000). The victims themselves suffered mightily. Many sterilized Native American women experienced severe depression; marriages were dissolved; and many women resorted to alcoholism and drug dependence (Lawrence 2000). Equally important were the consequences suffered at the collective level. In a population that was already decimated by disease, forced migration, expulsion from their lands, and disruption of their way of life, the communities in which large-scale sterilization occurred experienced a limiting of population size. Tribal governance was based upon a representative model, so a reduction in population would lead to reduced power for affected tribal communities. Native American activists began speaking of the situation as genocide (Carpio 2004; Lawrence 2000).

Coercive sterilization is by no means a problem of the past in the United States nor is it confined to only a few countries. For instance, approximately 150 incarcerated women in the State of California were sterilized for violating prison rules from 2006 to 2010 (Johnson 2013). The practice has been – and continues to be – used in countries around the world. Hundreds of thousands of individuals have been sterilized without their consent in every region of the globe, including Asia, Latin America, Europe, Africa, and North America (World Health Organization 2014). Mirroring US practices, agents of coercive sterilization around the world frequently focus on populations that are vulnerable due to poverty, mental illness, physical illness, or other attributes that are viewed by the society as undesirable. Countries have used numerous methods to coerce women to agree to sterilization, including offers of food, money, land, and housing, as well as threats, fines, and punishments, and governmental programs that provide rewards to health workers who meet sterilization targets. In many nations, sterilization procedures are carried out in unsafe and unhygienic conditions, often without proper follow-up care (World Health Organization 2014).

An example of present-day coercive sterilization can be found among South African, HIV positive women who have undergone sterilization procedures without their knowledge or consent (Strode, Mthembu, and Essack 2012). Strode and colleagues (2012), in a study of 22 HIV positive women in South Africa who underwent sterilizations, reported that many of the women thought the procedure could be reversed or were told it was in their best interests to be sterilized. Subjects stated, "They said they would sterilize me and I would be able to reverse it one day," and "I was told that if I got another child I would die" (Strode et al. 2012, 64). Most recently, allegations have been made by Catholic bishops in Kenya that two United Nations organizations have been sterilizing millions of girls and women, as an anti-tetanus shot administered to them secretly contained an anti-fertility agent (Weatherbe 2014). In India, a doctor has been arrested for the deaths of 13 women that he sterilized (Gowen 2014). The deaths of the women have raised concerns that they may have been coerced into undergoing the sterilization procedure (Gowen 2014). Since most of the victims were poor and received payment for the procedure, concerns have arisen about whether they were able to really consent, or chose freely, to such a procedure, since they were so destitute. An additional concern has arisen about the level of pressure these women may have been put under by the district family planning department, which has annual sterilization goals – despite the national government's claims that no official target number of sterilizations has been set (Gowen 2014).

There is a long history of discrimination that continues to this day associated with many nations' governmental and medical policies regarding intersex and transgender intersex persons. Intersex individuals are born with atypical sex characteristics – frequently with both male and female sex organs. It has been traditional medical practice to use "corrective" cosmetic surgery on infants' or children's reproductive organs so that the children appear as one sex or the other. These medically unnecessary procedures sometimes result in sterility. Transgender persons, such as Aleksa Lundberg, featured at the start of this chapter, have also been targets for compulsory sterilization targeted in many countries. For example, transgender persons wishing to obtain a birth certificate or other legal documents that match their preferred genders must submit to sterilization. In 2014, the State of New York relinquished the requirement that transgendered persons must offer proof of a surgical procedure in order for their birth certificate to be changed (Klepper 2014).

Further examples of sterilization for convicted offenders have emerged – generally male sex offenders or females who have killed their children. They have occasionally been offered the opportunity to "agree" to sterilization to obtain reduced sentences or to be considered for parole (Scott and Holmberg 2003). While some may contend that the offenders had the choice of declining, it is difficult to argue that this bargain does not involve coercion (Largent 2008).

In recent years, organizations around the world have begun to collaborate to stamp out the practice of coercive sterilization wherever it appears. As recently as 2014, the World Health Organization, in conjunction with seven other international human rights organizations, published a report entitled *Eliminating Forced, Coerced and Otherwise Involuntary Sterilization: An Interagency Statement*, emphasizing the continuing reality of coercive sterilization as a human rights issue that must be addressed by nations across the globe. The report offers specific and practical avenues for addressing this problem through legal, policy, and regulatory actions, improved training and education for health care providers, and supportive measures for individuals who might be targeted for such treatment (World Health Organization 2014).

GLOBAL PERSPECTIVES: The sterilization of women across the globe

According to the Open Society Foundation (2011), both forced and coerced sterilizations have been reported in South America, Africa, Asia, and Europe. Additionally, such sterilizations have also been reported to have taken place in countries such as the United Kingdom and Sweden (Zampas and Lamacková 2011). In Europe, mass sterilizations of women occurred with the Nazi eugenics movement beginning in the 1930s. Besides the atrocities inflicted on women by the Nazis, other women in Europe have also endured mass sterilizations. For instance, in Europe, the Romani are the largest ethnic minority, and Romani women have experienced forced and coerced sterilizations in the Czech Republic, Slovakia, and Hungary (Albert 2011; Zampas and Lamacková 2011). Women with mental disabilities may find themselves sterilized in countries such as Spain and Egypt (Open Society Foundation 2011). The Open Society Foundation (2011, 6) reports that "national law in Spain and other countries allows for the sterilization of minors who are found to have severe intellectual disabilities." If a woman, pregnant or not, is HIV positive, she may be coerced or forced into becoming sterilized, and such practices have been reported by women in Chile, the Dominican Republic, Mexico, Namibia, South Africa, and Venezuela (Open Society Foundation 2011).

Forced and coerced sterilizations of women have been and continue to be a problem for women across the globe. To help combat this problem worldwide, the International Federation of Gynecology and Obstetrics has recently adopted ethical guidelines on female sterilization. The guidelines state:

> 1) Sterilization should be considered irreversible and patients must be informed; 2) Consent to sterilization should never be a condition for access to medical care, HIV/AIDS treatment, natural or cesarean delivery, abortion, or to benefits such as medical insurance, social assistance, employment or release from an institution; 3) Sterilization for prevention of future pregnancy cannot be ethically justified on grounds of medical emergency and is not an emergency procedure; and 4) Article 23(1) UN Convention on the Rights of Persons With Disabilities imposes the duty upon states to ensure that persons with disabilities, including children, retain their fertility on an equal basis with others. (Albert 2011, 3)

The criminalization of abortion

Abortion is the intentional termination of a pregnancy through medical or surgical means resulting in the death of the fetus. Almost 90% of abortions are performed within the first trimester of pregnancy, the first 12 weeks. Only about 1.5% of abortions are performed at 21 weeks of pregnancy – about 5 months – or beyond (Solinger 2013). For much of Western history, the legal standing of abortion depended on theories of fetal development. Classical thought, reflected in the writings of Aristotle in the fourth century BC, stipulated that an embryo went through three stages of development – vegetable, animal, and then finally human – and that the acceptability of terminating a pregnancy depended upon the stage of fetal development (Graham 2014). Judeo-Christian doctrine stated that terminating a pregnancy was murder when the "unformed" fetus became "formed," although how that determination was made was not clear (Sachdev 1985). English common law drew the line for when abortion was acceptable at "animation," or entry of the soul (Sachdev 1985).

These were all gradualist approaches – in contrast to a more absolutist approach advocated by the Catholic Church. Catholic Church doctrine stipulates that life begins at conception, so any form of birth control that prevents an embryo from implanting in the uterine wall would be against its teachings. Given this perspective, the Catholic Church has outlawed abortions under all circumstances, the only exception being if the mother's life is in danger if the pregnancy continues (United States Conference of Catholic Bishops 2009). Other denominations take different positions with regard to the delicate balance between the rights of the developing fetus and the woman who is carrying it.

The nineteenth and twentieth centuries brought a spate of laws that criminalized abortion and restricted its use. Britain passed a restrictive abortion law in 1861, and about this period a more restrictive approach to abortion spread throughout many Western and emerging nations. By the end of World War II, most European countries had laws making abortion illegal, often with severe penalties associated with the crime (Reagan 1997). For instance, a Madame Giraud, a laundress who had performed 26 abortions in France, was executed for her crimes in February of 1942 (Sachdev 1985).

The United States reflected European trends until the mid-twentieth century when the women's liberation movement and the advent of effective birth control prompted rethinking of traditional women's roles. The 1973 *Roe v. Wade* **decision** was a landmark that underscored women's rights regarding matters of their reproduction while continuing to consider the issue of the fetus's potential for human life (Reagan 1997). Invoking the **Fourteenth Amendment**, the right to privacy, the Court ruled that women had total autonomy during the first trimester to terminate a pregnancy and then it defined different levels of "state interest" for the second and third trimesters. The Court determined that after the first trimester states had the right to regulate abortion in the interests of the viability of the fetus, so long as the health and life of the mother were protected (Linton 2012).

Roe v. Wade was a watershed for reproductive rights. Prior to this ruling, women in need of abortions had to undergo risky illegal procedures practiced by shady practitioners that sometimes led to permanent injury or even death (Johns 2013). Post-*Roe*, women seeking the termination of their pregnancies were able to obtain safe and legal abortions, a procedure that statistically is extremely low risk, from licensed practitioners in medically appropriate facilities. Women's health was immediately enhanced (Solinger 2013).

At the same time, many scholars view the *Roe v. Wade* decision as a turning point that sparked a tsunami of anti-abortion activism (Sachdev 1985). Ever since the decision, **anti-abortion activists** across the country have challenged and attempted to chip away at the ruling. Advances in medicine – such as imaging technology that enables parents to "view" their developing fetuses in utero and improved technologies for dealing with premature babies – have also prompted people to reconsider their views on abortion. For example, the courts had to rethink the notion of "viability," since premature newborns that would most certainly have perished had they been born at the time of the ruling are now being kept alive (Graham 2014).

The past 40 years have witnessed an enormous retrenchment in women's access to safe and legal abortions as state legislatures have engaged in efforts to regulate and restrict abortion. In many cases, these laws have been upheld upon challenge by higher courts, including the Supreme Court. Anti-abortion activists have lobbied for laws restricting virtually all aspects of the process of obtaining and funding abortions. These efforts have increased in severity and frequency over the decades, with the pace of legislation restricting abortion increasing exponentially within the second decade of the 2000s (Figure 4.2).

Anti-abortion activists and lawmakers have increasingly used the concept of fetal rights to criminalize behavior that injures or has the potential to injure a developing fetus, no matter how immature. Advocates for fetal rights argue that unborn fetuses are human life and are entitled to the same rights as any other human being. An example of one of these laws is the **Unborn Victims of Violence Act**, in which fetuses at any state of development may be treated as legal victims if they

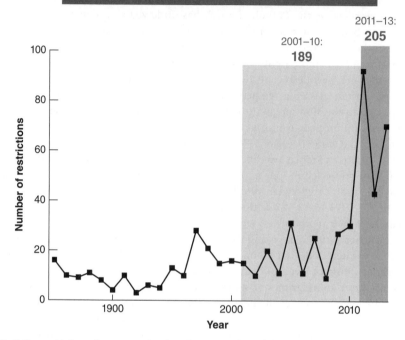

Figure 4.2 Statistics: restriction of access to abortion. *Source:* Nash et al. (2014).

are harmed or killed during the commission of certain state or federal crimes (Graham 2014). In 2004, Scott Peterson was convicted in California of first degree murder of his wife, Laci, and second degree murder for the death of their unborn child (Sahagun and Arax 2004). Laci was eight months pregnant at the time of her death. While laws such as these are intended to protect pregnant women from victimization, they also indirectly convey the implication that fetuses are lives with rights, thus calling into question the hard-won rights of women to choose to terminate pregnancies.

Laws limiting access to abortions have taken many forms. Some of the most widespread include laws that regulate the maximum number of weeks of pregnancy when women may obtain legal abortions. The most extreme is North Dakota's, which restricts legal abortions to women no more than six weeks pregnant, when a fetal heartbeat can first be detected (*New York Times* 2013). Other states, such as Florida, New York, California, and Michigan, have limited abortions to the first 22 weeks of pregnancy on the medically unproven assumption that the fetus starts to feel pain at this point (*New York Times* 2013).

In addition to restricting the length of time a pregnant woman can seek an abortion, other and perhaps more critical elements of the abortion process have been legislated. Various methods have been implemented that affect women seeking abortion, including restricting funds to pay for abortions, mandatory "counseling," waiting periods, and more.

The Guttmacher Institute (2014a) maintains detailed records of changes to laws governing abortion (Table 4.1). Its most recent 2014 report stipulates a range of tactics that have been used to restrict access to abortion. For example, funding for abortions has been heavily regulated. Nine states prohibit private insurance plans from covering abortion unless the woman's life is endangered, and almost all states allow individual health care providers to refuse to participate in funding abortions

Table 4.1 An overview of abortion laws, state policies in brief (as of November 2015).

State	Must be performed by a licensed physician	Must be performed in a hospital if at:	Second physician must participate if at:	Prohibited except in cases of life or health endangerment if at:	"Partial-birth" abortion banned	Public funding of abortion		Private insurance coverage limited
						Funds all or most medically necessary abortions	Funds limited to life endangerment, rape and incest	
AL	X	Viability	Viability	20 weeks*	▶		X	
AK	X	Viability	Viability		▶	X		
AZ	X	Viability	Viability	Viability	X	X		X
AR	X		Viability	20 weeks†	X		X	
CA				Viability		X		
CO		Viability		Viability			X	
CT				Viability		X		
DE	X	Viability		Viability			X	
DC							X	
FL	X	Viability	24 weeks	24 weeks	▶	X		
GA	X			Viability	Postviability		X	
HI	X			Viability				
ID	X	Viability	3rd trimester	Viability	▶		X	X
IL	X		Viability	Viability	▶	X		
IN	X	20 weeks	20 weeks	20 weeks*	X		X*	X
IA	X			3rd trimester	▶		X	X
KS	X		Viability	20 weeks*	X		X	X

(continued)

Table 4.1 (Continued)

State	Must be performed by a licensed physician	Must be performed in a hospital if at:	Second physician must participate if at:	Prohibited except in cases of life or health endangerment if at:	"Partial-birth" abortion banned	Public funding of abortion — Funds all or most medically necessary abortions	Funds limited to life endangerment, rape and incest	Private insurance coverage limited
KY	X	2nd trimester		Viability	▶		X	X
LA	X		Viability	20 weeks*	X		X	
ME	X			Viability			X	
MD	X			Viability$^\Omega$		X		
MA	X			24 weeks		X		
MI	X			Viability‡	X		X	X
MN	X		20 weeks	24 weeks		X		
MS	X$^\Phi$			20 weeks*	X		X$^\Omega$	
MO	X	Viability	Viability	Viability	▶		X	X
MT			Viability	Viability*	Postviability	X		
NE	X			20 weeks*	▶		X	X
NV	X	24 weeks		24 weeks			X	
NH	X				X		X	
NJ	X$^\xi$	14 weeks			▶	X		
NM	X				Postviability	X		
NY		20 weeks	24 weeks	24 weeks‡		X		
NC	X	20 weeks		20 weeks	X		X	
ND	X			20 weeks*	X		X	X
OH	X	Viability	Viability	Viability*	X		X	
OK	X	2nd trimester	Viability	20 weeks*	X		X	X

OR						X		
PA	X	Viability	Viability	24 weeks*			X	▶
RI	X			24 weeks‡	▶		X	▶
SC	X	3rd trimester	3rd trimester	3rd trimester	X		X	
SD	X	24 weeks		24 weeks	X		Life Only	
TN	X		Viability	Viability	X		X	
TX	X			20 weeks*			X	
UT	X	90 days		Viability†,Ω	X		X*	X
VT						X	X^Ω	
VA	X	2nd trimester	Viability	3rd trimester	X			
WA				Viability		X		
WV				20 weeks*	▶	X		
WI	X	Viability		Viability	▶		X*	
WY	X			Viability			X	X
Total	**38**	**19**	**18**	**43**	**19**	**17**	**32+DC**	**11**

Notes:

▶ Permanently enjoined; law not in effect.

*Exception in case of threat to the woman's physical health.

†Exception in case of rape or incest.

‡Exception in case of life endangerment only.

ΩException in case of fetal abnormality.

§Only applies to surgical abortion.

ΦLaw limits abortion provision to OB/GYNs.

(continued)

Table 4.1 (Continued)

| State | Providers may refuse to participate | | Mandated counseling includes information on: | | | Waiting period (in hours) after counseling | Parental involvement required for minors |
	Individual	Institution	Breast cancer link	Fetal pain	Negative psychological effects		
AL						48	Consent
AK	X	Private	X	X			Notice
AZ	X	X				24	Consent
AR	X	X		X^{Φ}		48	Consent
CA	X	Religious					▶
CO							Notice
CT	X						
DE	X	X				▶	Notice$^{\xi}$
DC							
FL	X	X				24	Notice
GA	X	X		X		24	Notice
HI	X	X					
ID	X	X				24	Consent
IL	X	Private					Notice
IN	X	Private		X		18	Consent
IA	X	Private					Notice
KS	X	X	X	X	X	24	Consent
KY	X	X				24	Consent

LA	X	X		X	X	24	Consent
ME	X	X					Notice
MD	X	X					
MA	X	X				►	Consent
MI	X	X			X	24	►
MN	X	Private		X^Φ		24	Notice[b]
MS	X	X	X			24	Consent[b]
MO	X	X		X^Φ		72	Consent
MT	X	Private				►	Notice
NE	X	X			X	24	Consent
NV	X	Private					►
NH	X	Private					Notice
NJ	X	Private					►
NM	X	X					►
NY	X	X					
NC	X	X			X	72	Consent
ND	X	X				24	Consent[b]
OH	X	X				24	Consent
OK	X	Private	X	X^Φ		24	Consent and Notice
OR	X	Private					
PA	X	Private				24	Consent
RI	X	X					Consent
SC	X	Private				24	Consent

(*continued*)

Table 4.1 (Continued)

State	Providers may refuse to participate		Mandated counseling includes information on:			Waiting period (in hours) after counseling	Parental involvement required for minors
	Individual	Institution	Breast cancer link	Fetal pain	Negative psychological effects		
SD	X	X		X	X	72◊	Notice
TN	X	X				48	Consent
TX	X	Private	X	X	X	24	Consent and Notice
UT	X	Private		XΦ	X	72◊	Consent and Notice
VT							
VA	X	X				24	Consent and Notice
WA	X	X					
WV					X	24	Notice[ξ]
WI	X	X				24	consent[ξ]
WY	X	Private					consent and Notice
Total	**45**	**42**	**5**	**12**	**9**	**28**	**38**

Notes:

▼Permanently enjoined; law not in effect.

ᵗEnforcement temporarily enjoined by court order; policy not in effect.

ΦFetal pain information is given only to women who are at least 20 weeks gestation; in Missouri at 22 weeks gestation.

ᵇBoth parents must consent to the abortion.

ξSpecified health professionals may waive parental involvement in certain circumstances.

◊In South Dakota, the waiting period excludes weekends or annual holidays and in Utah the waiting period is waived in cases of rape, incest, fetal defect or if the patient is younger than 15.

Source: Guttmacher Institute (2015).

if they so choose. Thirty-two states and the District of Columbia prohibit any public funds to be used for abortions unless the woman's life is in danger or she is the victim of rape or incest. Such restrictions weigh especially heavily on low-income women who may not have the means to pay for abortions or to select insurance plans that would cover this procedure (Guttmacher Institute 2014a).

Even if a woman is able to obtain funding for an abortion, before she can receive the procedure many states place multiple roadblocks in her path. For instance, 23 states require that women receive "counseling" on the risks and potential drawbacks of abortion prior to receiving the procedure. While it is not a bad idea for a woman contemplating a medical procedure to receive counseling, the information that some states require the counselor to review is not only intimidating but also downright fallacious. Doctors and counselors are required to cover "facts" that have no basis in science and are "blatantly untrue" such as purported links between receiving an abortion and later incidence of cancer, infertility, and suicide (Joffe 2013). Also, in 12 states, counselors are required to talk about when in the gestational period fetuses begin feeling pain, despite the fact that there is no medical documentation that this information is accurate (Guttmacher Institute 2014a). In other cases, states have mandated that women must be shown photographs or forced to watch videos of fetuses at the same gestational stage as her pregnancy. The reasoning behind such laws seems obvious – women who are led to believe that the abortion will have adverse effects on their future health or mental health or who are led to have more empathy for the developing fetus will do what lawmakers intend – they will choose not to have their abortions (Guttmacher Institute 2014a). A 2011 North Carolina law, which required abortion providers to supply ultrasound images of the fetus to the woman, was struck down in 2014 (Blythe and Jarvis 2014).

Additionally, 26 states have legislated **waiting periods** – generally 24 hours – between the time women receive pre-abortion counseling and when they may receive the procedure. In 10 of these states, women must make two separate trips to the abortion clinic. The outcome of these waiting period laws is to make the process of obtaining an abortion more cumbersome and complicated for women who are already stressed. Further, 39 states also have laws preventing minors from obtaining abortions without some level of involvement – either notification or consent – of the parents or legal guardians (Guttmacher Institute 2014a).

Other laws have placed restrictions on abortion providers. The state of Texas, for example, passed a 2013 law requiring doctors performing abortions in clinics to have admitting privileges to hospitals within 30 miles of the clinic. Many doctors were not able to obtain such privileges, so between 2011 and 2014 the number of clinics offering abortions in the state of Texas fell from 44 to 24 (Fernandez 2014). In September 2014, another part of the law reduced the availability of clinics even more. Beginning in September 2014, all abortion clinics were required to meet **surgical-center standards,** meaning that all abortions, including nonsurgical procedures, were required to be performed in hospital-style operating rooms. The result of such draconian laws has been that women seeking abortions in Texas have had to travel long distances to find a clinic that is still open. The shuttering of the one abortion clinic in McAllen, Texas, forced women seeking abortions to incur increased travel and hotel costs to obtain abortions 240 miles away in San Antonio or 310 miles away in Austin. The governor at the time, Rick Perry, stated that one of his goals was to "make abortion, at any stage, a thing of the past" (Fernandez 2014). "Increasingly, access to abortion depends on where you live," said Jennifer Dalven, director of the reproductive freedom project at the American Civil Liberties Union (Alford and Eckholm 2014). Most recently, in August of 2014, however, a federal judge struck down the requirement that abortion facilities must meet hospital-level building standards in Texas (Winter 2014). The US Supreme Court heard oral arguments on the constitutionality of the Texas law and will issue a ruling in 2016.

Non-physicians who attempt to assist women in obtaining abortions have also been prosecuted. Most recently, in 2014, a Pennsylvania mother was sentenced to a 12–18-month prison term for obtaining drugs that induced a miscarriage for her 16–year-old daughter who was pregnant (Dekok 2014). It seems that the mother violated the Pennsylvania law requiring all abortions to be performed by physicians.

It is instructive to compare the past four decades of abortion law and policy in the United States with the trends throughout the rest of the world. In the United States the *Roe v. Wade* decision brought abortion out of back alleys and enabled American women to obtain safe and legal abortions. In subsequent years women have retained access to safe and legal abortions; but the groundswell of anti-abortion activism has made getting abortions more difficult, costly, and complicated, especially for low-income women, in many states. The trend throughout much of the world has been toward more liberalized abortion law and policy. France, for example, passed legislation permitting women to obtain abortions during the first 12 weeks of pregnancy with no qualifying exceptions (Sifferlin 2014). Currently 74 countries, representing more than 60% of the world's population, permit abortion without restriction as to reason or on broad grounds. Over the past 20 years, more than 30 countries have liberalized abortion laws while only a handful have taken steps to restrict or make abortion more difficult (Center for Reproductive Rights 2014). Granted, abortion law in some countries is still more restrictive than that in the United States but, compared to the past, progress is being made.

To illustrate the types of changes that have occurred in nations across the globe, we will focus on abortion law in two countries on the continent of Africa. In 1996, South Africa adopted an abortion law that is similar to that in the United States – abortion is allowed without restriction during the first 12 weeks of pregnancy and on numerous grounds thereafter. Prior to that date, women in South Africa could only obtain legal abortions if their lives were in danger, to preserve mental health, or in cases of rape, incest, or fetal impairment. Another African country, Niger, adopted a far more limited law in 2006 – allowing abortion to save the life of the woman and in cases of fetal impairment. However, in Niger previous to 2006, abortion was completely prohibited under all circumstances. Since 1994 more than a dozen countries in Africa have liberalized their abortion laws by specifying additional grounds on which abortions are legal. In the same time period, no African country has added restrictions to women's access to abortion (Center for Reproductive Rights 2014).

There are countries that continue to severely restrict women's access to abortion. In 18 out of 47 Muslim countries (e.g., Afghanistan and Bangladesh), abortions are not permitted unless it is to save the life of the woman (Shapiro 2013). Even laws that have liberalized abortion in some countries have an extremely narrow range. Kuwait, for example, adopted a law in 1982 that permits women to have an abortion if they have been raped, but only if the abortion occurs within 120 days of the rape (Shapiro 2013).

⚖️ SPECIAL LEGAL ISSUES: One-child family policy in China and abortions

In 1979, China implemented its one-child family policy, which stipulated that each family in China was only permitted to have one child (Hesketh, Lu, and Xing 2005). Initially, the policy was intended to be a short-term measure to control population growth in the country and, despite the policy's name, there were exceptions to the rule. Primarily, the policy applied to families residing in urban areas and to all government employees (Hesketh et al. 2005). Women residing in rural areas might be permitted to have a second child after five years had passed since the birth of their first child and, in most cases, only if the first child was a girl (Hesketh et al. 2005). However, the policy permitted women from affluent families to bypass the policy by either paying a "social compensation fee" or by having their second child in another country such as in the United States (Sieczkowski

(continued)

2013). Those women that were not fortunate to bypass the policy often opted for sex-selective abortions if the fetus was a girl, since boys were "valued" more, or they endured forced abortions. The result of sex-selective abortions has resulted in a sex-ratio imbalance in China where men outnumber women. Hesketh and colleagues (2005) explain that the actual number of sex-selective abortions is impossible to obtain with any accuracy, but add that the sex-ratio imbalance has resulted in women being kidnapped and trafficked for marriage. Similarly, it is difficult to ascertain the exact number of forced abortions that pregnant Chinese women have experienced, as records, if they are kept, are not published – although plenty of examples of forced abortions have surfaced in the news. In September of 2013, officials from the Shandong Province Family Planning Commission forced their way into the home of Liu Xinwen (Sieczkowski 2013). Since Xinwen was already the mother of a 10-year-old son, her current pregnancy was not permitted. Xinwen was brought to the hospital and was administered a drug that caused her to abort her fetus (Sieczkowski 2013). She called the procedure "forced sterilization" and stated, "They don't have any humanity. They are not humans" (Sieczkowski 2013). In November of 2013, China declared it would ease the one-child policy; however, it would not be technically eliminated (Buckley 2013). The revised policy now allows families to have two children if the husband or wife is an only child. While this helps some women, it will likely not help all pregnant women who may be forced into obtaining abortions.

Criminalization of pregnant women

The barrier between the pregnant woman and developing fetus is **permeable** – developing fetuses are exposed to many of the substances that pregnant women consume, inhale, or inject. It has been known for many years that behaviors such as cigarette smoking and alcohol use during pregnancy can result in the exposed fetuses having health problems at birth and beyond. Historically, the decision as to whether to refrain from activities that may affect the environment of the developing fetus has been left with the pregnant woman. While there are warnings on packaging of many products against use by women who are or think they may be pregnant, historically it has been up to the woman to decide whether to smoke or drink during her pregnancy. Other women who may suffer from anxiety or depression and wish to continue to take their prescribed medications while pregnant may not have a choice, as they are either discouraged or prohibited from doing so by their physicians (Einarson and Koren 2007; Yonkers 2014).

This situation becomes a bit murkier when illegal drugs are involved. It is estimated that between 15% of babies born to women ages 15–17 and 7% of babies born to women ages 18–25 in the United States have been exposed to illicit, or illegal, drugs in utero (National Institute on Drug Abuse 2011). If a woman uses an illegal drug, she may be subject to arrest and conviction for this act. If that woman is carrying a fetus, her act of taking an illegal substance into her body means that her fetus has been exposed to the same illegal drug. Should the woman be held accountable for any harm her illegal actions may cause the developing fetus? In the past several decades, social policy, laws, and criminal justice enforcement practices to control the activities or punish women engaged in illegal drug use have proliferated. Pregnant women have been arrested, forced into drug treatment programs, confined to mental hospitals, and, in some cases, convicted for crimes as serious as murder for their use of illegal drugs during their pregnancies.

Legal attacks on pregnant women using illicit substances

For most of our nation's history, the criminal justice system in the United States paid little attention to women who abused drugs; but this situation changed as the popularity of crack cocaine increased in the mid-1980s (Campbell 2000). Crack, a form of cocaine, is an addictive stimulant that produces a "rush" and a short-term high followed by a "crash" and craving for more. Cocaine, which comes in powder form and is generally inhaled, was a drug of choice among the wealthy and powerful. Crack cocaine comes in the form of a "rock" that can be sold in small quantities for a low price and is delivered through smoking it in a pipe. Highly addictive, crack spread rapidly across the country and "hit women especially hard" (Inciardi, Lockwood, and Pottieger 1993, 12).

During the first few years of distribution, crack cocaine became characterized by the media as a serious menace to society and safety (Humphries 1999). Literally thousands of newspaper and magazine articles and television stories spread the word about the hazards of this drug. Crack was described as so powerful that users became immediately addicted, losing interest in anything but getting high and motivated to commit crime to support their habits (Inciardi et al. 1993). Women were as likely as men to use crack, a fact that particularly attracted media attention. Soon after the "epidemic" began, the media began running stories of **"crack mothers"** as being unfit mothers who had lost their maternal instincts (Gómez 1997). These stories resonated with the public who were horrified that vulnerable newborns were victims of their mothers' substance use.

Though there was relatively little medical evidence of the long-term impacts of crack cocaine on fetal development, the media played up the potential hazards to newborns affected by crack. Claims were made that "crack babies" were born prematurely or at low birth weights and had to endure the pains of withdrawal from the substance during their first days of life. Other adverse health effects, including miscarriage, birth defects and even infant mortality, were featured in these stories, despite scant medical evidence to substantiate many of these claims (Humphries 1999). Low income, minority, and inner-city women were especially targeted by media reports, further creating a "moral panic" and portraying women who used crack as not only irresponsible mothers but as a threat to the social order (Flavin 2009).

Race and class also played a role in how the media fomented social hysteria about crack cocaine. It is worth noting that chemically, crack cocaine and powder cocaine contain the same active ingredients and operate on the body in the same ways. Yet, the populations who used the different forms of this substance were quite different. Crack cocaine was more likely to be used by low-income minorities who lived in inner cities, while the media presented powder cocaine users as stressed-out professionals or wealthy college students who simply wanted to blow off steam and have a good time (Gómez 1997). Users of crack cocaine were portrayed in the media as dangerous, criminal, and irresponsible, and this portrayal reinforced attitudes that were dismissive and prejudicial toward the poor and racial minorities.

Drug researchers note that drug "epidemics" rise and fall in waves (Inciardi et al. 1993). Since the 1990s the popularity of crack cocaine has waned, to be replaced by another stimulant, methamphetamine, in the early 2000s and, more recently, with opioids such as the prescription drug oxycontin and the illegal drug heroin. The media has followed the trends of these drugs' ascension and has featured cases of women who have been subject to criminal justice sanctions for using these controlled substances during their pregnancies. Alicia Beltran, featured at the start of this chapter, is one of those women. Despite the fact that the criminal justice system continues to target substance-using pregnant women for punitive sanctions, the level of media attention since the early 2000s has never reached the fever pitch of the "crack mom" years (Flavin 2009).

Legal and criminal justice responses to pregnant women using drugs

In countries such as Canada and France, there have been no efforts to criminalize drug use during pregnancy (Fentiman 2009). However, in the United States, state legislatures and the criminal justice system began to respond to media accounts of the harms caused by using drugs during pregnancy as the media increased its coverage of "crack moms," stoking a moral panic among the general population. By the late 1980s, lawmakers and prosecutors realized that this issue was one that would garner support from their constituencies, so they began speaking out about the problem. Three approaches were taken. First, district attorneys prosecuted women by applying existing criminal laws, such as statutes penalizing defendants for delivering controlled substances to minors. A second approach was to create administrative policies within the social welfare system to force women into drug-free compliance during pregnancy or face adverse consequences. Finally, in some jurisdictions, legislators created new laws specifically targeted at women who passed illegal drugs to their fetuses.

Most states have approached the problem of prenatal substance abuse mostly by relying on criminal laws already on the books. Criminal laws that cover felony murder, manslaughter, and delivering a controlled substance to a minor have all been applied to pregnant women (Goodwin 2008). In 1977, the first criminal indictment was issued against Margaret Reyes for using the drug heroin while pregnant (Fentiman 2009). Reyes was charged with two counts of felony child endangerment. The first woman to be charged with manslaughter for using crack cocaine during pregnancy, in 1989, was Melanie Green, a 24-year-old poor, single mother from a working-class Black family in Rockford, Illinois, after her second child, Bianca, died. Green had tried to quit her drug use during her pregnancy but had not gained admission to a drug program in time. She ultimately gave birth to a daughter who tested positive for cocaine and was underweight and brain damaged. The infant died days after birth. Ultimately, a grand jury elected not to indict Green because it decided that Green had autonomy over her body as a constitutional right to privacy (Logli 1990). Alabama's and South Carolina's Supreme Courts have upheld convictions that women's substance use during pregnancy may be considered grounds for conviction for criminal child abuse (Dailard and Nash 2000).

An example of using existing laws to prosecute pregnant women is the case of Regina McKnight. In 2003, McKnight, who used cocaine during her pregnancy, gave birth to a stillborn baby. A South Carolina court found her guilty of homicide by child abuse and sentenced her to a 20-year incarceration term (Flavin 2009). The court's reasoning was that McKnight's addiction was the the cause of her baby's death. Even if infants are born healthy, pregnant women have been arrested for using drugs. Between 1990 and 2006 there were several hundred known cases where women who used substances during pregnancy were arrested even when their newborns showed no adverse health effects (Flavin 2009).

The second strategy – administrative procedures that restrict women's activity during pregnancy and invoke punitive sanctions for noncompliance – has been adopted by at least 15 states (Dailard and Nash 2000). In some states, women face losing custody of their newborns or existing children if it can be determined that they used substances during pregnancy, on the grounds that they are abusive and neglectful. Other states have adopted policies, allegedly to protect the fetus, authorizing civil commitment to a mental hospital or entrance into a drug treatment program for substance-using pregnant women (Dailard and Nash 2000).

A third approach in many jurisdictions was the creation of new laws that specifically targeted women who passed illegal drugs to their fetuses during pregnancy. Since the late 1980s a number of state legislators have proposed bills to criminalize drug use during pregnancy. In California alone, between 1986 and 1996, 57 bills were introduced concerning prenatal drug exposure (Gómez 1997). South Carolina has been particularly punitive in dealing with pregnant women who use drugs. For example, women at a Charleston hospital were secretly searched for evidence of drug use and, if a woman did test positive, she was reported to the police. In all cases such as these, the hospital and police department coordinated arrests on charges of possession, drug delivery, and child abuse (Flavin 2009). The law used to force Alicia Beltran to submit to an involuntary medical examination and to remain in custody at a drug treatment center against her will is the 1997 Wisconsin Act 292, informally dubbed "the cocaine mom act," which provides child welfare officials with the power to arrest and forcibly confine a pregnant woman who uses illegal drugs or alcohol for the length of her pregnancy, subject the woman to medical exams, and sometimes require her to stand trial for negligence. The Act gives Wisconsin courts jurisdiction over fertilized eggs, embryos, fetuses, and pregnant women at all stages of pregnancy where the woman "habitually lacks self control" in the use of alcohol or controlled substances such that there is "substantial risk" that the health of her subsequent newborn will be "seriously affected" (Eckholm 2013). Advocates for Beltran challenged the law in federal court, but the court dismissed the filing as moot (Advocates for Pregnant Women 2014).

Given the intense media attention and the rhetoric among lawmakers and prosecutors, one would expect that a raft of laws criminalizing drug use during pregnancy would have been passed. On the contrary, since the "crack war" scare of the mid-1980s there have been relatively few laws passed specifically criminalizing drug use during pregnancy. Of the 57 bills pertaining to pregnant drug-using women introduced into the California legislature, only about one third became law, and those laws focused on social services rather than criminal justice agencies to handle cases (Gómez 1997). In 2014, 15 states required that health care professionals report suspected prenatal drug abuse and 19 states support drug treatment programs targeted at pregnant women, in some cases providing priority access to pregnant women who seek treatment (Guttmacher Institute 2014b). The majority of states have opted for intervention by social service and medical agencies rather than the criminal justice system to deal with pregnant substance abusers. However, it should be noted that two states, Alabama and South Carolina, have passed laws allowing for criminal prosecution of pregnant women under child abuse codes (Scheller 2014) and Tennessee, in July of 2014, passed a new law that criminalizes drug use during pregnancy (Bassett 2014). A woman can now be "prosecuted for assault if she takes a narcotic drug while pregnant and the baby is born addicted, is harmed or dies because of the drug. The woman can avoid criminal charges if she completes a state treatment program" (Bassett 2014). Just a few days after the passage of the law, Mallory Loyola became the first woman arrested under the new law when her newborn daughter tested positive for methamphetamine (Kemp 2014).

The number of women who have actually been prosecuted for drug-related crimes committed against their fetuses during pregnancy has been quite low relative to the estimated millions of women who are likely to have ingested illicit substances during their pregnancies over the past decades. Paltrow and Flavin (2013, 299) attempted to identify all legal cases between 1973 and 2005 in which "a woman's pregnancy was a necessary factor leading to attempted and actual deprivations of a woman's physical liberty" and were able to identify only 413 cases in 44 states and the District of Columbia over a 32-year period.

There are three reasons why so few women have actually been prosecuted for using drugs when pregnant. One reason has to do with the women themselves. While they may have been portrayed by the media as "bad mothers," most women who use illegal substances during pregnancy are not hardcore offenders deserving of punishment. Murphy and Rosenbaum (1999) interviewed 120 women pregnant and postpartum women who were using heroin, crack cocaine, or methamphetamine during pregnancy. The women in their study could be characterized more as victims than as offenders. Most were "victimized and brutalized almost from birth," had experienced incest, molestation, rape, and battering (Murphy and Rosenbaum 1999, 130). Some were removed from their homes and others left in adolescence because of the chaotic and unstable environment. These women tried, within the range of options available to them, to be good mothers. For example, crack-using women "tried to separate drug use from parental responsibilities, budgeted money, and tried to get away from the crack scene" (Murphy and Rosenbaum 1999, 9). A second reason has to do with the medical evidence regarding the short- and long-term effects of exposure to drugs during pregnancy.

The dire predictions that drug-exposed babies inevitably experience seriously adverse health effects have been questioned by many medical researchers during the past two decades (Goodwin 2014). Thirdly, most prosecutors viewed many of the cases that came to their attention as weak cases. They would have difficulty proving that the women intended to harm their children or even knew of the connection between their drug use and potential harm (Gómez 1997).

Regardless of whether drug-using pregnant women are prosecuted or not, some have speculated that the fear of arrest or being reported to child protective services compromises the health of the unborn child by deterring pregnant women who use drugs from seeking prenatal health care. It is known that women who use drugs during pregnancy often receive little or no prenatal care (Roberts and Pies 2011). Recent research, however, questions the direct connection between fear of arrest and avoiding health services. Roberts and Pies (2011) found that drug-using women encounter many of the same barriers as non-drug-using women of the same backgrounds – poverty, homelessness, lack of transportation, inadequate knowledge, and difficulties scheduling appointments.

The situation for drug-using women in Norway may be viewed as equally coercive to that of women like Alicia Beltran, but in fact it may be quite different. Norway has enacted a law empowering the state to incarcerate, for the period of her pregnancy, any drug-using woman found to be pregnant (Ladegaard 2012). Advocates of this law claim that the mother and fetus are safer if they are locked up and if the mother is forced to detoxify from her drug use during her pregnancy. The pregnant addicts are not considered criminal per se, but their choices are severely restricted – they may remain confined to the institution or opt for an abortion. While there has been little research on the impact of this law, some women who have been confined as a result of it have been positive. According to one researcher, "What I hear again and again is that women experience life in the locked wards as very tough and hard to bear, and one even said it was worse than prison. But they are thankful in the end" (Ladegaard 2012).

Shackling of pregnant inmates giving birth

In 2013, there were estimated to be over 200,000 women serving time in local jails and state and federal prisons (AWHONN 2011); and of those, a rough estimate is that about 5% are pregnant (Ferszt 2011). Some will be released before their due dates, but many eventually give birth while incarcerated. While there has been no scientific study of the number of births that occur to prison inmates, a rough estimate is that more than 2,000 children are born to prison inmates each year (Doetzer 2008).

Childbirth is often the culmination of a time of great anticipation. Many women report that the experience of childbirth is one of the "peak experiences" of their lives. This scenario is far from the case for women who experience their pregnancies behind bars. These women are separated from family and friends, subject to prison rules and discipline, and are reliant on prison medical services for prenatal care. One element of the experience of pregnant women in prison is that when they are transported outside of prison walls to receive medical services or to give birth at a hospital, many are shackled. Also known as physical restraint, **shackling** is the use of devices to restrict an inmate's ability to move freely. Generally metal (or sometimes plastic) cuffs, similar to handcuffs, are affixed to inmates' ankles, leaving about 18 inches between them. These cuffs are generally connected by heavy chains to a waist belt, also metal, which is also attached to cuffs at the wrists. They not only restrict movement but are also uncomfortable and frequently painful. The use of restraints to manage inmates is common – inmates are shackled when they appear in court, are interviewed by attorneys, are transferred to a different facility, and so on. In many states, they are used on pregnant women not only during prenatal visits to hospitals but also immediately before, and sometimes even while, they are giving birth.

As early as 1955, the unregulated use of physical restraints on prison inmates – male and female – was determined to be an international human rights violation (Doetzer 2008). The United Nations Congress on Prevention of Crime and Treatment of Offenders set standards for the use of physical restraints, including: as a precaution against escape during a transfer; on medical grounds by direction of the medical officer; and in order to prevent a prison inmate from injuring himself/herself or others or from damaging property (Doetzer 2008). Nevertheless, shackling inmates during pregnancy – and for many up to and following the time they give birth – is still the norm in most states in the nation. As of June 2010, there were only 11 states that had passed legislation limiting or prohibiting the use of restraints for pregnant women (Ferszt 2011). The legislation varies considerably across states. Texas, for example, allows restraints during most of pregnancy, banning them only during labor and delivery. In contrast, Rhode Island prohibits use of restraints during the transport of pregnant women in their second and third trimester as well as during labor, delivery, and postpartum (Ferszt 2011). The shackling of pregnant incarcerated women is not a problem systemic to the United States. Most recently, an incarcerated pregnant woman on death row in Sudan was forced to give birth in chains in 2014 (Elbagir and Smith-Spark 2014).

As we saw from our case study at the start of the chapter, enduring the imposition of shackles during pregnancy can be both physically and emotionally damaging. Being placed in chains or other restraints is demeaning and an affront to human dignity, harking back to images of slavery. Equally significant, being shackled during labor certainly has short-term adverse effects and may have long-term or even permanent adverse health effects as well (Griggs 2011). In the short term, birthing a child is called "labor" for a reason – it is an uncomfortable process at best and frequently can be extremely painful. Having one's legs shackled together or to the hospital bed restricts the laboring woman from moving around. With chains holding her, she is unlikely to be able to find comfortable positions, and her restricted movement may delay the normal course of labor (Nelson 2006). Research has shown that walking and changing positions can result in "shorter labor, less severe pain, and less need for pain medications" (AWHONN 2011, 817). There can be more serious effects that compromise the health and life of the mother and fetus. For example, "In emergency situations such as maternal hemorrhage or abnormal fetal heart rate patterns, shackles may cause unnecessary delays in administration of potentially life saving measures" (AWHONN 2011, 817).

The ostensible reason for using shackles on prisoners is to maintain order and reduce the risk of escape. Shackling has been used for centuries on male inmates to control violence and flight potential of male inmates. Yet, there are a number of reasons why the arguments made for justifying restraints for male inmates do not hold in general for women prisoners, most especially when they are in the active stages of giving birth. Researchers have argued that females are less of a security risk than male prisoners because, compared to male inmates, women are serving shorter sentences, are more likely to be serving sentences for nonviolent crimes, have less history of violence, and, if they did commit a violent crime, it was frequently the result of their involvement in an abusive relationship with a violent man (Doetzer 2008). More pertinently, it is obvious that a person who is undergoing active labor and about to deliver a baby is in no physical position to launch an escape attempt. That being said, some corrections officials argue that shackling women during labor is necessary.

Shackling can lead to permanent injury, as we have seen with Shawanna Nelson. Nelson's shackling during most of her labor was not required by state or prison policy. According to the Arkansas Department of Corrections' regulations, shackles must be used "only when circumstances require the protection of inmates, staff or other individuals from potential harm or to deter the possibility of escape" (Liptak 2006b). Because Nelson was in such advanced stages of labor, the possibility that she would be an escape risk was virtually nil. It appears that Officer Turensky could – and should – have handled the situation quite differently. The regulations of her state required that the "officer responsible for transporting the inmate to a hospital 'use good judgment in balancing security concerns with the wishes of treatment staff and the medical needs of the inmate' before shackling an inmate (Liptak 2006b). Nevertheless, a statement from a spokesperson for the Arkansas Department of Corrections supported the officer's decisions: "Though these are pregnant women, they are still convicted felons, and sometimes violent in nature. There have been instances when we've had a female inmate try to hurt hospital staff during delivery" (Liptak 2006a).

In recent years, women's and human rights activists have attempted to end the shackling of women prisoners in the United States. Medical, nursing, and human rights organizations have all published policy position papers against shackling women (Sichel 2007). Arguments have been made that shackling violates the **Eighth Amendment** of the US Constitution barring cruel and unusual punishment and is a basic violation of human rights (Amnesty International 2000; Griggs 2011). A number of lawsuits by shackled women have sought redress through the courts. For example, Nelson filed a federal lawsuit claiming that her civil rights had been violated by the ADC as a result of her shackling. According to the *New York Times*, "partly as a consequence of Ms. Nelson's suit, Arkansas has started using softer, more flexible nylon restraints for prisoners deemed to be security risks. They are removed during the actual delivery" (Liptak 2006a).

Experts argue that changing legislation is ultimately more effective in eliminating this practice. The federal government, California, Illinois, and New York took the lead in passing laws banning the use of restraints on women prisoners during labor and delivery (Leveille 2008). The Illinois law, passed in 2000, is quoted in Sichel (2007, 228):

> no handcuffs, shackles or restraints of any kind may be used during her transport to a medical facility for the purpose of delivering her baby. Under no circumstance may leg irons or shackles or waist shackles be used on any pregnant female prisoner who is in labor. Upon the pregnant female prisoner's entry to the hospital delivery room, a county correctional officer must be posted immediately outside the delivery room.

Nevertheless, as of 2014, the University of Chicago issued a report that in many states shackling is still allowed and used widely. According to this report, "only 18 states have legislation in place that restricts the use of restraints on pregnant inmates, 24 states limit the use of restraints on pregnant inmates only through institutional policies, and 8 states do not have any form of regulation at all" (International Human Rights Clinic 2014). It also should be noted that other countries such as the United Kingdom rarely shackle pregnant women in labor and China does not shackle or chain pregnant women whatsoever (Ginn 2013; Tatlow 2012).

We must conclude, therefore, that at the present time there are hundreds of incarcerated women each year who have the experience of being shackled during childbirth. To a greater or lesser degree, they share the experience of one woman who said this about her childbirth experience while imprisoned:

> giving birth while incarcerated was one of the most horrifying experiences of my life. At the hospital I was shackled to a metal bed post by my right ankle throughout seven hours of labor, although a correctional officer was in the room with me at all times … Imagine being shackled to a metal bedpost, excruciating pains going through my body, and not being able to adjust myself to even try to feel any type of comfort, trying to move and with each turn having hard, cold metal restraining my movements. (Sichel 2007, 225)

Conclusion

This chapter has reviewed the long history of governmental intervention into the reproductive lives of women in the United States. Law, official policies, and informal practices enforced by criminal justice and social welfare agencies have affected women's reproduction at all stages. We have presented stories of women who were prevented from having children at all – or more children – through the mechanism of involuntary sterilization. It is shocking to consider the rapidity of the passage of laws authorizing sterilization in the early 1900s and governmental involvement in limiting fertility, especially among American Indians, as late as the 1970s. It is more shocking to consider that the practice continues around the world. While the frequency of sterilization to limit population growth among "undesirables" has waned in the past several decades in the United States, the story is different when it comes to pregnant women. In recent years, a plethora of laws have been passed regulating, restricting, and limiting the availability of abortion, with criminal penalties imposed for violating these laws. In some jurisdictions, pregnant women are increasingly viewed as incubators of developing fetuses whose rights may trump those of the person carrying them. The proliferation of anti-abortion laws in recent years may take our nation back to an earlier time of illegal abortions and increased danger to the health of women. A similar process is taking place in regulating the behavior of women who use controlled substances while pregnant. Perhaps even more starkly than the abortion issue, the issue of whether to penalize or regulate the behavior of drug-using women while they are pregnant seems to have struck a chord with the public. Finally, the section on shackling has explored a relatively infrequent condition but one in which women's reproduction is at the center. This demeaning, painful, and harmful practice affects some of society's most powerless individuals – women prison inmates.

We have brought up this issue throughout the chapter, but still it bears repeating. Not all women are equally affected by the laws and practices outlined in this chapter. Whether a woman is born into a wealthy or poor household and whether she is African-American or Caucasian may make the difference as to her likelihood of being involuntarily sterilized, prevented from obtaining an abortion, being punished for using drugs while pregnant, or being shackled during childbirth. As we have documented in this chapter, governmental punitive and restrictive practices pertaining to women's reproduction have been disproportionately applied to poor women and/or women of color. As time goes on our nation will become increasingly diverse and multicultural, and hopefully citizens will become increasingly informed about the potential harms to women of the restrictive laws and practices discussed in this chapter. In the coming decades we hope that citizens, lawmakers, and law enforcement officials will work to further protect the health and rights of girls and women regardless of their ethnicity, race, or income levels.

Suggested readings

Doetzer, Geraldine. 2007. "Hard Labor: The Legal Implications of Shackling Female Inmates during Pregnancy and Childbirth." *William & Mary Journal of Women and the Law*, 14: 363–392.

Flavin, Jeanne. 2009. *Our Bodies, Our Crimes: The Policing of Women's Reproduction in America*. Alternative Criminology Series. New York, NY: New York University Press.

Humphries, Drew. 1999. *Crack Mothers: Pregnancy, Drugs, and the Media*. Women and Health Series. Columbus, OH: Ohio State University Press.

Largent, Mark A. 2008. *Breeding Contempt: The History of Coerced Sterilization in the United States*. New Brunswick, NJ: Rutgers University Press.

Solinger, Rickie. 2013. *Reproductive Politics: What Everyone Needs to Know*. New York, NY: Oxford University Press.

Student engagement activities

1 Research abortion laws in your state/province and identify two areas where you think change is needed. Create draft bills that would implement those changes. Present your logic and proposals to the class.

2 Attend a meeting of a campus organization that has taken a position on abortion. Interview at least one member, letting the person know that you are doing this for a class project. Learn as much about the person's and organization's views. Then contrast/compare the position of the organization to your own views on abortion.

3 Find at least four newspaper articles about the criminalization of pregnant drug users. Read them carefully and select one that is especially powerful. Write a letter to that woman explaining how you feel about what she has done and what is happening/ has happened to her.

4 Identify one issue related to this chapter that has especially sparked your interest. Research the status of your state regarding that issue. Then frame and send a well-reasoned letter to the editor of your local newspaper.

Discussion questions

1 With medical science advancing the period of fetal viability, should states change abortion laws to restrict access to abortion to the very early weeks of pregnancy?

2 Imagine the future if women's access to abortion continues to be increasingly restricted. What will be the consequences? Will we have to go back to creating homes for unwed mothers? Will we start to resort to the dangerous practice of illegal abortion again? What other consequences can you envision?

3 Many would argue that women who use drugs during pregnancy have no business carrying children who are born addicted. What do you think? Consider a compassionate perspective on this issue – what would it be?

4 What is the appropriate role of social service agencies in counseling women about fertility? Consider the logic of social workers who tried to convince a woman to agree to long-term birth control or sterilization. What would you say to these social workers?

5 What does shackling women giving birth say about our prison system?

Key terms

Abortion
Anti-abortion activism
"Born criminal"
Buck v. Bell (1927)
Compulsory sterilization
"Crack mothers"
Eighth Amendment
Eugenics
Fourteenth Amendment
Institutionalized persons

Involuntary sterilization
Jim Crow laws
Marriage restriction laws
Permeable
Roe v. Wade (1973)
Shackling
Skinner v. Oklahoma (1942)
Surgical-center standards
Unborn Victims of Violence Act
Waiting periods

References

Albert, Gwendolyn. 2011. "Forced Sterilization and Romani Women's Resistance in Central Europe." *Different Takes*, 71: 1–4. http://popdev.hampshire.edu/sites/default/files/uploads/u4763/DT%20 71%20Albert.pdf

Advocates for Pregnant Women. 2014. "Wisconsin Alicia Beltran Case Federal District Court Avoids Ruling on Constitutionality." http://advocatesforpregnantwomen.org/blog/2014/09/wisconsin_ alicia_beltran_case.php

Alford, Jeremy, and Erik Eckholm. May 21, 2014. "With New Bill, Abortion Limits Spread in South." *New York Times*. Accessed September 29, 2014, http://www.nytimes.com/2014/05/22/us/politics/ new-bill-spreads-abortion-limits-in-south.html

Amnesty International. 2000. "Pregnant and Imprisoned in the United States." *Birth*, 27(4): 266– 271. DOI: 10.1046/j.1523-536x.2000.00266.x

AWHONN (Association of Women's Health, Obstetric & Neonatal Nursing). 2011. "Shackling Incarcerated Pregnant Women." *JOGNN: Journal of Obstetric, Gynecologic & Neonatal Nursing*, 40(6): 817–818. DOI: 10.1111/j.1552-6909.2011.01300.x

Bassett, Laura. April 30, 2014. "Tennessee Enacts Law to Incarcerate Pregnant Women Who Use Drugs." *Huffington Post*. Accessed September 8, 2014, http://www.huffingtonpost.com/2014/04/30/ tennessee-to-incarcerate-_n_5241770.html

Blythe, Anne, and Craig Jarvis. January 17, 2014. "Federal Judge Strikes Down NC's Ultrasound Abortion Law." *Charlotte Observer*. Accessed September 8, 2014, http://www.charlotteobserver. com/2014/01/17/4620543/federal-judge-strikes-down-ncs.html#storylink=cpy

Boies, Henry Martyn. 1893. *Prisoners and Paupers: A Study of the Abnormal Increase of Criminals and the Public Burden of Pauperism in the United States: The Causes and Remedies*. New York, NY: G. P. Putnam's Sons.

Buck v. Bell, 1927.

Buckley, Chris. November 15, 2013. "China to Ease Longtime Policy of 1-Child Limit." *New York Times*. Accessed September 8, 2014, http://www.nytimes.com/2013/11/16/world/asia/china-to-loosen-its-one-child-policy.html?pagewanted=all&_r=0

Campbell, Nancy, D. 2000. *Using Women: Gender, Drug Policy, and Social Justice*. New York, NY: Routledge.

Carpio, Myla Vicenti. 2004. "The Lost Generation: American Indian Women and Sterilization Abuse." *Social Justice*, 31(4): 40–53.

Center for Reproductive Rights. 2014. *Abortion Worldwide: 20 Years of Reform*. New York, NY.

Cepko, Roberta. 1993. "Involuntary Sterilization of Mentally Disabled Women." *Berkeley Journal of Gender, Law, & Justice*, 8(1): 122–165.

Dailard, Cynthia, and Elizabeth Nash. 2000. "State Responses to Substance Abuse among Pregnant Women." *The Guttmacher Report on Public Policy*, 3(6): 3–6.

Dekok, David. September 6, 2014. "Pennsylvania Mother Who Gave Daughter Abortion Pill Gets Prison. *Reuters*. Accessed September 8, 2014, http://www.reuters.com/article/2014/09/06/us-usa-crime-pennsylvania-abortion-idUSKBN0H10IR20140906

Doetzer, Geraldine. 2008. "Hard Labor: The Legal Implications of Shackling Female Inmates during Pregnancy and Childbirth." *William & Mary Journal of Women and the Law*, 14: 363–392.

Dugdale, Richard Louis. 1877. *"The Jukes": A Study in Crime, Pauperism, Disease and Heredity*. 3rd edn, rev. Vol. 14. New York, NY: G. P. Putnam's sons.

Eckholm, Erik. 2013. "Case Explores Rights of Fetus Versus Mother." *New York Times*, October 23, sec. US. http://www.nytimes.com/2013/10/24/us/case-explores-rights-of-fetus-versus-mother.html.

Einarson, Adrienne, and Gideon Koren. 2007. "Prescribing Antidepressants to Pregnant Women: What Is a Family Physician to Do?" *Cananadian Family Medicine*, 53(9): 1412–1414.

Elbagir, Nima, and Laura Smith-Spark. July 1, 2014. "Sudanese Christian Woman: 'There's a New Problem Every Day.'" *CNN*. Accessed September 8, 2014, http://www.cnn.com/2014/07/01/world/africa/sudan-apostasy-case/

Engs, Ruth Clifford. 2003. *The Progressive Era's Health Reform Movement: A Historical Dictionary*. Westport, CT: Praeger.

Fentiman, Linda C. 2009. "In the Name of Fetal Protection: Why American Prosecutors Pursue Pregnant Drug Users (And Other Countries Don't)." *Columbia Journal of Gender and Law*, 18(2): 647–669.

Fernandez, Manny. 2014. "Abortion Law Pushes Texas Clinics to Close Doors." *New York Times*, March 6. http://www.nytimes.com/2014/03/07/us/citing-new-texas-rules-abortion-provider-is-shutting-last-clinics-in-2-regions.html

Ferszt, Ginette G. 2011. "Who Will Speak for Me? Advocating for Pregnant Women in Prison." *Policy, Politics, & Nursing Practice*, 12(4): 254–256. DOI: 10.1177/1527154411424615

Flavin, Jeanne. 2009. *Our Bodies, Our Crimes: The Policing of Women's Reproduction in America*. Alternative Criminology Series. New York, NY: New York University Press.

Ginn, Stephen. 2013. "Women Prisoners." *British Medical Journal*, 1–4. DOI: 10.1136/bmj.e8318

Gómez, Laura E. 1997. *Misconceiving Mothers: Legislators, Prosecutors, and the Politics of Prenatal Drug Exposure*. Gender, Family, and the Law Series. Philadelphia, PA: Temple University Press.

Goodwin, Michele. 2008. "Prosecuting the Womb." *The George Washington Law Review*, 76: 1657–1746.

Goodwin, Michele. 2014. "Fetal Protection Laws: Moral Panic and the New Constitutional Battlefront." *California Law Review*, 102(4): 781–875.

Gowen, Annie. November 13, 2014. "Doctor Arrested after Botched Sterilizations in India Kill 13." *Washington Post*. Accessed November 14, 2014, http://www.washingtonpost.com/world/doctor-arrested-after-botched-sterilization-at-india-camp-kills-13/2014/11/13/a50991d6-6b06-11e4-a31c-77759fc1eacc_story.html

Graham, Ruth. 2014. "For Pregnant Women, 'Fetal Rights' Mean Two Sets of Rights in One Body – The Boston Globe." *BostonGlobe*. https://www.bostonglobe.com/ideas/2014/02/16/for-pregnant-women-two-sets-rights-one-body/5Pd6zntIViRBZ9QxhiQgFJ/story.html

Griggs, Claire Louise. 2011. "Birthing Barbarism: The Unconstitutionality of Shackling Pregnant Prisoners." *American University Journal of Gender Social Policy and Law*, 20(1): 247–271.

Guttmacher Institute. 2014a. "State Policies in Brief: An Overview of Abortion Laws." http://www.guttmacher.org/statecenter/spibs/spib_OAL.pdf

Guttmacher Institute – – –. 2014b. "State Policies in Brief: Substance Abuse during Pregnancy." Guttmacher Institute.

Guttmacher Institute. 2015. "State Policies in Brief: An Overview of Abortion Laws." Accessed November 5, 2015, http://www.guttmacher.org/statecenter/spibs/spib_OAL.pdf

Hesketh, Therese, Lu, Li, and Zhu Wei Xing. 2005. "The Effect of China's One-Child Family Police after 25 Years." *New England Journal of Medicine*, 353: 1171–1176. DOI: 10.1056/NEJMhpr051833

Humphries, Drew. 1999. *Crack Mothers: Pregnancy, Drugs, and the Media*. Columbus, OH: Ohio State University Press.

Inciardi, James A., Lockwood, Dorothy, and Anne E. Pottieger. 1993. *Women and Crack-Cocaine*. New York, NY: Macmillan.

International Human Rights Clinic. 2014. *Shackling of Pregnant Prisoners in the United States*. University of Chicago Law School.

Joffe, Carol. 2013. "Roe v. Wade and Beyond: Forty Years of Legal Abortion in the United States." *Dissent Magazine*. http://www.dissentmagazine.org/article/roe-v-wade-and-beyond-forty-years-of-legal-abortion-in-the-united-states.

Johns, Fran Moreland. 2013. *Perilous Times: An Inside Look at Abortion Before – and After – Roe vs. Wade.* New York, NY: YBK Publishers.

Johnson, Corey G. July 7, 2013. "Female Inmates Sterilized in California Prisons Without Approval." *The Center for Investigative Reporting.* Accessed October 2, 2014, http://cironline.org/reports/female-inmates-sterilized-california-prisons-without-approval-4917

Kemp, Joe. July 14, 2014. "Tennessee Mom Arrested under New Drug Law after Newborn Tests Positive for Meth." *New York Daily News.* Accessed October 21, 2014, http://www.nydailynews.com/news/crime/tennessee-mom-busted-new-drug-law-baby-tests-positive-meth-article-1.1865979

Klepper, David. June 9, 2014. "New York State Eases Transgender Policy." *Delaware News Journal Online.* Accessed October 1, 2014, http://www.delawareonline.com/story/news/health/2014/06/09/new-york-state-eases-transgender-policy/10232325/

Kluchin, Rebecca Marie. 2009. *Fit to Be Tied: Sterilization and Reproductive Rights in America, 1950–1980.* New Brunswick, NJ: Rutgers University Press.

Ladegaard, Isak. August 3, 2012. "For Norwegian Drug Addicts, Pregnancy Might Lead to Incarceration." *Sciencenordic.* Accessed September 29, 2014, http://sciencenordic.com/norwegian-drug-addicts-pregnancy-might-lead-incarceration.

Largent, Mark A. 2008. *Breeding Contempt: The History of Coerced Sterilization in the United States.* New Brunswick, NJ: Rutgers University Press.

Lawrence, Jane. 2000. "The Indian Health Service and the Sterilization of Native American Women." *The American Indian Quarterly*, 24(3): 400–419.

Leveille, Vania. 2008. "Bureau of Prisons Revises Policy on Shackling of Pregnant Inmates." *ACLU.* Accessed, September 8, 2014, https://www.aclu.org/blog/content/bureau-prisons-revises-policy-shackling-pregnant-inmates

Linton, Paul Benjamin. 2012. *Abortion under State Constitutions: A State-by-State Analysis.* 2nd edn. Durham, NC: Carolina Academic Press.

Liptak, Adam. 2006a. "Prisons Often Shackle Pregnant Inmates in Labor." *New York Times*, March 2, sec. National. http://www.nytimes.com/2006/03/02/national/02shackles.html

Liptak, Adam. 2006b. "Prisons Often Shackle Pregnant Inmates in Labor." *New York Times*, Late Edition (East Coast), March 2, sec. A.

Logli, Paul A. 1990. "Drugs in the Womb: The Newest Battlefield in the War on Drugs." *Criminal Justice Ethics*, 9(1): 23–29. DOI: 10.1080/0731129X.1990.9991869

Murphy, Sheigla, and Marsha Rosenbaum. 1999. *Pregnant Women on Drugs.* New Brunswick, NJ: Rutgers University Press.

Nash, Elizabeth, Gold, Rachel Benson, Rowan, Andrea, Rathbun, Gwendolyn, and Yana Vierboom. 2014. *Laws Affecting Reproductive Health and Rights: 2013 State Policy Review: State Trends for 2013 on Abortion, Family Planning, Sex Education, STIs and Pregnancy."* Washington, DC: Guttmacher Institute. Accessed September 15, 2014, http://www.guttmacher.org/statecenter/updates/2013/statetrends42013.html

National Institute on Drug Abuse. 2011. "Prenatal Exposure to Drugs of Abuse." National Institutes of Health.

Nelson, Rebecca. January 14, 2013. "Transgender People in Sweden No Longer Face Forced Sterilization." *Time.* Accessed September 8, 2014, http://newsfeed.time.com/2013/01/14/transgender-people-in-sweden-no-longer-face-forced-sterilization/

Nelson, Roxanne. 2006. "AJN Reports: Laboring in Chains." *The American Journal of Nursing* 106(10): 25–26.

New York Times. 2013. "Abortion Restrictions in States." http://www.nytimes.com/interactive/2013/06/18/us/politics/abortion-restrictions.html

Nourse, Victoria. 2008. *In Reckless Hands: Skinner v. Oklahoma and the Near-triumph of American Eugenics.* New York, NY: Norton.

Open Society Foundation. 2011. "Against Her Will: Forced and Coerced Sterilization of Women Worldwide." Accessed September 8, 2014, http://www.opensocietyfoundations.org/sites/default/files/against-her-will-20111003.pdf

Paillé, Helen. 2012. "Black Female Inmates' Reproductive Rights: Cutting the Chains of Colorblind Constitutionalism." *The William Mitchell Law Raza Journal*, 3(1): 1–20.

Paltrow, Lynn M., and Jeanne Flavin. 2013. "Arrests of and Forced Interventions on Pregnant Women in the United States, 1973–2005: Implications for Women's Legal Status and Public Health." *Journal of Health Politics, Policy and Law*, 38(2): 299–343. DOI: 10.1215/03616878-1966324

Reagan, Leslie J. 1997. *When Abortion Was a Crime: Women, Medicine, and Law in the United States, 1867–1973*. Berkeley: University of California Press.

Reilly, Philip. 1991. *The Surgical Solution: A History of Involuntary Sterilization in the United States*. Baltimore, MD: Johns Hopkins University Press.

Roberts, Sarah C. M., and Cheri Pies. 2011. "Complex Calculations: How Drug Use During Pregnancy Becomes a Barrier to Prenatal Care." *Journal of Maternal and Child Health*, 15(3), 333–341. DOI: 10.1007/s10995-010-0594-7

Roe v. Wade, 410 U.S. 113 (1973).

Sachdev, Paul. 1985. *Perspectives on Abortion*. Metuchen, NJ: Scarecrow Press.

Sahagun, Louis, and Mark Arax. November 12, 2004. "Scott Peterson Convicted in Murder of Wife Laci." *Los Angeles Times*. Accessed September 5, 2014, http://www.latimes.com/la-111204peterson_lat-story.html#page=1

Scheller, Alissa. 2014. "Where Laws Intended to Protect Women Are Used Against Them." *Huffington Post*. http://www.huffingtonpost.com/2014/04/04/arrests-of-pregnant-women_n_5083480.html

Scott, Charles L., and Trent Holmberg. 2003. "Castration of Sex Offenders: Prisoners' Rights Versus Public Safety." *Journal of the American Academy of Psychiatry and the Law*, 31(4): 502–509.

Shapiro, Gilla K. 2013. "Abortion Law in Muslim-Majority Countries: An Overview of the Islamic Discourse with Policy Implications." *Health Policy and Planning*, 8: 1–12 DOI: 10.1093/heapol/czt040

Sichel, Dana L. 2007. "Giving Birth in Shackles: A Constitutional and Human Rights Violation." *American University Journal of Gender, Social Policy & the Law*, 16: 223–256.

Sieczkowski, Cavan. April 10, 2013. "Chinese Mother Forced into Abortion at 6 Months Because of Nation's One-Child Rule." *Huffington Post*. Accessed September 5, 2014, http://www.huffingtonpost.com/2013/10/04/china-forced-abortion_n_4044446.html

Sifferlin, Alexandra. Aug. 6, 2014. "France Eases Abortion Restrictions in Sweeping Equality Law." *Time*. Accessed September 5, 2014, http://time.com/3086892/france-abortion-law-gender-equality/

Skinner v. Oklahoma, 1942.

Solinger, Rickie. 2013. *Reproductive Politics: What Everyone Needs to Know*. Oxford: Oxford University Press.

Strode, Ann, Mthembu, Sethembiso, and Zaynab Essack. 2012. "She Made Up a Choice for Me': 22 HIV-Positive Women's Experiences of Involuntary Sterilization in Two South African Provinces." *Reproductive Health Matters*, 20(39S): 61–69. DOI: 10.1016/S0968-8080(12)39643-2

Tatlow, Didi Kirsten. September 11, 2012. "Women in Prison Fare Better in China." *New York Times*. Accessed September 8, 2014, http://www.nytimes.com/2012/09/12/world/asia/12iht-letter12.html?pagewanted=all&_r=0

Tornkvist, Ann. 2011. "Sweden: Transgender Actress Mourns Her 'Forcible Sterilization.'" *GlobalPost*. Accessed September 5, 2014, http://www.globalpost.com/dispatch/news/culture-lifestyle/111101/sweden-transgender-LGBT-gay-lesbian-bisexual-sterilization.

United States Conference of Catholic Bishops. 2009. "Ethical and Religious Directives for Catholic Health Care Services." *USCCB.* Accessed September 5, 2014, http://www.usccb.org/issues-and-action/human-life-and-dignity/health-care/upload/Ethical-Religious-Directives-Catholic-Health-Care-Services-fifth-edition-2009.pdf

US Census Bureau. 2012. "Facts for Features: Mother's Day: May 13, 2012." https://www.census.gov/newsroom/releases/archives/facts_for_features_special_editions/cb12-ff08.html

Weatherbe, Steve. November 6, 2014. "'A Mass Sterilization Exercise': Kenyan Doctors Find Anti-Fertility Agent in UN Tetanus Vaccine." *Life Site News.* Accessed November 12, 2014, https://www.lifesitenews.com/news/a-mass-sterilization-exercise-kenyan-doctors-find-anti-fertility-agent-in-u

Winter, Michael. August 29, 2014. "Federal Judge Voids Key Piece of Texas Abortion Law." *USA Today.* Accessed September 5, 2014, http://www.usatoday.com/story/news/nation/2014/08/29/texas-abortion-law-struck-down/14822205/

World Health Organization. 2014. "Eliminating Forced, Coercive and Otherwise Involuntary Sterilization: An Interagency Statement." Accessed October 1, 2014, http://apps.who.int/iris/bitstream/10665/112848/1/9789241507325_eng.pdf?ua=1

Yonkers, Kimberly. October 9, 2014. "Stop Telling Pregnant Women to Go Off Their Antidepressants." *Washington Post.* Accessed October 11, 2014, http://www.washingtonpost.com/posteverything/wp/2014/10/09/stop-telling-pregnant-women-to-go-off-their-anti-depressants/

Zampas, Christina and Adriana Lamacková. 2011. "Forced and Coerced Sterilization of Women in Europe." *International Journal of Gynecology and Obstetrics,* 114: 163–166. DOI: 10.1016/j.ijgo.2011.05.002

CHAPTER 5

Sexual victimization

Student learning outcomes

After reading this chapter, you should be able to:

- Track changes in law pertaining to sexual assault and pinpoint elements of law that have improved outcomes for sexual assault victims.
- Discuss the extent of sexual assault in our society and why the official numbers may underestimate the problem.
- Explain why college campuses are high-risk environments for sexual assault and what is being done to change that.
- Compare and contrast the various theories about the causes of rape.
- Discuss the experiences of victims after being sexually assaulted and what programs are effective in assisting them.

Introduction

Steubenville, Ohio, is a decaying steel town on the Ohio River bordering West Virginia where football is venerated and the lucky ones go off to college. It is also a town where Steubenville's star quarterback and his favorite wide receiver were convicted of rape. On August 11, 2012, Trent Mays and Ma'lik Richmond, both 16, according to court testimony, had taken a 16-year-old girl from party to party, engaging in sex with her while she was too drunk to resist. Others at the party recorded the actions of these two young men, posting videos and photographs but doing little to stop the assault. Nor did anyone call the police. The victim, who was unconscious throughout most of the proceedings, had no memory of the assault. The assailants were arrested within days of the incident but few others came forward with information about what had happened, and some concealed information that they did have. Despite concern among some community members that further investigation would undermine the school's reputation, police initiated an investigation into others who might be partially responsible for the crime (Macur and Schweber 2012). Over a year later, on November 25, 2013, four adults, including the school superintendent, a former football coach, an elementary school principal, and the school's director of information technology were charged with crimes including providing alcohol to minors, obstructing justice, tampering with evidence, making false statements, and failing to report child abuse or neglect (Gabriel 2013). The decision to indict adults in conjunction with student criminal acts reflects a change in national attitudes about who is to be held responsible for sexual assault when teenagers are involved. It suggests the importance

---

Women, Crime, and Justice, First Edition. By Elaine Gunnison, Frances P. Bernat, and Lynne Goodstein.
© 2017 John Wiley & Sons, Ltd. Published 2017 by John Wiley & Sons, Ltd.

of bystanders taking active roles rather than turning the other way or concealing information when confronted with sex crimes.

In early 2001, Virginia Messick, from the small town of Baker, Florida, joined the Air Force and was assigned to an all-female training group under the supervision of Staff Sergeant Luis Walker. The 19-year-old was excited to be starting her military career at the Lakeland Air Force Base near San Antonio, Texas, but soon after beginning basic training, Sergeant Walker offered her access to a computer in his private office, a clear violation of military rules. On one occasion, he grabbed her and began to grope her but stopped when she resisted, assuring her that "it won't happen again." Soon after, however, Sergeant Walker ordered Messick to deliver towels to an empty floor in the trainee dorm. It was there that he raped her. Messick knew that what had happened to her was wrong and that she should tell someone. But she had also been told that if she had any problems she was to report them to her supervisor. Walker was her supervisor (Risen 2012). Therefore, she told no one about the April 2011 assault and completed her training, fearful of the consequences of speaking out. Messick moved on to an advanced training program in Mississippi when, later in 2011, she heard from a friend that she, too, was being harassed by Sergeant Walker. The friend spoke out about Walker to Air Force investigators, including reporting on what had happened to Messick. When called in to testify about Walker as part of a formal investigation, Messick was reluctant to reveal much about the incident. But by July of 2012, when Messick testified at Walker's court martial as one of 10 trainees who all claimed that Walker had victimized them, she did use the word rape. Sergeant Walker was convicted of 28 counts, including rape, sexual assault, and aggravated sexual contact and is serving a 20-year sentence for crimes involving 10 women.

Messick's testimony, along with that of 61 other trainees identified as victims of improper conduct, contributed to the court martials of at least seven Air Force instructors; more are under investigation. More importantly, this case has sparked a much larger discussion that has reached the highest levels of government. Congresswomen serving on federal committees, including Armed Services, have forced the issue of sexual assault in the military to the forefront from Capitol Hill to the White House, chairing investigations, authoring bills and publicly excoriating military leaders for their laxity in dealing with the problem (Steinhauer 2013a). Meanwhile, Messick, like so many victims of sexual assault, left the Air Force and moved back to Florida where she was diagnosed with **post-traumatic stress disorder (PTSD)** and joined a therapy program (Risen 2012).

 CASE STUDY: Sexual assault in India

On December 16, 2012 in a suburb of New Delhi, India, a young physiotherapy student and her male friend were returning from watching a movie, *The Life of Pi*, at a local theater. They boarded what they thought was a local passenger bus. Instead, inside the bus were six men who had laid a carefully planned trap. They brutally raped and sexually assaulted the woman with an iron rod and severely beat the young man until he was unconscious, then threw them out of a moving bus to bleed on the side of the road. No one came to their aid for precious minutes, and by the time they were taken to a hospital over two hours had elapsed. The young woman, critically injured in the attack, died days later. In a nation where violence against women is commonplace, the incident sparked a groundswell of protest from India's citizens. Hundreds of thousands of women staged days of demonstrations throughout the country, expressing their outrage at the slow response of the authorities and the lack of protection afforded women victims. The brutal rape not only galvanized India's populace but also prompted governmental leaders to respond (Timmons and

Gottipati 2012). Within three weeks of the rape a governmental commission issued a scathing indictment of the treatment of women in India, arguing that women are confronted on a regular basis with sexual violence and that the police and government had failed to enforce policies and laws to protect victims and prevent violence. The commission's report cut a wide swath in condemning India's treatment of women, covering not only sexual assault but also societal biases against daughters, workplace sexual harassment, child sexual abuse, the trafficking of women and children, and deep-rooted problems with Indian policing (Yardley 2013). Meanwhile, a year later, the defendants of the gang rape received their punishments. Four of the six defendants have received the death penalty, another is dead, and the sixth received the maximum sentence for a minor – three years in a reformatory (Vyawahare 2014a).

A few decades ago, rape and sexual assault were topics few people talked about. History buffs may have studied the Boston strangler or Jack the Ripper, notorious serial criminals who stalked unsuspecting women and then raped and murdered them. People might read about an unfortunate woman on her way home from work who was accosted by a stranger armed with a knife or gun and brutally raped after being forced into a dark alley. That was the model of rape – a masked stranger appearing out of the shadows, using the power of his larger size or weapon to overcome the woman's resistance, committing his violent act, and then fading away. The experience of the New Delhi couple mentioned in the text box – magnified by the fact that the crime was a gang rape with multiple perpetrators – reflects this model and underscores the terrifying reality that in the twenty-first century women are still targeted for violent victimization by strangers (Bryden 2000). At the same time, greater awareness has emerged that sexual assault perpetrators can also be known to the victim and may even be powerful entertainers. Recently, Bill Cosby has been in the news and is facing allegations of sexual assault from at least 15 different women (McCartney 2014).

Until recently, little was mentioned about what happened to victims after the fact. Rape, because it involved a sexual – instead of just a physical – assault, was viewed as a source of shame for the victim. Victims would worry that people would feel that they were somehow responsible for their victimization – by walking down the wrong street, being alone, or wearing alluring clothing. They worried about how they would be treated by their husbands or boyfriends, the police, hospital personnel, or legal authorities if they did report what had happened to them. Would sharing her story lead to a husband's coldness in response to learning that his wife had been violated by another man? If she did report her ordeal to the police would they believe her or treat her with suspicion and skepticism? When she went to the hospital for care would medical personnel know how to treat her with compassion while conducting an examination that would preserve evidence? More often than not, victims' worry was justified. Victims' experiences of sexual assault and its aftermath may still be much like those of victims from past decades and centuries. But what is different is the level of knowledge about the crime of sexual assault. The subject, one that received little scholarly or scientific investigation until the latter decades of the twentieth century, is now much better understood. Also, women's movement activists have influenced public opinion and successfully changed laws and social policy to better protect the rights and dignity of the victims. Practitioners who work with and treat rape victims and perpetrators have developed more effective methods. Yet these advances, as we will discuss in this chapter, are little consolation to the thousands of children and women who are victimized by rape and sexual assault every day in every country.

In this chapter, we define the term "sexual victimization," discuss the prevalence of sexual victimization, and describe the types of victimization that occur. We focus on the explanations for why sexual victimization may occur, and the role of police and courts in assisting victims. Finally, we offer suggestions as to what can be done to help support victims of sexual assault and how to go about creating a culture of support for those impacted by this violence.

Defining and prosecuting rape – then and now

Most crimes are relatively easy to define. Burglary involves a person entering someone else's home and taking their property. Embezzlement involves using one's work position to steal from an employer. Rape and sexual assault, however, are different matters. Over the centuries, the term "rape" has been defined quite differently.

Take a moment to consider what components should be included in a definition of rape. The elements of the crime that have received considerable attention over the years include: gender of victim and perpetrator; prior relationship between victim and perpetrator; the specific actions performed by the perpetrator; and the issue of victim consent. Let's examine one aspect of the debate regarding the definition of rape: the actions committed by the perpetrator that constitute rape. In thinking about this question, we need to be pretty graphic. Does rape need to involve penetration of the vagina by a penis, or can it be about penetration of another orifice – the mouth, the anus, or penetration by something other than the perpetrator's penis, such as a finger or inanimate object? Victim consent is yet another aspect of the definition to consider. Recently, CeeLo Green, a songwriter and record producer, came under fire for several tweets in which he provided his own interpretations of rape. Green tweeted that if a woman was raped she would certainly remember, and he also tweeted: "if someone is passed out they're not even WITH you consciously! so WITH Implies consent" (Zuckerman 2014). As you might imagine, his statements have raised a lot of concern and discussions have been abounding in the media and online regarding consent. If the victim consents to the sexual contact, most people might say it is not rape. However, it is difficult to know if the victim consented. In the case of the New Delhi woman, the fact that the assailants were all strangers to the victims and the extreme physical violence of the assault make it quite clear that there was no consent. In the case of the young woman raped by the Steubenville football players, there was documentary evidence that she was unconscious while the sexual penetration occurred and therefore could not actively provide consent. What if she had been conscious but so intoxicated that her judgment was extremely impaired? What about a woman who is conscious – how do we know if she is giving or not giving consent? If a woman does not consent to sex what does she have to do? Is saying "no" sufficient, or do we expect her to fight back or struggle?

Rape law – historical review

Historically – that is, prior to the 1970s – rape was defined as follows: "A man commits rape when he engages in sexual intercourse (in the old statues, 'carnal knowledge') with a woman not his wife; by force or threat of force; against her will and without her consent" (Estrich 1987). This definition implied that a man could not be arrested for raping his wife, a condition termed the **marital exemption**. The legal system also stipulated that the woman must exhibit **"utmost resistance"** in order to be believed as a credible victim. In some jurisdictions victims were required to provide corroborating information – a witness to the crime – to be considered credible. In other instances, the prosecution of an alleged rapist would not go forward if his victim had violated traditional norms of feminine morality and prudence – for example, by engaging in casual sex, drinking heavily, or hitchhiking

(Bryden 2000). If a case got to the prosecution stage, there were rules about the woman's "character for chastity" that gave the prosecution permission to cross-examine victims of **acquaintance rape** – sexual assault where the victim is acquainted with the perpetrator somehow – about their sexual histories in order to paint them as promiscuous. Prosecutors were bound by the **corroboration requirement** to present evidence in addition to the victim's testimony, such as a third-party witness who had observed the assault. Judges also often gave a **"cautionary instruction,"** sensitizing jurors to the assumption that accusations of rape were easy to fabricate. The inherent skepticism held by agents of the court about the credibility of victims' claims of rape is reflected in a frequently quoted statement from three centuries ago by English Lord Chief Justice Matthew Hale that rape is a charge "easily to be made and hard to be proved, and harder to be defended by the party accused, tho' never so innocent" (Hale 1847, 635).

Rape law reform

Beginning in the 1970s feminist scholars and activists advocated for changes in **rape laws** and **evidentiary rules** (Bevacqua 2000). By the early twenty-first century, modern reforms had largely eliminated these antiquated laws and evidentiary rules. Victims no longer must report their victimization promptly; the corroboration requirement has been dropped; judges no longer include the cautionary instruction; victims no longer must demonstrate "utmost resistance," and, with **rape shield laws**, defense attorneys may no longer bring up victims' prior sexual histories (Bevacqua 2000; Bryden 2000).

⚖️ **SPECIAL LEGAL ISSUES: Legislative changes in India**

The brutal rape described in the first text box not only prompted outrage among the citizenry but also pushed governmental leaders to institute legislative change. On February 4, 2013, India's government approved tough new laws against sexual violence ranging from a minimum of seven years in prison to the death penalty in cases where a victim dies or is left in a vegetative state (Timmons and Gottipati 2012). India's parliament also recognized the widespread nature of sexual victimization and attempted to develop new crimes that would address the multiple methods for enacting such violence. New crimes were created to punish stalking, acid violence, and voyeurism, all common in India. Stalking is particularly dangerous in India as it is seen as leading to more violent crime (Majumdar 2013). The laws also expanded the definition of rape, explicitly stating that victims need not physically struggle for an act of forced sex to be considered rape. In addition, the new laws prescribed penalties for police or other government agents who do not follow specific rules when rapes are reported (BBC News India 2013). Some activists praised the added protections, including access to appropriate health care and counseling, for survivors of sexual assault who may not have the financial means. On the other hand, critics of the government's response complained that these efforts will not address the underlying problem, a culture that supports violence against women. Some members of women's rights groups argued that the law is "piecemeal and fragmented" and that the laws were passed quickly simply to "appease public sentiment" (Yardley and Bagri 2013). Despite the recent attention to issues of sexual assault, not every type of rape is covered by Indian law. The Indian Penal Code does not recognize forced sexual intercourse by a man with his own wife over the age of 15 as rape. In a recent case in which a woman claimed to have been drugged and forced to have sex with her husband, the man was acquitted (Vyawahare 2014b).

In recent decades, legislatures have altered the definition of rape in several ways. It has made the crime **gender neutral** as to both perpetrator and victim – recognizing that males can be victims of rape as well as females. It has also broadened the definition of intercourse to include all types of sexual penetration, and it has abolished the marital exemption in most cases. Most states have eliminated the term "rape" from their books and created a new crime category called sexual assault. For example, some states now utilize language such as **criminal sexual conduct,** and it has been divided into degrees (Bryden 2000). Most recently, the FBI altered its definition of rape to "The penetration, no matter how slight, of the vagina or anus with any body part or object, or oral penetration by a sex organ of another person, without the consent of the victim" (US Department of Justice 2012).

We now would like to present what we see as a comprehensive and **contemporary definition of rape** developed by the Bureau of Justice Statistics (BJS) and used in the National Crime Victimization Survey. Those who crafted the definition addressed many of the criticisms of the historical definition, including gender of perpetrator and victim, relationship between victim and perpetrator, actions of the perpetrator, and the issue of victim consent. Note also the inclusion "use of psychological coercion" as well as "physical force" and the explicit reference to the inclusion of both homosexual and heterosexual rape.

> Rape is the unlawful penetration of a person against the will of the victim, with use or threatened use of psychological coercion and physical force, and forced sexual intercourse means vaginal, anal, or oral penetration by the offender. Rape also includes incidents where penetration is from a foreign object (e.g., a bottle), victimizations against male and female victims, and both heterosexual and homosexual rape. Attempted rape includes verbal threats of rape. (Planty et al. 2013, 2)

Continued challenges to rape prosecution

Yet even with the significant changes in rape laws, gaining justice for victims of sexual assault is challenging indeed. Rape victims, for reasons we will discuss later in the chapter, often do not report their assaults to the authorities in a timely fashion or at all. Hence, important rape scene evidence is not always available. Police and prosecutors may be reluctant to move a case forward, especially if – as is most common – the perpetrator is acquainted with the victim prior to the attack. In these situations, evidence frequently is of a "he said, she said" nature and thus may not be viewed as strong enough to stand up at trial. Even with rape reform, the circumstances surrounding the assault, such as whether the victim was drinking, voluntarily went with the perpetrator to a private room, and what the victim did to resist the assault, may be raised at trial. In sum, many victims who do seek justice through the courts must endure aggressive questioning, making it look like it is the victim, not the perpetrator, under investigation. One can easily understand why scholars and activists speak about the aftermath of rape for victims as a **"second rape"** (Dunn 2010; Holmstrom and Burgess 1978).

The measurement of sexual victimization

Over the past several decades, researchers have made strides in developing methods for estimating the extent of rape in the United States. Because of the difficulty in obtaining accurate estimates from police reports, researchers have instituted major national surveys to determine the extent of rape. Also, researchers have tried to be as explicit as possible as to the specific behaviors that they determined would constitute rape. For example, instead of asking general questions such as "have you ever been raped?" the surveys would describe the behavior of the assailant in detail – often in very explicit terms – and ask respondents to answer yes or no to whether that behavior had ever happened to them.

This survey tradition was started by Mary Koss (1987), who administered the Sexual Experiences Survey to women students in colleges and universities across the United States. Her work documented the extent of rape among college students and underscored the value of surveying victims directly. However, her work was limited to a small subgroup of the overall population. Two national surveys in particular have helped to provide important data about the incidence and prevalence of rape across the general population. The **National Violence Against Women Survey (NVAWS)** focuses specifically on sexual victimization (Tjaden and Thoennes 2006). The **National Crime Victimization Survey (NCVS)** assesses all property and violent crime victimization, including sexual victimization (Planty et al. 2013).

The NVAWS was a telephone survey of 8,000 women and 8,000 men that examined their experiences as victims of various forms of violence, including rape (Tjaden and Thoennes 2006). Researchers assumed that rape could happen to a woman or a man, so equal numbers of female and male respondents were included in the study. They carefully crafted screening questions covering the various methods by which a perpetrator could commit rape or sexual assault. Rape was defined as force or threat of force to penetrate the victim's vagina, mouth, or rectum. The survey has provided a wealth of information, not only on the incidence and prevalence of rape and sexual assault but also on the social, physical, and psychological consequences of rape victimization (Tjaden and Thoennes 2006).

TEXT BOX: National Violence Against Women definitions and survey questions

In the National Violence Against Women Survey (NVAWS), rape was defined as an event that occurred without the victim's consent that involved the use or threat of force in vaginal, anal, or oral intercourse. This definition closely resembles that used in the National Women's Study (NWS).[a] However, unlike NWS, NVAWS includes both attempted and completed rape. Thus, unless otherwise noted in this report, "rape" refers to both attempted and completed rape.

The survey included five behaviorally specific questions to screen for rape victimization. The first four questions are identical to those used in NWS and respectively screen for forced vaginal, oral, or anal penetration.[b] To collect information about attempted rape, NVAWS included a fifth question that screened for attempted forced penetration of the vagina, mouth, or anus. To minimize doubt in the respondent's mind about what was being measured, the questions incorporated explicit language. . . .

Respondents who replied "yes" to one or more of the screening questions were asked whether their rapist was a spouse, ex-spouse, male cohabiting partner, female cohabiting partner, relative, someone else they knew, or a stranger. To further delineate the victim-perpetrator relationship, interviewers asked respondents who disclosed rape victimization to specify which spouse/partner raped them (e.g., first ex-husband, current male cohabiting partner); or which relative raped them (e.g., father, brother, grandfather, mother, sister, aunt); or, in cases involving acquaintances, to specify the relationship they had with the rapist (e.g., date, boyfriend, girlfriend, boss, coworker, teacher, neighbor).

Respondents who disclosed rape were asked detailed questions about the characteristics and consequences of their rape, including the following:
- Where the rape occurred.
- Whether they or their rapist were using drugs or alcohol at the time of the incident.
- Whether their rapist used a gun, knife, or other weapon.

(continued)

- Whether their rapist verbally threatened them.
- Whether their rapist physically assaulted them.
- Whether they thought they or someone close to them would be seriously harmed or killed by their rapist.
- Whether they were physically injured and, if so, the types of injuries incurred.
- Whether they received medical services.
- Whether they received counseling from a mental health professional.
- Whether they lost time from routine activities such as school, work, volunteer endeavors, recreational activities, and household chores.
- Whether they reported their rape to the police.
- Whether they obtained a restraining order against their rapist and, if so, whether it was violated.
- Whether their rapist was criminally prosecuted.

These questions were posed for each type of offender (e.g., spouse, ex-spouse, boyfriend, grandfather) identified by the victim. Victims who were raped more than once by the same type of offender were asked to use their *most recent rape* as a reference point.

NVAWS generated information on both the prevalence and incidence of rape. *Prevalence* refers to the number of people within a demographic group (e.g., women or men) who are victimized during a specific time period, such as the person's lifetime or the previous 12 months. *Incidence* refers to the number of separate victimizations, or incidents, perpetrated against people within a demographic group during a specific time period. Incidence expressed as a victimization rate is obtained by dividing the number of victimizations perpetrated against people in the demographic group by the number of people in the group and setting the rate to a standard population base, such as 1,000 people.[c]

Notes

a. National Victim Center and Crime Victims Research and Treatment Center, *Rape in America: A Report to the Nation,* Arlington, VA: National Victim Center and Charleston, SC: Crime Victims Research and Treatment Center, 1992.
b. Ibid.
c. Koss, M.P., and M.R. Harvey, *The Rape Victim: Clinical and Community Interventions,* 2d ed., Newbury Park, CA: Sage Publications, 1991.

Source: Tjaden and Thoennes (2006).

The National Crime Victimization Survey (NCVS) is an annual national survey of many types of victimization. It is administered to persons age 12 or older from a representative sample of households in the United States. Trained interviewers visit people's homes and ask about the number and characteristics of victimizations that respondents have experienced within the past six months, both those reported and not reported to the police. Once a household is selected for the survey and the first in-home interviews have been conducted, the household remains in the sample for three years and eligible persons in the household are interviewed every six months. The number of respondents included in the NCVS is impressive. For example, in 2014, about 90,000 households and 158,000 individuals were interviewed (Truman and Langton 2015).

Prevalence of sexual victimization

In this section, a review of what criminologists know about the statistics associated with rape will be provided including: the prevalence of rape; the risk that any one person has of becoming a victim of rape or sexual assault; whether some persons are more at risk of rape or sexual assault than others;

and whether there are personal characteristics – such as gender, age, race, or ethnicity – that can make a person especially at risk of rape or sexual assault.

These are complex topics that are not easy to answer, in part, because of victims' reluctance to report and the tendency of some criminal justice officials to not take victims seriously. That being said, the surveys of victimization described above have helped tremendously in providing criminologists with data on the scope of rape. One way of looking at the scale of rape is to consider the **prevalence of rape victimization** by estimating the total number of individuals who have been victims at some point in their lives. NVAWS data from 1995 to 1996 estimate this number to be about 18 million women and almost 3 million men (Tjaden and Thoennes 2006). To place this in perspective, it would be as if every man, woman, and child in the cities of New York, Los Angeles, Chicago, Houston, Philadelphia, and Phoenix had been rape victims, and there would be victims left over.

Probably the most important statistic about the scope of rape is its extreme gender imbalance. In the vast majority of cases, victims of rape are female. For every one male victim of rape or sexual assault there are nine female victims (Tjaden and Thoennes 2006). For women, rape is an unfortunately common occurrence. The results vary somewhat across studies, but a conservative estimate by NVAWS is that 18% of women, or one in six, and 3% of men, or one in 33, are victimized by rape at some point in their lives (Tjaden and Thoennes 2006). Even though rape is now considered to be a gender neutral crime, changes in our understanding of the definition of rape have not changed the significantly greater likelihood that that victim will be a woman.

Another way of thinking about victimization is to estimate the percentage of people who are sexually victimized during a specified time period; this statistic is known as the **incidence of rape**. The National Crime Victims Survey estimates the number of victimizations that occur in a given year per 1,000 people (Truman and Langton 2015). This metric gives researchers the ability of comparing rape rates over time. The most recent estimate of the rate of rape is that 2.1 of every 1,000 women age 12 and above in the United States was a rape victim in 2010 (Planty et al. 2013) (Table 5.1).

A finding that may be surprising, given the publicity that the crime of rape receives, is that the rate of rape has declined in recent years – at least in the United States. Fifteen years earlier, in 1995, the rate of rape according to the NCVS was 5.0 per 1,000 women, meaning that the rape rate declined by 58% over that time period (Planty et al. 2013). The decline of the rate of rape also mirrors the decline of other criminal offenses, including child abuse, over the same time period (Conklin 2003). In other countries, such as India, the rape rate rose 70% from 2011 to 2013 (Pillai 2013).

Focusing on the perpetrators of sexual crimes, there is also a tremendous gender imbalance. Simply put, with rare exceptions, women do not commit rape. According to the NVAWS survey, nearly all of female victims (99.6%) and most of male victims (85.8%) were raped by men. There is no general agreement about why rape is almost exclusively a male crime, but some of the theories of rape that we will cover later in the chapter speak to this question. The cases mentioned earlier in the text reflect another fact about rape – it is a crime primarily perpetrated by someone known to the victim. In the years between 2005 and 2010, the NCVS found that 78% of sexual violence involved an offender who was a family member, intimate partner, friend, or acquaintance. Thus, about 8 in 10 rape victims are raped by people they know. The fact that so many rapes are committed against someone the perpetrator knows reflects larger issues of the situational and interpersonal dynamics that lead to sexual assault; we will address these points in the next section. Issues such as the proximity between perpetrator and victim, patterns of dominance and oppression in the household, the exercise of power and control, and misogynistic attitudes toward women make it logical that most rapes would occur between people who know one another.

Table 5.1 Rape and sexual assault victimization among females, 1994–2010.

Victim characteristic	Rate per 1,000 females age 12 or older		
	1994–1998	1999–2004	2005–2010
Total	4.2	3.1	2.1
Age			
12–17	11.3	7.6	4.1
18–34	7.0	5.3	3.7
35–64	2.3	1.8	1.5
65 or older	0.1!	0.2!	0.2!
Race/Hispanic origin			
White[a]	4.3	3.1	2.2
Black[a]	4.2	4.1	2.8
Hispanic/Latina	4.3	1.8	1.4
American Indian/Alaska Native[a]	6.4!	4.8!	4.5!
Asian/Pacific Islander[a]	2.5	1.2	0.7!
Two or more races[a]	~	6.6!	5.1!
Marital status[b]			
Never married	8.6	6.6	4.1
Married	1.3	0.7	0.6
Widowed	0.8	0.2	0.8
Divorced or separated	9.0	6.3	4.4
Household income			
Less than $25,000	6.1	5.6	3.5
$25,000–$49,999	3.3	2.7	1.9
$50,000 or more	2.9	2.0	1.8
Unknown	3.5	2.1	1.8
Location of residence			
Urban	5.1	4.0	2.2
Suburban	3.9	2.7	1.8
Rural	3.9	2.5	3.0

Notes:
! Interpret with caution; estimate based on 10 or fewer sample cases, or coefficient of variation is greater than 50%.
~Not applicable.
[a]Excludes persons of Hispanic or Latino origin.
[b]The NCVS collects information on respondent's marital status at the time of the interview, but it does not obtain marital status at the time of the incident or whether a change in marital status occurred after the incident.
Source: Bureau of Justice Statistics, National Crime Victimization Survey, 1994–2010. US Department of Justice.

The Steubenville case illustrates other facts about rape. The victim was young – still in high school – and both she and the perpetrators were drinking heavily. These elements of the case mirror the NVAWS findings that the risk of rape also is greater among younger people – more than half of female victims and 71% of male victims are raped before their 18th birthdays (Tjaden and Thoennes

2006). Moreover, drugs and alcohol play an important role in rape, with 67% of female victims and 59% of male victims reporting that the rapist used drugs or alcohol at the time of the rape (Tjaden and Thoennes 2006).

Let us summarize what we believe is most important to know about the incidence and prevalence of these crimes. Rape is a gender neutral crime, but it predominantly affects women. It affects approximately one in six women at some time during their lifetimes. A small minority of perpetrators commit the "classic" rape by targeting strangers, but most rape victims are acquainted with their assailants. Young women and adolescents are the most targeted group for sexual victimization. Finally, national surveys in the United States have shown found that the risk of being victimized by rape and sexual assault has declined over the past two decades, as have most other violent crimes (Catalano 2006).

Theories of rape

It is difficult to make sense of the crime of rape. After all, it is difficult to fathom the reasons which could explain why a violent and traumatizing crime appears to target young women who often know their perpetrators. When reflecting on the New Delhi gang rapists and murderers, the Steubenville high school athletes, and the Air Force sergeant, we can see that there were obviously very different circumstances involved in these three rapes. There are no doubt many different reasons why people make the decision to commit a violent crime, so there is probably no one theory that would even explain all rapes. Scholars have proposed a number of explanations.

Micro-oriented theories

Micro-oriented theories seek to differentiate – at the individual level – between those who would be prone to commit an act of sexual violence from those who would not. Many men have access to vans, but most would never think of using the van to stage a scenario that would lead to their perpetrating gang rape and murder. Using alcohol at a party is a commonplace occurrence among high school and college students, yet to most men the thought of sexual contact with a passed-out woman would be abhorrent. Why would some men, given the same circumstances, choose to commit sexual violence while others would not? Many theorists focus at the level of the individual, creating what are known as micro-oriented theories (Jasinski 2001). Many of the contributors to micro-level theories come from the disciplines of psychology or biology – they focus on the individual as the "unit of analysis." They would ask the question: What are the forces that caused an individual rapist to enact his violent crime?

Micro-level theoretical explanations cover a broad range of causes. Some theorists focus on influences in the environments – especially childhood environments – on men who become rapists. This is an example of the **Intergenerational Transmission of Violence Theory** (Straus 1991). Studies of incarcerated rapists have shown that the vast majority of men who are convicted of stranger rape endured extreme physical violence as children, either as witnesses of violence to others or as victims themselves (Bonnycastle 2012). The depiction of women as **sexual objects in the mass media** has also been identified by scholars as a cause for rape. The presentation of girls and women as sex objects is commonplace in US popular culture, as evidenced by advertisements such as Victoria Secret, mainstream magazines such as *Maxim* and the *Sports Illustrated* swimsuit edition, and other widely circulated publications that present both "soft" (*Playboy*) and "hard" (*Hustler*) pornography. Some men are especially drawn to or influenced by these types of videos, or by pornography that explicitly links sex and violence, causing them to become desensitized to victims' pain, fear, and humiliation and to associate sex with aggression (Ellis 1989).

Another approach is to think of rapists as inheriting or developing one or more forms of mental illness or psychological pathology. A **psychopathological explanation** would focus on personality factors or mental illness that would make individuals possessing these traits more likely to commit violence. These traits could have been inherited or they could have developed as a result of how these men were treated as children. Some theorists argue that men who commit sexual violence have low self-esteem, difficulties with anger management, or have depressive personalities (Jasinski 2001). Others have zeroed in on the role of **alcohol** in the crime of rape. Alcohol is the drug most commonly associated with all violent behavior (Tonry and Wilson 1990). The Steubenville rape case illustrates the role that alcohol use, both by the perpetrator and the victim, can play in the commission of rape. College campuses have been found to be settings of special danger to women due to the high levels of alcohol use (Schwartz and DeKeseredy 1997).

Macro-oriented theories

Macro-oriented theories look at societies or cultures as the entities that set the stage for sexual violence. They tend to be proposed by sociologists or use sociological perspectives. Macro-oriented theorists argue that there are specific elements in some cultures or societies that especially promote an acceptance of sexual violence. The implication is that if persons grow up within or become associated with cultures or organizations that are supportive of sexual violence, they become more likely to commit crimes of rape or sexual assault. The examples of the Steubenville and Air Force rapes reflect this type of macro-oriented theory. In both cases, perpetrators were involved in organizations that were predominantly or exclusively male, where women were demeaned, and where their own power and prestige were elevated by virtue of their roles within the organizations. Sociologists have targeted cultural institutions such as collegiate sports and the military as two arenas that allow and, in some cases, foster the victimization of women. We know, for example, that women who join the military have a higher risk of sexual assault (Chamberlain 2013; Hunter 2007; Nelson 2002) and that the incidence of rape among big-time college athletes is surprisingly high (Fisher, Daigle, and Cullen 2010; Pappas 2012).

Probably the most significant theories that have driven much of the research and anti-rape activism that have flourished over the past several decades are **feminist theories of rape and sexual victimization**. Literally thousands of books and articles have been written about sexual victimization from a feminist perspective. Hence there is no one general feminist theory of rape. Even the authors of this work do not always agree on every detail. That being said, there are many commonalities among the perspectives of feminist authors.

Feminists argue that most societies are **patriarchal**, or male dominated, and that most social institutions within societies are designed to perpetuate and maintain this male dominance. There are many examples to support feminist claims of patriarchy. In the United States, women historically have had less power than men. For much of our nation's history women could not own property, did not have the right to vote, were barred from admission to colleges and universities, and were paid less than men for doing the same jobs (French 1992). While efforts have been successful in rectifying some of the more egregious inequities, there are still many ways in which women are not afforded the same degree of power and privilege as men. Across the globe, patterns of gender inequality are played out in hundreds of nations, and in many countries the freedoms that Western women take for granted are far from reach for most women. Feminist theorists and criminologists argue that patriarchal culture promotes sexual violence as a mechanism for men to exert their power over women, thereby upholding a system of male dominance. These views were first applied to the crime of rape in the 1970s. Feminists argued that rape is not a sexual crime but a crime of violence and the exercise of power and domination (Brownmiller 1975). This perspective quickly became central to social scientists' explanations of sexual victimization.

Feminists argued that the mechanisms of teaching boys and girls from the youngest age to conform to appropriate sex roles – **sex role socialization** – resulted in males and females having very different perspectives on sex, love, and affection. Men learn to separate their sexuality from their needs for love and affection and to view women as sexual objects; while women learn to integrate sex, affection, and love, and to be sensitive to what their partners want (Russell 1975; 1984). These divergences in the ways in which males and females approach sexuality and relationships are thought to have profound consequences that ripple through the social fabric and reinforce gender inequalities in all aspects of social life, including the home, the workplace, media, politics and law, and economics (French 1992; Landrine and Klonoff 1997).

The **Male Peer Support Theory** integrates elements of a number of feminist theories (DeKeseredy and Schwartz 2013). The theory – which focuses specifically on male sexual and physical violence against women – posits that social support from peers is instrumental in perpetuating woman abuse. When men feel that their male authority is challenged by women, some seek out peers for advice and support. These peers reinforce patriarchal beliefs such as "an insistence of women's obedience, respect, loyalty, dependency, sexual access, and sexual fidelity" (DeKeseredy and Schwartz 2013, 56) that justify and encourage sexual and other violence against women. Two additional factors are at play in the **Male Peer Support Theory**. First, the theory targets extreme alcohol consumption – binge drinking – which can be associated with sexual aggression because it frequently occurs in the context of men's social groups, such as fraternities and sports teams, that embrace patriarchal ideology. Second, DeKeseredy and Schwartz argue that male perpetrators frequently feel that they commit rape because they can get away with it. Especially in settings such as college campuses where few assaults are reported, let alone prosecuted, men know that the likelihood of their being caught is so small. Hence, the men who hold patriarchal beliefs and have the support of their peers make calculated decisions to commit crimes against women.

Interrelationships between micro-oriented and macro-oriented theories

Obviously, there is a great deal of overlap between micro- and macro-level theories. Human beings are social animals, and, unless we are brought up on a desert island or in a cave, everything about us – what we know, how we think, what we believe, how we interact with other people – is influenced by our being part of a larger society. If a man grows up surrounded by rape-prone cultural influences, it is logical that he would be more likely to engage in sexual aggression than if he had not grown up with these influences. If a person is raised in a culture that does not support sexual violence but he happens to have inherited traits associated with sexual aggression, such as difficulties with anger management or poor impulse control, he may still be more prone to commit rape than a person who does not share these traits.

The **Biosocial Theory of Sexual Victimization** reflects the interrelationships between macro- and micro-oriented theory and stems from the disciplines of biology and anthropology. This theory focuses on why human females and males have evolved different physiological and psychological attributes, a process called **sexual selection** (Wrangham and Peterson 1996). The premise of this approach is that all living beings instinctually try to extend their genetic existence on the planet by passing their genes to the next generation. For the male of many species, this instinct is associated with the value of expressing aggression against and dominance over other males to "impress" the females and succeed in mating with them. Females in many species are the more selective maters. For them, the stakes are higher in selecting the ideal mate because females incur a greater cost in the process; they assume significantly more responsibility for carrying, bearing, and nurturing infants than males. Also, in many species females have fewer opportunities to pass their genes forward. This is especially true of human females, who only ovulate once per month during the limited number of years in which they are fertile. Because it is in the reproductive interests of males to spread their sperm widely, theorists argue that human males are less discerning about their sexual partners. Furthermore, in cases of males who experience difficulties finding willing partners, they argue that these males would be motivated to use their larger body size and aggressive instincts to force sex on unwilling women (Bonnycastle 2012). Evolutionary biologists have even claimed that patriarchy itself, argued by feminist scholars to be a cultural invention, is actually evolutionary in nature (Wrangham and Peterson 1996).

Regardless of whether one takes a micro-oriented, feminist, or evolutionary biology perspective on rape, there is a central truth about the commission of rape: rape is a crime in which (mostly) males exert power over (mostly) females by imposing their sexuality on unwilling partners. The existence of this act as a crime does not change regardless of whether one sees sexual assault as linked to humans' cultural fabric or our biological heritage. For those who are involved in helping victims of rape obtain the justice they seek or engage in the healing process, theories of why men rape are less important than understanding the impact of this crime on the victim. It is to this matter that we now turn.

The social context of rape

While there has been increased sensitivity in recent years to issues of sexual violence against women and children, rape is still a "hotly contested issue" in American society (Ullman 2010). Feminist theorists argue that, despite making ground and increasing public awareness about sexual assault, women exist within a **"rape culture"** (Buchwald, Fletcher, and Roth 1993) which leads rape victims to be treated differently from victims of other crimes. Scholars have characterized this culture as supporting **rape myths**, or false beliefs about rape. These myths are used to deny and justify male sexual aggression against women. Persons who subscribe to rape myths would agree that women are partially to blame for being sexually assaulted if they wear skimpy clothing, drink too much, or are not clear about whether they are willing to have sex or not. They would also suspect that women would lie about rape and that rape, when it happens, is not such a "big deal." Even if they have never heard the term "rape myth acceptance" or "rape culture," most victims are quite aware of the larger social climate regarding rape. These larger social influences significantly affect the responses of many victims to their victimization. In large part because the crime of rape **stigmatizes** victims in ways that other crimes do not, victims may have difficulty making sense as to what has happened to them and may be deterred from reporting the crime to the authorities.

Some victims experience confusion about the victimization itself; they may be reluctant to define what happened to them as a crime, as rape. This would be unlikely if the assault was committed by a stranger, as was the case with the New Delhi victim; but consider the other two case studies which represent the vast majority of rape victims who know their assailants. If a person is too intoxicated to consent, or if a person has been intimately involved with the assailant prior to being forced to have sex against her will, she might not immediately jump to the conclusion that she was criminally assaulted. For instance, one alleged rape victim of Bill Cosby reported that she knew she had been touched in some way by Cosby but she was unsure exactly what had occurred and since Cosby told her that he had been drunk, she was very unclear about what had actually occurred (Leopold and Brumfield 2014). Mary Koss described this as the **"hidden rape victim,"** referring to circumstances of victimization that would meet the legal definition for rape but where victims would respond "no" to questions about whether they had been raped (Koss 1987). The numbers

TEXT BOX: Common rape myths from the Illinois Rape Myth Acceptance Scale

Updated Illinois Rape Myth Acceptance Scale (IRMA)

	Strongly agree				Strongly disagree
	1	2	3	4	5
Subscale 1: She asked for it					
1. If a girl is raped while she is drunk, she is at least somewhat responsible for letting things get out of hand.					
2. When girls go to parties wearing slutty clothes, they are asking for trouble.					
3. If a girl goes to a room alone with a guy at a party, it is her own fault if she is raped.					
4. If a girl acts like a slut, eventually she is going to get into trouble.					
5. When girls get raped, it's often because the way they said "no" was unclear.					
6. If a girl initiates kissing or hooking up, she should not be surprised if a guy assumes she wants to have sex.					
Subscale 2: He didn't mean to					
7. When guys rape, it is usually because of their strong desire for sex.					
8. Guys don't usually intend to force sex on a girl, but sometimes they get too sexually carried away.					
9. Rape happens when a guy's sex drive goes out of control.					
10. If a guy is drunk, he might rape someone unintentionally.					
11. It shouldn't be considered rape if a guy is drunk and didn't realize what he was doing.					
12. If both people are drunk, it can't be rape.					
Subscale 3: It wasn't really rape					
13. If a girl doesn't physically resist sex—even if protesting verbally—it can't be considered rape.					
14. If a girl doesn't physically fight back, you can't really say it was rape.					
15. A rape probably doesn't happen if a girl doesn't have any bruises or marks.					
16. If the accused "rapist" doesn't have a weapon, you really can't call it rape.					
17. If a girl doesn't say "no" she can't claim rape.					
Subscale 4: She lied					
18. A lot of times, girls who say they were raped agreed to have sex and then regret it.					
19. Rape accusations are often used as a way of getting back at guys.					
20. A lot of times, girls who say they were raped often led the guy on and then had regrets.					
21. A lot of times, girls who claim they were raped have emotional problems.					
22. Girls who are caught cheating on their boyfriends sometimes claim it was rape.					

- Scoring: Scores range from 1 (strongly agree) to 5 (strongly disagree).
- Scores may be totaled for a cumulative score.
- Higher scores indicate greater rejection of rape myths.

Source: Payne, Lonsway, and Fitzgerald (1999); McMahon and Farmer (2011).

of victims who fail to self-label are quite high. Recent estimates are that anywhere from one half to two-thirds of women do not self-label as rape victims (Littleton, Rhatigan, and Axsom 2007).

Even if victims define what happened to them as rape, they may be unwilling to disclose their victimization to family and friends. Most people in our society consider sexuality a very private issue that they rarely talk about, even to people they know well. People are uncomfortable talking about sex in general, so victims of rape often have difficulty talking about matters dealing with sexuality and violation (Ullman 2010). Victims also fear reprisals or lack of support from family and friends. They may think that they will not be believed or that family members or friends will blame them for their victimization. These fears are linked to the social context for rape and the fact that rape myths still predominate in our culture. Victims worry that they could have done more to avoid the assault or that their actions – drinking too much, wearing suggestive clothing, and so on – would be viewed by others as making them responsible for the rape. Finally, victims worry, for good reason, about how reporting their victimization will be responded to by the authorities whose duty it is to uphold the law and enact justice. Recent research has shown that officials in the criminal justice and health systems responsible for dealing with victims often manifest resistance, skepticism, or rudeness (Martin 2005). Aware of these dynamics, victims may be quite reluctant to report to authorities and thereby subject themselves to this **"second assault"** (Williams and Holmes 1981). In one study over 90% of victims who did not report said that the police would not believe them (Kilmartin and Allison 2007). Perhaps they do not want to go through a trial or testify in court. The case of a 26-year-old victim of rape in 1992 in Texas may exemplify the fear that victims may have during the court process – particularly when the assailant is making outlandish claims and the public may not believe her. In the early 1990s, there was much AIDS awareness and education about the transmission of the HIV virus. One evening, the perpetrator of the sexual assault, Joel Rene Valdez, entered the victim's bedroom and held her at knifepoint (da Luz and Weckerly 1993). While the victim was held at knifepoint, she pleaded with Valdez to put on a condom as she was fearful of contracting AIDS. He did not have one, so she provided him with one. In **grand jury** testimony, Valdez argued that the sex was consensual since, after all, she provided him with condoms and asked him to wear one. The grand jury refused to **indict**, or issue a formal charge against, Valdez for the rape (da Luz and Weckerly 1993). When this occurred, the case garnered national attention. A second grand jury was convened and the second grand jury indicted Valdez. Valdez was subsequently convicted of the sexual assault (da Luz and Weckerly 1993). One can only imagine the turmoil that the victim went through with the various court proceedings.

Types of sexual victimization

As important as it is to present overall trends, it is also valuable to take a qualitative approach to understanding sexual assault. There are widely different circumstances under which rape can be perpetrated, with the classic "stranger rape" being the least common. Acquaintance rape is one of the most widely discussed types of rape, frequently occurring on college campuses.

Rape on college campuses

College campuses contain many risk factors for sexual victimization – a concentration of teenagers and young adults, unsupervised parties, abundance of alcohol and other drugs, students away from home for the first time, norms that allow for sexual contact without commitment, and so on. There are also campus organizations that appear to be linked to sexual assault, such as fraternities and sports teams (Pappas 2012; Sanday 1990). While researchers differ as to whether sexual assault rates are higher among college students (Fisher et al. 2010) or their non-college peers (Sinozich and Langton 2014), the scope of the problem is substantial. Between 20% and 25% of college women and 4% of college men have reported being sexually assaulted during their college years (Fisher et al. 2010).

The vast majority of perpetrators of campus sexual assaults, 80%, are known to the victim and commit their assaults while the victim is pursuing leisure activities away from home (Sinozich and Langton 2014). Campus rape victims often experience conflict in the aftermath of the assault. They may be conflicted about their part in what happened and whether to report the rape to the authorities. Most campus rape victims – 80% – do not report their assault to the authorities because they believe it is a "personal matter" or because they fear reprisal from the perpetrator. Most victims find themselves dealing with the trauma of the assault without the support of professionals trained to assist trauma victims. One study found that fewer than one in five campus victims received assistance from victim service agencies (Sinozich and Langton 2014).

Victims of campus sexual assault experience the same consequences that affect most rape victims, but there are certain circumstances unique to rape on college campuses that lead to special outcomes. Students are in college to obtain an education. The emotional stresses that accompany victimization may interfere with victims' ability to appear or concentrate in class and may reduce their ability to manage a regular course load, resulting in poorer academic performance. In many cases, victims fear encountering the perpetrator who is still on campus either because the victim did not report the assault or because the university did not take action to remove the perpetrator. Ultimately, it is not uncommon for victims to drop courses, transfer, or leave school altogether (Fisher et al. 2010).

Some victims who do report their victimization are also dissatisfied with the treatment they receive from campus authorities. Essentially there are two separate justice systems to handle campus rape cases. University campuses execute **administrative disciplinary procedures** that seek to determine whether conduct codes were violated, while the police and courts execute legally mandated investigative and prosecutorial procedures in an attempt to determine whether the perpetrator has committed a crime. Some scholars contend that university officials are "reluctant to refer incidents to the criminal justice system, and thereby yield control of the proceedings, opening them to public as well as media scrutiny" (American Association of University Professors 2012). Therefore, colleges may not refer cases to local law enforcement but rather attempt to apply campus disciplinary systems. Critics argue that these systems are not designed to handle conduct of the level of severity of sexual assault. Consequently, penalties for being found responsible for campus code violations may range widely, from simple relocation to another part of campus to suspension or expulsion. In many cases, these consequences are viewed by victims as far too lax for the severity of the perpetrator's behavior (Gonzales, Schofield, and Schmitt 2005).

This picture of lonely, traumatized college women who suffer in silence and who fear entering classrooms or dining halls is being upended by the power of a recent national movement. In recent years, sexual assault victims, families, and allies have advocated strongly for changes in the ways that colleges and universities deal with sexual assault. Across the nation, victims in far larger numbers than previously have gained the strength to publicly speak out about their assaults and have acted to hold colleges and universities accountable for their victimization. More campus women are reporting rapes than ever before (see National Public Radio 2010, Exhibit 3). These developments have influenced the ways that universities deal with publicizing campus crime, adjudicate cases of alleged crime on campus, and develop programs to prevent future crime.

This movement has gained the attention of the highest levels of the **federal government**. Changes to law regarding campus safety actually began in 1990 as a result of a gruesome murder of a coed on the Lehigh University campus. In 1986, Jeanne Clery, a 19-year-old freshman at Lehigh University, was raped and murdered in her campus residence hall by a stranger and visitor to campus who had gained access to Clery's room through an external door that had been propped open. In response, Congress passed a law to address campus crime that was then amended in 1992, 1998, and 2008. Together, these regulations are known as the Jeanne Clery Disclosure of Campus Security Policy and Campus Crime Statistics Act, or the **Clery Act** (National Public Radio 2010). The law requires that colleges and universities file annual reports with the federal government on campus crime, make this information available to prospective students, and develop prevention programs.

Another important federal law supporting anti-rape efforts is **Title IX** of the Education Amendments of 1972, which states that no person shall, "on the basis of sex, be excluded from participation in, be denied the benefits of, or be subjected to discrimination" in an educational program supported by the federal government (Pérez-Peña and Taylor 2014). Title IX, initially used to promote gender equity in college sports, has become the cornerstone in multiple efforts to hold universities accountable for campus rape prevention.

Title IX was invoked in the 2011 "Dear Colleague" letter, sent by the Education Department's Office for Civil Rights to every college and university in the nation. The letter emphasized that to be compliant with Title IX, universities and colleges are responsible for an effective response, when notified of sexual violence, and proactive efforts such as sexual assault prevention programs to reduce the incidence of sexual violence (Pérez-Peña and Taylor 2014).

Another important law was signed by President Obama in March 2013 – the Campus Sexual Violence Elimination (SaVE) Act. This Act, which was passed as part of the reauthorization of the Violence Against Women Act (VAWA), requires that all colleges and universities that accept federal student aid must take specific steps to reduce sexual violence and improve their handling of cases that do occur. They are expected to improve transparency about incidents of sexual violence, provide enhanced rights to victims, comply with federally mandated disciplinary procedures, and develop and implement campus-wide prevention education programs (Clery Center for Security on Campus 2015).

Legislators have focused not only on proceedings for adjudicating rape cases but also on changing standards of what would be considered "consent" to sexual activity. Not long ago the State of California passed a bill known as the "Yes Means Yes" law, requiring universities to set what is known as an "affirmative consent standard." To quote the bill,

> It is the responsibility of each person involved in the sexual activity to ensure that he or she has the affirmative consent of the other or others to engage in the sexual activity. Lack of protest or resistance does not mean consent, nor does silence mean consent. Affirmative consent must be ongoing throughout a sexual activity and can be revoked at any time. The existence of a dating relationship between the persons involved, or the fact of past sexual relations between them, should never by itself be assumed to be an indicator of consent. (State of California Legislature 2014)

Other states, such as New York (Fitzgerald 2015), have also expressed interest in adopting this standard.

So what has been the upshot of all of these legislative and policy changes? One indicator is the significant jump in the number of Title IX complaints filed against universities for inadequate handling of campus sexual assault. Universities from ivy leagues such as Harvard and Princeton to large state universities like Ohio State and Florida State are under federal investigation for their mishandling of sexual assault cases (Perez-Pena and Taylor 2014). In addition to the Office of Civil Rights, the Obama administration has expressed concern, stipulating that universities may not use the stricter "clear and convincing" rule in determining perpetrator responsibility but instead should use the "preponderance of the evidence" standard in deciding whether to hold an accused student responsible (Calmes 2014; Pérez-Peña and Taylor 2014).

There are other categories of sexual assault that have received considerable attention in recent years, including **marital rape**, **rape of children**, **rape in the military** and of citizens during wartime, and **rape among vulnerable populations**. These will be briefly discussed.

Marital rape

Until 1993 in the United States, a man could not be held legally culpable for raping his wife in many states (Bergen and Barnhill 2006; Estrich 1987), and in many countries around the globe this immunity provision still stands (Frank, Hardinge, and Wosick-Correa 2009). In many parts of the world, women are sexually violated by their husbands on a regular basis, and in most cases the perpetrator commits the crime with little fear of prosecution. Recently, in India, a court has ruled "that sex between a husband and wife, 'even if forcible, is not rape'" (Vyawahare 2014b). Marital rape is defined as "any unwanted intercourse or penetration (vaginal, anal, or oral) obtained by force, threat of force, or when the wife is unable to consent" (Bergen and Barnhill 2006, 1). By definition, the term "marital rape" excludes gay and lesbian couples. Research on lesbian partner sexual violence is scant; however, the little research that has emerged has revealed that lesbians also experience such violence in their relationships (see Girshik 2002). Marital rape survivors come from all social classes and races/ethnicities. Russell (1990), who conducted face-to-face interviews with approximately 900 women in San Francisco, found that African-American women experienced a higher rate of marital rape than Caucasian, Hispanic-American, and Asian-American women.

Studies of battered women have revealed that anywhere from 20% to 70% have reported sexual violence by their partner (Bergen and Barnhill 2006). While battered women often experience sexual violence along with physical violence, researchers caution that marital rape should not be lumped into the category of intimate partner violence, but rather it should be viewed as its own distinctive form of violence (Bergen and Barnhill 2006). That is, marital rape survivors may not be victims of domestic violence. Marital rape survivors may experience long-lasting physical injuries to their vaginal and anal areas of their bodies and also experience psychological consequences such as depression, fear, suicide ideation, and anxiety (Bergen and Barnhill 2006).

Rape of children

Statutory rape is sexual contact between an adult and another person, or a minor, who is below a required legal age to consent to the sexual contact. States set the legal age of consent so there are some differences in definitions across jurisdictions; however, the typical age of consent is 18 years of age. The 2012 criminal conviction of Penn State's former assistant football coach Jerry Sandusky for the rape and abuse of 10 young boys in the 1990s brought much attention to this form of sexual assault that is especially damaging to victims (Drape 2012). Sandusky was involved in college athletics and founded an organization for underprivileged boys. His actions reflected a pattern replicated by thousands of sexual predators who target vulnerable children in settings where they can establish close personal relationships to "groom" their victims for subsequent sexual contact. Other institutions that have been touched with similar scandals include the Boy Scouts and the Catholic Church.

As was the case with the Sandusky victims, generally male victims of sexual assault are targeted as children. Studies of adult male sexual assault victims have found that the vast majority – upwards of 90% – had been victimized before the age of 18 (Masho and Anderson 2009; McDonald and Tijerino 2013). Moreover, the scope of the problem for men is significant when one considers lifetime prevalence of victimization – Masho and Anderson estimate that more than 1 in 10 males are sexual assault survivors.

The trauma of childhood rape is exacerbated by the fact that childhood sexual abuse is virtually always perpetrated by individuals known to the victims and often in situations where both the children and family members view the adult as trustworthy. Childhood rape by persons familiar to the victim account for a relatively high percentage of the rapes reported by females, with the large majority of perpetrators being male (Douglas and Finkelhor 2005; Saunders et al. 1999). It is difficult to ascertain the exact number of children that are sexually victimized each year; however, various studies have found that girls are more vulnerable to this victimization than boys, with the range of victimization reports indicating that it is between 78% and 89% (Douglas and Finkelhor 2005). Both male and female victims of childhood sexual abuse experience long-term physical and psychological difficulties, including depression and post-traumatic stress disorder (Irish, Kobayashi, and Delahanty 2010; Paolucci, Genius, and Violato 2001).

Rape in the military

The military is another context in which sexual assault flourishes. Reports of sexual victimization have arisen not only in the armed forces but at the very institutions, such as the Air Force Academy and the Citadel, where women are training for careers in the military (Smith 2006; Thomas-Tucson 2003). It is estimated that one in three women in the military has been sexually assaulted, about twice the rate among civilian women. As many as 19,000 service members are assaulted each year, with women being more at risk of victimization than men (Risen 2012). In a highly hierarchical environment that still reflects a strongly masculine ethos, military women experience sexism, harassment, and demeaning behavior from their male colleagues, sometimes extending to sexual violence (Steinhauer 2013b). Those who complain about their victimization are often penalized, ridiculed, and harassed by superiors for coming forward. Thus, many victims may choose not to report their victimization or may be fearful to report their victimization – especially if the perpetrator is their superior. In a survey of 558 women military veterans, Sadler and colleagues (2003) found that only 28% of their sample who were rape victims formally reported their rape and about one-third of their sample did not know how to report their victimization formally. Frequently it is the victims who are penalized, ostracized, and prompted to terminate their military careers while their assailants remain.

Rape of members of vulnerable populations

Unfortunately, rape often occurs to vulnerable women in our society including street prostitutes, incarcerated women, elderly women, and poor immigrant women. Women involved in sex work become rape victims through a number of avenues. For street prostitutes who work under pimps, the pimps frequently use sexual violence and the threat of violence to prepare young women to enter sex work and then, later, to maintain control over them (Barry 1979; Sanders 2001). Also, prostitutes, whether in the United States or the United Kingdom, are vulnerable to violent rape from customers who feel that they can commit crime with impunity because prostitutes would not report victimization to the authorities (Burgess 1985; Church et al. 2001; Penfold et al. 2004). Prison inmates have been historically vulnerable to rape. In the case of women's prisons, perpetrators tend to be prison guards (Singer 2013). Whether the sexual assaults occur in a men's or women's prison, the consequences of disclosing the assaults can be retaliation and further victimization. Elderly women are also sometimes victims of sexual assault, and these attacks are often brutal (Pollock 1988). Del Bove, Stermac, and Bainbridge (2005) examined younger (15–30 years old) and older (55 years old and older) victims of sexual assault and found that older victims of sexual assault were more likely to be assaulted in their own home but that the injuries (e.g., physical trauma) that older victims received were similar to the injuries that younger victims experienced – although many older victims needed ambulance assistance. It is difficult to ascertain the exact number of elderly victims of sexual assault. Memory decay or dementia may contribute to the lack of ability of the victims to identify themselves as victims or perhaps to report the incident (Burgess 2006).

Millions of vulnerable and often poor immigrant girls and women across the globe are finding themselves thrust into the **sex trafficking** (forced prostitution) industry – a multi-billion-dollar industry (Balos 2004; Walker-Rodriguez and Hill 2011). Although victims of sex trafficking can be any age, gender, race, or ethnicity, they are often those who are most vulnerable and disadvantaged, such as the homeless, runaways, those with employment difficulties or limited education, or those with a history of prior sexual abuse, are the characteristics of girls and women that wind up in the horrific trade (Clawson et al. 2009). Lured by a promise of legitimate employment within their country or elsewhere, they may find themselves held hostage and forced to work in the sex industry (Watts and Zimmerman 2002). One female sex-trafficked worker in Turkey explained, "I came to Turkey to work in a good job; however, I was sold to a human trafficker who forced me to work as prostitute for one month. Then she set me free and bought my plane ticket to go back to my country. However, I did not go back" (Demir and Finckenauer 2010, 81). This victim returned to the sex trade in Turkey to support herself and her child. Other sex-trafficked workers have reported consenting, or choosing, to be part of the trade. One Ukranian sex-trafficked worker described her decision to work in the sex industry in Turkey:

> I used to work as a masseuse in my country. I heard from my friends several times that one could make a lot of money in sex work in Turkey. I heard about a woman pimp who was famous among women as a good person, had a wide network, and paid good money to the women working with her. Women working with her never had problems in money and living conditions. So, I decided to go to Turkey to find that woman. (Demir and Finckenauer 2010, 73)

For this sex worker, the decision to consent to the work was due to economic reasons; thus, it begs the question of how much choice she really had when she made her decision. For other women in the sex trade, such as in Cambodia, they neither are lured nor consent to the work, but rather they are brought into the sex-trafficking industry, and even managed, by family (McCauley, Decker, and Silverman 2010). Sex-trafficked victims are often unable to leave or escape due to the coercion (i.e., physical, mental, and sexual) used by their captors, surveillance by their captors, the absence of money or passports to flee, and fear (Bernat and Zhilina 2010). In addition to the sexual assault they experience with each unwanted and unsolicited sexual encounter with a customer, many sex-trafficking victims are physically beaten or raped by their pimps if they refuse to engage in sexual acts with customers (Balos 2004). Most likely, the "consenting" Ukrainian sex-trafficked worker mentioned earlier was victimized as she further immersed herself in the industry.

Technology has greatly assisted the perpetrators in operating their sex trade. The Internet has served as a tool for perpetrators to lure victims to travel to some destination for employment or to meet someone who will "help them" via chat rooms, or the perpetrators may "friend" a possible victim on Facebook and build a false friendship (Vanderschaaf 2013). Additionally, the Internet has facilitated the trading of victims through various websites or the posting of the "services" of victims on such sites as backpage.com (Vanderschaaf 2013). One researcher discusses how the internet allows both the pimp and the customer to remain anonymous:

> It makes it harder for police to track pimps and johns. It makes it harder for caregivers to establish when a pimp is targeting a young girl. There even exist ways in which a john can pay a pimp that guarantees him anonymity, through vehicles such as bitcoins, a virtual currency, which makes it nearly impossible for law enforcement officials to trace, and subsequently prove that an individual is either paying for or receiving income from human trafficking. (Vanderschaaf 2013, 136)

Thus, the Internet, while not used by all in the sex-trafficking industry, has certainly contributed to the increased sexual exploitation of girls and women across the world. Besides greater international awareness of sex-trafficking victims, there have also been attempts to combat the problem at the legislative level. In the United States, the **Trafficking Victims Protection Act** was passed in 2000 in an effort to combat the human-trafficking problem (Goździak and Bump 2008). The act has been reauthorized several times since its initial passing. Additionally, the United Nations has passed several acts over the past 60 years to address trafficking, with the most recent protocol, in 2003, called the **Protocol to Prevent, Suppress and Punish Trafficking in Persons, especially Women and Children** which seeks punishment for perpetrators and protection for victims (Balos 2004).

 GLOBAL PERSPECTIVES: Rape in wartime

Accounts of rape of women in wartime extend back literally thousands of years and unfortunately rape continues to be an instrument of warfare in contemporary times. While rape has been explicitly prohibited in such documents as the Geneva Convention of 1949, there are countless examples of rape being used in recent conflicts. For example, in 2014 Human Rights Watch issued *Here, Rape Is Normal: A Five-Point Plan to Curtail Sexual Violence in Somalia*. Two decades of civil conflict had created a large population of displaced persons and had destroyed state institutions normally responsible for protecting vulnerable citizens. The upshot has been that armed assailants commit "sexual assault, beat and stab women and girls inside camps and as they walk to market, tend to their fields, or forage for firewood" (Human Rights Watch 2014, 1).

In 2013, Dara Kay Cohen published an article on the extent of sexual violence during 86 major civil wars between 1980 and 2009 (Cohen 2013). Some of her most significant findings include the following:

- There were wide discrepancies in the extent and severity of rape in wartime, with some 53 conflicts reporting "widespread" or "numerous" rapes while in 15 wars there were no reports of rape.
- The worst sexual assaults were found in Bosnia Herzegovina, Burundi, Democratic Republic of the Congo, Georgia, India (Kashmir and the Northeast), Indonesia/East Timor, Iraq (Kurds), Liberia (NPFL), Rwanda, Sierra Leone, Somalia, Sudan, Tajikistan, Uganda, and Yugoslavia.
- Fighting groups – both state and insurgent – that are recruited through abduction have the lowest levels of internal social cohesion and are more likely to commit widespread rape than when fighters are recruited through voluntary methods.
- There was little evidence that rape was used as a "weapon of war" but instead is used to bond recruits together.

Rape asserts the power of the assailant and underscores the weakness of both the women who endure it and their countrymen who are powerless to prevent it. Other scholars argue that wartime rape is a form of genocide (Roth and Rittner 2012). In addition to the subjection to repeated assaults, victims of wartime rape who survive must deal with the consequences of having been raped by the enemy. Many become pregnant, contract sexually transmitted diseases, experience psychological trauma, and experience rejection by their families and communities (Branche and Virgili 2012).

The impact of rape on victims

In contrast to the rape myths outlined above, the reality of rape is devastating to victims. After homicide, rape is the ultimate violation, an invasion of the most private portion of a victim's body. In addition to the emotional and psychological impacts of sexual assault, victims may experience physical trauma such as bruising, lacerations, and broken bones in the course of their victimization. The consequences include long-term negative outcomes such as post-traumatic stress disorder (PTSD), substance abuse, suicidal ideation (and suicide), chronic physical health problems, depression, self-harm, eating disorders, and personality disorders (Brown and Walklate 2012). The severity of emotional and psychological consequences of rape is reflected in the number of memoirs written by rape victims about what happened to them. These accounts can be painful to read, but they provide a close-up perspective on the many ways that rape can disrupt and destabilize a victim's life (Francisco 1999).

TEXT BOX: "Remember My Name": A poem written by a rape victim

When you remember my walk upon this earth
Look not into my steps with pity.
When you taste the tears of my journey
Notice how they fill my foot prints
Not my spirit
For that remains with me.

My story must be told
Must remain in conscious memory
So my daughters won't cry my tears
Or follow my tortured legacy.
Lovin'
is a tricky thing
If it doesn't come
from a healthy place,
If Lovin'
Doesn't FIRST practice on self
it will act like a stray bullet
not caring what it hits

You may say:
Maybe I should've loved him a little less
Maybe I should've loved me a little more,
Maybe I should've not believed he'd never hit me again.
All those maybes will not bring me back – not right his wrong.
My life was not his to take.

As your eyes glance my name
Understand once I breathed
Walked
Loved
just like you.
I wish for all who glance my name
To know love turned fear – kept me there
Loved twisted to fear,
Kept me in a chokehold
Cut off my air
Blurred my vision
I couldn't see how to break free.

(continued)

I shoulda, told my family
I shoulda told my friends
I shoulda got that CPO
Before the police let him go
But all those shoulda's can't bring me back
when I lied so well
To cover the shame
To hide the signs.
If my death had to show
what love isn't
If my death had to show
that love shouldn't hurt
If my death had to make sure
another woman told a friend
instead of holding it in
If my death reminds you
how beautiful
how worthy
you really are
If my death reminds you
to honor all you are
daily
Then remember my name
Shout it
from the center of your soul
Wake me
in my grave
Let ME know
My LIVING was not in vain.

Source: Copyright Kimberly A. Collins, 1995.

Being the victim of rape shakes a victim to her very foundation. For many victims, their first reaction is "this cannot be happening to me." This reaction reflects a sense, some would say an illusion, of invincibility and invulnerability that in many ways is quite functional for getting through life. Feeling invulnerable allow us to trust other people, to take risks, to go to strange places, and to try new things. These actions are generally thought to enhance a person's quality of life and to make life more interesting and exciting. But for victims of rape and other violent crimes, their trauma disabuses them of their belief in their personal safety. Psychologically and emotionally they move from a position of safety to feeling like the world is a dangerous place. Specifically they fear a repeat rape; becoming a victim makes it easier to envision that one could become a victim again (Allison and Wrightsman 1993).

For most victims, the aftermath of rape brings extensive adverse cognitive, affective, behavioral, and physiological effects. Some show severe symptoms while for others the symptoms may not appear as severe, but all rape victims suffer. The combination of symptoms has commonly been called the **"rape trauma syndrome"** (Burgess 1985; 1988; 1991), a form of post-traumatic stress disorder (PTSD) (Ford 2009). Rape trauma syndrome is generally described as unfolding in two phases. Phase I, occurring immediately after the rape and lasting for a few hours to a few weeks, is often called the **acute crisis phase**. During this phase, victims experience an initial period of intense disruption in all areas of functioning; they are emotionally agitated and report feeling afraid, worried, terrified, and confused. Victims also report physical symptoms such as racing hearts, shaking or trembling, physical pain, tense muscles, rapid breathing, and numbness. Many victims have difficulty eating or sleeping and have trouble concentrating. Victims may also experience guilt or self-blame. Phase II, the **reorganization or recoil phase**, can last for months or even years. Victims must face the challenge of putting their lives back together, reinstituting a sense of comfort in their worlds, and come to terms with the emotions associated with what happened to them – sadness, grief, and anger. They may blame themselves. Many rape victims focus on the circumstances of their rape, playing over and over in their minds, "if I had not walked outside alone" or "if I had stopped drinking earlier" or "if I had not left the window open" (Janoff-Bulman 1985).

While victims work to restore their lives, they may also be experiencing longer-term impacts of the rape that are difficult to overcome. They may develop **phobias** – intense fears of objects or settings that they associate with the rape, such as a weapon or the location where the rape occurred. They may also develop more general fears and distrust of men or of being alone or going out at night. These fears can have serious adverse impacts on victims' lives and may result in some self-medicating by abusing alcohol or drugs or developing eating disorders. Some victims are compelled to move to another location; others change jobs or drop out of school. Recall that this is what happened to the victim of the Air Force sergeant – she left the military soon after the rape and moved thousands of miles across the country. Rape victimization can also take its toll on relationships. For some victims, withdrawal from the outside world is a coping strategy that shuts out good friends and family. Another problem is the response of friends and family to knowing that their loved one has been sexually violated. If the perpetrator is a family member or friend, persons close to the victim may be forced to choose sides and may side against the victim. In other cases, family and friends will unintentionally subscribe to rape myths themselves and blame the victim. Husbands or boyfriends may become angry or distant because the assault was sexual in nature. Even when responses of loved ones are supportive, over time friends and family may become impatient that the victim cannot just "get on with her life."

But healing does not always work that way. Victims heal at different rates and healing is not a simple, linear process. After one to three months most victims begin to see some improvement in their symptoms, although most victims are still experiencing some symptoms a year after the rape. Most victims cycle through better and worse periods, and symptoms that had disappeared may reappear later. Over time, most rape victims regain their equilibrium and are able to fully engage in the joys of life again. Unfortunately, a minority of victims, about 25%, report that they have not fully recovered several years after the rape; and some researchers caution that many victims will never make a complete recovery (Figley 1985).

Treatment of rape victims

The health care system is a critical service provider in assisting victims in dealing with trauma. When victims do receive effective health care, their recovery is enhanced; while if they are treated insensitively their sense of fearfulness, shame, and powerlessness can be magnified. Like victims who have negative experiences with police or court officials, they can also experience a "second rape" through the responses of insensitive or skeptical health care providers (Campbell 2012).

Health care providers are often the first professionals to respond to rape victims. Challenged to offer appropriate care to physical injuries and attend to the victim's emotional state, health care providers also are cognizant that evidence must be preserved in the event of a criminal prosecution. A rape victim's body is a crime scene, and the protocol for collecting evidence involves an extremely invasive physical examination. One method involves the use of a **rape kit** which includes materials and instructions to help nurses and doctors handle physical evidence in the course of performing an examination. Victims are asked to provide consent before receiving the examination, and some decline because they feel the process is too intrusive at a time when they already feel vulnerable. For those who consent, the examination involves the collection of fluids, examinations of body cavities, collection of clothing worn at the time of the rape, and collection of a blood sample. Other considerations that will be brought to the victim's attention by medical professionals involve the prevention of pregnancy and venereal disease through the administration of drugs such as Plan B and antibiotics (Campbell 2012).

TEXT BOX: Contents of a rape kit

DNA Evidence from a crime like sexual assault can be collected from the crime scene, but it can also be collected from your body, clothes, and other personal belongings. You may choose to have a sexual assault forensic exam, sometimes known as a "rape kit," to preserve possible DNA evidence and receive important medical care. You don't have to report the crime to have an exam, but the process gives you the chance to safely store evidence should you decide to report at a later time.

To find a location near you that performs sexual assault forensic exams, call the National Sexual Assault Hotline at 800.656.HOPE (4673) or talk to your local sexual assault service provider.

What is a rape kit?

You may have heard the term "rape kit" to refer to a sexual assault forensic exam. The term rape kit actually refers to the kit itself – a container that includes a checklist, materials, and instructions, along with envelopes and containers to package any specimens collected during the exam. A rape kit may also be referred to as a Sexual Assault Evidence Kit (SAEK). The contents of the kit vary by state and jurisdiction and may include:

- Bags and paper sheets for evidence collection
- Comb
- Documentation forms
- Envelopes
- Instructions
- Materials for blood samples
- Swabs

Preparing for a sexual assault forensic exam

If you're able to following an assault, try to avoid activities that could potentially damage evidence such as:

- Bathing
- Showering

- Using the restroom
- Changing clothes
- Combing hair
- Cleaning up the area

It's natural to want to go through these motions after a traumatic experience. If you have done any of these activities, you can still have an exam performed. You may want to bring a spare change of clothes with you to the hospital or health facility where you're going to have the exam.

In most cases, DNA evidence needs to be collected within 72 hours in order to be analyzed by a crime lab – but a sexual assault forensic exam can reveal other forms of evidence beyond this time frame that can be useful if you decide to report. Place your belongings, including the clothes you were wearing, in a **paper bag** to safely preserve evidence. If you have questions about the timeframe, you can call the National Sexual Assault Hotline at 800.656.HOPE (4673) or talk to your local sexual assault service provider.

How long is the exam?

The length of the exam may take a few hours, but the actual time will vary based on several different factors. It may be helpful to have someone to support you during this time. If you call the National Sexual Assault Hotline (800.656.HOPE) or contact a local sexual assault service provider, you may be connected with an advocate who can talk to you about the examination and offer support. The advocate may also be able to accompany you during the actual exam. Be aware that if you invite someone other than an advocate into the exam room, they could be called as a witness if you decide to report the crime.

What happens during a sexual assault forensic exam?

The steps below outline the general process for the exam. Remember, **you can stop, pause, or skip a step** at any time during the exam. It is entirely your choice.

- **Immediate care.** If you have injuries that need immediate attention, those will be taken care of first.
- **History.** You will be asked about your current medications, pre-existing conditions, and other questions pertaining to your health history. Some of the questions, such as those about recent consensual sexual activity, may seem very personal, but these questions are designed to ensure that DNA and other evidence collected from the exam can be connected to the perpetrator. You will also be asked about the details of what has happened to you to help identify all potential areas of injury as well as places on your body or clothes where evidence may be located.
- **Head-to-toe examination.** This part of the exam may be based on your specific experience, which is why it is important to give an accurate history. It may include a full body examination, including internal examinations of the mouth, vagina, and/or anus. It may also include taking samples of blood, urine, swabs of body surface areas, and sometimes hair samples. The trained professional performing the exam may take pictures of your body to document injuries and the examination. With your permission, they may also collect items of clothing, including undergarments. Any other forms of physical evidence that are identified during the examination may be collected and packaged for analysis, such as a torn piece of the perpetrator's clothing, a stray hair, or debris.

(continued)

- **Possible mandatory reporting.** If you are a minor, the person performing the exam may be obligated to report it to law enforcement. You can learn more about mandatory reporting laws in your state through RAINN's State Law Database.
- **Follow up care.** You may be offered prevention treatment for STIs and other forms of medical care that require a follow up appointment with a medical professional. Depending on the circumstances and where you live, the exam site may schedule a follow up appointment, or you can ask about resources in your community that offer follow up care for survivors of sexual assault. Someone from the exam site may also be able to provide information or resources about reporting options.

Who can perform the exam?

Not every hospital or health facility has someone on staff that is specially trained to perform a sexual assault forensic exam and interact with recent survivors of sexual assault. When you call the National Sexual Assault Hotline at 800.656.HOPE (4673) you will be directed to a facility that is prepared to give you the care you need.

- **Sexual Assault Nurse Examiners (SANEs)** – registered nurses who receive specialized education and fulfill clinical requirements to perform the exam
- **Sexual Assault Forensic Examiners (SAFEs)** and **Sexual Assault Examiners (SAEs)** – other healthcare professionals who have been instructed and trained to complete the exam

Why should you consider having a sexual assault medical forensic exam?

- **It won't cost you.** You should not be charged for the exam. The Violence Against Women Act requires states to provide sexual assault forensic exams free of charge if they wish to remain eligible for critical anti-crime grant funding. If you are charged for the exam, immediately contact your local sexual assault service provider.
- **You can have time to decide if you want to report.** The decision to report the crime is entirely yours. It may take some time to decide what to do. Having a sexual assault forensic exam ensures that the forensic evidence will be safely preserved if you decide to report at a later time.
- **It increases the likelihood of prosecution.** The importance of DNA evidence in sexual assault cases cannot be overstated. Not only does DNA evidence carry weight in court, but it may prevent future sexual assaults from occurring. Even if the perpetrator is not prosecuted, their DNA may be added to the national database, making it easier to connect the perpetrator to a future crime.
- **Your health matters.** Sexual assault can impact your physical health. You may have injuries and trauma related to the assaults that aren't immediately visible. During an exam you may be able to access treatment for these injuries, receive preventative treatment for STIs, and obtain emergency contraception to prevent pregnancy.

How long will the evidence be stored?

The amount of time an evidence kit will be stored varies by state and jurisdiction. A SANE, advocate, or law enforcement officer should let you know how long the evidence will be stored and the state's rules for disposing the kit. It's important to note that the amount of time the kit is stored doesn't necessarily match up with the amount of time that legal action can be taken against a perpetrator, also known as the statute of limitation. If you have questions about timing, statutes of limitation, or any other concerns, contact your local sexual assault service provider.

Source: Reproduced by permission of RAINN, www.rainn.org

Figure 5.1 The contents of a rape kit used by sexual assault nurses at the St Elizabeth Regional Medical Center's emergency room, Lincoln, Nebraska, March 2005. *Source:* Dior Azcuy/Lincoln Journal Star.

In recent years there has been growing interest in training emergency room nurses to become **sexual assault nurse examiners (SANE)**. These individuals provide emotional support and compassionate medical care to victims while keeping in mind the legal requirements to retain the necessary chain of evidence. SANE programs have been found to have positive effects on survivors' emotional recovery and may actually improve the prosecution rates of sexual assault (Campbell and Wasco 2005). Complementing the work of health care providers has been the success of anti-rape activists in developing full-service centers to support victims and provide community education. **Rape crisis centers** offer a range of services to assist victims. For some victims dealing with a rape that has just occurred, calling a rape crisis center's 24-hour hotline will be the first time she/he discloses to anyone what has happened to her/him. Centers offer victims support regarding medical and legal systems, trained and knowledgeable advocates to accompany victims to medical and legal appointments or court appearances, and group counseling to assist victims with their emotional distress.

Many different types of treatment programs have been offered to victims, some done individually and some in groups. Various theoretical approaches have also been tried. The good news is that when therapy is delivered by trained and competent clinicians, 7 in 10 victims become symptom-free and their improvement continues long after the therapy has been completed. While all therapy can be helpful, studies have found that **individual therapy** is more effective than **group therapy**, using "homework" is beneficial, and more structured therapy sessions tend to be most successful (Taylor and Harvey 2009).

One of the problems in addressing victims' symptoms is that a large proportion of victims, perhaps even the majority, do not seek rape crisis or advocacy services even if these services are readily available (Campbell 2012). The result is that some victims suffer from the after-effects of sexual assault for many years before seeking treatment (Crowell and Burgess 1996). This situation is so unfortunate for women who could otherwise be helped significantly through treatment.

Preventing sexual violence

It goes without saying that improving the type of treatment rape victims receive is an essential goal for professionals involved in the health care and criminal justice systems. But simply focusing on victims after the fact will do little to reduce the likelihood that others will be victimized. Therefore, it is important to focus also on efforts to prevent rape. Prevention efforts can occur at three levels. **Tertiary prevention**, or relapse prevention, are efforts to prevent a problem behavior from recurring once it has taken place. An example of a tertiary program would be intensive therapy for convicted rapists in a prison context (Bonnycastle 2012). Through **secondary prevention**, professionals attempt to identify individuals or organizations at high risk for the problem and then develop strategies to reduce these risk factors. Examples of secondary prevention would include educational programming for men in fraternities, athletic teams, or in the military, focusing on issues of hypermasculinity and violence prevention. **Primary prevention** involves working to reduce the incidence of a problem within the entire population. In the case of rape which appears to be caused in part by gender inequalities and gender socialization that promotes male dominance, primary prevention would involve efforts to develop new values and ways of thinking that promote gender equality and mutual respect among men and women.

Over the past decades, individuals and groups have initiated creative and effective prevention efforts, especially at the primary and secondary levels. Women activists have partnered with concerned men in developing a wide range of programs to address sexual violence. Because college campuses have been found to be settings conducive to acquaintance rape, they have been a target for a range of programs, from one-time awareness workshops and theatrical performances to ongoing, multi-session discussion groups or curriculum-based prevention interventions. Effective and popular programs that developed for delivery on college campuses use one or more of the following elements: peer mentoring, encouraging bystander intervention, leadership of men in delivering program information, and use of theatre and role-playing (Kilmartin and Allison 2007). A promising rape prevention strategy that has yielded positive results focuses on the concept of **bystander intervention**. It approaches women and men as potential witnesses to sexual violence and teaches them to intervene safely and effectively before, during, and after incidents of sexual victimization (Banyard, Moynihan, and Plante 2007).

Conclusion

Sexual assault is a world-wide phenomenon that has adversely impacted on the lives of women for millennia. It leads to both physical and psychological trauma that can be felt by victims for months and years following the assault. For the vast majority of victims, societal attitudes and rape myths supporting victim blaming and denial have further added to their trauma and isolation. For those who do report their assault, rape laws and criminal justice and health care procedures have a history of creating additional trauma for victims, resulting in what has been called a "second rape."

For the past four decades the veil of silence about sexual assault has been gradually lifting around the world. Feminist activists in the United States and other Western nations first brought the issue to public attention during the 1970s with the publication of books and articles arguing for compassion, respect, and justice for victims of rape. In response to shockingly brutal sexual assaults in other parts of the world, nations that have traditionally done little to support sex assault victims are beginning to approach the problem with new resolve. Today, there is much more knowledge about the crime of rape, its causes and consequences; and law, policy, practice, and treatment protocols relating to sexual assault have advanced accordingly. Yet, despite the fact that the rape crisis movement has existed for almost a half century, the laws are fairer, our practices are more victim friendly, and our treatment strategies are more effective, the old scripts that blame victims and set up obstacles to their recovery are still being played out throughout the United States and the world (Dunn 2010; Martin 2005).

There is still much to do to create a culture that does not support rape and where victims who do contact the legal or health care systems are treated with compassion and respect. Collaborative, multi-system innovations and evidence-based intervention programs such as the bystander intervention model are changing community responses. Attention to rape and associated crimes at the highest levels of government will hopefully prompt aggressive treatment and prevention efforts. A half century since the start of the anti-rape movement, there is a glimmer of hope that these efforts will be successful in reducing the incidence of the crime of rape and assisting those whose lives are blighted by this crime.

Suggested readings

Clay-Warner, Jody, and Mary E. Odem, 1997. *Confronting Rape and Sexual Assault*. Lanham, MD: Rowman & Littlefield Publishers.
Corrigan, Rose. 2013. *Up Against a Wall: Rape Reform and the Failure of Success*. New York: New York University Press.
Henry, Nicola, and Anastasia Powell. 2014. *Preventing Sexual Violence: Interdisciplinary Approaches to Overcoming a Rape Culture*. Basingstoke: Palgrave Macmillan.
Maier, Shana L. 2014. *Rape, Victims, and Investigations: Experiences and Perceptions of Law Enforcement Officers Responding to Reported Rapes*. Abingdon: Routledge.
Paludi, Michele A., and Florence L. Denmark. 2010. *Victims of Sexual Assault and Abuse: Resources and Responses for Individuals and Families*. Santa Barbara, CA: Praeger.
Raphael, Jody. 2013. *Rape Is Rape: How Denial, Distortion, and Victim Blaming Are Fueling a Hidden Acquaintance Rape Crisis*. Chicago, IL: Chicago Review Press.

Student engagement activities

1 Imagine that your university has asked you to create a bystander intervention program to prevent campus rape. Locate a website that addresses issues of campus rape prevention. University of New Hampshire is a leader in this arena and would be a good place to start. Create a presentation to give to your class explaining what the bystander intervention model is and outlining the goals of your proposed program.
2 Create a fictional "biography" of a victim of sexual assault. Based upon what you have learned in class, describe the circumstances of the assault and what happened afterwards. Then rewrite the biography from the time prior to the assault and describe a scenario in which the assault was prevented.
3 Make a visit to an office on campus or an organization in your town that focuses on violence prevention. Ask to speak with a volunteer about the work of that office. Prepare a one-page briefing statement addressing the following questions:
   a. What is the mission of the office or organization?
   b. Describe the staffing and organizational structure.
   c. What services does this office or organization provide?
   d. Describe the population served by this office or organization.
   e. What is your impression of the effectiveness of this office or organization in meeting its goals?

Discussion questions

1 The three stories at the start of the chapter are examples of situations of sexual assault. Thinking about what you know from reading newspapers, or from your own life, or the lives of friends or family, create a story of another rape that could have happened.
2 Historically, the crime of rape is considered as serious by the law as the crime of murder. Compare the crime of rape to the crime of robbery. What are the similarities and differences? Discuss why rape is such a serious crime.
3 Why do you think rape is such an underreported crime?
4 Some people argue that rape is primarily a sex crime while others argue that it is primarily a crime of power and control over victims. Which side do you take? Why?
5 Some people argue that reporting rape can be a mixed blessing for a victim. What are the positives and negatives about reporting rape to the criminal justice authorities?
6 Why would a victim feel apprehensive about reporting assault? Why might male victims be especially unlikely to report rape victimization? How could our society be changed to make victims more willing to come forward?
7 Consider the various theories of rape. Which one seems to make the most sense to you? Can they all be "true"?
8 What is a rape culture? Do you think we live in one? What are your reasons?
9 If you know someone who has been raped, what could you do to help this person as a friend or family member? What things might not be helpful?

Key terms

Acquaintance rape
Acute crisis phase
Administrative disciplinary procedures
Alcohol
Biosocial Theory of Sexual Victimization
Bystander intervention
"Cautionary instruction"
Clery Act
Contemporary definition of rape
Corroboration requirement
Criminal sexual conduct
Evidentiary rules
Federal government
Feminist Theory of Rape and Sexual
    Victimization
Gender neutral
Grand jury
Group therapy
"Hidden rape victim"
Incidence of rape
Indict
Individual therapy

Intergenerational Transmission of Violence
    Theory
Macro-oriented theories
Male Peer Support Theory
Marital exemption
Marital rape
Micro-oriented theories
National Crime Victimization Survey
    (NCVS)
National Violence Against Women Survey
    (NVAWS)
Patriarchal
Phobias
Post-traumatic stress disorder (PTSD)
Prevalence of rape victimization
Protocol to Prevent, Suppress and Punish
    Trafficking in Persons, especially Women
    and Children (2003)
Psychopathological explanation
Rape among vulnerable populations
Rape crisis centers
"Rape culture"

Rape of children

Rape kit

Rape laws

Rape in the military

Rape myths

Rape shield laws

"Rape trauma syndrome"

Reorganization or recoil phase

"Second assault"

"Second rape"

Secondary prevention

Sex role socialization

Sex trafficking

Sexual assault nurse examiners (SANE)

Sexual objects in the mass media

Sexual selection

Statutory rape

Stigmatizes

Tertiary prevention

Title IX

Trafficking Victims Protection Act (2000)

"Utmost resistance"

References

Allison, Julie A., and Lawrence S. Wrightsman. 1993. *Rape, the Misunderstood Crime*. Newbury Park, CA: Sage Publications.

American Association of University Professors. 2012. "Campus Sexual Assault: Suggested Policies and Procedures." http://www.aaup.org/report/campus-sexual-assault-suggested-policies-and-procedures

Balos, Beverly. 2004. "The Wrong Way to Equality: Privileging Consent in the Trafficking of Women for Sexual Exploitation." *Harvard Women's Law Journal*, 27: 137–175.

Banyard, Victoria L., Moynihan, Mary M., and Elizabethe G. Plante. 2007. "Sexual Violence Prevention through Bystander Education: An Experimental Evaluation." *Journal of Community Psychology*, 35(4): 463–481. DOI: 10.1002/jcop.20159

Barry, Kathleen. 1979. *Female Sexual Slavery*. Englewood Cliffs, NJ: Prentice-Hall.

Bernat, Frances P., and Tatyana Zhilina. 2010. "Human Trafficking: The Local Becomes Global." *Women and Criminal Justice*, 20(1–2): 2–9. DOI: 10.1080/08974451003641289

BBC News India. 2013. "Explaining India's New Anti-Rape Laws." *BBC News*, March 27. http://www.bbc.co.uk/news/world-asia-india-21950197

Bergen, Raquel Kennedy, and Elizabeth Barnhill. 2006. "Marital Rape: New Research and Directions." National Online Resource Center on Violence Against Women. Accessed June 3, 2014, http://vawnet.org/assoc_files_vawnet/ar_maritalraperevised.pdf

Bevacqua, Maria. 2000. *Rape on the Public Agenda: Feminism and the Politics of Sexual Assault*. Boston, MA: Northeastern University Press.

Bonnycastle, Kevin Denys. 2012. *Stranger Rape: Rapists, Masculinity, and Penal Governance*. Toronto: University of Toronto Press.

Branche, Raphaëlle, and Fabrice Virgili. 2012. *Rape in Wartime*. Basingstoke, UK; New York, NY: Palgrave Macmillan.

Brown, Jennifer, and Sandra Walklate, eds. 2012. *Handbook on Sexual Violence*. London; New York: Routledge.

Brownmiller, Susan. 1975. *Against Our Will: Men, Women and Rape*. New York, NY: Simon & Schuster.

Bryden, David P. 2000. "Redefining Rape." *Buffalo Criminal Law Review*, 3(2): 317–479. DOI: 10.1525/nclr.2000.3.2.317

Buchwald, Emilie, Fletcher, Pamela R., and Martha Roth. 1993. *Transforming a Rape Culture*. Minneapolis, MN: Milkweed Editions.

Burgess, Ann Wolbert. 1985. *Rape and Sexual Assault: A Research Handbook*. New York, NY: Garland.

Burgess, Ann Wolbert. 1988. *Rape and Sexual Assault II*. New York, NY: Garland.

Burgess, Ann Wolbert. 1991. *Rape and Sexual Assault III: A Research Handbook*. New York, NY: Garland.

Burgess, Ann Wolbert. 2006. *Elderly Victims of Sexual Abuse and Their Offenders*. Washington, DC: US Department of Justice. Accessed June 5, 2014, https://www.ncjrs.gov/pdffiles1/nij/grants/216550.pdf

Calmes, Jackie. 2014. "Obama Seeks to Raise Awareness of Rape on Campus." *New York Times*. Accessed January 22, 2014, http://www.nytimes.com/2014/01/23/us/politics/obama-to-create-task-force-on-campus-sexualassaults.html

Campbell, Rebecca. 2012. "Changing Community Response to Rape: The Promise of Sexual Assault Nurse Examiner (SANE) Programmes." In *Handbook on Sexual Violence*, edited by Jennifer Brown and Sandra Walklate, 458–474. London; New York, NY: Routledge.

Campbell, Rebecca, and Sharon M. Wasco. 2005. "Understanding Rape and Sexual Assault: 20 Years of Progress and Future Directions." *Journal of Interpersonal Violence*, 20(1): 127–131. DOI: 10.1177/0886260504268604

Catalano, Shannan M. 2006. *The Measurement of Crime: Victim Reporting and Police Recording*. Criminal Justice. New York, NY: LFB Scholarly Publishing LLC.

Chamberlain, Diane. 2013. *Conduct Unbecoming: Rape, Torture, and Post Traumatic Stress Disorder from Military Commanders*. Victoria, BC: FriesenPress.

Church, Stephanie, Henderson, Marion, Barnard, Marina, and Graham Hart. 2001. "Violence By Clients Towards Female Prostitutes in Different Work Settings: Questionnaire Survey." *British Medical Journal*, 322: 524–525. DOI: http://dx.doi.org/10.1136/bmj.322.7285.524

Clawson, Heather J., Dutch, Nicole, Salomon, Amy, and Lisa G. Grace. 2009. *Human Trafficking Into and Within the United States: A Review of the Literature*. Washington, DC: US Department of Health and Human Services. Accessed June 5, 2014, http://aspe.hhs.gov/hsp/07/humantrafficking/litrev/

Clery Center for Security on Campus. 2015. *The Campus Sexual Violence Elimination (SaVE) Act*. Accessed April 17, 2015, http://clerycenter.org/campus-sexual-violence-elimination-save-act

Cohen, Dara Kay. 2013. "Explaining Rape during Civil War: Cross-National Evidence (1980 2009)." *American Political Science Review*, 107(03): 461–477. DOI: 10.1017/S0003055413000221

Conklin, John E. 2003. *Why Crime Rates Fell*. Boston, MA: Allyn & Bacon.

Crowell, Nancy A., and Ann Wolbert Burgess, eds. 1996. *Understanding Violence Against Women*. Washington, DC: National Academy Press.

da Luz, Carla M., and Pamela C. Weckerly. 1993. "The Texas 'Condom-Rape' Case: Caution Construed as Consent." *UCLA Women's Law Journal*, 3(0): 95–104.

Del Bove, Giannetta, Stermac, Lana, and Deidre Bainbridge. 2005. "Comparisons of Sexual Assault Among Older and Younger Women." *Journal of Elder Abuse and Neglect*, 17(3): 1–18. DOI: 10.1300/J084v17n03_01

DeKeseredy, Walter S., and Martin D. Schwartz. 2013. *Male Peer Support and Violence Against Women: The History and Verification of a Theory*. Boston: Northeastern University Press.

Demir, Oguzhan O., and James O. Finckenauer. 2010. "Victims of Sex Trafficking in Turkey: Characteristics, Motivations, and Dynamics." *Women and Criminal Justice*, 20(1–2): 57–88. DOI: 10.1080/08974451003641081

Douglas, Emily M., and David Finkelhor. 2005. *Childhood Sexual Abuse Fact Sheet*. Crimes Against Children Research Center. Accessed June 3, 2014, http://www.unh.edu/ccrc/factsheet/pdf/childhoodSexualAbuseFactSheet.pdf

Drape, Joe. 2012. "Sandusky Guilty of Sexual Abuse of 10 Young Boys: [Sports Desk]." *New York Times, Late Edition (East Coast)*, June 23, sec. A.

Dunn, Jennifer L. 2010. *Judging Victims: Why We Stigmatize Survivors, and How They Reclaim Respect*. Boulder, CO: Lynne Rienner Publishers.

Ellis, Lee. 1989. *Theories of Rape: Inquiries into the Causes of Sexual Aggression*. New York, NY: Hemisphere Publishing.

Estrich, Susan. 1987. *Real Rape*. Cambridge, MA: Harvard University Press.

Figley, Charles R. 1985. *Trauma and Its Wake, Vol.1: The Study and Treatment of Post Traumatic Stress Disorder*. New York, NY: Brunner/Mazel.

Fisher, Bonnie, Daigle, Leah E., and Francis T. Cullen. 2010. *Unsafe in the Ivory Tower: The Sexual Victimization of College Women*. Los Angeles: Sage Publications.

Fitzgerald, Jim. 2015. "Cuomo Wants 'Yes Means Yes' Law For Private Colleges In New York." *Huffington Post*. Accessed January 18, 2015, http://www.huffingtonpost.com/2015/01/18/cuomo-yes-means-yes_n_6496786.html

Ford, Julian D. 2009. *Posttraumatic Stress Disorder: Scientific and Professional Dimensions*. Elsevier. http://www.sciencedirect.com/science/book/9780123744623

Francisco, Patricia Weaver. 1999. *Telling: A Memoir of Rape and Recovery*. New York, NY: Cliff Street Books.

Frank, David John, Hardinge, Tara, and Kassia Wosick-Correa. 2009. "The Global Dimensions of Rape-Law Reform: A Cross-National Study of Policy Outcomes." *American Sociological Review*, 74(2): 272–290. DOI: 10.2307/27736061

French, Marilyn. 1992. *The War Against Women*. New York, NY: Summit Books.

Gabriel, Trip. 2013. "Inquiry in Cover-Up of Ohio Rape Yields Indictment of Four Adults." *New York Times*, November 25, sec. US. Accessed January 5, 2014, http://www.nytimes.com/2013/11/26/us/steubenville-school-superintendent-indicted-in-rapecase.html

Girshick, Lori. 2002. *Woman-to-Woman Sexual Violence: Does She Call It Rape?* Boston, MA: Northeastern University Press.

Goździak, Elźbieta M., and Micah N. Bump. 2008. *Data and Research on Human Trafficking: Bibliography of Research-Based Literature*. Washington, DC: US Department of Justice. Accessed June 5, 2014, https://www.ncjrs.gov/pdffiles1/nij/grants/224392.pdf

Gonzales, Alberto, Schofield, Regina, and Glenn Schmitt. 2005. "Sexual Assault on Campus: What Colleges and Universities Are Doing About It". *NCJ 205521*. Washington, DC: National Institute of Justice. https://www.ncjrs.gov/pdffiles1/nij/205521.pdf

Hale, Matthew. 1847. *Historia Placitorum Coronae: The History of the Pleas of the Crown*. London: Professional Books.

Holmstrom, Lynda Lytle, and Ann Wolbert Burgess. 1978. *The Victim of Rape: Institutional Reactions*. New York, NY: Wiley.

Human Rights Watch. 2014. "'Here, Rape Is Normal': A Five-Point Plan to Curtail Sexual Violence in Somalia." Accessed May 25, 2014, http://www.hrw.org/sites/default/files/reports/somalia0214_ForUpload.pdf

Hunter, Michael. 2007. *Honor Betrayed: Sexual Abuse in America's Military*. 1st edn. Fort Lee, NJ: Barricade Books.

Irish, Leah, Kobayashi, Ihori, and Douglas L. Delahanty. 2010. "Long-term Physical Health Consequences of Childhood Sexual Abuse: A Meta-Analytic Review." *Journal of Pediatric Psychology*, 35(5): 450–461. DOI: 10.1093/jpepsy/jsp118

Janoff-Bulman, R. 1985. "The Aftermath of Victimization: Rebuilding Shattered Assumptions." In *Trauma and Its Wake, Vol. 1: The Study and Treatment of Post-Traumatic Stress Disorder*. New York, NY: Brunner/Mazel.

Jasinski, Jana. 2001. "Theoretical Explanations for Violence Against Women." In *Sourcebook for Violence against Women*, edited by Claire M. Renzetti, Jeffrey L. Edleson, and Raquel K. Bergen, 5–22. Thousand Oaks, CA: Sage Publications.

Kilmartin, Christopher, and Julie A. Allison. 2007. *Men's Violence Against Women: Theory, Research, and Activism*. Mahwah, NJ; London: Lawrence Erlbaum Associates.

Koss, Mary P. 1987. "The Hidden Rape Victim: Personality, Attitudinal, and Situational Character-istics." *Psychology of Women Quarterly*, 9(2): 193–212. DOI: 10.1111/j.1471-6402.1985.tb00872.x

Landrine, Hope, and Elizabeth A. Klonoff. 1997. *Discrimination Against Women: Prevalence, Conse-quences, Remedies*. Thousand Oaks, CA: Sage Publications.

Leopold, Todd , and Ben Brumfield. November 15, 2014. "Rape Allegations Haunt Bill Cosby in the Digital Age." *CNN*. Accessed December 9, 2014, http://www.cnn.com/2014/11/14/showbiz/tv/bill-cosby-rape-allegations/

Littleton, Heather, Rhatigan, Deborah, and Danny Axsom. 2007. "Unacknowledged Rape: How Much Do We Know About the Hidden Rape Victim?" *Journal of Aggression, Maltreatment & Trauma*, 14(4): 57–74. DOI: 10.1300/J146v14n04_04

Macur, Juliet, and Nate Schweber. 2012. "Rape Case Unfolds on Web and Splits City: [Sports Desk]." *New York Times, Late Edition (East Coast)*, December 17, sec. D.

Majumdar, Swapna. 2013. "New India Rape Law Hailed by Advocacy Groups for Stiffening Pun-ishments." *Huffington Post*. April 19. http://www.huffingtonpost.com/2013/04/19/indiaadvocacy-rape_n_3118504.html

Martin, Patricia Yancey. 2005. *Rape Work: Victims, Gender, and Emotions in Organization and Community Context*. New York, NY: Routledge.

Masho, Saba W., and Anderson, Lisa. 2009. "Sexual Assault in Men: A Population-Based Study of Virginia." *Violence and Victims*, 24(1): 98–110.

McCartney, Anthony. December 7, 2014. "LAPD Open Investigation into Bill Cosby Sex Abuse Claim." *Las Vegas Review Journal*. Accessed December 9, 2014, http://www.reviewjournal.com/entertainment/lapd-open-investigation-bill-cosby-sex-abuse-claim

McCauley, Heather L., Decker, Michele R., and Jay G. Silverman. 2010. "Trafficking Experiences and Violence Victimization of Sex-Trafficked Young Women in Cambodia." *International Journal of Gynecology and Obstetrics*, 110(3): 266–277. DOI: 10.1016/j.ijgo.2010.04.016

McDonald, Susan, and Adamira Tijerino. 2013. *Male Survivors of Sexual Abuse and Assault: Their Experi-ences*. Ottawa: Research and Statistics Division Department of Justice Canada.

McMahon, Sarah, and G. Lawrence Farmer. 2011. "An Updated Measure for Assessing Subtle Rape Myths." *Social Work Research*, 35(2), 71–81. DOI: 10.1093/swr/35.2.71

National Public Radio. 2010. "Campus Rape Victims: A Struggle for Justice." *NPR.org*. February 24. http://www.npr.org/templates/story/story.php?storyId=124001493

Nelson, T. S. 2002. *For Love of Country: Confronting Rape and Sexual Harassment in the U.S. Military*. New York, NY: Haworth Maltreatment and Trauma Press.

Paolucci, Elizabeth Oddone, Genius, Mark L., and Claudio Violato. 2001. "A Meta-Analysis of the Published Research on the Effects of Child Sexual Abuse." *Journal of Psychology*, 135(1): 17–36. DOI: 10.1080/00223980109603677

Pappas, Nick T. 2012. *The Dark Side of Sports: Exposing the Sexual Culture of Collegiate and Professional Athletes*. 1st edn. Maidenhead: Meyer & Meyer Sport (UK).

Payne, Diana L., Lonsway, Kimberly A., and Louise F. Fitzgerald. 1999. "Rape Myth Acceptance: Exploration of Its Structure and Its Measurement Using the Illinois Rape Myth Acceptance Scale." *Journal of Research in Personality*, 33(1): 27–68. DOI: 10.1006/jrpe.1998.2238

Penfold, Clarissa, Hunter, Gillian, Campbell, Rosie, and Leela Barham. 2004. "Tackling Client Vio-lence in Female Street Prostitution: Inter-Agency Working Between Outreach Agencies and the Police." *Policing and Society*, 14(4): 365–379. DOI: 10.1080/1043946042000286074

Pérez-Peña, Richard, and Kate Taylor. 2014. "Fight Against Sexual Assaults Holds Colleges to Account." *New York Times*, May 3. http://www.nytimes.com/2014/05/04/us/fight-against sex-crimes-holds-colleges-to-account.html

Pillai, Geetha S. December 25, 2013. "Rape Cases Increased by 70% in Three Years." *Times of India.* Accessed June 5, 2014, http://timesofindia.indiatimes.com/city/jaipur/Rape-cases-increase-by-70-in-three-years/articleshow/27871769.cms

Planty, Michael, Krebs, Christopher, Berzofsky, Marcus, and Hope Smiley-McDonald. 2013. "Female Victims of Sexual Violence, 1994–2010." *Journalist's Resource.* http://journalistsresource.org/studies/government/criminal-justice/female-victims-sexual violence-1994–2010

Pollock, Nathan L. 1988. "Sexual Assault of Older Women." *Annals of Sex Research*, 1(4): 523–532.

RAINN. 2014. *What Is a Rape Kit?* Accessed September 3, 2014, https://www.rainn.org/get-information/sexual-assault-recovery/rape-kit

Risen, James. 2012. "Military Has Not Solved Problem of Sexual Assault, Women Say: [National Desk]." *New York Times, Late Edition (East Coast)*, November 2, sec. A.

Roth, John K., and Carol Rittner, eds. 2012. *Rape: Weapon of War and Genocide.* 1st edn. St Paul, MN: Paragon House.

Russell, Diana E. H. 1975. *The Politics of Rape: The Victim's Perspective.* New York, NY: Stein and Day.

Russell, Diana E. H. 1984. *Sexual Exploitation: Rape, Child Sexual Abuse, and Workplace Harassment.* Beverly Hills, CA: Sage Publications.

Russell, Diana E. H. 1990. *Rape in Marriage.* New York, NY: Macmillan Press.

Sadler, Anne G., Booth, Brenda M., Cook, Brian L., and Bradley N. Doebbeling. 2003. "Factors Associated with Women's Risk of Rape in the Military Environment." *American Journal of Industrial Medicine*, 43, 262–273. DOI: 10.1002/ajim.10202

Sanday, Peggy Reeves. 1990. *Fraternity Gang Rape: Sex, Brotherhood, and Privilege on Campus.* New York, NY: New York University Press.

Sanders, Teela. 2001. "Female Street Sex Workers, Sexual Violence, and Protection Strategies." *Journal of Sexual Aggression*, 7(1): 5–18. DOI: 10.1080/13552600108413318

Saunders, Benjamin E., Kilpatrick, Dean G., Hanson, Rochelle F., Resnick, Heidi S., and Michael E. Walker. 1999. "Prevalence, Case Characteristics, and Long-Term Psychological Correlates of Child Rape among Women: A National Survey." *Child Maltreatment*, 4(3): 187–200. DOI: 10.1177/1077559599004003001

Schwartz, Martin D., and Walter S. DeKeseredy. 1997. *Sexual Assault on the College Campus: The Role of Male Peer Support.* Thousand Oaks, CA: Sage Publications.

Singer, Michael. 2013. *Prison Rape: An American Institution?* Westport, CT: Praeger.

Sinozich, Sofi, and Lynn Langton, 2014. *Rape and Sexual Assault Victimization Among College-Age Females, 1995–2013.* Washington, DC: National Institute of Justice Bureau of Justice Statistics.

Smith, Bruce. August 24, 2006. "Female Citadel Cadets Reports Assaults." *Washington Post.* Accessed June 3, 2014, http://www.washingtonpost.com/wp-dyn/content/article/2006/08/23/AR2006082300506.html

Steinhauer, Jennifer. 2013a. "Veterans Testify on Rapes and Scant Hope of Justice: [National Desk]." *New York Times, Late Edition (East Coast)*, March 14, sec. A.

Steinhauer, Jennifer. 2013b. "Pentagon Study Sees Sharp Rise in Sexual Assaults." *New York Times*, May 7, sec. US/Politics. http://www.nytimes.com/2013/05/08/us/politics/pentagon-study-sees-sharp-rise-in-sexual-assaults.html

State of California Legislature. 2014. *Student Safety: Sexual Assault.* Senate Bill No. 967, Chapter 748. Added as Section 67386 to the Education Code. Accessed April 17, 2015, https://leginfo.legislature.ca.gov/faces/billNavClient.xhtml?bill_id=201320140SB967

Straus, Murray A. 1991. "New Theory and Old Canards about Family Violence Research." *Social Problems*, 38(2): 180–197. DOI: 10.2307/800528

Taylor, Joanne E., and Shane T. Harvey. 2009. "Effects of Psychotherapy with People Who Have Been Sexually Assaulted: A Meta-Analysis." *Aggression and Violent Behavior*, 14(5): 273–285. DOI: 10.1016/j.avb.2009.03.006

Timmons, Heather, and Sruthi Gottipati. 2012. "Indian Women March: 'That Girl Could Have Been Any One of Us': [Foreign Desk]." *New York Times, Late Edition (East Coast)*, December 31, sec. A.

Tjaden, Patricia, and Nancy Thoennes. 2006. "Extent, Nature, and Consequences of Rape Victimization: Findings from the National Violence Against Women Survey – 210346.pdf." https://www.ncjrs.gov/pdffiles1/nij/210346.pdf

Tonry, Michael H., and James Q. Wilson. 1990. *Drugs and Crime*. Chicago, IL: University of Chicago Press.

Thomas-Tucson, Cathy Booth. May 6, 2003. "Conduct Unbecoming." *Time*. Accessed June 3, 2014, http://content.time.com/time/magazine/article/0,9171,428045-1,00.html

Truman, Jennifer L., and Lynn Langton. 2015. *Criminal Victimization, 2014*. Washington, DC: Bureau of Justice Statistics.

Ullman, Sarah E. 2010. *Talking about Sexual Assault: Society's Response to Survivors*. Washington, DC: American Psychological Association.

US Department of Justice. 2012. *Attorney General Eric Holder Announces Revisions to the Uniform Crime Report's Definition of Rape*. Washington, DC: FBI. Accessed June 5, 2014, http://www.fbi.gov/news/pressrel/press-releases/attorney-general-eric-holder-announces-revisions-to-the-uniform-crime-reports-definition-of-rape

Vanderschaaf, Victoria. 2013. "Spotlight on: How the Internet Facilitates Underage Victimization in Human Trafficking." *Children's Legal Rights Journal*, 34(1), 135–138.

Vyawahare, Malavika. 2014a. "High Court Upholds Death Penalty in Delhi Gang Rape Case." *India Ink*. March 13. http://india.blogs.nytimes.com/2014/03/13/high-court-upholds-death-penalty-in-delhi-gang-rape-case/

Vyawahare, Malavika. 2014b. "Indian Court Says Forced Marital Sex Is Not Rape." *New York Times*, May 12. http://www.nytimes.com/2014/05/13/world/asia/indian-court-says-forced-marital-sex-is-not-rape.html

Walker-Rodriguez, Amanda, and Rodney Hill. 2011. *Human Sex Trafficking: FBI Law Enforcement Bulletin*. Washington, DC: FBI. Accessed June 5, 2014, http://www.fbi.gov/stats-services/publications/law-enforcement-bulletin/march_2011/human_sex_trafficking

Watts, Charlotte, and Cathy Zimmerman. 2002. "Violence Against Women: Global Scope and Magnitude. *Lancet*, 359(9313), 1232–1237. DOI: 10.1016/S0140-6736(02)08221-1

Williams, Joyce E., and Karen A. Holmes. 1981. *The Second Assault: Rape and Public Attitudes*. Westport, CT: Greenwood Press.

Wrangham, Richard W., and Dale Peterson. 1996. *Demonic Males: Apes and the Origins of Human Violence*. Boston, MA: Houghton Mifflin.

Yardley, Jim. 2013. "Urging Action, Report on Brutal Rape Condemns India's Treatment of Women: [Foreign Desk]." *New York Times, Late Edition (East Coast)*, January 24, sec. A.

Yardley, Jim, and Neha Thirani Bagri. 2013. "Notorious Attack Spurs India to Approve New Rape Laws: [Foreign Desk]." *New York Times, Late Edition (East Coast)*, February 4, sec. A.

Zuckerman, Esther. September 2, 2014. "CeeLo Green Tweets that Only Women Who 'Remember' Can Be Raped." *Entertainment Weekly*. Accessed September 3, 2014, http://news-briefs.ew.com/2014/09/02/ceelo-green-tweets-that-only-women-who-remember-can-be-raped/

CHAPTER 6

Domestic violence

Student learning outcomes

After reading this chapter, you should be able to:

- Define domestic violence and distinguish among its various forms (physical, sexual, emotional).

- Explain the nature and extent of domestic violence.

- Identify the risk factors associated with domestic violence.

- Compare domestic violence incidents among various nations.

- Discuss criminal justice system and social service responses to domestic violence.

Introduction

Domestic violence garnered unusual public attention in the United States in 2013 when a woman was on trial for the murder of her boyfriend. Jodi Arias' capital murder trial, in Phoenix, Arizona, started in January 2013 and extended through April 2013. Arias had killed Travis Alexander in June 2008 by stabbing him 27 times, slitting his throat and shooting him in the head. She claimed that she killed him in self-defense and that she was a battered woman who suffered from post-traumatic stress and personality disorders (Skoloff 2013). The trial captured print and television news headlines as it extended over five months and resulted in her conviction of first degree murder. The penalty phase of the capital trial, however, resulted in a hung jury. Under Arizona State law, the court had to declare a mistrial in the penalty phase of the trial and that phase will need to be retried to determine whether she should be sentenced to death or given life imprisonment (Santos 2013). In 2015, she was sentenced to a life sentence without the possibility of parole (Kiefer 2015).

In 2012, police responded to a domestic assault call in Norristown, Pennsylvania. The female victim of domestic violence, Lakisha Briggs, had been hit with a brick by an ex-boyfriend and neighbors who heard the assault called the police for help. Briggs was told by police officers that she faced eviction because she had sought police help for a third time within a four-month period. Briggs had refrained from calling for police help after the first assault because she feared losing her home and having no place to live. In her city, a city ordinance empowers landlords to evict persons who have numerous police "domestic disturbance" calls to their home (Eckholm 2013). In 2013, the American Civil Liberties Union filed a lawsuit on behalf of Briggs claiming that the city violated

Women, Crime, and Justice, First Edition. By Elaine Gunnison, Frances P. Bernat, and Lynne Goodstein.
© 2017 John Wiley & Sons, Ltd. Published 2017 by John Wiley & Sons, Ltd.

her constitutional rights and the federal **Violence Against Women Act (VAWA)** which protects victims of domestic violence. Initially, the city rescinded the ordinance but almost immediately thereafter passed another similar ordinance in 2013. The new ordinance allows the city to levy fines on landlords if they do not evict tenants with numerous calls for police assistance even if the calls are for domestic violence. Norristown is not the only city with an eviction ordinance that negatively impacts victims of domestic violence who repeatedly seek police assistance. Milwaukee, Minnesota, for example, also has an ordinance which can target victims of domestic violence for eviction by classifying the calls as "nuisances" (Fais 2008).

To understand the complex family relationships that may be violent, we need to learn more about **domestic violence**. Domestic violence involves assaults and extremely controlling behavior within a domestic relationship. We usually categorize it as the physical assault by a husband on his wife but modern law includes abuse perpetrated against any partner, whether gay or straight, and regardless of marital status, age, socioeconomic status, or gender. What is interesting about the Jodi Arias news story, presented above, is that in convicting Jodi Arias the jury recognized that women can be the perpetrators of violence and did not believe that her male partner was the abusive instigator. The Briggs' news report indicates that communities have to provide better responses to victims of abuse and understand that all victims of violence need to be able to call the police for help without fear that they will be "punished." If victims of domestic violence do not get out of a violent relationship then the threat of death to the victim increases over time. All victims of domestic violence need criminal justice and social service support to end the violence.

Domestic violence

Domestic violence is also called "**intimate partner violence**" **(IPV)** but it also has been referred to by many other names. Among the most common terms used interchangeably with domestic violence and IPV are "family violence," "interpersonal violence," "domestic dispute," "wife abuse," "wife-beating," "spouse abuse," "marital violence," "marital rape," "intra-family violence," "child abuse and neglect," and "intimate abuse." In the past few decades, domestic violence has been extended to include dating violence, teen dating violence, intimate same-sex partner violence or abuse, elder abuse, and parental abuse. These definitional extensions show that it is important to understand that domestic violence is analyzed in terms of relationships and the violence that occurs within them. It is essential to understand the familial or social relationship between the people involved and to discern who the perpetrator of the violence is and who the recipient is.

The individual circumstances of domestic violence vary with each relationship. In some instances, physical violence is frequent and takes the form of both emotional and physical abuse. In other instances, there is only emotional violence, or an elder in the family is bilked out of life savings. A perpetrator can be a 17-year-old male student who just recently started to date another male student in high school and, while on a date, threatens to physically hurt or kill the boyfriend unless the date has sex. A perpetrator can be a 30-year-old husband who had not previously hit his wife, but, during her third month of pregnancy with their first child, he punches her in the stomach which results in a still birth. A perpetrator can be a woman who engages in abusive name-calling. In a small percentage of IPV cases, the violence is acute and may involve homicide, an attempt to kill the victim, rape, and/or emotional abuse. Domestic violence is not just about physical violence but is also about power and control.

The Power and Control Wheel is a common tool used to describe the experience of being battered. In recent years, persons who have been victims of domestic violence have consistently reported that, long after their physical scars have healed, the emotional trauma remains. Take a look at the wheel to see how an abuser uses emotional, physical, sexual or economic control and violence by to exert power over the family member or intimate partner (Figure 6.1). **Emotional**

Figure 6.1 Power and Control Wheel. *Source:* Domestic Abuse Intervention Project, www.duluth-model.org

abuse (psychological and verbal abuse) is displayed by intimidation and threats. The abuser may say, "I will kill you if you don't bathe the children by 8pm tonight," or, "I'll kill you and the children if you leave me," or even threaten to kill the family pet. Emotional abuse humiliates the victim and attacks the person's self-esteem by repeated name-calling, yelling, and social isolation of the victim from family and friends who otherwise might help. The name-calling demeans the victim and sends the message that victims deserve the abuse. **Physical abuse** can be exercised by "mild" forms of force (e.g., pushing, shoving, pinching, excessive tickling, throwing objects at a person) or by "serious" forms of physical force (e.g., the use of a weapon, stalking, choking, punching, or other forms of force that result in serious bodily injury). Physical abuse can result in the death of a victim. **Sexual abuse** involves the forced sexual assault or rape of a person and includes pressure to have sexual relations when a partner does not want to consent. **Economic abuse** includes the abusive control over another person's finances and not allowing a person to work to earn a living or get an education. It can also include the withholding of a person's work visa or passport. It can include threats that, if a victim reports domestic violence to police authorities, the victim will be deported and separated from her children. All of these forms of abuse result in the dependence of the victim on the abuser.

If you look closely at your daily newspapers, there will be many news reports about domestic violence but only the most notorious catch our attention. Sometimes, the report details a family homicide. Sometimes, the news story merely mentions that a person was arrested by the police for a family disturbance. Sometimes, the report is about a famous person being arrested and is accompanied by a mug shot showing the wealthy person in despair. Some reports capture special attention when the accused may have been involved in a particularly heinous act or when the state seems to dismiss the plight of victims. When are there enough reports that we put concentrated efforts into the eradication of domestic violence? More troubling, how do we eradicate a social phenomenon that goes unnoticed unless it is deemed "excessive" or "cruel" or "unusual?" This chapter aims to explain what domestic violence is, the history of domestic violence in the United States, and theories to explain domestic violence. Additionally, we examine the relationship between the victim and offender and describe the impact that violence has on the family – including on children. We also examine the risk factors for domestic violence as well as how laws have impacted victims. Finally, we describe what communities and the criminal justice system can do to protect victims and, hopefully, abate it. As the Arias and Briggs' news stories show, intimate partner violence may result in a homicide or it may result in a situation where victims of assault lack community understanding and police protection.

When did society start to consider domestic violence to be a crime?

Domestic assaults date to our earliest societies and were considered to be an acceptable method for men to keep their wives and children in check. The community acceptance of wife beating was even the subject of sixteenth-century ballads about overbearing women who needed to be punished for their assertiveness, and English church confessionals were replete with testimonies about the need of husbands to moderately correct wives (Butler 2007). The family mirrored the broader social hierarchical order with the father as its master and his wife and children as his property; consequently, it was protected from outside purview (Shahidullah and Derby 2009). In many nations, once married, a husband and wife were considered to be one legal entity. To understand how physical control over a wife evolved from an acceptable lawful right of a husband to a crime, we can trace the history of marriage and domestic violence in the common law.

This legal principle of marital unity in common law nations is part of the **doctrine of coverture** which existed into the nineteenth and twentieth centuries. The principle meant that wives could not enter into contracts, could not own their property as it was given to the husband upon the marriage, and could be physically punished by their husbands for misbehavior. Men, as the titular head of the family, were legally empowered to control their property with force whenever they deemed it necessary. Over time, the legal response to marital violence in England evolved from its medieval roots. By the nineteenth century, the doctrine of marital unity progressed into one in which husbands had the privilege of "chastisement" upon their marriage, and marriage entitled a man and woman to legal "privacy" within the home. This legal evolution was consistent with changes in legal philosophy, predominant during the Age of Enlightenment, which espoused that individuals had innate rights to control their own lives. Of course, this power to control one's life and have individual freedom and liberty was bestowed only upon men as the head of the family. Wives and children were expected to practice "domestic complacency and servitude" toward husbands and fathers (Rambo 2009). Such an enlightened notion of privacy enabled most forms of family violence to go unnoticed.

Similarly, in the United States, husbands were provided with both **impunity** to control their wives as part of their marital property and **immunity** to the use of violence to promote marital harmony and unity. Between the late nineteenth century and early twentieth century in the United States, many mothers found themselves at the mercy of the long arm of the law. According to

Gordon (2002), for example, in Boston, Massachusetts, if police or social workers were called to a home to check on wayward children, the mothers were held legally at fault for child neglect because they presumably failed to properly care for the physical and educational upbringing of their children. All the while, any physical signs of domestic violence exhibited on the women by husbands were ignored (Gordon 2002). Prejudices among the privileged class regarding the context of family violence and child abuse were tied to hostilities towards poor and ethnic minorities whose domestic disturbances were more likely to come to the attention of the police than abuse within privileged households.

During the early part of the twentieth century, the common law doctrine of coverture and other legal principles that empowered men to control their wives began to be eliminated as women fought for equal rights. In many common law nations, such as England, Canada, Australia, and the United States, women sought an end to domestic abuse as part of their struggle for civil rights. As a consequence, we begin to see during the first half of the twentieth century a change in the way Western society viewed domestic violence. It was slowly being considered to be a criminal offense and actionable against men who used physical violence against a member of their familial household. In an important case brought in the United States, Tracy Thurman sued the City of Torrington in 1984 because the police failed to protect her from her abusive spouse (*Thurman v. City of Torrington* 1984). The Federal District Court determined that her lawsuit should proceed and denied the city's motion to dismiss. Additionally, the court determined that police departments have an affirmative duty to protect all victims of assault, including victims of domestic violence. Moreover, the court recognized that men no longer have the common law right to hit their wives. By the end of the century, social, legal, and cultural changes were implemented to broaden the crime's definition and to proscribe many forms of intimate partner violence and family abuses. As can be seen in the Jodi Arias case, women as well as men can be convicted of domestic assaults, persons who are unmarried but in a relationship can be held legally accountable, and many forms of abuse are proscribed. Problematically, the Briggs case shows that communities still may not provide victims with supportive police services if they are poor.

How many people are affected by family violence?

No one really knows the exact number of victims of domestic violence either within the United States or worldwide – only that it is pervasive (Table 6.1). The **World Health Organization (WHO)** estimates that at least 35% of women worldwide experience violence in their lifetime and that 38% of women who are murdered are killed by an intimate partner (World Health Organization 2013). Among the common reasons for the lack of accurate domestic US and global numbers is that most victims do not report it, they deny that it happens, they may believe that they deserve it, and/or they may accept the abuse as commonplace within their family. Based upon US population numbers, it is estimated that a woman is the recipient of domestic violence every nine seconds. In the United States, these estimates are generated by looking at various forms of crime data: calls to the police, arrest and conviction statistics, emergency room statistics, calls to domestic violence hotlines and shelter statistics, and other methods of crime and victimization data analysis such as information gleaned from the annual **National Crime Victimization Survey (NCVS)**, **National Violence Against Women Survey (NVAWA)**, and the **National Incidence Based Reporting System**. In developing nations, domestic violence estimates are based upon understandings of the cultural norms of the community and small research studies that attempt to generate reliable numbers estimating victimization (see Adekeye, Abimbola, and Adeusi 2011; McQuigg 2011; Shahidulla and Derby 2009; Yosihama, Parekh, and Boyington 1998).

Table 6.1 Rate of violent victimization, by victim characteristics and victim–offender relationship, 2003–2012.

Demographic characteristic	Domestic violence				Well–known/ casual acquaintance	Stranger
	Total	Intimate partner[a]	Immediate family[b]	Other relative		
Total	5.6	3.9	1.1	0.6	8.4	10.2
Sex						
Male	2.8	1.4	0.9	0.5	8.9	14.2
Female	8.4	6.2	1.4	0.8	7.9	6.4
Age						
12–17	5.0	1.1	2.6	1.2	26.9	15.2
18–24	11.6	8.7	1.8	1.2	14.0	19.9
25–34	8.7	7.3	0.7	0.7	7.5	14.5
35–49	6.4	4.7	1.2	0.5	6.4	9.7
50–64	2.9	1.5	1.0	0.5	4.8	5.9
65 or older	0.6	0.2	0.2	0.1	1.3	1.6
Race/Hispanic origin						
White[c]	5.7	3.9	1.2	0.6	8.6	9.7
Black[c]	6.7	4.7	0.7	1.2	10.1	12.3
Hispanic/Latino	4.0	2.8	0.6	0.6	6.3	10.4
Other race[c,d]	3.7	2.3	1.3	0.2!	4.6	8.4
Two or more races[c]	22.5	16.5	4.4	1.6	24.6	26.7
Marital status						
Never married	7.0	4.4	1.7	0.9	15.6	17.1
Married	2.0	1.0	0.6	0.4	3.7	5.9
Widowed	2.3	0.6	1.5	0.2!	2.2	2.3
Divorced	13.8	11.4	1.5	0.9	11.4	12.9
Separated	49.1	44.7	2.8	1.6	13.9	16.0

Note: Victimization rates are per 1.000 persons age 12 or older. In a small percentage of victimization, the victim-offender relationship was unknown or the number of offenders was unknown These estimates are not shown.
! Interpret with caution. Estimate based on 10 or fewer sample cases, or coefficient of variation is greater than 50%.
[a]Includes, current or former spouses, boyfriends, and girlfriends.
[b]Indudes parents, children, and siblings.
[c]Excludes persons of Hispanic or Latino origin.
[d]indudes American Indian, Alaska Native, Hawaiian, Asian, and other Pacific Islander.
Source: Truman and Morgan (2014).

Who can be a victim of domestic violence and who are the offenders?

Victimization studies show that victims of domestic violence can be of any age, sexual orientation, gender, race, ethnicity, or socioeconomic level. The infamous assault on Rihanna by Chris Brown before the 2009 Grammy Awards shows that violence does not just occur in a marital relationship or in poor families; it can happen to an affluent, unmarried, and successful working woman. Most crime researchers find that the impact of intimate family violence is disproportionately experienced

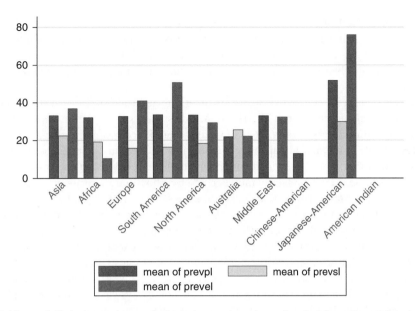

Figure 6.2 Mean of lifetime prevalence of physical, sexual, and emotional violence by continent or country. *Source:* Alhabib et al. 2010. Reproduced with permission of Springer Print and Business Media. *Note:* prevpl = prevalence of lifetime physical violence; prevel = prevalence of life time emotional violence; prevsl = prevalence of lifetime sexual violence.

by women at the hands of male partners but also that women may engage in mild assaults on family members (see Auchter and Moore 2013; Straus 2005) (Figure 6.2). A study of family violence by the Bureau of Justice Statistics reports that, while females comprised slightly more than half the US population, they comprised 73% of the recipients of family violence between 1998 and 2002 (Durose et al. 2005). Catalano (2012) estimates that in 2010 there were slightly more than 900,000 female victims, 12 years of age or older in the United States; more recent figures indicate that 1.3 million US women are victimized by an intimate each year (Do Something 2014). In their National Intimate Partner and Sexual Violence Survey, the **Center for Disease Control (CDC)** found among other things that one in four females and one in seven males have been the victim of severe physical violence by an intimate partner; female domestic violence victims experience fear 72% of the time and men 18% of the time. The CDC found that severe physical intimate partner violence impacts women more than men: women show post-traumatic stress disorder (PTSD) symptoms 63% of the time and men 16% of the time; 62% of women feared for their safety compared to 16% of men; and female domestic violence victims experienced multiple forms of trauma.

Some people, citing Straus and Gelles' seminal work on family violence, assert that men and women are equally violent, and they believe that female violence is overlooked and ignored; others assert that males are more violent than females (Feder and Henning 2005; Hines and Malley-Morrison 2005; Mills 2008; Minakeer and Snider 2006). The issue of female batterers has received some attention since the 1970s when research was published on male victimization, and dual arrest data show an increase in the number of women being brought into the criminal justice system for domestic assaults (Abel 2001). It appeared reasonable to assume that women and girls were as seriously violent as men since the percentages of their arrests went up dramatically and a "moral panic" regarding violent females was initiated. However, Minakeer and Snider (2006) explain that, as women became more successful at instituting legal and social changes to redress power inequities in the system, particularly as it pertained to domestic violence, the discourse of "equality" was used as a backlash against women. They found that the majority of domestic violence victims are women and the majority of aggressors are male (Minakeer and Snider 2006). Approximately 1.5 million US women are physically assaulted or raped by their intimate partner each year (Shahidullah and Derby 2009).

To understand domestic homicides, let's look at recent homicide statistics in the United States. According to the *Uniform Crime Report* in 2014, homicide statistics show that in cases where the victim–offender relationship was known, 36% of victims were killed by an intimate partner or family member (FBI 2014). In a longitudinal study of homicides in the United States, between 1980 and 2008, it was found that where the victim–offender homicide relationship was known, 10% were committed by a spouse, 12% by a family member, 6% by a boyfriend/girlfriend, 22% by a stranger, and 49% by an acquaintance (Bureau of Justice Statistics 2011). If we then focus on the gender of the victims and offenders then we see that females are more likely to be killed than to kill. In 2000, the number of females killed by family violence was almost three times the number of males killed: 1,300 female compared to 500 male familial homicide victims (Adams 2007). Despite moral panics over women who kill, women resort to serious forms of physical violence in a relationship less than men, and when they resort to violence against a partner it is usually not self-initiated but in response to violence already present in the home. It is not always easy to know who initiated the violence and who the violent partner is – that is why police training and legal education on domestic violence are important.

 GLOBAL PERSPECTIVES: Domestic violence across the globe

Domestic violence statistics vary widely from nation to nation due to legal and cultural differences about domestic violence. However, statistics show that females are primarily the recipients of intimate personal violence. The World Health Organization (WHO) considers domestic violence to be a major world health threat for women aged 15 to 44 (Alhabib, Nur, and Jones 2010). WHO (2013), in their study of 80 nations, found that some nations have higher levels of domestic violence than others and that 20% of women and 5–10% of men reported experiencing child abuse. Leung (2014) states that women battering in Hong Kong is considered to be a serious problem as evidenced by a 74% increase in police reports between 1999 and 2008, a rise from 1,679 to 6,483 cases reported to the police. In India, female domestic violence may be underreported in some communities and victimization rates may be as low as 6% or as high as 60% (Shahidullah and Derby 2009). To get a better understanding of domestic violence, Shahidullah and Derby (2009) surveyed women at work and in the marketplace and found that 39% of women in India reported being a victim of domestic violence. In Japan, Kim et al. (2010) found that 77% of Japanese women reported being a victim of at least one interpersonal violent incident. In Nigeria, Adekeye et al. (2011) found that between 56% and 65% of Nigerian women reported being a victim of domestic violence. WHO (2013) indicates that for women in many developing nations physical and sexual abuse is a serious problem: 71% of women in Ethiopia reported physical or sexual violence by an intimate, and women in rural Tanzania (17%), rural Peru (24%) and rural Bangladesh (30%) report that their first sexual experience was by force. Worldwide statistics are difficult to use because women who are physically assaulted may not identify themselves as victims of domestic violence, may feel shame, may believe that they deserve to be hit and "corrected" by their husbands, and in some non-Western nations, women may view domestic violence as a private matter (Alhabib et al. 2010).

The reasons why women are victimized by family members vary widely across cultures. It is estimated by WHO (Alfred 2014) that, worldwide, 40% of all female murder victims are killed by a partner. The United Nations reports that between 40% and 70% of female murder victims are killed by their intimate partner in Australia, Canada, Israel, South Africa, and the United States (United Nations 2014). In some nations, women may be killed within the family in order to preserve the family honor. For example, in Pakistan, there are problems in distinguishing between a marital rape and an honor killing; if a woman cannot prove that she was raped by bringing forth four witnesses, then she herself is viewed as an offender. These honor killings are accepted by the formal legal system as a private matter that is accepted by tribal and local customary laws (Bhatti et al. 2011). Sometimes, these customs and traditions are brought to Western nations, and immigrant families will commit honor killings in their new country of residence. For example, in Canada, an Afghan father killed his three daughters for dating in 2012 (Austen 2012). In Belgium, a Pakistani girl was killed for not going through with an arranged marriage in 2011 (AFP 2011). In the United States, the number of honor killings is rising among Muslim families and immigrants. Worldwide, the number of honor killings is estimated to be at least 5,000 per year (Chesler 2010).

Theory and domestic violence

In 1979, Lenore Walker developed the **Cycle Theory of Violence** from her counseling practice while working with victims of domestic violence (Walker 1984). This theory, consisting of three phases, helps to explain violence within domestic relationships. Phase One is tension building. An abusive person is unable to effectively deal with stress, tension builds, and he/she gets very angry. Phase Two is explosion. When the abusive person reaches his/her tipping point, he/she will explode and become violent. Phase Three, the final phase of the cycle, is loving contrition. In this phase, the batterer is sorry for the abuse and apologizes. Despite any physical injuries, a victim of domestic abuse will want to believe that the batterer will never do it again, that he/she will change, that he/she loves the victim, and that the abuse was an isolated event. Yet, the abusive cycle will start over, leading the victim to officially be considered a battered woman/man, having gone through at least two cycles of violence. Over time, the violent episodes will intensify, and the level of the victim's fear will ultimately replace any prior feelings of love. The level and intensity of violence and the amount of time between explosive phases will vary from couple to couple. In some families, the assaults can be a daily or weekly event while in other families the physical violence is irregular. Intensified violence in the home is associated, according to Walker (1984), with learned helplessness, the inability to leave because victims learn that there is nothing they can do to stop the abuse and accept it.

Since the Cycle Theory of Violence was first proposed, some social scientists and legal scholars have challenged it. Some scholars say that there is no evidence that all battered women experience all phases of the cycle and that battered women may experience different effects after their abuse; some challenge the viability of the learned helplessness concept; and some challenge the use of battered women syndrome as a defense of female offending behaviors (Biggers 2003; Coughlin 1994; Rothenberg 2002). Despite the criticism that has been levied at it, it remains a powerful legal explanation for why women stay in abusive relationships and is used as part of the **Battered Women Defense** by courts to explain why some women may kill their batterers. The theory has been modified to analyze intergenerational family abuse patterns, explained using a Cycle of Violence Theory (see Jennings et al. 2013; Jewkes, Levin, and Penn-Kekana 2002), and post-traumatic stress disorder (PTSD) which underscores the psychological dimension that inhibits women from leaving an abusive relationship and the impact of violence on their emotional and physical wellbeing (see Bergman and Brismar 1991; Walker and Browne 1985).

Why do men hit their female partners?

Domestic violence is typically understood from the view that husbands abuse their wives. In general, as noted above, when men perceive that they have to exert power and control in a relationship to maintain their masculinity then an abusive relationship is likely to occur. According to Hattery (2009) male battering ensues under two common scenarios. First, men might feel the loss of their masculinity when their role of the breadwinner has been diminished. Male batterers may be threatened by their inability to provide for their family, threatened by women in the workplace, or threatened if their partner earns more money than they do. Second, male batterers may have a heightened view about their sexual prowess and their right to have sex with many women and thereby demand sex from their partners. In another internationally publicized case, Lorena Bobbitt cut off her American husband's penis after he raped her and fell asleep in 1993. He was convicted of rape; she was tried for aggravated assault and found not guilty by reason of temporary insanity (Margolick 1994). According to Lorena Bobbitt, when she was married to John Bobbitt, her husband purportedly had a number of affairs and believed that he was entitled to demand sex from her. She says that he raped her several times prior to the time when she cut off his penis. Men with heightened sexual entitlement views are threatened if they feel that other men find their partner sexually attractive or if their partner refuses to have sex with them. The use of physical violence is a way that these men may achieve a restoration of balance to their masculinity. Violence committed on a partner enables the batterer to restore the patriarchal state that had been threatened (Hattery 2009).

These threats to the male social identity can lead to violence when some common factors are present: poverty or economic strain, conservative and traditional family structure, strongly patriarchal culture, and intoxication. The focus on wife abuse arises from an initial awareness of the problem in the 1960s and 1970s when White women sought treatment and help. Today, many forms of domestic violence and risks of family violence are recognized globally. The trial of Jodi Arias is a testament to the fact that men can be brutalized at the hands of the women they love or are dating.

When and why might females be the abusive partner?

To understand the dynamics of female-perpetrated battering, current research has attempted to distinguish levels of violence within a relationship and the reasons for which it occurs. Female batterer relationships have been narrowed to three types: mutual combative relationships, retaliatory violence (self-defense), and female aggressor relationships. In a mutual combative relationship, the level of physical violence is usually depicted by mutual hitting or slapping and other low or high levels of force. Johnson (2008) calls this situational violence. In retaliatory violence, the male is a violent partner and the female retaliates in self-defense (Miller 2001). Miller (2001) found that many probation and social workers who work with women convicted of battering their partner believe that women who use physical force against their partner do so for one of two reasons: they are frustrated by being battered by their partner or they are attempting to defend themselves at the time. These criminal justice actors have found that usually the male partner is also under their supervision for domestic violence and that the police may be over-enforcing laws against domestic violence. In this regard, probation and social workers in Miller's study found that the women arrested for domestic violence were not representative of a myth that "women are getting more violent"; rather, the women were predominantly reacting to the lack of power in their relationship and abuse by their partner (Miller 2001).

Some females, albeit a small number, are like Jodi Arias; they are indeed the aggressors and mirror patterns of the Power and Control Wheel in their interactions with their partners. These relationships qualify as female aggressor relationships (Hines and Malley-Morrison 2005; Johnson 2008). Men, who are the victims in female aggressive relationships, stay for the same reasons that women stay in abusive relationships (Brennen 2015). They stay because of love, fear, their children, a lack of support services available to them, the police do not believe that they are the victims, they have no place to go, shame, and/or low self-esteem. This third form of female battering is about power and control. To understand the dynamics of a violent female in a relationship, Ferreira and Buttell (2014) studied women who had been ordered to attend batterer intervention programs. They found that women who were exposed to violence as children have a high propensity for being violent as an adult. However, they also found that domestic violence programs that have been designed for male batterers may not be successful in assisting abate female battering. Ferreira and Buttell (2014) suggest that programs should be developed and tailored to intervene and target female battering.

Some self-defense cases receive public attention when the female victim of domestic violence has killed her abuser, as seen in the debate over the case of Jodi Arias. If a battered woman is charged with the homicide or assault then she might claim **battered women syndrome defense**; the defense's viability depends on the state's criminal law and legal defenses. When Lorena Bobbitt was tried for assault, the battered women syndrome defense did not apply to her actions because she responded to the rape after it had occurred; for self-defense she would have had to react (kill him) during the rape. These homicide cases bring attention to the fact that some women do engage in very violent acts towards their partners, including acts that can result in their death. When women act in a very aggressive manner, then the public begins to believe that women are becoming more violent and that women's domestic violence propensity is the equivalent of men's. However, in reviewing the literature on physical assaults committed by women and reviewing the research methodology that gives rise to the conclusions from those studies, Saunders (2002) found that when studies accounted for methodical deficiencies (e.g., failure to consider stalking behaviors or include violence perpetrated by divorced or separated individuals) then women are not as violent as men. Instead, women were more likely to be victims of domestic violence (Saunders 2002). He also found that some research studies are flawed because they fail to account for women of color (e.g., Black women may need to defend against violence on their own) or because the researchers do not adequately ask questions about self-defense (Saunders 2002). He concluded that while there is no general consensus among the scientific community in regard to women who abuse their partners, the research has generally shown that women are more likely to be victims of domestic violence, be affected both physically and psychologically by domestic violence, and require more resources to deal with their victimization than men.

 SPECIAL LEGAL ISSUES: Battered women syndrome defense in other countries

The battered women syndrome defense was first used in the late 1970s in the United States. Other countries have also permitted the use of the battered women syndrome defense as a justification for homicide due to psychological abuse or distress. In a Supreme Court decision in Canada in 1990, the battered women syndrome defense was permitted for use by women accused of homicide or aggravated assault (Regehr and Glancy 1995). Women in Australia may legally use self-defense against their batterer. Tarrant (1990, 148) explains that this defense is legally permissible "when a person is unlawfully assaulted in such a way as to cause reasonable apprehension of

(continued)

death or grievous bodily harm and the person assaulted believes on reasonable grounds that (s)he cannot otherwise be saved, there is justification for using deadly force against the assailant." New Zealand also permits the use of self-defense for battered women engaging in force but does not require the women to be in imminent danger for the defense to be utilized (Sheehy, Stubbs, and Tolmie 2012). In an analysis of self-defense case outcomes for accused battered women in Canada, Australia, and New Zealand from 2000 to 2010, Sheehy and colleagues (2012) found that New Zealand had the highest conviction rate for battered women when compared to the other countries. The researchers also found that Canada had the highest acquittal rate for battered women during this time period.

Other countries have been reluctant to adopt the battered women syndrome defense or refuse to consider such a defense. In the United Kingdom, for example, battered women syndrome has not been considered as evidence in a self-defense claim (Belew 2010). Rather, the courts allow for the use of provocation as a partial defense for women who kill their batterers (Belew 2010). Marginalized women in other countries such as in the Middle East are not permitted to utilize the battered women syndrome defense when killing their abuser.

What are the risk factors associated with domestic assault?

Among the common factors associated with family violence are poverty or economic strain (see Kishor and Johnson 2006; Jewkes 2002; Mishra et al. 2014; Wesely and Wright 2009). Arrests for domestic violence occur more often among low-income and minority groups (Sherman, Schmidt, and Rogan 1992), and poor women are more likely than wealthier women to show up in the emergency rooms or be hospitalized (see Kernic, Wolf, and Holt 2000; Kishor and Johnson 2006). More research on economic inequality is needed as traditional family homes are more likely to experience violence (see Jewkes et al. 2002). In India, for example, Mishra et al. (2014) found that domestic violence victimization (physical, sexual, and psychological) was more prevalent among housewives than among women with a profession. They posit that when families in India experience economic strain then family violence will ensue but in families where there is more income and women are educated then female education and financial independence are protective factors against abuse. Globally, lower levels of education, associated with poverty, are a factor associated with family violence. As women in developing nations become educated and have a more equalitarian family relationship, they are less likely to report physical abuse than rural and uneducated women.

Family history of violence is a factor associated with intimate partner violence. Husbands who physically hurt their wives may believe that it is necessary, may believe that they are not using excessive force, may blame the wife for the physical violence, and may be surprised to learn that their violence is their "fault." Wives who are physically hurt may be shocked at its initial onset but will eventually accept responsibility for the violence perpetrated on them. Sometimes the onset of violence will occur on a first date, sometimes on a wedding night, sometimes upon a pregnancy; often, it is because the male partner feels a loss of control and that the relationship is threatened. Jealousy can also play a role in the abuse; men who fear that their partners are having an affair may resort to violence to exert their ownership and domination over the female. Violent relationships contain frequent verbal arguments and high levels of family conflict (Jewkes 2002). Consequently, marital discord and male sexual entitlement play a role in risk for sexual violence in a family.

CASE STUDY: Case A. Homicide–parasuicide involving a man killing his spouse

Born and raised in Yugoslavia, A., aged 28, immigrates to the Netherlands. He finds work as a factory employee but fails to learn Dutch. At the age of 35, he marries a girl 16 years his junior in a pre-arranged wedding. In their marriage, three children are born. A. considers himself to be the head of the household, responsible for the well-being of his wife and children. He is authoritarian and expects his family members to adhere to his rules.

Over time, A.'s health deteriorates. As a consequence, he is on sickness benefit, which he perceives as a failure. Simultaneously, his wife starts to work, speaks Dutch fluently, and becomes acquainted with others outside the family home. In the meantime, his children become older and less dependent on their father. The independence of his wife and children, his perceived failure as a skilled worker, and his wife's social contacts make him feel humiliated, rejected, and angry. Referring to his wife visiting friends without his consent: "She did not have the right to treat me like that. I did everything for her." He feels powerless and unable to control his wife and children. More and more often, he lashes out violently against his wife, accusing her of adultery.

A. feels increasingly tense, afraid that his wife will leave him. One night, she refuses sexual intercourse. He interprets her refusal as evidence of her adulterous behavior and as soon as she is asleep, he stabs her multiple times. "For a moment, I felt relieved [...] She shouldn't have rejected me." When he comes to realize she is dead, he stabs himself: "I did not want to live without her. She was mine and mine alone [...] I wanted to die, too." He is found by the police and remains in a coma for several months.

Source: Liem (2010, 253).

Violence in families may go undetected because domestic violence is kept a secret and an abuser could be a respected person in the neighborhood or well established in the community as a lawyer, police officer, chief executive officer, or member of the clergy. The abuser may appear to members outside the family to be a nice person, who is helpful and has a loving family. A victim lives in fear that her/his family and friends will find out about the abuse. If they know about it, then they might get tired of telling her/him to leave and not want to hear her/his "complaints" anymore. Female victims may fear reporting domestic abuse because they are afraid that it will result in them being ostracized by their church, families, and neighbors (see Lichtenstein and Johnson 2009). The social isolation may, in extreme cases, turn into physical isolation too and may be experienced in excessive ways: no phone in the home, lack of available transportation, locked in a room while the abusive spouse is out, and so on. Victims may not report the victimization to the police and social service agencies because they think that they will not be believed or taken seriously (see Jewkes 2002) and children in violent homes may also remain silent and afraid (O'Brien et al. 2013). When abuse is made public, neighbors, friends, family, and work colleagues may be surprised because it had appeared that the family was happy and loving; the truth about the violence makes it sometimes difficult for persons who are not the recipients of the violence to comprehend how the abuser, this nice person, could engage in emotional, physical, or sexual abuse. Even close family members might not want to believe that abuse has occurred within the family and blame the victim who reports it as causing trouble and lying. Silence can be deadly. In Hong Kong, women's silence about domestic assault is believed to increase their risk of being killed by an abusive husband (Leung 2014). In Turkey, poor women may know that their daughters are victims of incest but are unable to intervene due to their economic and social vulnerabilities. Kardam and Bademci (2013) explain that while domestic violence and incest are not exclusive to poor families, as they exist in any socioeconomic family, poor women may be more likely to come to the attention of social service professionals because families with higher socioeconomic backgrounds can hide family abuse. In Turkey, Kardam and Bademci (2013) found that mothers may help hide abuse and incest as a method of family unity, no matter what level of abuse occurs. As in other parts of the world, Kardam and Bademci report that in Turkey, 39% of women report domestic violence in their lifetime; 44% report emotional abuse and 15% report sexual violence.

Physical and sexual abuse are more likely to occur when the abusive partner is intoxicated either through alcohol or drugs than when sober (Jewkes 2002; Mishra et al. 2014). Research shows mixed results as to whether intoxication causes men to be violent or if violent men are just more prone to resort to violence when intoxicated. Some research has shown that male partner violence may occur if the intoxicated man also has higher levels of antisocial personality or an abuse-prone personality trait (Hines and Malley-Morrison 2005). Further, women victims are more likely to drink heavily. A study of abused women in South Africa found that the abused women were more likely to drink alcohol, particularly if they had experienced physical violence within the past year (Jewkes et al. 2002). Mishra et al. (2014) also found that in India domestic violence is more likely when alcohol is present, whether consumed by the male or the female.

Why are children violent?

Children who experienced or witnessed family violence may engage in violent acts as they age. This perpetuation of violence from one generation to another has been termed the Cycle of Violence Theory. Some research shows that girls from violent homes may be verbally abusive, boys who were hit by a parent are much more likely to resort to violence in their adult relationships, and, if boys both witness and experience physical violence, they are highly likely to become abusers as adults, compared to boys who did not have these experiences (Mills 2008). Children who experience childhood abuse may also engage in a variety of offending behaviors, including drug use and abuse, and may exhibit early abusive tendencies by abusing pets (Fagan 2005; Zilney 2007). In some cases, the abused child might kill a parent. Stacey Ann Lannert killed her father in 1990 when she was 18, after years of being sexually abused by him. She says the abuse started when she was a very young girl and became more frequent in her teenaged years. At her trial, she raised the issue of self-defense and insanity but the jury convicted her of first degree murder and she was sentenced to life imprisonment. The jury had not been made aware of the years of sexual abuse that Stacey had experienced or that she had feared that her father had been also sexually abusing her younger sister. Although her conviction and sentence were upheld on appeal, the Governor of Missouri, Matt Blunt, commuted her sentence just before his term ended and she was released from prison in 2009 (Martelli 2009). While the overall number of children who kill their fathers or mothers is low in the United States, boys are more likely to kill their parents than girls (see Bourget, Gagne, and Labelle 2007). The reasons that youth give for killing a parent are smoldering resentments built up from long-term abuse, shame, and disrespect and humiliation that they experienced at the hands of their parents (Hart and Helms 2003; Malmquist 2010).

Interracial couples and physical violence

There is a paucity of research on interracial domestic violence. Hattery (2009) found that, in interracial couples, White women were more likely to experience physical abuse from their Black male partners than Black women did from their Black male partners in same-race couples. Black women experienced the least amount of violence when they were in relationships with White men. This difference between White and Black women may exist because Black women have generally been unwilling to report family violence to the police or use the services of shelters; they wait to call for help until the situation has escalated to near-lethal violence (Lichtenstein and Johnson 2009; Potter 2008). Thus, the underreporting of domestic violence in the United States by Black women skews data on racial differences, and it is difficult to accurately determine the role of race. More global research is warranted to understand the effect of race, and interracial relationships, on domestic violence and a victim's willingness to seek help and report it.

Domestic violence and other domestic relationships

As we learn more about domestic violence and its intergenerational effects, we begin to realize that it is not limited to husbands and wives and their children. Other types of relationships should also be studied and offenders held accountable. In recent years, research has examined dating violence, violence in the lesbian, gay, bisexual, and transsexual (LGBT) community, and elder abuse.

Violence in a dating relationship, even among teenagers, has been the subject of some recent research and interest in the criminal justice community. Abusive partners may blame their victims and receive support from their friends for their violent behavior (McCarry 2010; Wright and Fagan 2013).The propensity to be violent towards one's dating partner can be seen in various attitudes and behaviors of both young men and women. The common methods of dating violence are akin to marital violence: threats of suicide, use of weapons, pushing, hitting, shoving, sexual violence, name-calling, blaming the victim, and demands that the victim break off any familial relationships or friendships that the abusive partner perceives to threaten the continuation of the couple's own relationship (Gamache 1998). The use of cigarettes, marijuana, and/or alcohol has been shown to increase the risk of dating violence for both perpetrators and victims (Reingle et al. 2013).

Throughout the twentieth century, domestic violence focused on heterosexual couples and there was a general belief that homosexual couples were non-violent. Some people believe that the LGBT community did not want to discuss intimate partner violence because the community faced other forms of social and legal stigmas and did not wish to raise other problems which could harm their ability to seek legitimacy and recognition. However, some research into domestic violence in the LGBT community has shown that they are not immune from interpersonal violence. Within the LGBT community, lesbian couples are more likely to report domestic violence (including verbal, physical, and sexual violence) than gay, bisexual, or transgendered couples (Hines and Malley-Morrison 2005). Although lesbian batterers become more violent as their partners become more submissive and dependent, among all LGBT couples, mutual verbal abuse is a common predictor of domestic violence. As with other domestic violence families, substance abuse, poverty, low self-esteem, and a history of child abuse and neglect and/or a history of family violence (mother was abused) are predictive factors in LGBT violence (Hines and Malley-Morrison 2005). Difficulty in assessing violence in LGBT communities stems from disagreement as to whether the same theories that are used to explain violence in heterosexual relationships can be used to explain violence in non-traditional family relationships. According to Koeppel and Bouffard (2014), non-heterosexual victims report significantly higher drug use and adverse health effects while heterosexual couples report significantly higher levels of depression and alcohol use. These impacts of domestic violence are higher than reported by similarly situated non-domestic violence victims. More research on violence in LGBT relationships is needed.

Elder abuse is another type of family violence that has generated discussion because more and more persons are living longer and the forms of abuse are quite diverse. The risk factors for elders being abused by their children or spouses are: female, over 75 years of age, mental or physical infirmity (Alzheimer's disease is the common mental infirmity associated with family violence), alcohol use, low socioeconomic status, social isolation, lack of social support, and past conflict between the parent and the child (Carp 2000). Offenders seem to exhibit caregiver stress, whether they are spouses or children. Sons and husbands are likely to hit, punch, slap, and may use knives, canes, or other forms of weaponry. Daughters (or daughters-in-law) who resort to violence tend to yell and verbally abuse the elders in their care (Carp 2000). Some elders also experience sexual abuse.

Intimate partner violence and victim responses

Do you understand why someone would stay if they are abused by a "loved" one? It is not uncommon for abused women to say that they can get over the physical pain soon enough, but the emotional pain is long lasting. The reasons for staying are complex. Some women initially stay because they believe that they can change the abusive partner, that they love him, and that his violent persona is not his true self. Also, the level of violence, the type of violence, and the frequency of physical and sexual violence can differ. Johnson (2008) explains that, in homes where victims experience domestic terrorism, the level and intensity of the violence is acute; in homes that experience situational violence, where violence can be irregular, there is wide variation in whether victims will accept the violence and whether the family will stay together. In very abusive homes, those described as exhibiting "domestic terrorism," women are six times more likely to experience such regular physical assaults as to consider it normal (Stark 2009). In families where the violence changes from one situation to another, victims may come to think about getting out and the families break apart (Johnson 2008).

Many victims provide similar reasons for staying in a violent relationship. Some women victims of domestic violence believe that they deserve the battering or mistakenly believe that they are strong and can handle the abuse. Some women stay because they have no other place to go and have no money or resources. Some women stay for the family pets or perhaps they have older male children who are not able to join them in a shelter. In communities where religion and community notions about gendered roles dictate that women are to remain silent and take abuse, women feel that they have no options. In nations where family honor is to be preserved and the patriarchal social order demands female subservience, women stay because of cultural norms and the legal system's failure or inability to acknowledge the abuse as illegal.

Regardless of whether victims come to expect violence and think that it is normal, people who are in abusive relationships need help in recognizing it and its patterns (Mills 2008). Victims who live in very violent homes need to realize that as the abuse in the home escalates in duration and severity, the victim's life and her children's safety are endangered. At some point, a victim will realize that she cannot change the abusive partner and the threat to her life becomes real and her love is replaced by fear, fear of death, and the loss of her children. Women who are physically abused experience shame and guilt; they are likely to indicate that they are afraid, that their relationship is not good, and that some physical forms of aggression are an appropriate method to resolve disputes (see Jewkes et al. 2002). Abuse impacts the victims' self-esteem and other aspects of their wellbeing. Kernic et al. (2000) found, for example, that abused women were at an increased risk for attempting suicide, having a mental disorder, and experiencing digestive system problems.

What has been done legally?

As seen in the Pennsylvania case at the beginning of this chapter, some women may be kicked out of their apartment and have no place to live if they are repeatedly visited by the police. These victims might think twice about calling for police help and might wait until the violence is extreme before seeking police assistance. Severe violence victims may not even call the police if they viewed the prior police response to be unjust (see Dichter 2013; Felton et al. 2002). Police responsiveness and the laws regarding domestic violence matter (Xie, Lauritsen, and Heimer 2012). If laws and policies are in place to enable abuse victims to get assistance and protection for their children then more victims may leave abusive homes.

In the United States, laws have been created at the state and national level to punish domestic violence offenders and to provide services for victims. Every state proscribes domestic violence in their statutes. These statutes give authority to the police to arrest persons who abuse a family member or dating partner. To recognize the severity and frequency of domestic violence at the federal level, the Violence Against Women Act (VAWA) was passed by the US Congress in 1994 and reauthorized in 2000, 2005, and 2013. The VAWA is credited with helping to bring the issue of domestic violence to national attention and supporting much needed services for diverse victims. The initial act has been modified to address inadequacies in the law and to improve criminal justice responses, particularly for Native American and immigrant women (Kwong 2002). Immigrant women need help because they may not understand the US legal system and may fear the police, they may not speak English, and may have been threatened by the abusive spouse with deportation. Such fears and threats may immobilize immigrant women and federal laws will protect victimized women regardless of their immigration status. The VAWA also seeks to add assistance for elderly victims, rural victims, LGBT victims, and dating victims, and to fund evaluation of prevention and protection efforts (Auchter and Moore 2013). The extension of legal protections to these historically overlooked victims aims to recognize that anyone can be a victim of intimate partner violence and that such violence is unacceptable in the United States.

Where can victims get legal help?

In the twenty-first century, many Western nations have looked to community groups (shelters and domestic violence programs), academics, law enforcement, lawyers, and judges to promote social and legal change. These groups have aimed to educate themselves and the community about the negative impact of domestic violence and to promote changes in laws and legal responses that will protect victims, treat offenders, and provide multidimensional responses to women of color. These efforts have seen mixed results; some research has shown that the changes have reduced violence across the board while others argue that victims who lack power and prestige have still been largely ignored (Eisikovits and Buchbinder 2000; Hines and Malley-Morrison 2005; Mills 2008; Riger et al. 2002; Roberts 2002). In non-Western nations, cultural and local legal practices may determine if and when help may be provided. Shelters and domestic violence treatment programs for victims or offenders are rare in poor, third world nations.

What if the police and courts don't believe victims?

There are a number of reasons why women do not report their domestic victimization to the police, but the primary reasons continue to consist of dissatisfaction with the criminal justice system and a failure to consider the incident serious enough as to require police attention (Gover et al. 2013). Police agencies, too, are concerned about domestic violence and how to respond to calls for assistance. Larger police departments may have greater access to a variety of community resources for victims and be able to respond to calls with specially trained officers. In Phoenix, Arizona, for example, there is a special unit of the city's police department that responds to domestic violence calls. Small towns and communities may not have enough police personnel to respond to domestic calls with two officers as proposed by national standards (Schafer and Giblin 2010). The differences between what might be appropriate community and police responses can vary, but victims, victims' advocates, and police responders agree that police–victim communication is important. If the victim does not believe that she/he will be taken seriously by the police and legal system and if the police do not believe that the victim will follow up with abuse allegations, then both sides may be reluctant to follow through on subsequent calls for assistance.

Courts have implemented a number of different programs to address concerns that they do not know how to process domestic violence cases. These court responses aim to ensure victim protection and adherence to new laws criminalizing domestic violence and attempt to find effective programs to abate violence in the home. In some urban communities, specialized domestic violence courts have been created; judges in these courts are educated to understand the latest research on battering relationships and the community programs and resources that are available to assist both batterers and their families. Another major initiative for misdemeanor domestic violence convictions is to require batterers to attend **group battering programs**. Labriola, Rempel, and Davis (2008) found that victims like having the batterer sentenced to a treatment program even if the results of their study showed that the treatment did not reduce violence in the home.

What type of legal help do immigrant women need to deal with domestic violence?

Immigrant women in the United States who are victims of domestic violence pose unique concerns for the police and the courts. While they may be willing to receive help from governmental agencies, they may not be able to communicate effectively with the criminal justice personnel due to language and cultural barriers. In their study, Sokoloff and Pearce (2011) found that the participating immigrant women knew that domestic violence was illegal in the United States but did not want the criminal justice system to punish their husbands; they only wanted to stop the abuse. However, the criminal justice system is designed to handle crimes and punishments and may not be the most effective avenue for addressing the remedies expected by immigrant communities. Immigrant women in Baltimore, for example, when faced with court processing of their victimization cases, chose to be deported back to their home nations even if they had a very sympathetic judge hearing their cases (Sokoloff and Pearce 2011). To address their needs, some US law schools provide legal assistance to immigrant women via clinics which provide information about the legal availability of **U-Visas** (a visa for victims of violence) to enable the women to stay in the United States. These clinics also help law students to understand the issue of domestic violence, especially as it pertains to immigrants (Barasch and Lutz 2002). U-visas are helpful for immigrants without permanent residence or citizenship because the victims might not be able to return to their home country for any number of reasons (e.g., there is war in their homeland, or their family would view the women with disdain for breaking away from her husband).

Necessary criminal justice policy responses and domestic violence

Criminal justice system responses to domestic violence must be designed with sensitivity to race/ethnicity, class, gender/sexual orientation, age, and immigration status. Although the US and Western law have been broadened over the past 50 years to include more forms of victimization and to redress prior inadequacies in the legal system, biases against victims of domestic violence remain intact. These biases are manifestations of the criminal justice system administrators' views of domestic violence which are also framed by their own cultural and familial backgrounds and view of women and familial relationships. People in the United States and in various parts of the world are willing to acknowledge that abuse exists, has a harmful impact on the family, and can contribute to subsequent criminal conduct. However, such changes are "worthless if it still deprives the true victims of access to legal remedies early enough to prevent the tragedies" that may result in victims' incarceration or the inability to get effective help (Buel 2003, 349). The criminal justice system must understand that victims do not always wish to follow through with their complaints and may want to retract them. In these cases, it is incumbent on the court to proceed in the interest of protecting domestic violence victims and their family.

Courts should not quickly dismiss cases based upon the unwillingness of a victim to proceed. If a person is convicted of misdemeanor domestic violence, a court can order the batterer to vacate the home, provide support for the family, and stay away from the victim and the family for a period of up to one year. Federal US law, 18 U.S.C. § 922(g)(9), provides that if a person is convicted of a domestic violence crime then the person can be prohibited from possessing firearms. In 2014, the US Supreme Court unanimously ruled in *United States v. Castleman* that the federal law applied to persons even if they are convicted of a misdemeanor domestic violence crime. Castleman pled guilty in the State of Tennessee to intentionally and knowingly causing bodily injury to a woman who was the mother of his child. The Court's decision recognizes that domestic violence crimes do not necessarily have to cause serious injury or involve violent physical force. Rather, the Court stated that, in many cases, the offender may use pushing, shoving, biting, or pinching actions but that these assaults are nonetheless assaults which can lead to life-threatening situations, and the federal law sought to prevent these.

To get immediate legal assistance from an abusive partner, in all jurisdictions, a victim can ask the court for an immediate **order of protection** from her/his abuser. This is a civil, not a criminal, proceeding that generally results in the perpetrator being restricted from seeing, calling, texting, or emailing the victim for a brief period of time. To extend the order, the civil court must allow the person against whom the order is directed an opportunity to be heard. If the judge agrees to this at the conclusion of a hearing, or, if the batterer fails to appear, a permanent order of protection can be imposed. An order of protection, while helpful in legally acknowledging violence in a home, should not be the sole source of protection for victims. It is, after all, a piece of paper and cannot stop violence if victims and batterers come into contact. However, the order of protection can enable the police to arrest a batterer if he/she violates its conditions, and the VAWA allows protective orders to be recognized across the United States. In addition to conditions to stay away from the victim, protection orders may include support for the family, custody arrangements, and required attendance at group counseling or a batterer intervention program. The order of protection is usually for one year, but, if extreme violence and threats are found, a court can impose the order for up to three years in many jurisdictions. Nonetheless, as found by a study in the United Kingdom, "the criminal justice system has its own difficulties inhibiting victim protection" when victims do not come to court to pursue orders of protection or when they initiate an order of protection but fail to come back to court to pursue it (Bettinson 2012).

Necessary social service agencies and medical professional responses to domestic violence

Community and social service agencies are also needed to protect victims of family violence. Most persons who work with domestic violence victims – whether they are in law enforcement, prosecuting attorney offices, legal clinics, courts, social services, or mental or medical health care – agree that coordinated responses are needed. Victims need to be heard and helped even if they decide to stay with abusive partners. When dealing with minority communities, including LGBT and immigrant communities, active participation from members of those communities is necessary to ensure appropriate understanding of the dynamics of abuse and the willingness/unwillingness of victims to come forward and to seek help.

A major source of assistance to victims of domestic abuse came in the form of the shelter movement of the 1970s. Formed by community activists who recognized victims' needs for support beyond what law enforcement could provide, shelters provided women and their children with a safe place to reside and hide from abusive spouses. Starting with one battered women's shelter opening in Arizona in 1973 and another in Minnesota in 1974, within a few years the movement had grown and, by 2005, there were over 2,000 shelters throughout the United States (Hines and Malley-Morrison 2005; Mills 2008; Potter 2008; Roberts 2002). The shelter movement, along with an increasing number of social scientists who began studying domestic violence during this time period, is also credited with many of the legal changes previously discussed (e.g., criminalizing domestic violence, recognizing battered women defense in the courts, the VAWA, etc.). Still, there continue to be inequities in the manner in which these benefits have been experienced by victims. Low-income, minority, non-English speaking, and gay and lesbian victims have not benefited from these innovations to the same extent as White women. There are many social and legal support services available to victims of domestic violence but not all victims know about them or want to use them. Shelters help victims know what services might exist in a community to help them to safely leave a violent home or relationship.

Victim counseling

Counseling is always recommended so that victims understand the dynamics of abuse, realize that it is not their fault, and can find safe avenues to either leave the relationship or understand the abuse that is happening should they remain in the home. Some battered women will take criminal responsibility for their violent partners, particularly if the violent partner is facing prison time if convicted of another offense. The impact of battering on trends in female offending must be incorporated into our understanding of violent relationships (Whaley et al. 2007). As discussed above, Black women may not want to call the police for help until the battering in their relationship is acute, and immigrant women may not understand the dynamics of an abusive relationship because, in their culture, violence may be accepted to keep women "in their place."

Counseling should be individually tailored to the needs of specific victims. Despite some research to the contrary, for example, not all victims of dating violence have experienced violence in their families. For some girls, dating violence is the first time that they have experienced it. These girls need help in understanding that the violence is not their fault and that it is not acceptable. If girls have experienced domestic violence within their families, then early intervention counseling can help thwart later abusive relationships (Jennings et al. 2013). For youth in immigrant communities, having other teenagers speak to them in their own language and explain the intersections of gendered relationships, violence, and culture can be effective in helping them realize that they are not alone and that support is available. In lesbian communities, outreach groups led by adult lesbians can help eliminate social isolation that teen lesbians may feel and provide them with a place to be free from harassment and prejudice. Thus, coordinated community and family responses are important and effective in helping young victims realize that they are not to blame and have support from parents and community resources (Gallers and Lawrence 1998; Levy and Lobel 1998; Prato and Braham 1998; Yosihama et al. 1998; Zimmer 1998).

If a victim does not want to call the police or know how to find a shelter then how can she or he find help?

Victims who do not know how to obtain help may decide to use a phone or the Internet to contact domestic violence hotlines. Many of these hotlines have access to personnel who can speak the language of the victims so that immigrant and non-English speaking victims can receive assistance.

The hotlines can help victims determine what to do and if they have a safe shelter to go to for help. If the police or medical help is needed, then hotline personnel usually recommend that the person hang up and call emergency assistance right away. Each nation can set up their particular emergency number so it is wise to know what it is: in North America the emergency number is 911, in the UK and some parts of Africa the emergency number for police is 999, in the European Union and China the number is 112, in other parts of Asia the number might be 117 or 119, in New Zealand it is 111; a person can check online to see what emergency number to call. Emergency calls for assistance may be pre-programed for mobile phones and have GPS tracking capability to enable police and medical responses.

Whether victims decide to leave the abusive home, it is a good idea to have a safety plan. A safety plan is advisable because when victims attempt to leave violent relationships, the likelihood of extreme violence by batterers attempting to prevent victims from fleeing is high. Service providers offer essential advice to victims to ensure their safety during the especially dangerous time when victims plan to leave their abusers. For instance, victims may be told to delete calls from their phone lists and online-use histories to avoid their partner's awareness of their efforts to obtain help. They will also be instructed in the creation of a safety plan, including collecting critical pieces of information such as pictures or other evidence of the abuse, medical records, marriage and birth certificates, children's immunization and school records, and social security cards and passports (if available), saving money, practicing how to leave with children, and having phone numbers of family, friends, or domestic violence programs that can help. Continued counseling of persons who have left an abusive partner can help empower victims to change the patterns that might keep them in abusive relationships, to prevent them from choosing one abusive partner after another, and to help them to reconcile the fact that they loved someone who harmed them.

What programs exist for offenders?

Because domestic violence is so pervasive, there simply is not enough jail and prison space for all offenders who hit, punch, verbally and emotionally assault their family members and intimate partners. Creative and consistent solutions are needed. Treatment goals for abusers include having the offender take responsibility for the abuse, recognize his/her inability to control anger, and find effective mechanisms to reduce stress and aggression. The pattern of abuse in a relationship may not be so linear as "she did this, so I did that"; thus, counselors are cautioned not to isolate one factor when working with batterers because batterers may have many ready-made excuses for why they hurt their family member or partner (Eisikovits and Buchbinder 2000). As Fagan (2005) notes, because the cycle of violence is found to continue when a child is abused, more treatment and services are needed for child victims of abuse so that they do not offend as adults. Auchter and Backes' (2013) analysis of the research on domestic violence treatment programs of offenders shows that we still need to examine what works in treating offenders because "one size does not fit all" and many questions still exist on what should be done to change violent behavior.

Conclusion

Every country varies in its understanding of domestic violence and its impact on the family, the community, and the society. With an established sociological perspective, Westernized nations are continuing to change laws and implement programs and policies to respond to the needs of victims.

In non-Western societies, nations are at varying stages of acknowledging the need to change laws, customs, and policies. Cultural traditions and religion are used to justify domestic violence in African and Asian nations in order to maintain the patriarchal family structure. In every nation, women blame themselves for the abuse while the various nations' social traditions may serve to reinforce the cultural norm of controlling "unruly" women.

Taken as a whole, the stories of domestic violence appear to be a "women's issue." However, beginning in the nineteenth century, feminists have argued that family violence is a socio-political and economic issue that affects millions of women, men, and children annually. Their fight for change has resulted in new laws that define domestic violence as a criminal act and new police policies that empower law enforcement agencies to treat victims of domestic violence as they would other victims of assault. Now, international scholars are utilizing the knowledge and research gained from decades of work in the United States and other Western nations to address domestic violence from the perspectives of their nations' cultures, traditions, and laws.

As we have seen in this chapter, legal change is not enough to alter attitudes and beliefs about domestic violence. Collaborative work is both encouraged and necessary among and between police agencies, social service agencies, researchers, counselors, and others. We have to prioritize the best intervention practices and refine the laws for the protection of victims of domestic abuse. Abusers, too, need help so they can recognize that the abuse is their responsibility, their fault, and perhaps they will begin to abate their violent tendencies. One day, with hope and hard work, these laws and practices will not be required, and family violence will become a thing of the past.

Suggested readings

Alfred, Charlotte. 2014. These 20 Countries Have No Law Against Domestic Violence. *Huffington Post*, March 8, 2014. Accessed April 25, 2014, http://www.huffingtonpost.com/2014/03/08/countries-no-domestic-violence-law_n_4918784.html

Berry, Dawn Bradley. 2007. *The Domestic Violence Sourcebook*. New York, NY: McGraw-Hill.

Buzawa, Eve S., Buzawa, Carl G., and Evan D. Stark. 2012. *Responding to Domestic Violence: The Integration of Criminal Justice and Human Services*. Thousand Oaks, CA: Sage.

Fontes, Lisa Aronson. 2005. *Child Abuse and Culture: Working with Diverse Populations*. New York, NY: Guilford Press.

World Health Organization. 2013. "WHO Multi-country Study on Women's Health and Domestic Violence Against Women." Accessed April 25, 2014, http://www.who.int/gender/violence/who_multicountry_study/summary_report/en/

Student engagement activities

1 Compare and contrast how Western and non-Western nations conceptualize domestic violence.

2 Develop a blog on recent instances of interpersonal violence in your community. (http://blog.ted.com/2013/01/25/5-brave-personal-stories-of-domestic-abuse/).

3 Compare an instance of family violence in the community to the wheel; what information was depicted that shows evidence of the attributes described on the wheel? (http://www.domesticviolence.org/violence-wheel/).

4 Develop a public service announcement for dating violence for your campus or community and indicate how victims can get help.

Discussion questions

1 What type of a safety plan would you have if you are a victim of DV? (http://www.domestic violence.org/personalized-safety-plan/).
2 Read several news stories that raise the issue of domestic violence and discuss the type of domestic abuse experienced. What are the warning signs that it is an abusive relationship? (http://www .hiddenhurt.co.uk/may_domestic_abuse_story.html).
3 Explain why children might engage in dating violence or more extreme forms of violence such as killing their mother or father. (http://www.pendulumfoundation.com/parricidefacts.html).

Key terms

Battered women defense
Battered women syndrome defense
Center for Disease Control (CDC)
Cycle Theory of Violence
Doctrine of coverture
Domestic violence
Economic abuse
Emotional abuse
Group battering programs
Immunity
Impunity

"Intimate partner violence" (IPV)
National Crime Victimization Survey (NCVS)
National Incidence Based Reporting System
National Violence Against Women Survey (NVAWS)
Order of protection
Physical abuse
Sexual abuse
U-Visa
Violence Against Women Act (VAWA)
World Health Organization (WHO)

References

Abel, Eileen Mazur. 2001. "Comparing the Social Service Utilization, Exposure to Violence, and Trauma Symptomology of Domestic Violence Female 'Victims' and Female 'Batterers.'" *Journal of Family Violence*, 16(4): 401–420. DOI: 10.1023/A:1012276927091

Adams, David. 2007. *Why Do They Kill? Men Who Kill Their Intimate Partners*. Nashville, TN: Vanderbilt University Press.

Adekeye, Olujide A., Abimbola, Oluremi H., and Sussan O. Adeusi. 2011. "Domestic Violence in a Semi-Urban Neighbourhood." *Gender & Behaviour*, 9(2): 4247–4261.

AFP. December 13, 2011. "Belgian Honour Killing: Pakistani Family Sentenced to Prison." *Express Tribune*. Accessed May 16, 2014, http://tribune.com.pk/story/305893/belgiums-first-honour-killing-trial-ends-sends-family-to-prison/

Alfred, Charlotte. 2014. These 20 Countries Have No Law Against Domestic Violence. *Huffington Post*, March 8, 2014. Accessed April 25, 2014, http://www.huffingtonpost.com/2014/03/08/countries-no-domestic-violence law_n_4918784.html

Alhabib, Samia, Nur, Ula, and Roger Jones. 2010. "Domestic Violence Against Women: Systematic Review of Prevalence Studies." *Journal of Family Violence*, 25: 369–382. DOI: 10.1007/s10896-009-9298-4

Auchter, Bernard, and Bethany L. Backes. 2013. "NIJ's Program of Domestic Violence Research: Collaborative Efforts to Build Knowledge Guided by Safety for Victims and Accountability of Perpetrators." *Violence Against Women*, 19(6): 713–736. DOI: 10.1177/1077801213494703

Auchter, Bernard, and Angela Moore. 2013. "Mounting and Sustaining the Violence Against Women Research and Evaluation Program at the National Institute of Justice." *Violence Against Women*, 19(6): 687–712. DOI: 10.1177/1077801213494702

Austen, Ian. January 29, 2012. "Afghan Family, Led by Father Who Called Girls a Disgrace, Is Guilty of Murder." *New York Times*. Accessed May 16, 2014, http://www.nytimes.com/2012/01/30/world/americas/afghan-family-members-convicted-in-honor-killings.html?_r=0

Barasch, Amy P., and Victoria L. Lutz. 2002. "Innovations in the Legal System's Response to Domestic Violence." In *Handbook of Domestic Violence Intervention Strategies*, edited by Albert R. Roberts, 173–201. Oxford: Oxford University Press.

Belew, Christine. 2010. "Killing One's Abuser: Premediation, Pathology, or Provocation." *Emory Law Journal*, 59(3): 769–808.

Bergman, Bo, and Bo Brismar. 1991. "A 5-Year Follow-up Study of 117 Battered Women." *American Journal of Public Health*, 81(11): 1486–1489. DOI: 10.2105/AJPH.81.11.1486

Bettinson, Vanessa. 2012. "Restraining Orders Following an Acquittal in Domestic Violence Cases: Securing Greater Victim Safety?" *Journal of Criminal Law*, 76: 512–527.

Bhatti, Nadeem, Jamali, Muhammad B., Phulpoto, Najma N., Mehmood, Teriq, and Faiz. M. Shaikh. 2011. "Domestic Violence Against Women: A Case Study of District Jacobabad, Sindh Pakistan." *Asian Social Science*, 7(12): 146–162.

Biggers, Jacquelyne R. 2003. "A Dynamic Assessment of the Battered Woman Syndrome and Its Legal Relevance." *Journal of Forensic Psychology Practice*, 3(3): 1–22. DOI: 10.1300/J158v03n03_01

Bourgett, Dominique, Gagne, Pierre, and Mary-Eve Labelle. 2007. "Parricide: A Comparative Study of Matricide Versus Patricide." *Journal of the American Academy of Psychiatry and the Law*, 35(3): 306–312.

Brennen, Barrington H. 2015. "Why Do Men Stay in Abusive Relationships?" *Sounds of Encouragement*. Accessed March 17, 2015, http://www.soencouragement.org/whymenstay.htm

Buel, Sarah M. 2003. "Effective Assistance of Counsel for Battered Women." *Harvard Women's Law Review*, 26: 217–350.

Bureau of Justice Statistics. 2011. *Homicide Trends in the United States, 1980–2008*. US Department of Justice, November 2011, NCJ 236018. Washington, DC.

Butler, Sara M. 2007. *The Language of Abuse: Marital Violence in Later Medieval England*. Leiden: Brill.

Carp, Frances Merchant. 2000. *Elder Abuse in the Family: An Interdisciplinary Model for Research*. New York, NY: Springer Publishing Company.

Catalano, Shannan. November 2012. "Intimate Partner Violence, 1993–2010." NCJ 239203. US Department of Justice: Washington, DC.

Chesler, Phyllis. 2010. "Worldwide Trends in Honor Killings." *Middle East Quarterly*, 17(20): 3–11.

Coughlin, Anne M. 1994. "Excusing Women." *California Law Review*, 82: 1–93.

Dichter, Melissa E. 2013. "'They Arrested Me – And I Was the Victim': Women's Experiences with Getting Arrested in the Context of Domestic Violence." *Women & Criminal Justice*, 23(2): 81–98. DOI: 10.1080/08974454.2013.759068

Do Something. 2014. "11 Facts about Domestic and Dating Violence." Accessed April 23, 2014, https://www.dosomething.org/facts/11-facts-about-domestic-and-dating-violence

Durose, Matthew R., Wolf, Caroline H., Langan, Patrick A., Motivans, Mark, Rantala, Ramona R., and Erica L. Smith. 2005. *Family Violence Statistics: Including Statistics on Strangers and Acquaintances*. US Department of Justice, Bureau of Justice Statistics.

Eckholm, Erik. August 16, 2013. "Victims' Dilemma: 911 Calls Can Bring Eviction." *New York Times*. Accessed May 16, 2014, http://www.nytimes.com/2013/08/17/us/victims-dilemma-911-calls-can-bring-eviction.html?pagewanted=all

Eisikovits, Zvi, and Eli Buchbinder. 2000. *Locked in a Violent Embrace: Understanding and Intervening in Domestic Violence*. Thousand Oaks, CA: Sage Publications.

Fagan, Abigail A. 2005. "The Relationship Between Adolescent Physical Abuse and Criminal Offending: Support for an Enduring and Generalized Cycle of Violence." *Journal of Family Violence*, 20(5): 279–290. DOI: 10.1007/s10896-005-6604-7

Fais, Cari. 2008. "Denying Access to Justice: The Cost of Applying Nuisance Laws to Domestic Violence." *Columbia Law Review*, 108(5): 1181–1225.

FBI (Federal Bureau of Investigation). 2014. *Uniform Crime Report*. Washington, DC.

Feder, Lynette, and Kris Henning. 2005. "A Comparison of Male and Female Dually Arrested Domestic Violence Offenders." *Violence and Victims*, 20(2): 153–171. DOI: 10.1891/0886-6708.2005.20.2.153

Felton, Richard B., Messner, Steven F., Hoskin, Anthony W., and Glenn Deane. 2002. "Reasons for Reporting and Not Reporting Domestic Violence to the Police." *Criminology*, 40(3): 617–647. DOI: 10.1111/j.1745-9125.2002.tb00968.x

Ferreira, Regardt J., and Frederick P. Buttell. 2014. "Can a 'Psycholosocial Model' Help Explain Violence Perpetrated by Female Batterers?" *Research on Social Work Practice*: 1–10. DOI: 10.1177/1049731514543665

Gallers, Johanna, and Kathy J. Lawrence. 1998. "Overcoming Post-Traumatic Stress Disorder in Adolescent Date Rape Survivors." In *Dating Violence: Young Women in Danger*, edited by Barrie Levy, 172–183. Seattle, WA: Seal Press.

Gamache, Denise. 1998. "Domination and Control: The Social Context of Dating Violence." In *Dating Violence: Young Women in Danger*, edited by Barrie Levy, 69–83. Seattle, WA: Seal Press.

Gordon, Linda. 2002. *Heroes of Their Own Lives: The Politics and History of Family Violence, Boston 1880–1960*. Urbana, IL: University of Illinois Press.

Gover, Angela R., Welton-Mitchell, Courtney, Belknap, Joanne, and Anne DePrince. 2013. "When Abuse Happens Again: Women's Reasons for Not Reporting New Incidents of Intimate Partner Abuse to Law Enforcement." *Women & Criminal Justice*, 23(2): 99–120. DOI: 10.1080/08974454.2013.759069

Hart, Jessica L., and Jeffrey L. Helms. 2003. "Factors of Parricide: Allowance of the Use of Battered Child Syndrome as a Defense." *Aggression & Violent Behavior*, 8: 671–683. DOI: 10.1016/S1359-1789(02)00103-9

Hattery, Angela J. 2009. *Intimate Partner Violence*. Lanham, MD: Rowman & Littlefield Publishers.

Hines, Denise A., and Kathleen Malley-Morrison. 2005. *Family Violence in the United States: Defining, Understanding, and Combating Abuse*. Thousand Oaks, CA: Sage Publications.

Jennings, Wesley G., Richards, Tara N., Tomsich, Elizabeth, Gover, Angela, and Rachael A. Powers. 2013. "A Critical Examination of the Causal Link Between Child Abuse and Adult Dating Violence Perpetration and Victimization from a Propensity Score Matching Approach." *Women & Criminal Justice*, 23(3): 1–17. DOI: 10.1080/08974454.2013.802271

Jewkes, Rachel. 2002. "Intimate Partner Violence: Causes and Prevention." *The Lancet*, 359: 1423–1429. DOI: 10.1016/S0140-6736(02)08357-5

Jewkes, Rachel, Levin, Jonathan, and Loveday Penn-Kekana. 2002. "Risk Factors for Domestic Violence: Findings from a South African Cross-sectional Study." *Social Sciences & Medicine*, 55: 1603–1617.

Johnson, Michael P. 2008. *A Typology of Domestic Violence: Intimate Terrorism, Violent Resistance, and Situational Couple Violence*. Boston, MA: Northeastern University Press.

Kardam, Filiz, and Emine Bademci. 2013. "Mothers in Cases of Incest in Turkey: Views and Experiences of Professionals." *Journal of Family Violence*, 28: 253–263. DOI: 10.1007/s10896-013-9495-z

Kernic, Mary A., Wolf, Marsha E., and Victoria L. Holt. 2000. "Rates and Relative Risk of Hospital Admission Among Women in Violent Intimate Partner Relationships." *American Journal of Public Health*, 90(9): 1416–1420.

Kiefer, Michael. April 13, 2015. "Jodi Arias Sentenced to Natural Life in Prison." *The Arizona Republic*. Accessed March 25, 2016, http://www.usatoday.com/story/news/nation/2015/04/13/jodi-arias-sentencing/25691575/

Kim, Bitna, Titterington, Victoria B., Kim, Yeonghee, and William Wells. 2010. "Domestic Violence and South Korean Women: The Cultural Context and Alternative Experiences." *Violence and Victims*, 25(6): 814–830. DOI: 10.1891/0886-6708.25.6.814

Kishor, Sunita, and Kiersten Johnson. 2006. "Reproductive Health and Domestic Violence: Are the Poorest Women Uniquely Disadvantaged?" *Demography*, 43(2): 293–307. DOI: 10.1353/dem.2006.0014

Koeppel, Maria, and Leanna Bouffard. 2014. "Sexual Orientation and the Effects of Intimate Partner Violence." *Women & Criminal Justice*, 24(3): 126–150. DOI: 10.1080/08974454.2013.842517

Kwong, Deanna. 2002. "Removing Barriers for Battered Women: A Comparison of Immigrant Protections under VAWA I & II." *Berkeley Women's Law Journal*, 17: 137–152.

Labriola, Melissa, Rempel, Michael, and Robert C. Davis. 2008. "Do Batterer Programs Reduce Recidivism? Results from a Randomized Trial in the Bronx." *Justice Quarterly*, 25(2): 252–282. DOI: 10.1080/07418820802024945

Leung, Lai-ching. 2014. "It's a Matter of Trust: Policing Domestic Violence in Hong Kong." *Journal of Interpersonal Violence*, 29: 82–101. DOI 10.1177/0886260513504645

Levy, Barrie, and Kerry Lobel. 1998. "Lesbian Teens in Abusive Relationships." In *Dating Violence: Young Women in Danger*, edited by Barrie Levy, 203–208. Seattle, WA: Seal Press.

Lichtenstein, Bronwen, and Ida M. Johnson. 2009. "Older African American Women and Barriers to Reporting Domestic Violence to Law Enforcement in the Rural Deep South." *Women & Criminal Justice*, 19(4): 286–305. DOI: 10.1080/08974450903224329

Liem, Marieke C. A. 2010. "Homicide–Parasuicide: A Qualitative Comparison with Homicide and Parasuicide." *The Journal of Forensic Psychiatry & Psychology*, 21(2): 247–263. DOI: 10.1080/14789940903335144

Malmquist, Carl P. 2010. "Adolescent Parricide as a Clinical and Legal Problem." *Journal of American Academy of Psychiatry and the Law*, 38(1): 73–79.

Margolick, David. January 22, 1994. "Lorena Bobbitt Acquitted in Mutilation of Husband." *New York Times*. Accessed May 16, 2014, http://www.nytimes.com/1994/01/22/us/lorena-bobbitt-acquitted-in-mutilation-of-husband.html

Martelli, Joan. March 26, 2009. "Convicted Murderer Released After 18 Years in Prison." *ABC News*. Accessed May 16, 2014, http://abcnews.go.com/2020/story?id=7168291

McCarry, Melanie. 2010. "Becoming a 'Proper Man': Young People's Attitudes about Interpersonal Violence and Perceptions of Gender." *Gender and Education*, 22(1): 17–30. DOI: 10.1080/09540250902749083

McQuigg, Ronagh J. A. 2011. "What Does the Council of Europe Convention on Violence Against Women Hold as Regards Domestic Violence?" *International Journal of Human Rights*, 16(7): 947–962. DOI: 10.1080/13642987.2011.638288

Miller, Susan L. 2001. "The Paradox of Women Arrested for Domestic Violence: Criminal Justice Professionals and Service Providers Respond." *Violence Against Women*, 7: 1339–1376. DOI: 10.1177/10778010122183900

Mills, Linda G. 2008. *Violent Partners: A Breakthrough Plan for Ending the Cycle of Abuse*. New York, NY: Basic Books.

Minakeer, Joanne C., and Laureen Snider. 2006. "Husband Abuse: Equality with a Vengeance?" *Canadian Journal of Criminology and Criminal Justice*, 48(5): 753–780.

Mishra, Ashok, Patne, S. K., Tiwari, Ranjana, Srivastava, Dhiraj Kumar, Gour, Neeraj, and Manoj Bansal. 2014. "A Cross-sectional Study to Find Out the Prevalence of Different Types of Domestic Violence in Gwalior City and to Identify the Various Risk and Protective Factors for Domestic Violence." *Indian Journal of Community Medicine*, 39: 21–25.

O'Brien, Kristy L., Cohen, Lynne, Pooley, Julie Ann, and Myra F. Taylor. 2013. "Lifting the Domestic Violence Cloak of Silence: Resilient Australian Women's Reflected Memories of Their Childhood Experiences Witnessing Domestic Violence." *Journal of Family Violence*, 28: 95–108.

Potter, Hillary. 2008. *Battle Cries: Black Women and Intimate Partner Abuse*. New York, NY: New York University Press.

Prato, Laura, and Regina Braham. 1998. "Coordinating a Community Response to Teen Dating Violence." In *Dating Violence: Young Women in Danger*, edited by Barrie Levy, 153–163. Seattle, WA: Seal Press.

Rambo, Kirsten S. 2009. *"Trivial Complaints": The Role of Privacy in Domestic Violence Law and Activism in the U.S. New York, NY: Columbia University Press.*

Regehr, Cheryl, and Graham Glancy. 1995. "Battered Woman Syndrome Defense in Canadian Courts." *Canadian Journal of Psychiatry*, 40(3): 130–135.

Reingle, Jennifer M., Jennings, Wesley G., Maume, Michael O., and Kelli A. Komro. 2013. "The Substance-Related Etiology of Teen Dating Violence Victimization: Does Gender Matter?" *Women & Criminal Justice*, 23(3): 1–23. DOI: 10.1080/08974454.2013.802269

Riger, Stephanie, Bennett, Larry, Wasco, Sharon M., Schewe, Paul A., Frohmann, Lisa, Camacho, Jennifer M., and Rebecca Campbell. 2002. *Evaluating Services for Survivors of Domestic Violence and Sexual Assault*. Thousand Oaks, CA: Sage Publications

Roberts, Albert R. 2002. "Myths, Facts, and Realities Regarding Battered Women and Their Children: An Overview." In *Handbook of Domestic Violence Intervention Strategies: Policies, Programs, and Legal Remedies*, edited by Albert R. Roberts, 3–22. Oxford: Oxford University Press.

Rothenberg, Bess. 2002. "The Success of the Battered Woman Syndrome: An Analysis of How Cultural Arguments Succeed." *Sociological Forum*, 17(1): 81–103. DOI: 10.1023/A:1014593523666

Santos, Fernanda. May 9, 2013. "After Verdict, Sentencing Is a New Trial for Jurors." *New York Times*. Accessed May 16, 2014, http://www.nytimes.com/2013/05/10/us/after-conviction-of-jodi-arias-deciding-on-the-death-penalty.html

Saunders, Daniel G. 2002. "Are Physical Assaults by Wives and Girlfriends a Major Social Problem? A Review of the Literature." *Violence Against Women*, 8(12): 1424–1448. DOI: 10.1177/107780102237964

Schafer, Joseph A., and Matthew J. Giblin. 2010. "Policing Intimate Partner Violence in Rural Areas and Small Towns: Policies, Practices and Perceptions." *Women & Criminal Justice*, 20(4): 283–301. DOI: 10.1080/08974454.2010.512226

Shahidullah, Shahid M., and C. Nana Derby. 2009. "Criminalisation, Modernisation, and Globalisation: The US and International Perspectives on Domestic Violence." *Global Crime*, 10(3): 196–223. DOI: 10.1080/17440570903079923

Sheehy, Elizabeth, Stubbs, Julie, and Julia Tolmie. 2012. "Defences to Homicide for Battered Women: A Comparative Analysis of Laws in Australia, Canada and New Zealand." *Sydney Law Review*, 34: 467–492.

Sherman, Lawrence W., Schmidt, Jannell D., and Dennis P. Rogan. 1991. *Policing Domestic Violence: Experiments and Dilemmas*. New York, NY: Free Press.

Skoloff, Brian. May 8, 2013. "Jodi Arias Convicted of First-Degree Murder." *Desert News*. Accessed May 16, 2014, http://www.deseretnews.com/article/765629077/Jodi-Arias-convicted-of-first-degree-murder.html?pg=all

Sokoloff, Natalie J., and Susan C. Pearce. 2011. "Intersections, Immigration, and Partner Violence: A View from a New Gateway – Baltimore, Maryland." *Women and Criminal Justice*, 21(3): 250–266. DOI: 10.1080/08974454.2011.584468

Stark, Evan. 2009. *Coercive Control: How Men Entrap Women in Personal Life*. Oxford: Oxford University Press.

Straus, Murray A. 2005. "Women's Violence Toward Men Is a Serious Social Problem." In *Current Controversies on Family Violence*, 2nd edn, edited by D. R. Loseke, R. J. Gelles, and M. M. Cavanaugh, 55–77). Newbury Park, CA: Sage Publications.

Tarrant, Stella. 1990. "A Feminist Perspective." *Legal Service Bulletin*, 15(4): 147–150.

Thurman v. City of Torrington, 595 F. Supp. 1521, D. Conn, 1984.

Truman, Jennifer L, and Rachel E. Morgan. 2014. *Nonfatal Domestic Violence, 2003–2012*. US Department of Justice, Bureau of Justice Statistics.

United Nations. 2014. "Facts and Figures: Ending Violence Against Women: A Pandemic in Diverse Forms." United Nations Entity for Gender Equality and the Empowerment of Women. Accessed on April 24, 2014 at http://www.unwomen.org/en/what-we-do/ending-violence-against-women/facts-and-figures#notes

United States v. Castleman, 572 US ___, 2014.

Walker, Lenore E. 1984. *The Battered Woman Syndrome*. New York, NY: Springer Publishing Company.

Walker, Lenore E., and Angela Browne. 1985. "Gender and Victimization by Intimates." *Journal of Personality*, 53(2): 179–195. DOI: 10.1111/j.1467-6494.1985.tb00363.x

Wesely, Jennifer K., and James D. Wright. 2009. "From the Inside Out: Efforts by Homeless Women to Disrupt Cycles of Crime and Violence." *Women & Criminal Justice*, 19(3): 217–234. DOI: 10.1080/08974450903001552

Whaley, Rachel Bridges, Moe, Angela M., Eddy, J. Mark, and Jean Daugherty. 2007. "The Domestic Violence Experiences of Women in Community Corrections." *Women & Criminal Justice*, 18(3): 25–45. DOI: 10.1300/J012v18n03_02

World Health Organization. October 2013. *Violence Against Women: Intimate Partner and Sexual Violence Against Women*. Fact sheet no. 239. Accessed April 24, 2014, http://www.who.int/mediacentre/factsheets/fs239/en/

Wright, Emily M., and Abigail A. Fagan. 2013. "The Cycle of Violence in Context: Exploring the Moderating Roles of Neighborhood Disadvantage and Cultural Norms." *Criminology*, 51(2): 217–249. DOI: 10.1111/1745-9125.12003

Xie, Min, Lauritsen, Janet L., and Karen Heimer. 2012. "Intimate Partner Violence in U.S. Metropolitan Areas: The Contextual Influences of Police and Social Services." *Criminology*, 50(4): 961–992. DOI: 10.1111/j.1745-9125.2012.00284.x

Yosihama, Mieko, Parekh, Asha L., and Doris Boyington. 1998. "Dating Violence in Asian/Pacific Communities." In *Dating Violence: Young Women in Danger*, edited by Barrie Levy, 185–195. Seattle, WA: Seal Press.

Zilney, Lisa Anne. 2007. *Linking Animal Cruelty and Family Violence*. Youngtown, NY: Cambria Press.

Zimmer, Bonnie. 1998. "Felicia: Working with a Teen Mother in an Abusive Relationship." In *Dating Violence: Young Women in Danger*, edited by Barrie Levy, 164–171. Seattle, WA: Seal Press.

CHAPTER 7

Victimization enabled by technology

Cyberbullying and related crimes

Student learning outcomes

After reading this chapter, you should be able to:

- Distinguish among cyberbullying, cyberstalking, and cyberharassment offenses.
- Describe the relationship between bullying and cyberbullying behaviors.
- Explain why victims of cyberharassment might commit suicide.
- Indicate appropriate criminal justice and community responses to cyberbullying.

Introduction

It was a school day that seemed like any other September day in 2013. The sun was shining and the school buses picked up and delivered children to schools in Polk County, Florida. But September 10, 2013, was not just any other day for one girl, Rebecca Sedwick (Allen 2013). The young girl decided that she had had enough. Rebecca Sedwick was 12 and had been bullied by two female classmates for one and a half years over a boy at her middle school. Rebecca had dated the boy in middle school and after they broke up he started dating someone else. Because the new girlfriend was jealous of Rebecca, the new girlfriend began to taunt her and encouraged others at the school to do likewise.

Rebecca's mother did not know that her daughter planned to kill herself that day, thinking that she was heading to school in the morning. Rebecca, however, had other ideas swimming around in her mind as she changed her online screen name to "That Dead Girl," climbed to the top of an abandoned concrete plant, and jumped to her death (Allen 2013; Stanglin and Welch 2013). She had tried at least once before to take her life when in December, 2012, she slit her wrists. Perhaps because the prior attempt did not work, she decided to take a surer path to her death by jumping off the tall building, or maybe by selecting an abandoned tower she would not be stopped. It is possible that she wanted to be stopped; she had messaged a male friend that she was going to jump just before leaving her home (Stanglin and Welch 2013). What is clear is that she was depressed, suicidal, felt terrorized by the bullying, and wanted to die.

Women, Crime, and Justice, First Edition. By Elaine Gunnison, Frances P. Bernat, and Lynne Goodstein.
© 2017 John Wiley & Sons, Ltd. Published 2017 by John Wiley & Sons, Ltd.

The bullying that Rebecca experienced follows an all-too-familiar pattern. One of the bullies was her former best friend. Not unusual, the bullying Rebecca received involved other students and former friends who either participated in it or did nothing to stop the assault on Rebecca's character and help her to cope. One report said that at least 15 girls bullied her (Stanglin and Welch 2013). In an attempt to get away from the bullying, Rebecca had changed schools but, in a virtual world, face-to-face school bullying can be augmented by going online (Allen 2013). In Rebecca's case, the last straw might have been the online bullying. Two girls seem to have been the primary attackers who pushed Rebecca too far. Just prior to the suicide, her former best friend, aged 12 at the time Rebecca died, and a 14-year-old teenager, who was dating Rebecca's former boyfriend, hacked into Rebecca's Facebook account (Stanglin and Welch 2013). They posted pictures of condoms, modified a picture of Rebecca, and posted messages that Rebecca would have sex with anyone who came to her house, and said that she was a slut. One month after the suicide, the two teens did not believe that they had done anything wrong (Stanglin and Welch 2013).

State law enforcement authorities considered whether the two females who hacked into Rebecca's Facebook page should be criminally charged with a crime other than bullying – aggravated stalking – because Florida did not have a law against bullying. So the authorities were contemplating whether some other statutory crime would fit the behavior (Stanglin and Welch 2013). The former best friend knew Rebecca's password so it was not difficult for the girls to get into her account and alter her page. Rebecca's mother believes that it was the cumulative "abusive" behavior of the children that contributed to her daughter's depression, suicidal thoughts, and ultimate death. The state attorney in Florida, however, found that there was not enough evidence to proceed with criminal charges of aggravated stalking and dropped them. It was not until the criminal charges were dropped that the former best friend said that she wanted to be part of an anti-bullying campaign. This desire, of course, is too late for Rebecca, but it is what we want our youth to do. We want them to acknowledge that their bullying words and actions can hurt and if a bullied victim is depressed, feels alone, and ganged up on then it can lead to suicide. The former best friend said that she had been bullied herself but continued to claim that her behavior was not online "stalking." The 14-year-old, who was dating Rebecca's former beau and was jealous of Rebecca because the boy had continued to say nice things about her despite the breakup, posted a defiant message online that said that she did not give a "F" that Rebecca killed herself.

When Rebecca jumped to her death, she was not and will not be the first youth to ever commit suicide, nor even the first to commit suicide due to cyberbullying. In the 12 months leading up to Rebecca Sedwick's death, the following girls committed suicide due to online bullying in the United States, England, and Ireland: Ciara Pugsley, aged 15, died in September 2012; Erin Gallagher, aged 13, died in October 2012; her sister Shannon Gallagher, aged 15, died several weeks later in December 2012; Jessica Laney, aged 16, died in December 2012; Hannah Smith, aged 14, died in August 2013; and still the deaths continue (Edwards 2013). What do these deaths have in common and what is cyberbullying and cyberstalking?

How does technology impact criminal victimization and what can the criminal justice system do? This chapter explores how technology enables female victimization. We will examine how technology has created new venues for victimization and attempt to discern how the criminal justice system can respond to questions about crime definitions, evidentiary proof, and what policies and programs can be utilized to handle emerging methods of victimization.

Bullying behavior and victimization

Understanding cyberbullying victimization requires us to step back a moment and look at the baseline offense of bullying. When we consider the root crime of bullying, some clear trends emerge about age and gender. Bullying behavior is primarily associated with young, immature persons who repeatedly engage in acts of verbal, emotional, or physical assaults on a targeted victim. Some victims are targeted because they appear different from their peer group: they may be from a different ethnic or racial group; they may be homosexual; they may be small or appear to be frail; and they may be smart or have a learning disability. If a person is targeted because of their race, gender, ethnicity, or sexual orientation then they may be considered to be a victim of a **hate crime**. The Bullying Statistics organization (2014) reports that in the United States about 160,000 youth miss school each year because they are being bullied and feel afraid. In the Western world, however, we find that bullying occurs in our schools, neighborhoods, and workplaces (Brewer and Whiteside 2012; Chapell et al. 2004; Espelage, Bosworth and Simon 2001). Bullying is not limited to children in a playground and can be found in adult workplaces where persons who are "different" are targeted, teased, and harassed.

Researchers in Europe and North America have found that young males tend to be victims and aggressors of physical bullying behavior more than females, but if verbal aggression is taken into account then gender differences may abate (Frisén, Jonsson and Persson 2007). In Sweden, for example, 39% of students reported bullying victimization, 20% said that they bullied others and 13% reported being both a bully and bullying other students (Frisén, Jonsson and Persson 2007). In Ireland, over 60% of school youth indicated that other students at the school were bullied a little bit and 15% said that other youth were bullied a lot (McGuckin and Lewis 2006). Thus, if we examine bullying as part of youth development then we should not be surprised to find that middle school and high school males and females self-report either being a bully or being bullied during the school year.

It is important to understand that bullying is not something that a person might just grow out of doing, and that bullying can have dire consequences on the physical, social, and mental health of the targeted person – female or male. Wolke et al. (2013) indicate that bullying is not harmless fun that is a "rite of passage" from childhood into adulthood. Rather, they assert that young bullies are usually strong and healthy male children who have problematic home situations and may engage in criminal acts as they age. In their longitudinal study that tracked children into adulthood in North Carolina, they also found that victims of bullies may come from dysfunctional families and be predisposed to emotion or psychiatric problems in their youth. As they compared bullies and victims, they found that if a person was neither a victim nor a bully then the person was not likely to have any negative adulthood problems in terms of his/her health, wealth, and social relationships, and would not engage in criminal or risky lifestyle behaviors (felonies, drug use, or one-night stands with strangers). However, if a person was a bully-victim then the person experienced the most negative outcomes in terms of his/her adult health, wealth, and social relationships; if a person was a bully only then he/she was more likely than other group of persons to engage in risky and illegal behavior and also experience some negative impact on his/her health, wealth, and social relationships; if a person was only a victim of a bully then he/she experienced some negative impact on his/her health, wealth, and social relationships and might also engage in some illegal behavior. Chronic victims of bullying have elevated levels of problems with social relationships, poor educational achievements, and economic problems as adults.

TEXT BOX: Statistics: Bullying statistics 2010

New bullying statistics for 2010 revealed that about one in seven students in grades kindergarten through 12th grade is either a bully or has been a victim of bullying. Sometimes a teen or child who has been bullied eventually becomes the bully as a way to retaliate. In fact, revenge for bullying

(continued)

is one of the strongest motivations for school shootings, according to recent bullying statistics. A reported 61% of students said they believe students shoot others at school because they have been victims of physical violence at home or at school. This is a true indicator that bullying can occur in all forms by other students, children, and teens as well as adults. According to various bullying studies, many teens and children act out violently on their peers through acts of bullying because they are abused at home.

Other bullying statistics

- Over half, about 56%, of all students have witnessed a bullying crime take place while at school.
- A reported 15% of all students who don't show up for school report it to being out of fear of being bullied while at school.
- There are about 71% of students that report bullying as an on-going problem.
- Along that same vein, about 1 out of every 10 students drops out or changes schools because of repeated bullying.
- One out of every 20 students has seen a student with a gun at school.
- Some of the top years for bullying include 4th through 8th grades in which 90% were reported as victims of some kind of bullying.
- Other recent bullying statistics reveal that 54% of students reported that witnessing physical abuse at home can lead to violence in school.
- Among students of all ages, homicide perpetrators were found to be twice as likely as homicide victims to have been bullied previously by their peers.
- There are about 282,000 students that are reportedly attacked in high schools throughout the nation each month.

Source: Bullying Statistics organization: http://www.bullyingstatistics.org/content/bullying-statistics-2010.html

Accordingly, bullying is a group behavior which becomes a normative part of an environment and can be easily found at any age. As youth progress from elementary to secondary schools, they are able to discern unwanted aggression from their peers and articulate their feelings of anxiety. Youth want to fit into their school environments and feel stress as they begin to grow and mature. Interestingly, bullying may be associated with a school's pecking order. In small rural middle schools, for example, students may engage in bullying behavior to maintain their social status in small, isolated schools where every student knows the others and some level of peer status was developed in the earlier grade levels (Farmer et al. 2011). Bullying behavior and victimization have been found to exist in higher levels when youth are in middle school and as they transition from middle school and the 9th grade into the 10th and 11th grades (Goldweber, Wassdorp, and Bradshaw 2013; Poteat and DiGiovanni 2010; Seals and Young 2003). It is during times of transition that children and adolescents may increase their aggression to maintain dominance over others. Bullies may also engage in other forms of deviant behavior, crime, and may perform poorly in school. Some persons never "grow out of" being a bully. Bullying behavior is found among college students and faculty and continues into other workplace settings; a study in the United Kingdom found an association between youth who were bullied or who bullied others as youth and subsequent bullying in the workplace (Chapell et al. 2004; Matthiesen and Einarsen 2007).

Gender, bullying, and victimization

Bullying behavior affects bullies and their victims. Being a bully in Western nations has been associated with the following psychosocial problems: low self-esteem, problems at home or school, jealously towards the victim, anger, peer pressure, depression, impulsivity, suicide and suicide attempts, and prior victimization (Espelage et al. 2001; Frisén et al. 2007; Lösel and Bender 2011; Luukkonen et al. 2009; Seals and Young 2003).

The self-esteem of both offenders and victims is lower than among youth not associated with any bullying activity. Farrington and colleagues (2011) found that being a bully increased the likelihood of engaging in delinquency by two-thirds. If a youth indicated that he was a bully at age 10, then by age 11 or 12 the boy was significantly likely to also be involved in minor criminal offenses. The effect of being a bully can also impact the emotional development of the child. Both boy and girl bullies show signs of being under emotional distress; although girl bullies may experience greater levels of depression than boys (Farrington et al. 2011; Lösel and Bender 2011).

Girls who bully others or who are bullied are at an increased risk for attempting suicide (Luukkonen et al. 2009). We should not be surprised then that Rebecca Sedwick was bullied by a group of youth from her school, that these bullies were as young as 12 years of age, or that she was targeted because of jealousy, to maintain a pecking order as the youth transitioned from one grade level to another, or that the bullies were female. The new girlfriend was jealous of Rebecca and encouraged Rebecca's school peers to repeatedly engage in targeted verbal aggressions directed against Rebecca. Not all victims of bullying commit suicide, but all victims do experience emotional problems, depression, social withdrawal, and low self-esteem. Rebecca experienced all of these symptoms, the most obvious expression of which was her first suicide attempt in 2012. Some victims of bullying act out as aggressors to others and bully their peers who they perceive as weak or vulnerable. Still other victims of bullying behavior engage in very serious assaults on the community. Recent examples of youth who killed classmates and teachers on US college campuses and secondary schools is evidence that there can be a reciprocal relationship between bullying victimization and physical aggression on others (Chapell et al. 2004).

Who are the offenders and victims of cyberbullying?

Cyberbullying is generally defined as bullying behavior committed through the use of electronic media. It can be committed with a computer, smart phone, text message, Instagram, email, personal digital assistant (PDA), or other social communication methods on the Internet. It can be committed by a direct victimization where a person is targeted with repeated, unwanted text or photo images; or by the sending of information or images of a victim to others with the aim of causing the victim injury, discomfort, or ridicule from others.

The bullying creates a hostile environment where the victim is demeaned and the offender is empowered. Nuccitelli (2012) listed 28 cyberbullying tactics used to victimize children electronically (although these tactics are also used against adults) and are as follows:

1 **Bash boards:** Online bulletin boards that demean a person or peer group with hateful comments.
2 **Chicanery:** A victim is tricked into divulging private secrets and publishing them online.
3 **Cyber drama:** Spreading gossip online about a victim that is spread to a few persons and then stopped.
4 **Cyberharassment:** Repeated offensive messages.
5 **Cyberstalking:** Use of a personal online environment to repeatedly threaten the victim with harm and intimidation; the victim feels tremendously fearful and unsafe.
6 **Denigration:** Putting the victim down and sending or posting untrue rumors and gossip.
7 **Email and cell phone image dissemination:** Sending a pornographic or sexual image to a victim and then resending it to others within a social network.
8 **Email threats and dissemination:** Posting a message to a victim and spreading it to others.
9 **Exclusion:** Keeping a person out of an online group.

10 **Exposure:** Posting or sending material about a person that was meant to be kept private, including images that are sexual.

11 **Flaming:** Angry, rude, or vulgar text or email messages.

12 **Griefing:** Cyberbullying that is intended to cause a victim or the victim's peers to feel grief, or to keep a victim out of an interactive game.

13 **Happy slapping:** Posting of an embarrassing video or a video of a physical assault of a victim in an online or social network site.

14 **Image and video:** Posting videos and images of a victim on YouTube or other public web space.

15 **Impersonation:** Pretending to be a victim and posting materials which make that person look bad.

16 **Instant messaging:** Using IM to send harassing messages or messages filled with hate towards a targeted victim.

17 **Interactive game harassment:** Using profane and harassing language to persons playing interactive games over the internet.

18 **Password theft lockout:** Stealing the victim's password and pretending to be the victim while sending provocative messages or images.

19 **Phishing:** Tricking a victim to reveal information about themselves and then disseminating it online, or using the victim's password to engage in unauthorized postings or purchases.

20 **Pornography and marketing list inclusion:** Signing a child victim up to receive numerous emails and instant messages from pornographic and marketing lists.

21 **Pseudonym:** A false name – for example, used online to hide a person's identity from his/her victim.

22 **Screen name mirroring:** Creating a screen name that is similar to a victim's screen name so as to create confusion.

23 **Sending malicious code:** Sending malware or viruses to a victim; usually victims are skilled in advanced computing technology.

24 **Sexting:** Inducing a person to send sexual pictures which can then be distributed to others.

25 **Text wars and text attacks:** Group of bullies gang up on a victim by sending hundreds of emails or text messages to the victim.

26 **Voting/polling booths:** Creating an online poll to embarrass persons by being voted a derogatory title such as "the ugliest" or "most promiscuous."

27 **Warning wars**: Making a false allegation against a victim that she or he is posting illicit information so that an internet provider will issue a warning or suspend the victim from service.

28 **Website creation:** Creating a website that is designed to demean and belittle a victim or a peer group.

Hence, there are a myriad of methods for cyberbullies to utilize to carry out their attacks. What makes cyberbullying behavior different from traditional bullying is the ability of offenders to be anonymous and for the comments to be spread fast and widely to others. In many instances, the images and postings are difficult, if not impossible, to remove (Maras 2015). Because the materials are posted electronically and passed from one person's device to another, the negative posts or pictures can last indefinitely. Youth are worried about being cyberbullied by having pictures being texted or sent through other electronic means (Bernat and Rodriguez 2014). Dir and colleagues (2013) found that females were more likely to report negative experiences from receiving sexting messages than males, and that single persons reported more negative experiences from sexting than persons in a relationship. Consequently, cyberbullying victims feel powerless and the intensity of the shame and embarrassment can be overwhelming as victims fear that the embarrassing and demeaning pictures, videos, and messages may arise at any time in their near or distant future to haunt them. Interestingly, Tarapdar and Kellett (2011) found that young children in the United Kingdom may report the cyber-victimization to parents and older youth will talk about it with their friends; younger persons were more likely to be victimized by abusive emails and texts or prank calls and older youth experienced more aggressive cyberbullying tactics such as the exchange of sexually explicit images, death threats, computer viruses, hate websites, or happy slapping.

One of the reasons that people think that cyberbullying is more pervasive than bullying is because of news stories reporting suicides, which have alarmed school officials and parents. Indeed, most cyberbullying studies are primarily performed in middle school and high schools. These studies have found that many youth report having been a victim of cyberbullying, with more females reporting cyberbullying victimization than males (Floros et al. 2013; Li 2008; Mark and Ratliffe 2011). Hinduja and Patchin (2012) argue that cyberbullying is not really an "epidemic" because traditional bullying in the schools is more commonplace. In their review of 35 journal publications on cyberbullying, Hinduja and Patchin (2012) found that, overall, 24% of youth reported being a victim and 17% reported being a bully. In addition, they reported that about 10% of students self-reported being both a cyber-victim and a cyberbully. (See Table 7.1.)

Even if bullying behavior is more commonplace than cyberbullying, cyberbullying is gaining national and international attention. Li's (2008) cross-cultural comparison of cyberbullying in China and Canada found that more middle school students in both countries self-reported higher levels of traditional bullying victimization than cyberbullying victimization. Not surprisingly, fewer students reported being a bully or a cyberbully than being a victim. In Canada, bullying victimization was 55%, cyberbullying victimization was 25%, being a bully was 31%, and being a cyberbully was 15%; in China, bullying victimization was 65%, cyberbullying victimization was 33%, being a bully was 34%, and being a cyberbully was 7% (Li 2008). In their study of three middle schools in Hawaii, Mark and Ratliffe (2011) found that girls had a higher self-report incidence of cyberbullying victimization than boys, and that a higher incidence rate was found in the larger public school followed by the private girls school, with the least amount of reported cyberbullying in the public charter school. Bernat and Rodriguez's (2014) study of cyberbullying victimization in a college sample of students in the southern United States found that 12% said that they were a victim of cyberbullying, 14% said they were a victim of cyberstalking, and 15% said that they were harassed online; 32% said they used offensive language in a chat room, and 26% said that they used offensive language in online gaming. While most of these college students did not report any negative consequences from being cyberbullied and did not report it, if they did tell someone it was most likely their parents or a best friend.

Table 7.1 Statistics: cyberbullying.

Cyber Bullying Statistics	Data
Percent of students who reported being cyber bullied	52%
Teens who have experienced cyberthreats online	33%
Teens who have been bullied repeatedly through their cell phones or the internet	25%
Teens who do not tell their parents when cyber bullying occurs	52%
Percent of teens who have had embarrassing or damaging pictures taken of themselves without their permission, often using cell phone cameras	11%

Source: Statistic Brain Research Institute (2013).

GLOBAL PERSPECTIVES: Cyberbullying in the United Kingdom

Recent studies have examined the nature and extent of cyberbullying behavior. The statistics that are reported show some varying rates of victimization but in the United States and in Europe, cyberbullying is considered to a pervasive, but underreported, problem. For example, Tarapdar and Kellett (2011, 15) examined cyberbullying in the United Kingdom and found that "in recent European comparative data, focusing on online bullying, 8% of those in the UK were bullied, placing it sixth out of 25 countries." This cyberbullying rate was higher than in other European countries such as Spain and France (see Livingstone et al. 2011). Upon further inspection of online bullying data in the United Kingdom, one study reported that approximately 20% of children were bullied online (AVG 2010). However, other research reports that these rates might be higher – as high as 31% (see Bryce 2009). While the exact rates of cyberbullying in the United Kingdom are difficult to calculate, it is clear that cyberbullying is a problem in this country. More recently, research has surfaced stating that over 5 million children are potential victims of cyberbullying in the United Kingdom via Facebook, Twitter, and Ask.fm (Ellis 2013). The same report identifies Facebook as being the biggest contributing source to online bullying and notes that females and males are at equal risk of being bullied online (Ellis 2013).

Cyberbullying and the GLBT community

In the Western world, little research has been completed on the relationship between homophobia and bullying. The research that has been conducted shows a relationship between one's sexual orientation and bullying behavior and victimization. Gays and lesbians indicate that they are repeatedly called derogatory names, experience physical assaults, and are frequently teased because of their sexual orientation. Gay slurs could be considered to be a form of social bantering, particularly among males who may use derogatory gay names against other males, but the impact of such verbal aggression can be severe. While we tend to think that only males use derogatory homophobic verbal aggression, females also engage in gay name-calling behaviors. The male or female aggressor's use of gay slurs is not directed only or singularly at gay and lesbian individuals, as victims might be either homosexual or heterosexual. What is important is that this verbal aggression may not be about one's sexual identity (although it might be), but that gay bashing or name-calling behavior is used to demean the victims and intimidate them. Consequently, gay naming-calling behavior seems to impact males more than females as males show higher signs of depression when called a gay slur than females – although females exhibit higher levels of social withdrawal than male victims (Poteat and Espelage 2007).

Males who have had homophobic words repeatedly used against them show high levels of anxiety, depression, and a lack of belonging or connection to the schools that they attend. In some cases, gay bashing leads to violence in the school setting by the male victims or by youth who fear being associated with a gay student. When Brandon McInerney, for example, was a 14–year-old middle school student in California, he shot and killed a 15-year-old openly gay classmate in 2008 in the school computer lab because McInerney feared that his peer, Larry King, had a crush on him (Saillant 2011). The tragedy is that McInerney planned the killing by carrying a loaded gun into the classroom, and, after taking his seat behind King, he shot him in the head. Years later, he said that he realizes now, way too late, that he acted out because he feared being thought of as gay. McInerney was small for his age and teased in school; he shot King twice in the head because he did not like being asked by King to be his Valentine. After pleading guilty to second degree murder in 2011, McInerney was sentenced to 21 years in prison (Saillant 2011).

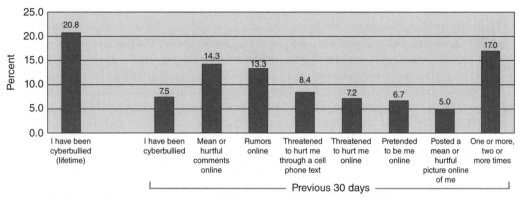

Note: N = 4441 Random sample of 10-18 year-olds from large school district in thesuthern U. S.

Figure 7.1 Cyberbullying victimization. *Source:* Cyberbullying Research Center, cyberbullying.org

More research on the relationship between bullying and gay bashing needs to be performed. Studies have shown that large percentages of homosexual school-aged children report being harassed verbally or hearing homophobic slurs and comments. While bullying and homophobia are linked, the fact that males are more likely than females to use gay slurs to demean others regardless of their sexual orientation evidences the use of homophobic words among males to establish their power over their peers (Poteat and Espelage 2005). Adolescent boys who engage in bullying tend to use words that are sexually biased to prove their "manhood" and heterosexuality, particularly as they transition through high school. Bullying and dominance then are connected in that adolescent males who express high levels of anti-gay attitudes also tend to use "biased language" outside of bullying incidents (Poteat and DiGiovanni 2010). Prejudice against homosexual persons and youth can be moderated when sexually biased words are limited but it does not necessarily end bullying behavior. Bullying behavior can be a separate form of aggression that may augment prejudicial views against homosexuals and be used to demean victims of bullying (Figure 7.1).

What are the risk factors associated with cyberbullying?

Western researchers studying cyberbullying behaviors agree that cyberbullying is a problem in our primary, secondary, and post-secondary schools. According to Snell and Englander (2010, 510), some researchers have said that cyberbullying "has reached epidemic proportions," "cyberbullying may become – or may already be – the dominant form of bullying behavior among children," and that among undergraduate college students surveyed by the Massachusetts Aggression Reduction Center "60% admitted to being victimized online." Patchin (2013) found after 10 years of research into cyberbullying that almost 15,000 middle and high school students reported being cyberbullied in 80 different US schools. It is thought that bullying victims may feel helpless in their neighborhoods and schools and have a sense of power when bullying others online or through other electronic mediums. In general, research shows that females may be more likely to be both victims and offenders of cyberbullying. The reasons provided for this gender disparity are that females may be more likely to use electronic means to express their displeasure with another person – the female may not wish to engage in face-to-face confrontation and hides behind the veil of a computer; that female victims of face-to-face bullying may resort to the electronic bullying against persons that they perceive to be "weaker" than themselves to vent their own frustrations at being the target of a school bully; that the Internet provides an easy venue to convey gossip, rumors, and threats about others; that females may be online and in chat rooms more frequently than males (Snell and Englander

2010). Floros et al. (2013) found that although we might not know the actual number of children who are cyberbullied, the impact felt by victims can be serious. Greek adolescents in their study revealed that victims and cyberbullies reported having lower grades than in a previous semester. The male youth, who reported more bullying behaviors than female youth, reported higher levels of impulsive, pathological Internet usage which included online gaming and online pornography.

In general, victims of cyberbullying feel depressed, isolated and alone, threatened, and have low self-esteem. Many female victims do not tell their parents that they are cyberbullied or harassed and attempt to cope with their anger, hurt, and depression on their own. That girls like Rebecca Sedwick would take their life after being repeatedly cyberbullied should now be understandable, even if it is difficult to fathom the depths of despair that she felt as she climbed the tower and jumped. Many cyberbullies also feel alone and depressed and have impulsive online behaviors which may be pathological.

 CASE STUDY: Cyberbullying suicide in Italy

Do you have a Facebook account? Most likely you have one and perhaps have had it for a while. What about an Ask.fm account? Perhaps you have never heard of this social media cite. Ask.fm is a popular social media website in Europe that has over 100 million registered users across the globe (Lepido 2014). If you haven't heard of Ask.fm, it is a website where you can ask others on the web questions and receive responses.

In February of 2014, a 14-year-old Italian schoolgirl named Nadia posed a question on Ask.fm using the alias "Amnesia" (Lepido 2014). Apparently, she was having some emotional difficulties and asked her online virtual peers for help. Unfortunately, Nadia did not receive the help she needed – rather, she was cyberbullied. Responses from cyberspace included insults written on her cyber-wall and comments such as "Kill Yourself" (Lepido 2014). Such hurtful comments pushed Nadia over the edge, and she took her own life by jumping to her death from the tenth floor of an abandoned hotel (Lepido 2014). Her suicide is yet another example that female victims of cyberbullying are not just found in the United States but these victims can be found across the world. This case has lawmakers in Italy considering a new bill to increase punishment for online cyberbullying (BBC News 2014).

Cyberbullying laws

The use of technology to engage in social networking is commonplace around the world. The Internet has provided new venues for cyber-victimization such as cyberbullying, cyberharassment, and cyberstalking. As noted earlier, the definitions of these crimes are not clear either within the United States or around the world. Consequently, although the impact of these offenses can traumatize victims, victims might not know where to turn for help if offenders are anonymous online contacts or lie about their true identify in online forums. In 2006, for example, Lori Drew, the mother of a Missouri teenage girl, was worried that Megan Meier, a 13-year-old girl, was saying negative things about her daughter online. To see if Meier was engaged in spreading the rumors, Drew created a false identity in MySpace by pretending to be a male teenager who liked Meier. When the "boy" began to send negative messages to Meier through MySpace, Meier became very depressed and ultimately committed suicide (Maag 2007). Because state laws, at the time, did not proscribe the behavior, federal prosecutors indicted Drew on violation of federal law that prohibited unauthorized access of a computer to intimidate another; the intentional unauthorized access was argued to be the creation of a fake identity. After her misdemeanor conviction, a federal district court on appeal set aside the guilty verdict because the court found that the federal law did not explicitly criminalize the access provided to Drew when she created the fake name on her account with MySpace (McCarthy and Michels 2009). In response to the gap in US state and federal law, many states enacted cyberbullying or cyberharassment laws (Hinduja and Patchin 2014). These laws aim to protect minors who are bullied online or through other electronic messaging means.

European nations are beginning to enact laws to deal with cyberbullying and cyberharassment in order to protect victims. Internationally, as within the United States, each nation's laws have to be viewed to determine if someone has engaged in cyberbullying – most likely, the laws that can be used to proscribe electronic victimization are those that pertain more specifically to harassment or stalking behaviors. The European Union, for example, is currently seeking to implement cyberbullying and harassment laws while also working with Facebook and MySpace in an attempt to explore ways to protect minors. In the United Kingdom, England and Scotland have both cyberbullying and harassment laws. It is expected that nations without laws will consider enacting legislation since cyberbullying is becoming a global issue; one poll found that 1 in 10 children are cyberbullied worldwide (Skye 2014). To address cyberbullying in other nations, the United Nations and UNICEF are asking that nations coordinate their efforts to promote governmental action to address cyber hate crimes (http://www.cybersmile.org/advice-help/category/cyberbullying-and-the-law).

Jurisdiction and the law

In addition to the creation of laws that will specifically address various cyberbullying behaviors, gaps in legal processes need to be filled if laws are to have any salience for deterring cybercrime and preventing victimization. One problem for nations seeking to proscribe cybercrime concerns **jurisdiction**. Because a cyber-victim might live in one community and the offender might be a person living in another, it is difficult to prosecute these behaviors when each site does not see the problem as something that they have jurisdiction over, particularly if the nature of the offense appears to be "minor" or the monetary damages minimal (see Bernat and Godlove 2012). International law may generally allow victims to proceed with prosecutions in the home communities, the locus of their victimization, but finding and extraditing offenders can be difficult. In addition to the technical problems of identifying online anonymous offenders, nations may not wish to assist in the extradition of their citizens if the nation's own laws do not classify the behavior as illegal within its borders. Such jurisdictional problems must be addressed and resolved in favor of victims but, to do so, the legal communities across the US and across nations have to work together to broaden the long arm of the law to enable each one to assert jurisdiction over the case. If cyberbullying offenses are to be taken seriously, then offenders cannot hide behind an anonymous or false identity posting and need to be transferred to the jurisdiction of the victim for prosecution. As cyberharassment and cyberstalking offenses become recognized as criminal in nations outside the Western world then, perhaps, problems of detection and prosecution of these behaviors can be mollified and governmental responses coordinated.

Necessary criminal justice policy responses to cyberbullying

A primary criminal justice agency that must address their policies and procedures for responding to cybercrime, in general, and cyberbullying behavior, in particular, is law enforcement. Law enforcement officers are on the front line when a child commits a suicide because of cyberbullying, not only because they have to investigate the nature of the death and respond to inquiries from the child's family but because the community will look to the police to make appropriate arrests and to explain the laws and legal processes that could prevent future deaths.

To address cyberbullying and provide appropriate law enforcement responses, each police department should have police **cybercrime forensic specialists** who can investigate allegations and collect evidence of cyberbullying. If a department cannot afford to hire an internal person(s) then the agency should work with other nationwide or statewide law enforcement teams. To start, the police should work with Internet service providers to identify cyberbullies or use reverse email lookup (Maras 2015; Orton 2011). If identified, and depending on one's nation, the process by which officers can search and seize computers and digital evidence may vary. If computers and other devices are seized, then cybersecurity law enforcement forensic specialists may be able to perform computer forensics to determine if offensive content is stored on a suspect's computer or other technological devices (Maras 2015; Orton 2011). Even if materials are deleted, forensic experts may be able to retrieve the data or find other evidence of criminal wrongdoing stored electronically. Ideally, the local police who confiscate the devices (smart phones, IPads, computers) will not attempt to turn them on in the belief that they can find incriminating evidence. Turning on a smart phone, for example, may delete important ISP information. It is best to leave computer forensics to a professional who can secure the device, save stored information and then begin the long and tedious task of mining it for data.

Police investigations in the United States require the police to be attentive to constitutional rights of both alleged offenders and victims. If the constitutional rights of a suspect are violated then the evidence could be suppressed and the case against the defendant dismissed. Among the constitutional issues that arise in the United States for cybercrime investigations are a person's right of privacy and a person's right not to be the subject of a search or seizure without probable cause or a warrant. The **right of privacy** is of concern because a person may argue that their private communications (including emails, text messages, and private chat room conversations) are protected under the Fourth Amendment to the US Constitution from unreasonable searches and seizures by the government. The privacy right aims to protect a person's ability to think and act, within bounds of the law, without governmental intrusion into their private life. In the United States, officers will need to submit an affidavit indicating who is to be arrested and for what offense(s) or particularly describe the technological devices (e.g., computers, smart phones, gaming consoles, memory cards or chips) that are believed to have been used in a cybercrime(s) and where they are to be located. In general, a person might have a right of privacy as to their own computer but this right can be limited if the computer is shared with others. If the computer is owned by an employer or the victim, then a suspect may not be able to claim a right of privacy to prevent the forensic analysis of the computer or digital materials (Orton 2011).

In their investigations, the police can be proactive and detect cyberbullies by pretending to be a victim. Officers can set up false profiles and pose as a youth victim in gaming communities and post messages on youth-oriented bulletin boards or in other online venues that the victim used to intercept communications and bullying behaviors (Maras 2015). Such tactics will not violate the law but officers should be careful not to lead or direct a person to commit a crime; providing a person with the opportunity to engage in a crime is all right, but entrapment is a legal defense in the United States and could result in a not guilty verdict.

In addition to the investigation of cyberbullying offenses and the securing of evidence, the police can play a role in preventing suicides due to cyberbullying by helping to educate the community on the importance of contacting the police and reporting cyberbullying before victims become despondent. Upon a report of cyberbullying, the police can help to empower victims by taking the reports seriously and providing information to the victim and the victim's family about community support services that are available. The police can also reach out to local schools and college campuses to educate teachers, students, and administrators about the laws and why cyberbullying threats will be taken seriously. During such outreach sessions, the police can indicate what victim support services are available. Other information that the police should provide includes advising parents of youth how to set their email and internet accounts to block offensive content and offensive emails as well as privacy screens for their social media accounts.

TEXT BOX: Cyberbullying: What we know, What can we do?

Figure – statistics and the legal framework

Whether in the US or Europe, statistics and figures tend to broadly agree. **Between one and five and one in three children tend to experience cyberbullying at some point in their lives.** Also, most cyberbullying perpetrators are girls.

While many **teens talk to a friend** about such incidents, which is a very positive development, a much lower proportion talks about their experience with cyberbullying to adults (parents or teachers). The reasons vary but often it is out of fear that their technology privileges might be taken away from them. However, the help and support of adults can be key to ensure that victims are assisted in dealing with cyberbullying appropriately.

Bullies often feel anonymous and 'distanced' from the incident when it takes place online and 'bystanders' can easily become perpetrators by forwarding cyberbullying. The FOSI (Family Online Safety Institute) GRID initiative was developed to assess whether the internet was getting safer and what were the risks and challenges globally in all 194 countries around the world. The study identified 26 global risks and challenges and the **number one risk was cyberbullying**.

In addition to building resilience in children, **parents need to be more empowered** in their use and understanding of new technologies. According to a FOSI survey, while 84% of parents felt they used appropriate filtering for their teens, when checking the configurations, only 37% had a suitable filtering in place.

The **effects of cyberbullying** on victims are well known. It affects their self-esteem, academic achievement, it can cause absenteeism; it feeds moderate school delinquency and violence, and can even lead to suicidal thoughts and attempts. Cyberbullying also has an impact on perpetrators, bystanders (who don't feel safe in school wondering if they will be cyberbullied next), parents (the family environment), and schools (especially the school learning environment).

A **positive school climate** greatly influences the prevalence of incidents such as cyberbullying and can therefore be an important step to prevent it. Examples for creating a positive school climate include: curriculum enhancements (resources and lessons about conflict resolution, socio-emotional learning), peer mentoring and social norming (changing mentality about what is acceptable behavior), and the development of an anti-bulling policy or charter for the school, jointly by the teaching staff and the pupils.

Whilst there are no laws dedicated to cyberbullying specifically, there is **much legislation development in harassment**, violence, sexting and so on. In many US states, there was also progress in bullying related legislation, notably by ensuring that **school policies** include measures against bullying and cyberbullying.

Source: European Conference on Cyberbullying (2013, 4).

Necessary social and community responses to cyberbullying

Cyberbullying and bullying are generally seen as a social and community concern. School officials are developing policies to identify appropriate responses that can be taken if the behavior occurs in schools or with school property. Many schools in the United States and Europe are developing programs to raise awareness among the youth about the dangers of bullying and cyberbullying behaviors and are providing counseling to youth who are victims of bullies. Some non-profit organizations (NGOs) are taking on the issue of bullying and cyberbullying and developing training and awareness programs and services. In Europe, for example, some NGOs have implemented a **Safer Internet Day**, which encourages an international activity to bring awareness to cyberbullying, some have developed interactive board games that educate youth, parents, and teachers about cyberbullying, and some have television ads and training sessions that reach out to communities, parents, and youth (European Conference on Cyberbullying 2013). Because youth who are bullied may not want to talk about it out of fear or feelings of embarrassment, it is important to help them reach out for help and assistance to deal with their depression and potentially suicidal thoughts.

Parents, as seen in some of the stories presented above, may not know that their child is a victim of cyberbullying and are shocked when their child kills himself/herself. Consequently, parents need to learn about safe computing and safe texting behaviors and what to look for in youth who are being cyberbullied. In the 1990s and early 2000s, parents were told that for their children to be safe from Internet predators, their computers should be kept in open areas of a home, not in the child's bedroom, so that computer usage and communications could be monitored. However, this advice is no longer feasible since many youth have smart phones and iPads that enable them to be engaged in nefarious conversations while sitting next to parents in a living room. Rather, it is the changed demeanor of a youth, their depression, and other signs of withdrawal that parents need to watch for. Keeping open lines of communication with a child and educating youth about safe use of the Internet and why sexting and offensive texts are harmful and illegal may be a more appropriate message to provide to parents than merely advising parents that the computer should be in a common area of the home. Taciturn and withdrawn children should not be regarded as anti-establishment youth who are exerting their "independence" from parents as they grow up; parents need to be aware that such youth may be withdrawing because they are being bullied.

Conclusion

Cyberbullying laws are being passed throughout the United States and are being considered in nations around the world. If a nation does not have a particular cyberbullying law, other laws that proscribe harassment, illicit electronic communications, or child pornography may be used to prosecute cyberbullies. Cyberbullying laws, however, are not enough to deter the myriad of behaviors which victimize youth and adults. Communities need to educate parents, school personnel, and law enforcement on the dangers associated with cybercrime victimization and how offensive texts and pictures can follow persons throughout their lives. It is very difficult to redact something that is in cyberspace and the intensive feelings of shame and guilt that victims face can lead them to commit suicide.

More research on the dynamics associated with cybercrime and the norms associated with texting, sexting, and technology need to be performed. Although an inexperienced child may initially think that sending a sexually provocative text or picture is acceptable, as the youth ages then he/she may be faced with having that message or picture used against him/her and be bullied by groups of people who have access to it. The ability of the Internet to pass images and messages to multiple recipients and transcend time means that a victim of cyberbullying may not be able to escape from it. What seems to help victims is the development of close ties to parents, teachers, and others who can help them maintain a positive attitude towards school and their workplace. Schools, homes, and workplaces should be places of refuge and safety. When the Internet and technology assist in a person's victimization, then these places of refuge become places of victimization. When persons believe that the cyber-victimization is persuasive and perpetual, then victims may take their life to end their misery.

Suggested readings

Hirsch, Lee, Bower, Cynthia, and Dina Santorelli. 2012. Bully: *An Action Plan for Teachers, Parents, and Communities to Combat the Bullying Crisis*. Philadelphia, PA: Weinstein Books.
Ivester, Matt. 2011. *IOL…OMG!: What Every Student Needs to Know about Online Reputation Management, Digital Citizenship and Cyberbullying*. Reno, NV: Serra Knight Publishing.

Student engagement activities

1 Create a model statute that distinguishes the crimes of cyberharassment and cyberstalking and addresses issues of jurisdiction (i.e., that the offender and victim may exist in different communities or nations).
2 Develop a YouTube video that can help victims of cyberbullying who are suicidal or create a website like Cybersmile, http://www.cybersmile.org/, or join national campaigns, like http://www.ncpc.org/cyberbullying, for youth to get support.
3 Explain why adults might engage in cyberharassment.
4 Develop a blog to talk about cyberbullying and what youth, parents, and schools can do to help deter these offenses.

Discussion questions

1 What type of family and school policies help to identify bullies and victims of cyberbullies?
2 Explain why bullying may lead some victims to commit suicide.
3 Distinguish various forms of cyberbullying victimization and discuss whether we should continue to use the word "cyberbullying" to characterize these behaviors.

Key terms

Bash boards
Chicanery
Cyber drama
Cybercrime forensic specialists
Cyberharassment
Cyberstalking
Denigration
Email and cell phone image dissemination

Email threats and dissemination
Exclusion
Exposure
Flaming
Griefing
Happy slapping
Hate crime
Image and video

Impersonation

Instant messaging

Interactive game harassment

Jurisdiction

Password theft lockout

Phishing

Pornography and marketing list inclusion

Pseudonym

Right of privacy

Safer Internet Day

Screen name mirroring

Sending malicious code

Sexting

Text wars and text attacks

Voting/polling booths

Warning wars

Website creation

References

Allen, Stephanie. September 10, 2013. "Lakeland Girl Commits Suicide After 1½ Years of Being Bullied." *The Ledger*. Accessed May 26, 2014, http://www.theledger.com/article/20130910/news/130919963?p=4&tc=pg

AVG. 2010. *Digital Playground, Amsterdam and London: Research Now and AVG*. United Kingdom.

BBC News. February 12, 2014. "Cyberbullying Suicide: Italy Shocked by Amnesia Ask.fm Case." *BBC News: Europe*. Accessed May 20, 2014, http://www.bbc.com/news/world-europe-26151425

Bernat, Frances P., and Nicholas Godlove. 2012. "Understanding 21st Century Cybercrime for the "Common" Victim." *Criminal Justice Matters*, 89(1): 4–5. DOI: 10.1080/09627251.2012.721962

Bernat, Frances P., and Nicholas Rodriguez. 2014. "Cyber-Harassment, Cyber-Bullying and Cyber-Stalking: What Are Our College Kids Doing and What Do They Know?" Paper presented at the 51st annual Academy of Criminal Justice Sciences meeting, February 21, Philadelphia, PA.

Brewer, Gayle, and Emma Whiteside. 2012. "Workplace Bullying and Stress Within the Prison Service." *Journal of Aggression, Conflict and Peace Research*, 4: 76–85. DOI: 10.1108/17596591211208283

Bryce, Jo. 2009. *Internet Years Project*. London: Orange UK.

Bullying Statistics. 2014. "Bullying Statistics 2010." Accessed May 8, 2014, http://www.bullyingstatistics.org/content/bullying-statistics-2010.html

Chapell, Mark, Casey, Diane, De la Cruz, Carmen, Ferrell, Jennifer, Forman, Jennifer, Lipkin, Randy, Newsham, Megan, Sterling, Michael, and Suzanne Whittaker. 2004. "Bullying in College by Students and Teachers." *Adolescence*, 39(153): 53–64.

Dir, Allyson L., Coskunpinar, Ayca, Steiner, Jennifer L., and Melissa A. Cyders. 2013. "Understanding Differences in Sexting Behaviors Across Gender, Relationship Status, and Sexual Identity, and the Role of Expectations in Sexting." *Cyberpsychology, Behavior, and Social Networking*, 16(8): 568–574.

Edwards, Jim. September 16, 2013. "Users on this Web Site Have Successfully Driven Nine Teenagers to Kill Themselves." *Business Insider*. Accessed May 26, 2014, http://www.businessinsider.com/askfm-and-teen-suicides-2013-9

Ellis, Mark. October 2, 2013. "Cyber-Bullying: 5.4m Kids in UK Are Potential Victims on Facebook, Twitter and Ask.fm." *Mirror*. Accessed May 28, 2014, http://www.mirror.co.uk/news/uk-news/cyber-bullying-facebook-twitter-askfm-2328238

Espelage, Dorothy L., Bosworth, Kris, and Thomas R. Simon. 2001. "Short-Term Stability and Prospective Correlates of Bullying in Middle-School Students: An Examination of Potential Demographic, Psychosocial, and Environmental Influences." *Violence and Victims*, 16(4): 411–426.

European Conference on Cyberbullying. 2013. *Conference Report, Madrid, 28 May 2013*. Accessed May 20, 2014, http://deletecyberbullying.files.wordpress.com/2013/09/euconference-cyberbullying-28-may-madrid-conference-final-report1.pdf

Farmer, Thomas W., Hamm, Jill V., Leung, Man-Chi, Lambert, Kerrylin, and Maggie Gravelle 2011. "Early Adolescent Peer Ecologies in Rural Communities: Bullying in Schools that Do and Do Not Have a Transition During the Middle Grades." *Journal of Youth Adolescence*, 40(9): 1106–1117. DOI: 10.1007/s10964-011-9684-0

Farrington, David P., Loeber, Rolf, Stallings, Rebecca, and Maria M. Ttofi. 2011. "Bullying Perpetration and Victimization as Predictors of Delinquency and Depression in the Pittsburgh Youth Study." *Journal of Aggression, Conflict and Peace Research*, 3: 74–81. DOI: 10.1108/17596591111132882

Floros, Georgios D., Siomos, Konstantinos E., Fisoun, Virginia, Dafouli, Evaggelia, and Dimitrios Geroukalis. 2013. "Adolescent Online Cyberbullying in Greece: The Impact of Parental Online Security Practices, Bonding, and Online Impulsiveness." *Journal of School Health*, 83(6): 445–453. DOI: 10.1111/josh.12049

Frisén, Ann, Jonsson, Anna-Karin, and Camilla Persson. 2007. "Adolescents' Perception of Bullying: Who Is the Victim? Who Is the Bully? What Can Be Done to Stop Bullying?" *Adolescence*, 42: 749–761.

Goldweber, Asha, Wassdorp, Tracy Evian, and Catherine P. Bradshaw. 2013. "Examining Associations Between Race, Urbanicity, and Patterns of Bullying Involvement." *Journal of Youth Adolescence*, 42: 206–219. DOI: 10.1007/s10964-012-9843-y

Hinduja, Sameer, and Justin W. Patchin. 2012. "Cyberbullying: Neither an Epidemic Nor a Rarity." *European Journal of Developmental Psychology*, 9(5): 539–543. DOI: 10.1080/17405629.2012.706448

Hinduja, Sameer, and Justin W. Patchin. 2014. *State Cyberbullying Laws: A Brief Review of State Cyberbullying Laws and Policies*. Cyberbullying Research Center. http://cyberbullying.us/Bullying_and_Cyberbullying_Laws.pdf

Lepido, Daniele. March 5, 2014. "Another Teen Suicide Linked to Ask.fm Leaves Questions." *Bloomberg*. Accessed May 27, 2014, http://www.bloomberg.com/news/2014-03-05/another-teen-suicide-linked-to-ask-fm-leaves-questions.html

Li, Qing. 2008. "A Cross-Cultural Comparison of Adolescents' Experience Related to Cyberbullying." *Educational Research*, 50: 223–234. DOI: 10.1080/00131880802309333

Livingstone, Sonia, Haddon, Leslie, Gorzig, Anke, and Kjartan Olafsson. 2011. *Risks and Safety on the Internet: The Perspective of European Children*. London: London School of Economics, EU Kids Online. http://www.lse.ac.uk/media@lse/research/EUKidsOnline/EU%20Kids%20II%20(2009-11)/National%20reports/UKReport.pdf

Lösel, Griedrich, and Doris Bender. 2011. "Emotional and Antisocial Outcomes of Bullying and Victimization at School: A Follow-Up from Childhood to Adolescence." *Journal of Aggression, Conflict and Peace Research*, 3: 89–96. DOI: 10.1108/17596591111132909

Luukkonen, Anu-Helmi, Räsänen, Pirkko, Hakko, Helinä, and Kaisa Riala. 2009. "Bullying Behavior Is Related to Suicide Attempts But Not to Self-Mutilation Among Psychiatric Inpatient Adolescents." *Psychopathology*, 42: 131–138. DOI: 10.1159/000204764

Maag, Christopher. November 28, 2007. "A Hoax Turned Fatal Draws Anger But No Charges." *New York Times*. Accessed May 27, 2014, http://www.nytimes.com/2007/11/28/us/28hoax.html?_r=0

Maras, Marie-Helen. 2015. *Computer Forensics: Cybercriminals, Laws, and Evidence*, 2nd edn. Burlington, VT: Jones & Bartlett Learning.

Mark, Lauren, and Katherine T. Ratliffe. 2011. "Cyber Worlds: New Playgrounds for Bullying." *Computers in the Schools*, 28: 92–116. DOI: 10.1080/07380569.2011.575753

Matthiesen, Stig Berge, and Ståle Einarsen. 2007. "Perpetrators and Targets of Bullying at Work: Role Stress and Individual Differences." *Violence and Victims*, 22: 735–753.

McCarthy, Tom, and Scott Michels. July 2, 2009. "Lori Drew MySpace Suicide Hoax Conviction Thrown Out." *ABC News*. Accessed May 27, 2014, http://abcnews.go.com/TheLaw/story?id=7977226

McGuckin, Conor, and Christopher Alan Lewis. 2006. "Experiences of School Bullying in Northern Ireland: Data from the Life and Times Survey." *Adolescence*, 41: 313–320.

Nuccitelli, Michael. 2012. "2012 Cyber Bullying Tactics." *The Forensic Examiner*, 21(3): 2012: 24–27.

Orton, Ivan. 2011. "The Investigation and Prosecution of a Cybercrime." In *Cybercrime: The Investigation, Prosecution and Defense of a Computer-Related Crime*, 3rd edn, edited by Ralph D. Clifford, 105–200. Durham, NC: Carolina Academic Press.

Patchin, Justin W. 2013. "Cyberbullying Research: 2013 Update." Accessed February 2, 2014, http://cyberbullying.us/cyberbullying-research-2013-update/

Poteat, V. Paul, and Craig D. DiGiovanni. 2010. "When Biased Language Use Is Associated with Bullying and Dominance Behavior: The Moderating Effect of Prejudice." *Journal of Youth Adolescence*, 39: 1123–1133. DOI 10.1007/s10964-010-9565-y

Poteat, V. Paul, and Dorothy L. Espelage. 2005. "Exploring the Relation Between Bullying and Homophobic Verbal Content: The Homophobic Content Agent Target (HCAT) Scale." *Violence and Victims*, 20: 513–528.

Poteat, V. Paul, and Dorothy L. Espelage. 2007. "Predicting Psychosocial Consequences of Homophobic Victimization in Middle School Students." *The Journal of Early Adolescence*, 27(2): 175–191. DOI: 10.1177/0272431606294839

Saillant, Catherine. November 22, 2011. "Gay Teen's Killer Takes 21-Year Deal." *Los Angeles Times.* Accessed May 26, 2014, http://articles.latimes.com/2011/nov/22/local/la-me-1122-gay-shooting-20111122

Seals, Dorothy, and Jerry Young. 2003. "Bullying and Victimization: Prevalence and Relationship to Gender, Grade Level, Ethnicity, Self-Esteem, and Depression." *Adolescence*, 38: 735–747.

Skye, Jared. 2014. *Cyber Bullying Statistics.* Accessed February 10, 2014, http://safety.lovetoknow.com/Cyber_Bullying_Statistics

Snell, Patricia A., and Elizabeth Englander. 2010. *Cyberbullying Victimization and Behaviors Among Girls: Applying Research Findings in the Field.* MARC Publications. Paper 4. http://vc.bridgew.edu/marc_pubs/4

Stanglin, Doug, and William M. Welch. October 16, 2013. "Two Girls Arrested on Bullying Charges After Suicide." *USA Today.* Accessed May 26, 2013, http://www.usatoday.com/story/news/nation/2013/10/15/florida-bullying-arrest-lakeland-suicide/2986079/

Statistic Brain Research Institute. 2013. *Cyber Bullying Statistics.* Accessed May 26, 2014, http://www.statisticbrain.com/cyber-bullying-statistics/

Tarapdar, Saima, and Mary Kellett. 2011. *Young People's Voices on Cyberbullying: What Can Age Comparisons Tell Us?* London: The Diana Award.

Wolke, Dieter, Copeland, William E., Angold, Adrian, and E. Jane Costello. 2013. "Impact of Bullying in Childhood on Adult Health, Wealth, Crime, and Social Outcomes." *Psychological Science*, XX: 1–13. DOI: 10.1177/0956797613481608

CHAPTER 8

Women and law enforcement

Student learning outcomes

After reading this chapter, you should be able to:

- Describe the history of women entering the police profession.
- Summarize the nature of police work for women today.
- Describe the issues that female police officers encounter on the job.

Introduction

September 11, 2001. This is a date that will be forever burned into the memories of US citizens who were either alive when the terrorist attacks occurred or were born afterwards and have read accounts of the attacks in history books. Without a doubt, there were many heroes, including fire-fighters and police officers, who bravely sacrificed their lives to help others at the World Trade Center (Towers 1 and 2) in New York City and at the Pentagon in Washington, DC. Among the many who bravely sacrificed their lives were 23 New York Police Department officers who were killed during the rescue attempts of citizens at the World Trade Centers (Lestch and McShane 2012). Of the 23 officers killed, one was a female officer named Moira Smith. After the first hijacked plane hit the World Trade Center, she courageously reported to the World Trader Centers and plunged herself into the rescue efforts. In fact, she was one of the earliest responders to the scene. She assisted survivors to safely escape out of the towers, and then returned to a blocked stairwell in Tower 2. Officer Smith did this to not only help restore order, but to establish a sense of calm in the utter madness and mayhem that was unfolding around everyone. When survivors were asked what they remembered about her, they mentioned her calm voice saying over and over again, "Don't look. Keep moving" (Hamill 2013). Ultimately, even while knowing that staying in the stairwell to help others would put her own life at grave risk, she was responsible for saving hundreds of lives (Hamill 2013). Moira, a New York City police officer, a mother of a 2-year-old daughter, and a wife, was killed when Tower 2 fell on her. For her bravery, she was posthumously awarded the New York Police Department Medal of Honor (Hamill 2013).

In 2011, Linda Gotham and Lynn Whitey, police officers (now retired) on the Los Angeles Police Department (LAPD), sued the police department for discrimination and harassment (Candido 2013). The two officers, who are also lesbians, claimed senior administrators did not intervene to stop harassment they were receiving from their supervisor about their sexual orientation. Apparently, the officers

Women, Crime, and Justice, First Edition. By Elaine Gunnison, Frances P. Bernat, and Lynne Goodstein.
© 2017 John Wiley & Sons, Ltd. Published 2017 by John Wiley & Sons, Ltd.

were the recipients of vulgar sexual comments about their sexual orientation, and their supervisor had also made sexual propositions towards them (Rubin 2013). It was not until after the officers filed their lawsuit that an internal investigation into their claims was even launched. In 2013, the officers received a $1.25 million settlement for the harassment and discrimination that they endured (Rubin 2013).

In this chapter, we provide a historical overview of women in policing and provide current statistics as to the number of women working in the profession today. We will describe how women police officers in the United States may be similar and/or different from women officers around the world. Next, we will examine the many challenges that women police officers encounter on the job and include discussion on the role that gender, race, and sexual orientation have in these challenges. Finally, we discuss the effectiveness of women as police officers.

 CASE STUDY: Malalai Kakar

At the international level, one often does not hear about female police officers in other countries. One of the most high-profile female officers in Afghanistan, who garnered international attention, was Malalai Kakar (Burns 2008). Kakar joined the police force in 1982, but she was forced from her position in the mid-1990s when the Taliban captured the city of Kandahar (Burns 2008). The Taliban, a terrorist organization, did not believe that women should be able to work. Thus, Kakar was forced to leave her job as an officer. When the Taliban were finally driven out from the city and country in 2001, she quickly resumed her role as an officer. In fact, she was the first female police officer to return to work in Afghanistan. Eventually, she held the position of captain in Kandahar's Department of Crimes Against Women (Burns 2008). Due to her high profile, she received many death threats. In 2008, she was gunned down in Kandahar by Taliban terrorists, and she died. It has been reported that she was in her forties and a mother of six children (Burns 2008).

History of women in policing

Due to policing being a very much male-dominated profession, females' entry into the profession was slow in the United States. In the mid-1800s, in response to mounting pressure from various women's organizations that promulgated that women should be hired to handle and oversee women and girls held in custody in either jails or prisons, two female **police matrons** were appointed to serve in two prisons in New York City (Higgins 1951). Thus, early female police matrons found themselves assigned to work in correctional institutions rather than out in their communities as we would see policewomen working today. Police matrons' work assignments in the United States were similar to those of female police matrons who began their work in the United Kingdom in 1883 (Emsley 1996). Early police matrons in the United Kingdom, for example, were to interact with incarcerated women or assist in the searching of women and children held in custody (Emsley 1996). It was not until 1893 in Chicago that the first policewoman, Marie Owens, was appointed to the Chicago Police Department. However, it should be noted that her official title was "patrolman." As a female "patrolman," Owens assisted detectives with cases involving women and children (Higgins 1951). Following her appointment, other police departments recognized the need for women to assist in the department on cases involving women and children. However, these early female officers, or police matrons, lacked the full power and authority of male police officers. Why do you think that early female police officers did not have the same authority as male officers?

Figure 8.1 Alice Stebbins Wells of the Los Angeles Police Department, considered to be the first police-woman in the United States. *Source:* Topical Press Agency/Getty Images.

In 1910, Alice Stebbins Wells was appointed officially as a "policewoman" by the Los Angeles Police Department (LAPD); thus, some have credited her as the first official policewomen to be hired in the United States (Higgins 1951) (Figure 8.1). Wells, a social worker in Los Angeles, gained this position by petitioning the police commissioner as well as the Los Angeles city council to be admitted to the force. It was her belief that as a policewoman she could better assist women and children who were victims of crime. Additionally, in her role, she provided sexual education to women and girls. Why do you think Wells was called on to perform such a duty as a police officer? Primarily, her duties consisted of not only enforcing laws in public facilities such as dance halls and skating rinks, but also providing advice pertaining to appropriate moral behavior. For example, when Wells came into contact with women or girls in such facilities, she would discourage them from engaging in premarital sex and encourage them to remain "pure." Reforming morals was a key aspect of early female police officers. Another change that Wells' role as a policewoman brought about was having a desk alongside her male colleagues at the police department. This was a rarity, as many police departments established offices for female police officers outside of the main police department. This was due to police departments believing that women police officers could better help women and girls in an office that was more "homey" or felt more inviting. In 1915, Wells, as a pioneer of women in the law enforcement profession, would found and establish the International Association of Police Women (Higgins 1951). With Wells' hiring into the LAPD police department, many other departments followed their lead and began hiring more women in their departments. Shortly after Wells' appointment, the first female police officer, Sofia Stanley, was hired in the United Kingdom in 1919 (Camber 2009).

By 1922, there were 500 policewomen working in the United States (Shulz 1995). However, this would only be a small victory, as early hires were relegated to working solely with women and juveniles and in support positions to male officers. That is, policewomen were viewed as social workers instead of officers because being on the streets fighting crimes was too "dangerous" for these "fragile" individuals. Female police officers in the United Kingdom, for example, were required to ask for male officer assistance if they observed crime and were not given full powers to arrest until 1923 (Camber 2009). Not only were police women not permitted to patrol in the United States, but many of the early policewomen hired were also required to be more educated than their male counterparts and were not allowed to compete with male officers for promotions (Milton 1972). There were many reasons why police departments did not want female police officers patrolling the streets alongside male officers. It was often the case that male officers resented working with female police officers. The resentment that women faced from their male colleagues included a lack of support on the job and even sexual harassment (Brown and Heidensohn 2000; Hunt 1990). These early female officers were paid less than male officers and their selection (e.g., written exams and oral interviews) onto the police force differed from the selection process utilized for males (Martin and Jurik 2007).

It was not uncommon for female police officers to be removed from the police force if they married (Prenzler 2002). Additionally, the majority of policewomen that were hired were Caucasian. African-American females were rarely hired and, when they were, there were assigned to work with women and children of color. Thus, females' entry into the policing profession was fraught with discrimination and bias. The practice of discrimination against women in policing continued throughout the 1960s and 1970s.

 GLOBAL PERSPECTIVES: Entry into policing and roles

For women pursuing law enforcement careers in other first world countries, their entry was very similar to those of their US colleagues. The first female police officer was hired in Germany in 1903, with other countries such as Denmark, the United Kingdom, and Australia following soon after (Martin and Jurik 2007). Like female officers in the United States, these early female police officers were relegated to clerical work or working with women and children and regulating the sexual conduct of women. The hiring of female officers in other continents, such as Asia, also mirrored similar trends in the United States and Europe. For instance, recruitment of female officers in mainland China began in the 1930s and early female officers found themselves performing clerical work, public sanitary education, and some undercover work (Yang 1985). In Taiwan, the first female officers joined the force in 1948, but women were not actively recruited to join the police force until the late 1970s (Chu and Sun 2006). Early female officers in Taiwan also found themselves performing clerical work and working with women and juveniles (Chu 2013). Women entered the policing profession in Ghana, a country in Africa, in the 1950s, and until the 1990s they primarily performed administrative roles (Becker et al. 2012). In Latin America, women entered the force in the 1970s and represent about 5% of the total force while, in Afghanistan, women represent 1% of the total force and have only recently been able to be frontline police officers (Donaido and Manzottta 2010; Graham-Harrison 2013; Johnson, Forman, and Bliss 2012) (Figure 8.2).

Due to differences in cultural values and expectations about the roles which women perform in the society, integrating women into the policing profession to work alongside men is not always ideal (Natarajan 1996). For instance, in one state within India, during the 1990s, all-women police units were established (Natarajan 2001). The establishment of such policing units was thought to be a solution to assist women in finding a gratifying role within the profession. However, women's role in policing in this country is still often defined by their gender. These officers primarily assist women and, in particular, women who have been victims of violence due to problems with dowries or broken engagements (Natarajan 2001). However, these specialized units may also perform some law and order functions such as crowd control, escorting prisoners, and providing protection for high-ranking officials (Natarajan 2001). Female officers in Bahrain, an Arab country, began working in their profession in the 1970s. At the time, it was thought that female police officers were needed to assist women and children in the society. Like many female officers in India, they work in gender-segregated units and prefer to do so out of respect for cultural values and traditions.

While policing roles have expanded for many women police officers across the globe, they do share two key similarities. Female police officers represent a smaller number of officers in their respective departments, and they are less likely to be represented in upper administrative ranks (Silvestri 2012; Strobl 2008).

Figure 8.2 Female Afghan police officers to be sent to Turkey in order to receive security assistance from Turkish police line up during training in Kabul, Afghanistan, on October 29, 2014. *Source:* Haroon Sabawoon/Anadolu Agency/Getty Images.

TEXT BOX: Female police in Latin America

Although they represent only 5.5 percent of civil police staff, women have become an increasingly common sight in Latin America's police forces. Initially, some belonged to separate auxiliaries, but the overwhelming trend has been to integrate them into the broader corps, often helping victims of gender-based violence. However, women are increasingly found in professional specialties and management assignments.

Chile has employed female detectives since the 1940s. Uruguay admitted commissioned officers in 1971, and Bolivia created the National Police Female Brigade in 1973. Peru admitted women into its Civil Guard in 1977 and into the Republican Guard in 1984. Ecuador accepted women into its police forces in 1977, and Argentina admitted women to the Federal Police Cadet School in 1978 and as commissioned officers in the National Gendarmerie in 2009. Paraguay's police opened its doors to females in 1992, El Salvador in 1993, and Guatemala in 1997.

Uruguay has the highest proportion of female police, who represent 25.6 percent of all personnel. Chile's Investigation Police are 23.4 percent female. Bolivia, Guatemala, Paraguay, and Peru all have about 11 percent female representation in their forces (see chart below).

Source: Johnson et al. (2012, 13). © Center for Strategic and International Studies

(*continued*)

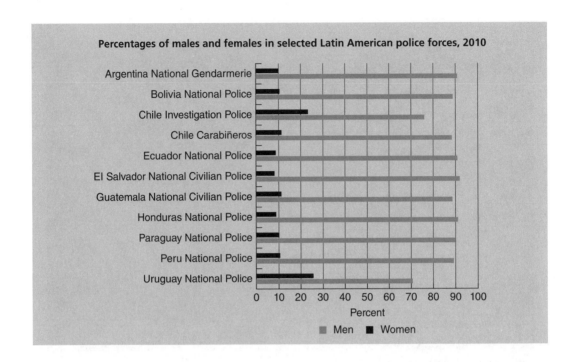

In the 1960s, there was both a need for improvements in the policing profession and a growing social awareness in the United States of discrimination impacting individuals in society based on their race or gender. This era fostered a greater awareness of the plights of the disenfranchised within US society, leading to a demand for improvements in the policing profession. The policing profession was in a crisis in the 1960s due to many violent and deadly confrontations between citizens and police officers and rising crime rates (Martin and Jurik 2007). With the policing profession viewed as ineffective and out of control by both the public and politicians, several presidential commissions recommended the establishment of personnel standards in regard to recruiting and hiring of officers. These personnel standards included specific recommendation of hiring more women and persons of color (Martin and Jurik 2007). The impact of the recommendations was positive and helped women gain entry into the policing profession in greater numbers, as by 1960 more than 5,600 women were working in the police force in the United States (Shulz 1995). With greater social awareness, individuals starting bringing issues of discrimination to the forefront of the US court system and many landmark cases paved the way to making employment in policing less discriminatory. One piece of legislation that assisted women was the **Equal Pay Act of 1963** which required that men and women be given equal pay for equal work. This legislation helped to better align the pay that women were receiving in their positions as officers with their male colleagues. Another legislative ruling that assisted women in the police profession was **Title VII of the Civil Rights Act of 1964**. Title VII prohibits employer discrimination on the bases of race and color, as well as national origin, sex, and religion. It applied to employers with 15 or more employees, including state and local governments (US Equal Employment Opportunity Commission 2013). This legislation assisted women in the policing profession to some extent as a few police departments were assigning female officers to patrol. In 1968, the Indianapolis Police Department became the first department in the nation to assign two women to regular patrol duties in a marked police car. However, many police departments were still reluctant to hire women or, when they did, refrained from assigning females to patrol duty. As women were being hired in greater numbers to the police force, there still were distinct differences between female and male officers. Judith Lewis describes her entry onto the Los Angeles Sheriff's Department in 1969 as follows: "'When I joined the department … we were called 'lady deputies.' Our uniform was a skirt, high heels, and a blouse. We went through a 10-week academy vs. a 20-week academy for men. We got a 2-inch gun to carry in our purse. I was a deputy in an administrative job'" (Scoville 2012). As previously mentioned, many police departments refrained from assigning females to patrol duty. Indeed, in 1971, in the United States, there were only *seven* policewomen on patrol (Gates 1976). The lack of women on patrol was due to both the police culture and, in many cases, women choosing not to work on patrol. Lewis explains, "'I didn't want to go to patrol at that time because I had three small kids. Patrol wasn't what I joined the job for, and neither did most women. Opinion was mostly negative in the department to do that'" (Scoville 2012). Perhaps early policewomen, such as Lewis, did not really have a choice to pursue patrol as part of their jobs. The lack of support from the department and lack of flexibility by the department to assist female officers who often were mothers too may have decreased the desire for women to pursue patrol, thereby contributing to the low numbers of women on patrol.

The biggest shift in the policing profession for women occurred in the 1970s. Throughout the 1970s, the feminist movement was well underway and continued to draw attention to the plight of women in US society. With increasing attention being directed towards female inequity in the workplace (as well as to other groups in society), lawsuits were filed and additional legislation was implemented, which resulted in women entering the law enforcement profession in greater numbers (Sulton and Townsey 1981). At this point in time, women only represented 2% of the policing profession (Martin and Jurik 2007). One significant barrier that prevented women from entering the policing profession included common standards required by police departments in regard to physical attributes such as weight and height and physical fitness standards. If women did not meet a particular height or weight requirement for a police department, they were unable to apply to the department for an officer position. Additionally, the physical fitness standards, established for men, were not modified for females, regardless of any differences in physical abilities (e.g., the standards were the same in regard to push-ups, sit-ups, or running times) (Sulton and Townsey 1981). Because of the biased standards, women began to file lawsuits to challenge them (Martin and Jurik 2007). In a historic Supreme Court ruling, *Griggs v. Duke Power Company* **(1971)**, the court ruled that businesses, including the police profession, cannot establish a policy that has a detrimental impact on the hiring of a particular group in society. It was only after the *Griggs* ruling that police departments had to modify their employment standards (i.e., suspend or modify height, weight, and physical fitness standards) for females and that ruling finally facilitated a larger number of women to enter the policing profession. What do you think about different physical standards for men and women in this profession? While such modifications may have been made for women attempting to enter the police profession, it did not eliminate the discrimination that they experienced in actually getting hired or promoted. The discrimination was now shifting from the application process to the police academy. Patty Fogerson, a policewoman hired with the Los Angeles Police Department in 1969, recalls the discrimination she experienced in the police academy when she went through training to be assigned to patrol six years later. "'In 1975, I experienced some double standards in the academy,' says Fogerson. 'Physical training instructors in the academy didn't want us there, and they made life as difficult as possible for us. One guy changed my time on the obstacle course. I had won medals in the Police Olympics, so I had done well. But he read off my time as being slower than the slowest person there'" (Scoville 2012).

Besides lawsuits that created some change for women, legislation was also critical in carving a pathway for women into the policing profession. The **Equal Employment Opportunity Act of 1972** sought to strengthen Title VII of the Civil Rights Act of 1964 by again asserting that those seeking employment should be treated fairly and should not be discriminated against based on their

Figure 8.3 Kathleen O'Toole, Chief of the Seattle Police Department. *Source:* Seattle Police Department.

race, sex, religion, color, or national origin. This legislation single-handedly resulted in a significant increase in the number of women hired into the policing profession (Sulton and Townsey 1981). An additional provision of the Equal Employment Opportunity Act of 1972 was the creation of the **Equal Employment Opportunity Program**, which instituted policies such as affirmative action (e.g., specific quotas of females to be hired in a given department) and offered assistance to those who may have been discriminated against. Do you think women could have entered into the policing profession without such legislation? How do you feel about affirmative action policies instituted in the policing profession?

While lawsuits and legislation opened the door for women to enter the policing profession in the 1970s, the number of women in the policing profession has not grown at a particularly quick pace. In 2008, combined from local, state, and federal agencies there were just over 1 million law enforcement officers, with women representing merely 100,000 officers of that figure (Langton 2010; Reaves 20112008). Today, women represent just 10% of the police force in the United States. If these figures are further dissected, women are also underrepresented at the upper administrative ranks, such as chief. In fact, it was not until 1985 that the first female police chief was hired in Portland, Oregon (Felperin 2004). Most recently, in Seattle, in 2014, Kathleen O'Toole was hired as the first female police chief in the history of the city (Miletich 2014) (Figure 8.3). The most recent survey of women working in 247 police agencies in 2001 conducted by the National Center for Women in Policing (2002) found that women held only 9.6% of supervisory positions and 7.3% of top command positions. Such findings are even more troubling when you take into consideration that female officers are better educated, or have higher education levels, on average, compared to male officers (Lonsway et al. 2003; Sklansky 2006). There are many explanations as to why women have had a hard time breaking into upper administrative ranks. One possible explanation could be due to the evaluation process of female officers (Anderson 2003). As evaluations are subjective, it may be the case that women police officers are not receiving as high evaluations as their male colleagues, resulting in them getting knocked out of the running for these coveted and competitive upper administrative positions. Additionally, it may be that there are just not a sufficient number of women applying for top positions (Cordner and Cordner 2011). Another explanation can be due to the sheer lack of women in the upper administrative ranks. Without mentors or role models, it can be harder for more junior-level policewomen to advance in their careers and learn the steps they need to take to make it to the next rank (Cordner and Cordner 2011; Felperin 2004). Female police officers may also hit a **glass ceiling**, or brass ceiling. That is, as they move further up the ranks, there are fewer positions open to them to apply for, or it may take many years before they are able to climb the ladder (Rabe-Hemp 2008). Finally, it could also be due to policewomen choosing not to take promotional exams to move up the ranks. This could be due to the perceived burden that the position, if obtained, could impose on their personal and family relationships (Felperin 2004). Today, the policing profession is much more heterogeneous than it once was, but a greater diversity of officers (i.e., gender, race, ethnicity, and sexual orientation) is still needed in departments.

⚖️ **SPECIAL LEGAL ISSUES: Legal pathways for female officers in South Africa**

It was not until the early 1970s that women entered the police profession in South Africa, and they did so in very small numbers – 100 female officers versus 50,000 male officers (Morrison 2004). With the disbandment of apartheid and the instatement of the first democratic elections in South Africa in 1994, the pathway for women entering the profession increased tremendously. The new Constitution of South Africa, Act 108, 1996 included a Bill of Rights section that prohibited discrimination (Morrison 2004). By including the equality clause, women were finally able to enter the police profession in greater numbers. However, despite this legislation, the nation of South Africa is very patriarchal in nature, and female police officers have not necessarily been welcomed with open arms onto the police force. Morrison (2004, 239) states, "Men do not like to accept women's authority which results in oppositions from their male colleagues. They face overt hostility from men as well as experiencing double standards." Recently, South Africa presented the Women Empowerment and Gender Equality Bill to Parliament to combat the current discrimination facing women in the workplace in South Africa (Goko 2013). The Bill was passed in 2014 and requires government agencies and companies to fill at least 50% of all senior positions with women, beginning in 2015 (All Africa 2014; Goko 2013).

Women and their employment in law enforcement

Police culture and women's contribution to law enforcement

When you think of the culture of policing, what comes to mind? Do images from television shows such as *COPS* pop in your mind? What about the role of women in the police culture? How might it differ from televisions shows such as *Cagney and Lacey*, a popular show featuring two fictional law enforcement officers (i.e., before reality television was born) in the 1980s? What about current television shows depicting policewomen such as *CSI*? Oftentimes, the representations of women as police officers in television shows and reality-based shows are skewed. That is, either female officers are not predominately featured, or, if they are, they are either portrayed as crime fighters or not at all as crime fighters. Television shows such as *Law and Order* and *Criminal Minds* tend to portray female officers almost exclusively as crime fighters and to be harder working than male officers. On the other hand, reality television shows paint a different picture of female police officers. In an analysis of the portrayal of female officers in *COPS*, Monk-Turner and colleagues (2007) reported that women officers were rarely featured, and, when they were, they were not portrayed as having a major role in the policing incident/event that was presented in episodes. Rabe-Hemp (2011) performed a content analysis on the reality television show called *Female Forces*, which follows female officers on the job. Not surprisingly, she found that female officers were stereotypically portrayed as nurturers or caretakers and less as crime fighters. Evans and Davies (2014), who examined the depictions of female officers on television shows from 1950 to 2008, state that these shows often depict a large number of women and more women of color on the force – at levels that are not consistent with the reality of women working in the profession today. Further, in an examination of 112 "cop genre" films, Wilson and Blackburn (2014) found that key issues impacting female police officers (i.e., harassment or gender discrimination) were not highlighted in the films and that female officers were often depicted as having traumatic past histories. In any of the previously mentioned shows or films, there are certainly no accurate depictions or portrayals of the police culture, including the role that female officers have within police departments and the challenges they face on the job.

It is probably not surprising that the media does not more accurately portray female officers given its role of enhancing viewership through sensational reporting or altering reality for the purposes of entertainment. Because of media manipulation as well as the police culture, it is no wonder the public lacks a firm grasp on the realities of policing for women. Much of policing occurs behinds closed doors and out of the view of the public. Sure, we do see police officers patrolling, assisting in accidents, or sometimes making an arrest. The public may even get a glimpse of the police subculture every now and again. Balko (2013) reports on various slogans printed on t-shirts worn by police officers across the nation. Examples include: "Save the police time, beat yourself up"; "Math for Cops … 2 to the chest + 1 to the head = problem solved"; and "Cops make good roommates … they're used to taking out the trash" (Balko 2013). However, the policing profession is rather isolating for officers. After all, police officers are not friends of the public, but, rather, their goal is to protect the public while reducing crime. In order to achieve this goal, police officers and their respective departments remain silent on ongoing investigations and what measures they may be taking to help root out crime in various neighborhoods across a city. This distance, often referred to as the blue wall of silence, may be perceived by members of the public as the police being "out to get them" (Inciardi 1990).

Because of the gap between the police and the public and the stress of police work, a police culture develops. A **police culture** refers to attitudes and values within the policing profession that officers internalize in the police socialization process that begins in the training academy. Common examples of attitudes and values instilled in all officers would be to exhibit loyalty to the department and follow department policies and procedures. Apart from the overall police culture, a police subculture also develops whereby fellow officers instill in one another shared values and views of the world, and as well as attitudes regarding their roles in relation to one another (Inciardi 1990). For example, police subcultural attitudes may include: "cover your ass," "don't rat out another officer," or "don't trust the public" (Paoline, Myers, and Worden 2000). Other attributes that may be values are exerting masculinity (i.e., being tough, strong, and aggressive). As for these same values applying to female officers, when it comes to asserting masculinity, it can be rather tricky. On the one hand, if women officers do not exude toughness to their colleagues, they may be perceived as weak. On the other hand, if they exert too much masculinity, their male colleagues may try to strip them of it by calling them "butch" or "lesbian." Thus, women police officers might find it difficult to fit within this culture. The police culture has been reported by women officers as being one of misogyny, sexism, and even racism. It is one of many challenges that female law enforcement officers experience on the job and may, perhaps, contribute to their lower ratings of job satisfaction when compared to their male colleagues (Kakar 2002).

Challenges faced by women

One clear challenge that female officers have faced on the job is police culture. Historically, policing was considered to be a "man's job" and women were not welcome. The challenge for acceptance still continues to this day. In regard to the police culture, female officers are sometimes isolated from it or degraded as part of the culture through forms of offensive language and harassment. For example, they have been referred to as "lesbians" or "bitchy" – perhaps due to exerting too much masculinity or maybe as an insult (Balkin 1988; Poole and Pogrebin 1988). Other examples of the police culture that women may experience are receiving the silent treatment from male colleagues or failure to receive any recognition for a job well done. In the mid-1980s, rumors were circulating around the Los Angeles Police Department, in particular, that the culture towards women officers was hostile. It was reported that several male officers banded together to create the "**Men Against Women**" **(MAW)** organization. As part of the organization, male officers would harass and intimidate their female colleagues in an attempt to compel them to quit (Harris 1997). Examples of the negative culture towards female officers include male officers refusing to speak to women officers during training or splashing gasoline in their face (Harris 1997). Male officers who did not participate in MAW were also ostracized by their colleagues. Caruso (1997) explains, "Male officers found guilty of fraternizing with females were 'sentenced' to punishments such as a week of 'silent treatment' or 'the back,' where other male officers would turn their backs on the offender." The leader of the MAW organization was Mark Fuhrman, the lead detective in the O. J. Simpson murder case in the early 1990s. He claimed that MAW had 145 members over several of the city's police divisions (Caruso 1997; Harris 1997). A few of Fuhrman's most infamous quotes about women as police officers are as follows (Caruso 1997):

> Take every female officer, take them out of the field. You would not see a difference in the impact on crime. You would see a hell of a lot more morale.

> You've got to be able to shoot people, beat people beyond recognition, and go home and hug your little kids. [Women] don't pack those qualities. Almost no women do, and if they do, they are either so ugly or they're a lesbian or they're so dyke-ish that they are not women anymore.

While an internal investigation in the department uncovered the MAW organization in the mid-1980s, claims by top administrators that they shut down the organization were untrue as it reportedly operated for 10 years (Caruso 1997). Why do you think this behavior was tolerated for so many years? Unfortunately, the hostility that female police officers experienced from male colleagues in the past is still alive and an inherent feature of the police culture in many police departments today across the nation.

Harassment in policing has crossed the line further from lewd unprofessional comments to sexual harassment, which is defined by the US Equal Opportunity Employment Commission (2002) as follows: "Unwelcome sexual advances, requests for sexual favors, and other verbal or physical conduct of a sexual nature constitute sexual harassment when this conduct explicitly or implicitly affects an individual's employment, unreasonably interferes with an individual's work performance, or creates an intimidating, hostile, or offensive work environment." Sexual harassment in policing experienced by female officers includes improper touching, sexist and racist comments, having their personal property destroyed, and having sexual materials (e.g., pornography) placed on their office desks. In 1985, Ramona Arnold, an African-American police officer in Seminole, Oklahoma, brought further attention to the plight that female officers experienced on the job. She sued the city of Seminole due to the discrimination she experienced on the job, which included sexual harassment, and termination due to her voicing the discrimination claims. When she was hired in 1977, her supervisor told her that he did not believe women should be police officers, refused to speak to her, and even stated he would harass her until she quit or was fired. Arnold was passed over for promotions that ultimately went to male officers with less experience and seniority. She was victorious in her lawsuit in 1985 (*Ramona Arnold v. City of Seminole, Oklahoma*), and was awarded back pay and reinstatement. However, it is important to note that such incidents are not an artifact of the past, but rather an example of incidents that still occur today. More recently, a female police officer in the New York Police Department, Shemalisca Vasquez, has filed a lawsuit against the department claiming sexual harassment from her supervisor. She reports that in 2010 her supervisor exposed himself to her and even sent graphic text messages to her (Marzulli 2012). In terms of the prevalence of sexual harassment experienced by female police officers, the exact number is difficult to ascertain. Researchers have estimated that anywhere from 55% to 77% of female police officers have experienced some form of sexual harassment on the job (Bartol et al. 1992; Nichols 1995).

When you think about it, accurate estimates of harassment are difficult to obtain – after all, female officers may refrain from filing a complaint about the harassment that they are enduring.

Female police officers may not report the harassment as they view it to not be serious enough to report, fear retaliation for filing a claim, or because the perpetrator may be their supervisor. In an examination of sexual harassment experienced by both male and female police officers, Lonsway, Paynich, and Hall (2013) report that female officers explained that the harassment they experienced included dirty jokes or stories being told, pornography displayed, or negative remarks made based on their gender or sexual orientation. One female officer recalled a comment made to her by a captain who believed that women did not belong in the policing profession: "Why don't you go home and be a normal woman barefoot and pregnant in the kitchen?" (Lonsway et al. 2013, 191). Lonsway and colleagues (2013, 191) report that other female officers described ongoing unwanted sexual remarks as follows:

> I was the undercover officer for a high profile prostitution escort service. An Assistant Chief and Lieutenant said "I'd pay to fuck that." Over 20 years the number of times is too long to list. I have never filed a complaint.

> Co-workers and supervisors alike elude [sic] to sexual situations or jokes [on a] nearly daily basis. I would not file a complaint and typically am not offended – if you do complain this would make you an outcast/untouchable.

Apart from the sexist language, one quarter of the female officers in their study reported experiencing unwanted sexual contact and coercion for sex. One female officer stated, "Once a Captain told me that my life could be real simple or it can be quite difficult and grabbed my breast when he shut the door (closing me in his office). I walked out and my career has been HELL" (Lonsway et al. 2013, 192). The National Center for Women in Policing (1998, 4) reports that sexual harassment in police departments is pervasive and "that supervisors and commanders not only tolerate such practices by others, but also are frequently perpetrators themselves." While much of the sexual harassment experienced by female officers is from their colleagues, it is also not uncommon for the female officer to be the recipient of unsolicited sexual attention from members of the public – usually from intoxicated males (Lonsway et al. 2013). Apart from occasional sexual harassment that female law enforcement officers may face on the job from citizens, another challenge that female law enforcement officers encounter is getting respect from members of the public. Think about the ways in which the public may not respect female law enforcement officers. Female police officers may be viewed as women first and officers second by members of the public. A female campus police detective stated, "If I had a dollar for everybody who said, 'Hey, you want to come over and search me?' I would be a rich woman" (Rabe-Hemp 2009, 122). Additionally, one female municipal patrol officer recalled, "There's some people where as soon as you get out of the car, they'll whistle or say 'Hey baby' or 'You look good in those pants'" (Rabe-Hemp 2009, 122). In other instances, a citizen may simply ignore a female officer on the scene or may request a male officer be summoned so that the citizen can file his/her report (Gossett and Williams 1998).

Despite the strides that women have made to reduce discrimination in policing due to legislation and lawsuits, it appears many departments have found methods to circumvent anti-discrimination laws and policies (e.g., hiring) and instead institute informal methods of discrimination (Garcia 2003). For instance, female officers may experience lower performance marks on their evaluations. These lower ratings have an impact on their future training and promotion opportunities. Additionally, it appears that despite many affirmative action policies in police departments, these policies may not actually be enforced (Lee 2005). Female officers report that the discrimination they experience is not overt as it once was in the past (Gossett and Williams 1998). As one female officer puts it, "It is not blatant. It is not something that occurs on a daily or routine basis. It will be something along the line of even though we have an outlined system for transfers, someone will get a position in what we deem the 'good ole boy system'" (Gossett and Williams, 1998, 63). Despite such findings, female African-American officers have reported experiencing discrimination on a higher level due to both their gender and race (Price 1996). Examples of the discrimination reported by this group include being sent into high crime areas (White female colleagues are not) or difficulties in securing desired job assignments (Price 1996). Female African-American police officers often experience **double discrimination** – discrimination for both their gender and race. The fear of speaking up or retaliation is a factor in the decision by female officers not to report much of the abuse or discrimination they experience. One female African-American police officer with several decades of service recalls that in her early years on the force, she was very reluctant to report her negative experiences. She recalled, "I'm on probation, so I'm concerned about retaliation, and so a lot of times that is a big important factor. You don't have the department's support. I believe you can be discriminated against, but you won't seek help because of fear of retaliation" (Haarr and Morash 2013, 405). Another difference between Caucasian female police officers and other minority officers may be in the level of sexual harassment that is experienced between the groups. Haarr and Morash (2004) state that female African-American officers report experiencing higher levels of sexual harassment than female Caucasian officers. While female African-American officers certainly experience negative incidents at the hands of male officers, you might be surprised to learn that these female officers also report male African-American officers as not only the perpetrators, but also non-supportive (Texeira 2002). Why would fellow male African-American officers engage in such behaviors against female African-American officers? Perhaps it is due to the masculine culture of the police department or because male officers are fighting for survival in a department that may discriminate against them due to their race or view female African-American officers as competition for coveted spots in the department (Dodge and Pogrebin 2001).

Discrimination of police officers has also crossed sexual-orientation lines. Historically, lesbian officers were often banned from being hired onto police departments. With **sodomy laws** in existence, many departments likened hiring lesbian or gay applicants to hiring criminals (Buhrke 1996). This viewpoint, however, on hiring lesbian or gay applicants changed for many departments when they were sued for discrimination. One lawsuit that not only brought attention to the plight of lesbian applicants but also paved the way for lesbians to be hired by police departments was *England v. The City of Dallas, Mack Vines, and the State of Texas* **(1990)**. In 1989, Mica England, a lesbian applicant, was denied employment at the Dallas Police Department due to her sexual orientation. When she was interviewed for the position, she was asked if she was a lesbian. She replied that she was. Because of her answer, she was immediately disqualified for a position, as the Dallas Police Department had hiring policies that denied employment to gays and lesbians. Specifically, the hiring policy at the Dallas Police Department stated that applicants should not have had sexual relations with a member of the same sex since the age of 15. One female officer with approximately 15 years on the force sued her department for civil rights violations and contract violations in order to garner protection from losing her job due to her status as a lesbian. She recalls, "There was no state statute for the law or anything to protect gays and lesbians. And they [the police department] were actually quoting different individuals from throughout the state that had been fired for that reason. So I knew my life was over. The chief at the time said to an officer that he was going to rid the department of all the lesbians and that he could start with [officer name], meaning me" (Haarr and Morash 2013, 16). Lesbian officers, like other minorities, experience double discrimination – gender and sexual orientation. All too often, lesbian officers hide their sexual orientation due to fear of rejection, harassment, or discrimination (Buhrke 1996).

Within the field of policing, stress and strain are experienced by both male and female police officers (Greene and del Carmen 2002). Reflect for a moment on the types of strains that female officers' experience and how the strains and stressors may be similar and/or different between male and female officers. Female officers share with male officers the strains that are inherent in police work on a daily basis. The policing profession is dangerous; thus, both genders must cope with the strain of ensuring their personal safety. The stressors and strains take a toll on the physical and mental health of police officers, resulting in them being at risk for high blood pressure, insomnia, heart disease, **post-traumatic stress disorder** (PTSD), and even suicide (Joseph et al. 2009; Violanti 2010; Violanti et al. 2007). In a study of 41 women and 70 male officers in a mid-sized urban department, Violanti et al. (2008) reports that female police officers experienced higher rates of suicide ideation and depression than both their male colleagues and those in the general population. Additionally, female officers also experienced high levels of PTSD symptoms. Some studies have revealed that female police officers report higher levels of stress than male officers (Dowler and Arai 2008; Pendergrass and Ostrove 1984). Gachter and colleagues (2011) report that **tokenism** and low levels of perceived fairness by female officers are the root causes of strain for them and suggest that the environment in which female officers work compromises their ability to employ effective coping mechanisms to ameliorate their experienced strains. Why do you think that female police officers are experiencing such strains? Violanti and colleagues (2008) speculate that the shifts, or the times in which women work, may play a role. The researchers found that female police officers most often work during the day and that "it is possible that women officers may tend to feel more uneasy and stressed in a daytime male dominated work environment due to more frequent peer and public interaction" (Violanti et al. 2008, 765). It may also be that the strains and pressures of the police culture and the worries of childcare arrangements could compound the stress and strains of police work for them.

Race, gender, and sexual orientation can indeed impact the levels of stress that female police officers experience on the job. In a study of approximately 1,200 female and male patrol officers of various races/ethnicities and sexual orientations in Milwaukee, Hassell and Brandl (2009) found that African-American female officers and Latina female officers experience more negative workplace experiences (e.g., lack of opportunity, perceptions of bias, or vulgar language) than other patrol officers. In fact, the researchers found that female African-American officers reported experiencing higher levels of stress than other officers. Additionally, the researchers found that lesbian, gay, and bisexual officers reported experiencing more perceptions of vulgar language than heterosexual officers. Colvin (2009), in a study of 66 lesbian and gay police officers, reports that a majority of the officers indicated that they experience social isolation and being subjected to homophobic language. These experiences, along with other organizational barriers such as a lack of opportunity for promotion, may add to their stress and lead to job dissatisfaction, increasing the chance of them ultimately deciding to resign from the police force.

It does appear that health conditions such as pregnancy do create a strain for female police officers. How might pregnancy be a strain for women in society who are not law enforcement officers? Why would it be a strain for female police officers? Motherhood is also stressful for female officers. What types of strain might a female police officer encounter on the job in regard to being a mother? Cowan and Bochantin (2009) interviewed 15 female officers about pregnancy and motherhood and how they frame these experiences in the course of their jobs. Results from the interviews showed that female officers frame these issues as follows: (1) pregnancy and motherhood is risky; (2) police organizations view pregnancy as a "crime" or "illness"; (3) mothering skills are not valued; and (4) it is a struggle to balance family and work responsibilities. The risky aspect of pregnancy and motherhood was explained by the officers as unwelcomed by the department or their colleagues and the officers felt that pursuing motherhood could be harmful to their career:

> Janice explains her department's attitude after finding out she was pregnant, "They told me at one point that they were not going to hold my job … people were saying that I should've known before I got the job, now I will need all this time off and I'm pretty much screwing everyone else over." (Cowan and Bochantin 2009, 26)

Being a mother may also make it more difficult to level up for a promotion, and hence, is another risk for their careers. With the demands of childcare, female officers may be reluctant to pursue a promotion that may negatively impact their current work schedule that is favorable to their childcare arrangement (Whetstone 2001). Also, female officers, after becoming mothers, began to question whether they wanted to continue to risk their lives for fear of their children growing up without them.

> Kelly explains, "When I came back to work after having the baby I had a really hard time with it. I kept asking my husband, 'how can I do this? I am a mother. What kind of mother am I that I have to worry about dying every night? How can I put myself in harm's way?'" (Cowan and Bochantin 2009, 26)

Pregnancy was viewed as a "crime" by some police departments who did not know where to place female officers once discovering they were pregnant. Janice explains,

> I was the first woman in the department to have children. All of the other women had children before they started. I was only one month pregnant and they sent me home because they didn't know what to do with me. They wouldn't give me light duty because they didn't consider it an injury so I just had to wait at home until they figured out what to do. There were a lot of people who were mad that I wanted both a job and a family. (Cowan and Bochantin 2009, 27)

In another study of 21 policewomen, one woman with 30 years' experience on the force recalled how her pregnancy was essentially considered a crime. Single and pregnant, virtually everyone in her department avoided her, most criticized her for her status, and many claimed, "she would never be promoted and that she was a poor role model for women" (Haarr and Morash 2013, 15). In other instances, police departments viewed pregnancy as an illness due to the **Family and Medical Leave Act (1993)**. This act requires employers to provide 12 weeks of leave to new mothers and also requires employers to hold the position for the woman upon her return from leave. Perhaps like working women in other occupations, female police officers did not view their skills as mothers to be valued by their colleagues and organization and struggled to balance work and family life. Cowan and Bochantin (2009) report that female officers often expressed that they were implicitly or explicitly devalued by their departments due to their status. Further, female officers recognized that it was tough to be a "superstar" both at work and at home and "having it all" was extremely difficult. Many female officers in their sample chose to make sacrifices in their work life to accommodate their home life – which they often valued more. As one female officer stated in regard to not seeking a promotion, "I feel as though I would be promoted because I am a token female in the department. The demands placed on me from my family are also very high which means I would not be able to be completely committed to the position" (Archbold, Hassell, and Stichman 2010). It appears that the policing profession, at least when it comes to female police officers, is not "family friendly" (Cordner and Cordner 2011).

 GLOBAL PERSPECTIVES: Shared experiences/distinct differences

Female officers across the globe share many challenges and strains with their US colleagues in regard to stress, discrimination, and harassment. Researchers have reported on such challenges experienced by female officers from a wide range of countries including Afghanistan, Brazil, England, Ghana, India, Wales, and South Africa (Becker et al. 2012; Bezerra, Minayo, and Constantino 2013; Brown 1998; Collins and Gibbs 2003; Graham-Harrison 2013; Pienaar and Rothmann 2006;

(continued)

Selokar et al. 2011). Examples of shared stressors include internal and external work environments, shifts, and harassment. In regard to female officers in India and South Africa, researchers have reported that they are more likely to experience mental health issues than their male colleagues due to the occupational stress.

In Ghana, female officers share similar struggles with female officers in the United States as well as some distinct struggles. For instance, female police officers in Ghana struggle to overcome gender stereotypes such as policing being viewed as a physical job – best suited to men (Becker et al. 2012). They also experience sexual harassment and are pressured into engaging in sexual relations out of fear of being isolated or publicly humiliated. Additionally, female officers experience struggles with arranging childcare, particularly when working night shifts. One difference between female officers in Ghana and female officers in the United States is their personal safety. Female officers in Ghana may be called upon to patrol dangerous areas of the city at night, by themselves. Becker and colleagues (2012, 47) state that "a female officer was reportedly raped while seeking shelter after her night shift." Clearly, this is one horrific victimization that female police officers in the United States do not incur. Female police officers in Afghanistan are currently fighting to have women-only restroom facilities installed in police stations (Graham-Harrison 2013). Graham-Harrison (2013) explains,

> Women are often targeted by predatory colleagues while using shared toilets in isolated corners of stations, said an international adviser to the police force ... Afghan and foreign women say the lack of basic facilities is just one part of a wider culture of disrespect that discourages prospective female police officers. It also has wider, societal implications, because without female officers, there are concerns there may not be as much progress on promises to tackle rampant violence against women.

Effectiveness of women officers

While many in policing or even the public may not have valued or currently value female officers, women officers do indeed play an important and valuable role in the policing profession. Concerns have arisen about whether female police officers could cope with danger effectively, could command authority over the public, or refrain from being too emotional. Despite such concerns, female police officers have many qualities that contribute to their effectiveness in their jobs. With women being stereotyped as being too emotional, some researchers have set out to determine if their emotionality has resulted in more harm to them on the job. Research has found that female officers are more likely to use their communication skills, rather than reach for their weapon, to de-escalate violent encounters between officers and citizens and conflicts between citizens (Price 1985; Lonsway et al. 2003). The use of communication skills rather than lethal force by female officers has not translated into a higher rate of female officer deaths, as some have speculated. In 2013, 27 police officers were killed in the line of duty, with two of these deaths being female police officers (FBI 2013). Thus, females may be better at de-escalating violent situations, perhaps due to having stronger verbal skills than male officers, thereby resulting in a lesser likelihood of injury on the job. Research on female police officers also appears to support this assertion. In a study of 531 female officers, Seklecki and Paynich (2007, 26) report that officers in their study believed that they were more capable of applying interpersonal skills in policing situations than their male colleagues, and that they were "equally as capable" as male officers of physically dealing with hostile citizens. Their use of verbal skills carries over into other facets of their positions such as interacting with crime victims. One female officer with approximately 15 years of experience states,

> I think a lot of the younger guys and even some of the sergeants realize the importance of women in police work. We can do more things than people said, and I really think that we talk and tend to be better with the victims … I think we have a very important niche because after everything is settled we can go ahead and have, at least most of us, we can go in and help the actual person or victim and explain things and be there to listen. (Morash and Haarr, 2012, 14)

Women police officers are *indeed* effective in their jobs, whether patrolling the streets or providing assistance to victims of crime – even if their styles of carrying out their duties tend to be a bit different from those of male officers. While the presence of women police officers has been met with resistance, it is clear that their entry into the policing profession has resulted in not only an overall improved image of policing in general, but they have also assisted police departments in many facets, from crime reduction to service to their communities.

Conclusion

In this chapter, we provided a historical overview of women in policing. It has been a struggle for women to enter the policing profession and the struggle continues today, with policing still being a very male-dominated profession. The role of women in policing has improved somewhat due to legislation. However, the police culture stymies the experiences of women working in the profession today and, in many departments, contributes to continued harassment and discrimination of women law enforcement officers. Even though women have "proved" their worth and effectiveness as police officers, they are still unwelcome or begrudgingly accepted into police departments. Female police officers have unique skills, such as solid communication skills, that are both an asset for their male colleagues and for helping those in their communities. With better training in police departments, removal of any police officer, male or female, that may be engaging in harassment and discriminatory practices, and the creation of shift schedules that help to balance work and life for all officers, the policing profession may become a better place for women to work in. It is imperative that law enforcement agencies recognize the assets of females and recruit more women into their agencies and promote those women that have exemplified quality policing and administrative skills. However, recruitment and promotion alone are not enough – rather, there need to be organizational changes and attitudinal changes in order for the goal of gender equity to be achieved in policing today.

Suggested readings

Eisenberg, Adam. 2009. *A Different Shade of Blue: How Women Changed the Face of Police Work*. Lake Forest, CA: Behler Publications, LLC.

Lunneborg, Patricia. 2004. *Women Police: Portraits of Success*. Lincoln, NE: iUniverse.

Snow, Robert L. 2010. *Policewomen Who Made History: Breathing through the Ranks*. Lanham, MA: Rowman & Littlefied Publishers.

Wells, Sandra K., and Betty L. Alt. 2005. *Police Women: Life with the Badge*. Westport, CT: Praeger.

Student engagement activities

1 Research the history of entry for women into policing in the state/province/county in which you reside. Be sure to search for newspaper articles that may have reported on it. Write a one-page

summary of the history of women entering policing in your state/province/county and critically analyze how women were portrayed at this time in the newspaper reports. Also, be sure to discuss the types of duties they performed when they entered the police force and note whether their entry and duties were similar and/or different than other women entering the policing profession across the nation.

2 Watch two episodes of *Female Forces* (on TV, iTunes, or Xfinity). Record how women in policing are being portrayed in terms of their duties and roles within the policing profession. What do you notice about the images of female police officers as the introduction of the show opens? How about the interactions between the officers and their colleagues and citizens? Write a one-page summary of your observations.

3 Research a country (besides the United Kingdom) where women work as police officers. Write a five-page essay covering the history of women entering the force, the current number of women working as police officers, and describe any challenges that they may face on the job. Within your essay, compare the similarities and differences between female police officers in the United States with female police officers in your chosen country.

Discussion questions

1 What legislation helped women enter the policing profession in greater numbers?
2 How does the police culture impact women working as law enforcement officers? Provide examples of the culture that present visible and invisible barriers to these working professionals.
3 Given the challenges that many female law enforcement officers face in juggling family and their careers, what do you think could/should be done to assist women (or even men) working in this profession? What policies would you recommend? Why?

Key terms

Double discrimination
England v. The City of Dallas, Mack Vines, and the State of Texas (1990)
Equal Employment Opportunity Act of 1972
Equal Employment Opportunity Program
Equal Pay Act of 1963
Family and Medical Leave Act (1993)
Glass ceiling

Griggs v. Duke Power Company (1971)
"Men Against Women" (MAW)
Police culture
Police matrons
Post-traumatic stress disorder (PTSD)
Sodomy laws
Title VII of the Civil Rights Act of 1964
Tokenism

References

All Africa. March 5, 2014. "South Africa: National Assembly Approves Gender Bill." *SANews.gov.za.* Accessed February 9, Allafrica.com/stories/201403051114.html

Anderson, Laura. September 19, 2003. *Women in Law Enforcement.* Accessed September 22, 2013, http://www.emich.edu/cerns/downloads/papers/PoliceStaff/Police%20Personnel%20(e.g.,%20 Selection,%20%20Promotion)/Women%20in%20Law%20Enforcement.pdf

Ramona Arnold v. City of Seminole, Oklahoma (1985).

Archbold, Carol A., Hassell, Kimbeley D., and Amy J. Stichman. 2010. "Comparing Promotion Aspirations Among Female and Male Police Officers." *International Journal of Police Science & Management*, 12 (2): 287–303. DOI: http://dx.doi.org/10.1350/ijps.2010.12.2.175

Balkin, Joseph. 1988. "Why Policemen Don't Like Policewomen." *Journal of Police Science and Administration*, 16: 29–38.

Balko, Radlye. June 21, 2013. "What Cop T-Shirts Tell Us about Police Culture." *Huffington Post.* Accessed October 1, 2013, http://www.huffingtonpost.com/2013/06/21/what-cop-tshirts-tell-us-_n_3479017.html

Bartol, Curt R., Bergen, Goerge T., Volckens, Julie S., and Kathleen M. Knoras. 1992. "Women in Small-Town Policing: Job Performance and Stress." *Criminal Justice and Behavior*, 19: 240–259. DOI: 10.1177/0093854892019003003

Becker, Jenny, Brown, Caroline B., Ibrahim, Aisha F., and Akosua Kuranchie. 2012. "Freedom Through Association: Assessing the Contributions of Female Police Staff Associations to Gender-Sensitive Police Reform in West Africa." *The North South Institute.* Accessed September 1, 2013, http://www.nsi-ins.ca/wp-content/uploads/2012/10/2011-Freedom-through-Association-Assessing-the-Contributions-of-Female-Police-Staff-Associations-to-Gender-Sensitive-Police-Reform-in-West-Africa.pdf

Bezerra, Claudia M., Minayo, Maria C., and Patrícia. 2013. "Occupational Stress Among Female Police Officers." *Cien Saude Colet*, 18(3): 657–666. DOI: 10.1590/S1413-81232013000800011

Buhrke, Robin A. 1996. *A Matter of Justice: Lesbians and Gay Men in Law Enforcement.* New York, NY: Routledge.

Burns, John F. September 28, 2008. "Taliban Claim Responsibility in Killing of Key Female Afghan Officer." *New York Times.* Accessed July 6, 2014, http://www.nytimes.com/2008/09/29/world/asia/29afghan.html?_r=0

Brown, Jennifer M. 1998. "Aspects of Discriminatory Treatment of Women Police Officers Serving in Forces in England and Wales." *British Journal of Criminology*, 38(2): 265–282. DOI: 10.1093/oxfordjournals.bjc.a014235

Brown, Jennifer, and Frances Heidensohn. 2000. *Gender and Policing: Comparative Perspectives.* New York, NY: Palgrave Macmillan.

Camber, Rebecca. November 24, 2009. "90 Years of Girls in Blue: And in 1919 They Weren't Even Allowed to Make Any Arrests!" *Daily Mail.* Accessed June 23, 2014, http://www.dailymail.co.uk/news/article-1230562/The-girls-blue-Met-celebrates-90-years-WPC.html

Candido, Sergio N. March 23, 2013. "Lesbian LAPD Officers Get $1.2 Million Settlement Over Alleged Discrimination." *South Florida Gay News.* Accessed August 11, 2013, http://southflorida-gaynews.com/articles/lesbian-lapd-officers-get-1-2-million-settlement-over-alleged-discrimination/110223

Caruso, Michelle. April 28, 1997. "Fuhrman Led 'Klan' vs. Female Officers in Tapes, O.J. Trial Cop Tells of 'Tribunals.' *New York Daily News.* Accessed August 12, 2013, http://www.nydailynews.com/archives/news/fuhrman-led-klan-female-officers-tapes-o-trial-tells-tribunals-article-1.757959

Chu, Doris C. 2013. "Gender Integration in Policing: A Comparison of Male and Female Police Officers' Perceptions in Taiwan. *International Journal of Comparative and Applied Criminal Justice*, 37(2): 143–157. DOI: 10.1080/01924036.2012.721202

Chu, Doris C., and Ivan Y. Sun. 2006. "Female Police Officers' Job-Related Attitudes: A Comparative Study of Taiwan and the United States. *Women & Criminal Justice*, 18: 107–130. DOI: 10.1300/J012v18n01_04

Collins, Pamela A., and A. C. C. Gibbs. 2003. "Stress in Police Officers: A Study of the Origins, Prevalence, and Severity of Stress-Related Symptoms Within a County Police Force." *Occupational Medicine*, 53: 256–264. DOI: 10.1093/occmed/kqg061

Colvin, Roddrick. 2009. "Shared Perceptions Among Lesbian and Gay Police Officers: Barriers and Opportunities in the Law Enforcement Work Environment. *Police Quarterly*, 12(1): 86–101. DOI: 10.1177/1098611108327308

Cordner, Gary, and AnnMarie Cordner. 2011. "Stuck on a Plateau? Obstacles to Recruitment, Selection, and Retention." *Police Quarterly*, 14: 207–226. DOI: 10.1177/1098611111413990

Cowan, Renee L., and Jaime E. Bochantin. 2009. "Pregnancy and Motherhood on the Thin Blue Line: Female Police Officers Experiences in a Highly Masculinized Work Environment." *Women & Language*, 32: 22–30.

Dodge, Mark, and Mark Pogrebin. 2001. "African American Policewomen: An Exploration of Professional Relationships." *Policing: An International Journal of Police Strategies and Management*, 24: 550–562. DOI: 10.1108/13639510110409601

Donaido, Marcela, and Cecila Manzotta. 2010. *Women and the Armed and Police Forces in Latin America*. Red de Seguridad y Defensa de America Latina.

Dowler, Kenneth, and Bruce Arai. 2008. "Stress, Gender and Policing: The Impact of Perceived Gender Discrimination on Symptoms of Stress." *International Journal of Police Science and Management*, 10(2): 123–155. DOI: 10.1350/ijps.2008.10.2.81

Emsley, Clive. 1996. *The English Police: Apolitical and Social History*. Longman: London.

England v. The City of Dallas, Mack Vines, and the State of Texas (1990).

Evans, Lorraine, and Kim Davies. 2014. "Small Screens and Big Streets: A Comparison of Women Police Officers on Primetime Crime Shows and in U.S. Police Departments, 1950 to 2008." *Women and Criminal Justice*, 24(2): 106–125. DOI: 10.1080/08974454.2013.842513

Family & Medical Leave Act (1993).

FBI (Federal Bureau of Investigation). 2013. *Officers Feloniously Killed*. Accessed March 26, 2016, https://www.fbi.gov/about-us/cjis/ucr/leoka/2013/officers-feloniously-killed/felonious_topic_page_-2013

Felperin, Jon. May 18, 2004. "Women in Law Enforcement: Two Steps Forward, Three Steps Back." *PoliceOne*. Accessed August 12, 2013, http://www.policeone.com/police-recruiting/articles/87017-Women-in-Law-Enforcement-Two-steps-forward-three-steps-back/

Gachter, Martin, Savage, David A., and Benno Torgler. 2011. "Gender Variations of Physiological and Psychological Strain Amongst Police Officers." *Gender Issues*, 28: 66–93. DOI: 10.1007/s12147-011-9100-9

Garcia, Vanessa. 2003. "'Difference' in the Police Department: Women, Policing, and 'Doing Gender.'" *Journal of Contemporary Criminal Justice*, 19(3): 330–344. DOI: 10.1177/1043986203254530

Gates, Margaret J. 1976. "Occupational Segregation and the Law." In *Women and the Workplace*, edited by Martha Blaxall and Barbara Reagan, 61–74. Chicago, IL: University of Chicago Press.

Goko, Colleen. August 19, 2013. "New Gender Equality Bill Aims to 'Change Landscape' for SA Women." *Business Day*. Accessed July 7, 2014, http://www.bdlive.co.za/business/2013/08/19/new-gender-equality-bill-aims-to-change-landscape-for-sa-women

Gossett, Jennifer L., and Joyce E. Williams. 1998. "Perceived Discrimination Among Women in Law Enforcement." *Women & Criminal Justice*, 10(1): 53–73. DOI: 10.1300/J012v10n01_03

Graham-Harrison, Emma. April 24, 2013. "Afghanistan's Female Police Officers Fight for Women-Only Toilets." *Guardian*. Accessed August 2, 2013, http://www.theguardian.com/world/2013/apr/24/afghanistan-female-police-officers-toilet

Greene, Helen T., and Alejandro del Carmen. 2002. "Female Police Officers in Texas: Perceptions of Colleagues and Stress." *Policing: An International Journal of Police Strategies and Management*, 25(2): 385–398. DOI: 10.1108/13639510210429428

Griggs v. *Duke Power Company* (1971).

Haarr, Robin N., and Merry Morash. 2004. "Police Workplace Problems, Coping Strategies and Stress: Changes from 1990 to 2003 for Women and Racial Minorities." *Law Enforcement Executive Forum*, 4, 165–185.

Haarr, Robin N., and Merry Morash. 2013. "The Effect of Rank on Police Women Coping with Discrimination and Harassment." *Police Quarterly*, 16(4), 395–419.

Harris, Scott. May 15, 1997. "A Slow Change in Attitudes for the LAPD." *Los Angeles Times*. Accessed August 12, 2013, http://articles.latimes.com/1997-05-15/local/me-59067_1_lapd-officers

Hamill, Denis. March 8, 2012. "Manhattan Playground Is Perfect Tribute to 9/11 Hero Moira Smith." *New York Daily News*. Accessed July 17, 2013, http://www.nydailynews.com/new-york/manhattan-playground-perfect-tribute-9-11-hero-moira-smith-article-1.1034731

Hassell, Kimberly D., and Steven G. Brandl. 2009. "An Examination of the Workplace Experiences of Police Patrol Officers: The Role of Race, Sex, and Sexual Orientation." *Police Quarterly*, 12: 408–430. DOI: 10.1177/1098611109348473

Higgins, Lois. 1951. "Historical Background of Policewomen's Service." *Journal of Criminal Law & Criminology*, 41: 822–835.

Hunt, J. 1990. "The Logic of Sexism Among Police." *Women and Criminal Justice*, 1(2), 3–30.

Inciardi, James A. 1990. *Criminal Justice*, 3rd edn. San Diego, CA: Harcourt Brace Jovanovich.

Johnson, Stephen, Forman, Johanna M., and Katherine Bliss 2012. *Police Reform in Latin America: Implications for U.S. Policy*. Washington, DC: Center for Strategic and International Studies. Accessed July 7, 2014, http://csis.org/files/publication/120228_Johnson_PoliceReform_web.pdf

Joseph , P. Nedra, Violanti, John M., Donahue, Richard, Andrew, Michael E., Trevisan, Maurizio, Burchfiel, Cecil M., and Joan Dorn. 2009. "Police Work and Subclinical Atherosclerosis." *Journal of Occupational and Environmental Health*, 51: 700–707. DOI: 10.1097/JOM.0b013e3181a02252

Kakar, Suman. 2002. "Gender and Police Officers' Perceptions of Their Job Performance: An Analysis of the Relationship Between Gender and Perceptions of Job Performance." *Criminal Justice Policy Review*,13(3): 238–256. DOI: 10.1177/0887403402013003003

Langton, Lynn. 2010. *Women in Law Enforcement, 1987–2008*. Washington, DC: Bureau of Justice Statistics.

Lee, Tazinski P. 2005. "The Myth and Reality of Affirmative Action: A Study Using the Perceptions of Female Police." *Race, Gender & Class in Public Policy, Planning, & Administration*, 12(3/4): 56–72.

Lestch, Corrine, and Larry McShane. March 10, 2012. "Moira Smith, 9/11 Hero Cop, Memorialized with Joy at Manhattan Playground Named Renamed for Her." *New York Daily News*. Accessed July 17, 2013, http://www.nydailynews.com/news/moira-smith-9-11-hero-memorialized-joy-manhattan-playground-named-renamed-article-1.1036870

Lonsway, Kim, Carrington, Susan, Aguirre, Patricia, Wood, Michelle, Moore, Margaret, Harrington, Penny, Smeal, Eleanor, and Katherine Spillar. 2003. "Equality Denied: The Status of Women in Policing, 2001." *National Center for Women & Policing. Feminist Majority Foundation*. Accessed August 22, 2013, http://www.womenandpolicing.org/PDF/2002_Status_Report.pdf

Lonsway, Kimberly A., Paynich, Rebecca, and Jennifer N. Hall. 2013. "Sexual Harassment in Law Enforcement: Incidence, Impact, and Perception." *Police Quarterly*, 16, 177–210. DOI: 10.1177/1098611113475630

Martin, Susan E., and Nancy C. Jurik. 2007. *Doing Justice, Doing Gender: Women in Legal and Criminal Justice Occupations*, 2nd edn. Thousand Oaks, CA: Sage Publications.

Marzulli, John. August 15, 2012. "Cop Sues for $30M Over Claims Her Lieutenant Exposed Himself to Her and Sent Explicit Texts and Photos." *New York Daily News*. Accessed August 215, 2013, http://www.nydailynews.com/new-york/sues-30m-claims-lieutenant-exposed-explicit-texts-photos-article-1.1137297

Miletich, Steve. June 23, 2014. "O'Toole Promises a Police Force 'Second to None.'" *Seattle Times*. Accessed June 24, 2014, http://seattletimes.com/html/localnews/2023913628_chiefvotexml.html

Milton, Catherine. 1972. *Women in Policing.* Washington, DC: Police Foundation.

Monk-Turner, Elizabeth, Martinez, Homer, Holbrook, Jason, and Nathan Harvey. 2007. "Are Reality TV Crime Shows Continuing to Perpetuate Crime Myths." *Internet Journal of Criminology.* Accessed August 12, 2013, www.internetjournalofcriminology.com

Morash, Merry, and Robin N. Haarr. 2012. "Doing, Redoing, and Undoing Gender: Variation in Gender Identities of Women Working as Police Officers." *Feminist Criminology*, 7: 3–23. DOI: 10.1177/1557085111413253

Morrison, Cherita J. 2004. "Towards Gender Equality in South African Policing." In *Policing in Central and Eastern Europe: Dilemmas of Contemporary Criminal Justice*, edited by Gorazd Mesko, Milan Pagon, and Bojan Dobovsek, 238–244. Slovenia: University of Maribor.

Natarajan, Mangai. 1996. "Towards Equality: A Report on Women Policing in India." *Journal of Women and Criminal Justice*, 8(2): 1–18. DOI: 10.1300/J012v08n02_01

Natarajan, Mangai. 2001. "Women Police in a Traditional Society: Test of a Western Model of Integration." *International Journal of Comparative Sociology*, XLII (1–2): 211–233. DOI: 10.1163/156851801300171760

National Center for Women in Policing. 1998. *Equality of Policing: The Status of Women in Policing, 1998.* Accessed August 9, 2013, http://www.womenandpolicing.org/status1998.html

National Center for Women in Policing. 2002. *Equality Denied: The Status of Women in Policing, 2001.* Accessed August 9, 2013, http://womenandpolicing.com/PDF/2002_Status_Report.pdf

Nichols, David. 1995. "The Brotherhood: Sexual Harassment in Police Agencies. *Women Police*, 29(2): 10–12.

Paoline, Eugene A., Myers, Stephanie M., and Robert E. Worden. 1990. "Police Culture, Individualism, and Community Policing: Evidence from Two Police Departments." *Justice Quarterly*, 17(3), 575–605.

Prenzler, Tim. 2002. "Sex Discrimination." In *Police Reform: Building Integrity*, edited by Tim Prenzler and Janet Ransley, 67–82. Sydney, Australia: Federation Press.

Pendergrass, Virginia E., and Nancy M. Ostrove. 1984. "A Survey of Stress in Women in Policing." *Journal of Police Science and Administration*, 12: 303–309.

Pienaar, Jacobus, and Sebastiaan Rothmann. 2006. "Occupational Stress in the South African Police Service." *South African Journal of Industrial Psychology*, 32(3): 72–78.

Pregnancy Discrimination Act. 1978.

Poole, Eric, and Mark Pogrebin. 1988. "Factors Affecting the Decision to Remain in Policing: A Study of Women Officers." *Journal of Police Science and Administration*, 16: 49–55.

Price, Barbara R. 1985. "Sexual Integration in American Law Enforcement." In *Police Ethics: Hard Choices in Law Enforcement*, edited by William C. Heffernan and Timothy Stroup, 205–214. New York, NY: John Jay Press.

Price, Barbara R. 1996. "Female Police Officers in the United States." *Policing in Central and Eastern Europe.* Slovenia: College of Police and Security Studies. Accessed August 25, 2013, https://www.ncjrs.gov/policing/fem635.htm

Rabe-Hemp, Cara. 2008. "Survival in an 'All Boys Club: Policewomen and Their Fight for Acceptance.'" *Policing: An International Journal of Police Strategies & Management*, 31(2): 251–270. DOI: 10.1108/13639510810878712

Rabe-Hemp, Cara. 2009. "POLICEwomen or PoliceWOMEN? Doing Gender and Police Work." *Feminist Criminology*, 4(2): 114–129. DOI: 10.1177/1557085108327659

Rabe-Hemp, Cara. 2011. "Female Forces: Beauty, Brains, and a Badge. *Feminist Criminology*, 6: 132–155. DOI: 10.1177/1557085111398471

Reaves, Brian A. 2011. *Census of State and Local Law Enforcement Agencies, 2008.* Washington, DC: Bureau of Justice Statistics.

Rubin, Joel. March 20, 2013. "L.A. OKs $1.25-Million Payout to Two Lesbian LAPD Officers." *Los Angeles Times.* Accessed August 29, 2013, http://articles.latimes.com/2013/mar/20/local/la-me-0321-gay-lapd-lawsuit-20130321

Scoville, Dean. September 21, 2012. "The First Female Patrol Officers." *Police.* Accessed August 9, 2013, http://www.policemag.com/channel/women-in-law-enforcement/articles/2012/09/the-first-female-patrol-officers.aspx

Seklecki, Richard, and Rebecca Paynich. 2007. "A National Survey of Female Police Officers: An Overview of Findings." *Police Practice and Research*, 8(1): 17–30. DOI: 10.1080/15614260701217941

Selokar, Deepak, Nimbarte, Sanjay, Ahana, Satyanarayan, Gaidhane, Abhay, and Vasant Wagh. 2011. "Occupational Stress Among Police Personnel of Wardha City, India." *Australasian Medical Journal*, 4(3): 114–117. DOI: 10.4066/AMJ.2011.562

Shulz, Dorothy M. 1995. *From Social Worker to Crime Fighter: Women in the United States Municipal Policing*. Westport, CT: Praeger.

Silvestri, Marisa. 2012. *Women in Charge: Policing, Gender, and Leadership*. New York, NY: Routledge.

Sklansky, David A. 2006. "Not Your Father's Police Department: Making Sense of the New Demographics of Law Enforcement." *The Journal of Criminal Law & Criminology*, 96(3): 1209–1243. DOI: 0091-4169/06/9603-1209

Strobl, Staci. 2008. "The Women's Police Directorate in Bahrain: An Ethnographic Exploration of Gender Segregation and the Likelihood of Future Integration." *International Criminal Justice Review*, 18(1): 39–58. DOI: 10.1177/1057567708315642

Sulton, Cynthia G., and Roi D. Townsey. 1981. *Progress Report on Women in Policing*. Washington, DC: The Police Foundation.

Texeira, Mary T. 2002. "Who Protects and Serves Me? A Case Study of Sexual Harassment of African American Women in One U.S. Law Enforcement Agency." *Gender and Society*, 16: 524–545. DOI: 10.1177/0891243202016004007

US Equal Employment Opportunity Commission. 2002. *Facts about Sexual Harassment*. Washington, DC. Accessed February 9, 2016, www.eeoc.gov/facts/fs-sex.html

US Equal Employment Opportunity Commission. 2013. *Title VII of the Civil Rights Act of 1964.* Accessed August 24, 2013, http://www.eeoc.gov/laws/statutes/titlevii.cfm

Violanti, John M. 2010. "Police Suicide: A National Comparison with Fire-Fighter and Military Personnel." *International Journal of Police Strategies & Management*, 33: 270–286. DOI: 10.1108/13639511011044885

Violanti, John M., Andrew, Michael, Burchfiel, Cecil M., Hartley, Tara A., Charles, Luenda E., and Diane B. Miller. 2007. "Posttraumatic Stress Symptoms and Cortisol Patterns Among Police Officers." *Policing: An International Journal of Police Strategies and Management*, 30: 169–188. DOI: 10.1108/13639510710753207

Violanti, John M., Charles, Luenda E., Hartley, Tara A., Mnatsakanova, Anna, Andrew, Michael E., Fekedulegn, Desta, Vila, Bryan, and Cecil M. Burchfiel. 2008. "Shift-Work and Suicide Ideation Among Police Officers." *American Journal of Industrial Medicine*, 51(10): 758–768. DOI: 10.1002/ajim.20629

Whetstone, Thomas S. 2001. "Copping Out: Why Police Officers Decline to Participate in the Sergeant's Promotional Process." *American Journal of Criminal Justice*, 25: 147–159. DOI: 10.1007/BF02886842

Wilson, Frankin T., and Ashley G. Blackburn. 2014. "The Depiction of Female Municipal Police Officers in the First Four Decades of the Core Cop Film Genre: "It's a Man's World." *Women and Criminal Justice*, 24(2): 83–105. DOI: 10.1080/08974454.2013.842521

Yang, Dung-Ju. 1985. "Women in Policing: A Comparative Study of the United States and the Republic of China." *Police Studies: The International Review of Police Development*, 8(3): 125–131.

CHAPTER 9

Women in the courts

Student learning outcomes

After reading this chapter, you should be able to:
- Explain the history of women in the legal profession.
- Define the nature of legal practice and how it has changed since the nineteenth century.
- Analyze the gendered nature of the legal profession.
- Compare and contrast the experiences of legal practice for women around the globe.

Introduction

Fashion and the practice of law are two terms that most individuals do not think about in tandem. For many female attorneys, however, their work attire is often scrutinized. US District Judge Barbara Lynn in the Northern District in Texas reports wearing a vest jumpsuit in the 1980s when she made an appearance as a litigator in court (Farmer 2010). Her choice of dress in court was not traditional attire for female lawyers, and the majority of her colleagues viewed her decision to wear the jumpsuit as analogous to career suicide (Farmer 2010). Judge Lynn explains that "women lawyers were usually careful in those days to stick to skirt suits that hovered below the kneecap. Their wardrobes, including their affinity for conservative suits (usually navy, gray, or black) and plan, white button-down shirts, mimicked professional menswear to a large extent" (Farmer 2010, 4). The fashion breakthrough that Judge Lynn achieved in the 1980s did not end the attention that female lawyers experienced in regard to their dress. Rather, the focus on the attire of female lawyers continued in the 1990s. One of the most infamous female prosecutors in the 1990s was Marcia Clark. Clark rose to sudden international "fame" when she served as the lead prosecutor in the O. J. Simpson murder trial in Los Angeles in 1995. Simpson, a retired NFL football player, was accused of murdering his ex-wife, Nicole Brown Simpson, and her friend Ron Goldman. Because of Simpson's fame and the crime he was charged with, his case received international attention. His trial was also televised. It is through the televised trial that most people became acquainted with Clark. It did not take long for attention to be turned to Clark's attire rather than to her skills as an attorney (Hall 1995). What women wear in their professional and personal lives is an area of focused attention for female lawyers and affects how they are viewed by judges, juries, and the public. In 2014, US District Judge of Nebraska, Richard Kopf, expressed on his blog that female

---

Women, Crime, and Justice, First Edition. By Elaine Gunnison, Frances P. Bernat, and Lynne Goodstein.
© 2017 John Wiley & Sons, Ltd. Published 2017 by John Wiley & Sons, Ltd.

lawyers should dress more conservatively, and how he felt a sexual attraction to one female lawyer in his court (Gershman 2014). He said:

> True story. Around these parts there is a wonderfully talented and very pretty female lawyer who is in her late twenties. She is brilliant, she writes well, she speaks eloquently, she is zealous but not overly so, she is always prepared, she treats others, including her opponents, with civility and respect, she wears very short skirts and shows lots of her ample chest. I especially appreciate the last two attributes. (Gershman 2014)

Thus, the firestorm of what female attorneys should wear is scrutinized by the media and their colleagues, and, in some cases, they bear the blame for others' inappropriate sexual attraction towards them.

Not only do female attorneys face sexism in regard to their appearance, but others have faced outright discrimination. Francine Griesing, a female attorney who had worked in the law firm Greenberg Traurig (GT) in Philadelphia, filed a federal class action lawsuit against her former employer in 2012, citing discrimination that she and other female attorneys had experienced at the firm based on their gender (Brinkmann 2012). According to Griesing, her employment with the firm was terminated when she voiced her concerns not only about the discrimination she was facing at the firm but also about acts of discrimination that many of her female attorney colleagues were facing as well (Brinkmann 2012). Specifically, her lawsuit alleged that the law firm "pays women less, promotes them at lower rates than men and virtually freezes them out from high-level managerial positions" (Zaretsky 2012). Problematically, getting ahead may not have been about legal competency: according to the lawsuit, "GT has one exception to its general practice of denying women professional development opportunities and compensating women less than men. GT prioritizes, pays and promotes women who have intimate relationships with Firm leaders or who acquiesce to sexualized stereotypes" (Zaretsky 2012). In 2013, she settled her $200 million class action lawsuit with her former employer for an undisclosed sum (McAfee 2014). Whether it is their attire or discrimination on the job, female lawyers experience a wide range of barriers today. The purpose of this chapter is to explore the historical underpinnings of the rise of women into the profession in the late nineteenth and early twentieth centuries and to explore the many barriers that women working in the legal profession experience today. What women can do or how they can thrive in a male-dominated and -defined profession is as important an issue today as it was in the past. To better understand these issues, this chapter will look at women in the legal profession.

 CASE STUDY: Kate Baker

Regardless of which country a female attorney is practicing law in, she is not immune to potential discrimination and harassment within her place of employment. In early 2013, Kate Baker, an attorney employed at the law firm Follett Stock in the United Kingdom, voiced her concerns to the Employment Tribunal (similar to the Equal Employment Opportunity Commission in the United States) regarding her experiences of sexual harassment, sexual discrimination, and unfair termination (Reynolds 2013). Baker claimed that her boss bullied her and instructed her to remain single and to refrain from having children (Reynolds 2013). When Baker entered into a serious relationship, she was dismissed from the law firm. The law firm claimed that she was dismissed due to mistakes she made on the job. Baker disagreed and stated that her dismissal was due to gender discrimination (Reynolds 2013). Later in 2013, Baker entered into a settlement with her former employer – the terms of the settlement have not been disclosed (Baksi 2013).

History of women as lawyers and jurists

Worldwide, nations from ancient times and into the twentieth century had social and cultural norms, reinforced by law, which prevented women from full social and political participation. Married women, limited by the **doctrine of coverture**, could not own or inherit property, work outside the home, or vote, and were barred from serving on juries and engaging in public life. It was believed that it was against human nature for women to be intellectual and engage in academic pursuits or to be engaged in civic affairs and politics. To ensure that women did not become lawyers at a time in the nineteenth century when law was developing from a trade into a profession, many countries where women first sought a right to practice law had statutes which limited the practice of law to men: Australia, Belgium, England, France, Italy, and the United States (Mossman 2008). In addition, women were only provided with limited opportunities to become educated, and were barred from earning degrees at many universities. It was generally believed that women and men were biologically destined to live in separate spheres, and that the practice of law required intellectual aptitude to which the female sex was not fit.

The legal limits placed on women's lives were based on long-standing views on the proper roles for men and women in civil society and justified on the basis of religious scripture and cultural norms. As women (and progressive men) pushed for equal rights, they argued that European **Enlightenment** philosophy meant that "all" people were born with inalienable rights to life, liberty, and property/happiness. The substantive eighteenth- and nineteenth-century changes in political philosophy, from an emphasis on **natural law** in which men and women's capabilities were highly differentiated to an emphasis on enlightenment liberalism in which men were endowed with inalienable rights, provided nineteenth- and early twentieth-century women with a legal basis for demanding equal rights and full participation in civil life, including employment in the legal profession (see Jordan 2009; Mossman 2008; Tani 2012).

Prior to the nineteenth century, while nations may not have thought of law as a profession requiring regulation, nations still viewed employment outside the home, particularly law, as a province within the male domain. This predominant exclusion of women from the legal profession did not mean that women were totally excluded from the practice of law, as some worked alongside male relatives or "practiced" law without a license. The first woman to be formally empowered to act as an estate executor and lawyer in the American colonies was Margaret Brent, who, in 1638, represented the estate of the late governor of colonial Maryland in 124 actions (Bernat 1992). Because legal rules allowed persons to represent themselves in a court of law, women might also argue their cases *pro se*. But, women's formal admission to the legal profession, worldwide, began to coincide with the advancement of women's civil and human rights. These efforts were spearheaded by women (and supportive men) in the United States after the slave trade and slavery were outlawed (Mossman 2008).

In the late nineteenth and early twentieth century, in Western societies, the first women lawyers were among the educated class of women who fought for equality. These first women were unique in that they sought independent careers, self-sufficient lives, and an education in the law. In 1869, Arabella Mansfield became the first woman to be a licensed attorney in the United States in the state of Iowa, and most likely in the world (Jordan 2009; Mossman 2008). During the nineteenth century, the practice of law became more formalized and in an effort to distinguish the legal profession from trades, states within the United States, European countries, and common law nations governed by England began to require a license to practice. Regulatory laws governing legal practice enabled men to sit for the bar exam and become practicing lawyers. Iowa's regulatory statute also used the word "male" to define those persons who might be qualified to sit for the bar examination. However, Mansfield was encouraged by a sympathetic and supportive member of the state's judiciary, Judge

Springer, to take the exam after she had admirably studied in her brother's law firm for two years. The judge ruled that the term "male" in the statute governing attorney licensing included "females." While Mansfield passed the exam with high marks and was subsequently sworn into the profession, other women were not so successful. Without statutory changes of the word "male" to be "person" or some other gender-neutral language, many bar associations in the United States and other parts of the world refused to admit women into the profession. Mansfield herself never practiced law and was content to be an educator but her admission to the state bar of Iowa encouraged other women to challenge their exclusion from the legal field.

 GLOBAL PERSPECTIVES: Entry into the legal profession for women across the globe

For women pursuing careers in the legal profession in other countries across the world, their entry occurred after Mansfield's foray into the profession. For example, in India, Cornelia Sorabji was trained at Oxford and after moving to India she argued claims before British judges in 1896. Ethel Benjamin in New Zealand and Clara Brett Martin in Canada both had the easiest time among these first women because the statutes governing bar admission had been changed to include women one year prior to their successful applications in 1897. In England, Eliza Orme was never formally admitted to the bar but opened a law office in 1875 on Chancery Lane in London where she practiced for many years. Jeanne Chauvin, in France, had to wait from 1897 until the nation's law was changed in 1900 before she was admitted to the bar; and in Australia, Grata Flos Greig gained admission in 1905 when Australia finally removed the gender barrier in its laws (Mossman 2008). Although women in the United States led the way in gaining admission to the bar, by 1900 only 20 women were admitted to practice before the US Supreme Court and, in other nations, women found themselves to be the sole female practicing member of the profession in the early years of the twentieth century (Mossman 2008; Norgren 2013). Mossman (2008) comments that Chauvin (in France) could not fully support herself as a lawyer and instead she became a teacher, Benjamin (in New Zealand) claimed to be the only female lawyer in the southern hemisphere and was excluded from many lawyer social activities, which hurt her ability to practice, and Orme (in England) worked in a law office but legal statutes prohibited women from being lawyers in England until after 1900. In 1922, following the removal of the gender disqualification of women to be lawyers in England, four women were admitted to practice in England (BBC 1997).

American women lawyers in the nineteenth century

Women lawyers in the United States in the nineteenth century are noted for their "firsts" because they tended to find more success than women in other nations. Although their numbers were low, as the nineteenth and early twentieth centuries progressed, they were able to band together for guidance and support. Thus, as noted earlier, the first woman to be admitted to a state bar association was Arabella Mansfield, 1869. Other first women in law included the first woman to graduate from law school, Ada Kepley, 1870; the first African-American woman to practice law, Charlotte Ray, 1872; and the first woman to be admitted to practice before the US Supreme Court, Belva Lockwood, 1879 (Jordan 2009; Norgren 2013). Not surprisingly, women who had fought for the abolition of slavery in the mid-nineteenth century were unhappy with their **disenfranchisement** and inability to obtain equality, which they believed was endowed to all humans. Having helped to fight for equality for African-Americans and an end to slavery, American women were appalled that they remained "enslaved" after the Civil War. To achieve social equality and political rights, notable women sought avenues of redress in law by appealing to first the courts and then the legislature for change. To facilitate women's claims for equality under the law, women realized that they needed to work on the inside of the system as lawyers (Jordan 2009).

In the nineteenth century, the primary avenue to become a lawyer in the United States was through a clerkship (apprenticeship). But as the profession developed and wished to distinguish itself from other trades, schools of law opened to educate persons in the practice of law and legal reasoning. For clerkships, prospective lawyers worked alongside a person who was admitted to a state bar, a practicing lawyer. When "he" felt prepared, usually within a year or two, the prospective lawyer petitioned the state bar association to sit for examination. If the clerk passed, then he could be admitted to practice in the state. Male lawyers, however, generally did not believe that women were capable of performing legal work and did not allow them to clerk in their offices (Bernat 1992; Jordan 2009).

Exceptions occurred for women in the western territories of the United States, where there was a need for more persons practicing law and women were more likely to find progressive male lawyers in whose offices they could learn the practice of law; many of these male lawyers were their fathers or husbands (Bernat 1992). Yet, state bar associations still presented a hurdle that prevented some women trained or educated in the law from legal practice (Brundige 2012). One year after Mansfield's admission to a state bar in 1869, Ada H. Kepley became the first woman to graduate from a law school in Chicago in 1870. However, she was not admitted to the Illinois state bar, which had been reluctant to admit women. She did not even try to be admitted upon her law school graduation because she knew that she would be barred on account of her gender (Jordan 2009: Morello 1986).

Ada Kepley's contemporary Myra Bradwell had clerked in the legal office of her husband and sought Illinois state bar admission but was denied on the grounds that she was female. The state court ruled that under the doctrine of coverture she was unable as a married woman to enter into contracts and that the practice of law was deemed fit for men only (Bernat 1992; Jordan 2009; Morello 1986). Undeterred by the state court's blatant sexism, Bradwell appealed her case to the US Supreme Court. A supportive male lawyer argued her petition on the basis of the Fourteenth Amendment's privileges and immunities clause. He asserted that women, as citizens of the United States, had the right to enjoy the civil right of employment of their choice. The US Supreme Court upheld the state supreme court's decision to deny Bradwell admission to the practice of law. While the majority decision narrowly focused on the meaning of the privileges and immunities clause, the concurring opinion by Justice Bradley lays bare the sexism of the time. Bradley asserted that it was unnatural for women to engage in legal thinking and practice law. He maintained that natural law provided for women to be mothers in the home and that women were unfit to be lawyers (Bernat 1992; Jordan 2009).

However, the opinion gave women renewed optimism, because within the decision was the germ of hope that if state legislatures changed the law, then state law would prevail and women could gain admission to the legal profession. Women who wanted to practice law, and supportive male lawyers, began to work on changing state laws that denied women the right to a legal license to practice law. Women's nineteenth- and early twentieth-century challenge to become members of the legal profession was not easy; some women had to be "content" to serve the legal profession in other capacities such as advocates for women's rights, legal managers within a law firm, news reporters, or educators. Bradwell never was admitted into the legal profession, even after Illinois changed its statute to eliminate the gender disqualification. Instead, she edited a legal newspaper that published judicial opinions and informed the legal community about injustices, suffrage, and important gains for women in legal practice.

TEXT BOX: *Bradwell v. State of Illinois*, 83 U.S. 130 (Wall., 1872)

Mr. Justice MILLER delivered the opinion of the court.

The record in this case is not very perfect, but it may be fairly taken that the plaintiff asserted her right to a license on the grounds, among others, that she was a citizen of the United States, and that having been a citizen of Vermont at one time, she was, in the State of Illinois, entitled to any right granted to citizens of the latter State …

The fourteenth amendment declares that citizens of the United States are citizens of the State within which they reside; therefore the plaintiff was, at the time of making her application, a citizen of the United States and a citizen of the State of Illinois.

… In this latter proposition we are not able to concur with counsel. We agree with him that there are privileges and immunities belonging to citizens of the United States, in that relation and character, and that it is these and these alone which a State is forbidden to abridge. But the right to admission to practice in the courts of a State is not one of them …

JUDGMENT AFFIRMED.

Mr. Justice BRADLEY:

I concur in the judgment of the court in this case, by which the judgment of the Supreme Court of Illinois is affirmed, but not for the reasons specified in the opinion just read …

The claim that, under the fourteenth amendment of the Constitution, which declares that no State shall make or enforce any law which shall abridge the privileges and immunities of citizens of the United States,… assumes that it is one of the privileges and immunities of women as citizens to engage in any and every profession, occupation, or employment in civil life. It certainly cannot be affirmed, as an historical fact, that this has ever been established as one of the fundamental privileges and immunities of the sex. On the contrary, the civil law, as well as nature herself, has always recognized a wide difference in the respective spheres and destinies of man and woman. Man is, or should be, woman's protector and defender. *The natural and proper timidity and delicacy which belongs to the female sex evidently unfits it for many of the occupations of civil life. The constitution of the family organization, which is founded in the divine ordinance, as well as in the nature of things, indicates the domestic sphere as that which properly belongs to the domain and functions of womanhood.* The harmony, not to say identity, of interest and views which belong, or should belong, to the family institution is repugnant to the idea of a woman adopting a distinct and independent career from that of her husband. So firmly fixed was this sentiment in the founders of the common law that it became a maxim of that system of jurisprudence that a woman had no legal existence separate from her husband, who was regarded as her head and representative in the social state; and, notwithstanding some recent modifications of this civil status, many of the special rules of law flowing from and dependent upon this cardinal principle still exist in full force in most States. One of these is, that a married woman is incapable, without her husband's consent, of making contracts which shall be binding on her or him. This very incapacity was one circumstance which the Supreme Court of Illinois deemed important in rendering a married woman incompetent fully to perform the duties and trusts that belong to the office of an attorney and counsellor.

It is true that many women are unmarried and not affected by any of the duties, complications, and incapacities arising out of the married state, but these are exceptions to the general rule. The paramount destiny and mission of woman are to fulfil the noble and benign offices of wife and mother. This is the law of the Creator. And the rules of civil society must be adapted to the general constitution of things, and cannot be based upon exceptional cases.

The humane movements of modern society, which have for their object the multiplication of avenues for woman's advancement, and of occupations adapted to her condition and sex, have my heartiest concurrence. But I am not prepared to say that it is one of her fundamental rights and privileges to be admitted into every office and position, including those which require highly special qualifications and demanding special responsibilities. In the nature of things it is not every citizen of every age, sex, and condition that is qualified for every calling and position. *It is the prerogative of the legislator to prescribe regulations founded on nature, reason, and experience for the due admission of qualified persons to professions and callings demanding special skill and confidence.* This fairly belongs to the police power of the State; and, in my opinion, in view of the peculiar characteristics, destiny, and mission of woman, it is within the province of the legislature to ordain what offices, positions, and callings shall be filled and discharged by men, and shall receive the benefit of those energies and responsibilities, and that decision and firmness which are presumed to predominate in the sterner sex.

For these reasons I think that the laws of Illinois now complained of are not obnoxious to the charge of abridging any of the privileges and immunities of citizens of the United States.

Mr. Justice SWAYNE and Mr. Justice FIELD concurred in the foregoing opinion of Mr. Justice BRADLEY.

The CHIEF JUSTICE dissented from the judgment of the court, and from all the opinions.

[Emphasis added.]

Women lawyers in the twentieth century

Bradwell, her supporters, suffragettes, and others who believed in female equality began working in earnest to change the state statutes that discriminated against women. The struggle to change the laws preventing women's equality was not settled by the end of the nineteenth century. It took several decades into the twentieth century for some gains to be won. Suffrage did not provide women with equal rights in the United States or in Europe. The right of women to vote was established under the Nineteenth Amendment to the US Constitution, in 1920; however, equal rights were fought on a case by case basis throughout the twentieth century. In England, even when the British law was changed to enable women to be admitted to legal practice in 1922, it was an uphill battle for women to support themselves as lawyers. To be a practicing member of the British legal profession required lawyers to pay annual fees that most women could not afford; many parents might pay the fees for their sons but did not do so for their daughters (BBC 1997).

In the first half of the twentieth century, apprenticeships in law offices were phased out as law schools gained acceptance as the preferred method of legal study. In the United States, Harvard Law School graduates began to have success once admitted to the bar. These lawyers were trained in legal reasoning and studied cases to determine the prevailing legal arguments in litigation. Other law schools soon followed Harvard's model and state bar associations realized that a legal education was a better method of establishing qualified persons to sit for the bar exam than clerkships. However, many law schools had charters that were specifically written to prohibit admission to women. Slowly, law schools began to change their prohibitive admission standards and, by 1950, Harvard Law School became the last school to remove the gender exclusion language (Bernat 1992).

Graduating from a prestigious law school affects a person's ability to be hired by a prestigious firm, obtain a high salary, and obtain upon graduation some status in the profession. In this regard, clerks to US Supreme Court justices and law school faculty are most likely to have graduated from one of the prestigious law schools in the United States (Campos 2013). Corresponding with the high value placed on top-tier law schools is the increased cost of tuition. Campos (2013) found that the cost of attendance at Harvard Law School has always been high but that, correspondingly, the first year salaries of its graduates are also amongst the highest in (New York) law firms. Having access to a legal education, including at previously all-male bastions of learning, was an important hurdle to be eliminated for women to gain entrance to the practice of law, but others remained.

As women gained admission to all law schools in the first half of the twentieth century, their numbers were still fairly low as legal practice was considered best suited for the male gender. Law is traditionally viewed as an aggressive, intellectual profession, and so its characteristics are at odds with the stereotypical characteristics of the female gender: passive and emotional. The first women at Harvard and other law schools that reluctantly opened up their doors found that they were not necessarily accepted into the law school classes and that their professors might aim to embarrass them (Bernat 1992). For example, women attending law classes were often not called on until "Ladies Day" – almost a full year into the academic year in the spring. The few women in the class were told on a Friday by male professors to prepare for "Ladies Day" on the following Monday, when they would be called on. To their horror, the only questions that were posed to the women in the class surrounded questions of marital property law (Mullarkey 2004).

As women proved themselves intellectually, and showed themselves to be adept in law school, women lawyers had to continue to pry open doors that had previously been closed to them in their fight for gender equality and social justice. The twentieth century saw the rise of the corporate lawyer and the further stratification of the profession (Mossman 2003). Yet, women were still excluded on the basis that they did not belong in the corporate world, nor in the "commodified" world of the legal profession. It was thought that women's sensibilities were not aligned with harsh cut-throat legal tactics. Justice Bertha Wilson, who served on the Supreme Court in Canada, said that as women gained admission, lawyers had to re-examine the profession to determine if the quest for money tarnished the profession and lawyers needed to examine whether the profession was "still noble and learned" (Mossman 2003, 155). In this regard, law schools began to change their views on legal practice and devote some time to legal ethics. Although the percentage of female law professors is small, the entrance of women into law schools as students and professors meant that the legal profession needed to change. In addition to new courses in law schools on ethics and female legal concerns (family law, civil rights, women and the law), the practice of law stratified into new legal avenues for work.

Women sought jobs in the public sector as prosecutors, defense counsel, government attorneys, or attorneys for non-profit organizations. In private practice, women focused on family law issues and helped to argue for changes in laws which discriminated against women and minorities. By the 1970s, federal laws were passed to eliminate discriminatory practices on the basis of gender (**Equal Pay Act of 1963** and **Title VII of the Civil Rights Act of 1964**). Thus, by the end of the 1970s, law school classes did not use gender as a reason to admit women or as a disqualifier to exclude them from the profession. About one-third of the law school classes were comprised of women in the late 1970s and law school curriculums included classes on women in the law. By the end of the century about one-half of any given law school class was comprised of women.

It took 112 years for women to progress from legal practice and access to legal education to prominent judge positions, including in the US Supreme Court. In 1981, Mary Morgan was the first openly lesbian judge appointed to the San Francisco Superior Court and is considered to be the first openly lesbian judge in the nation (Egelko 2011). The honor of being appointed to the US Supreme Court was bestowed in 1981 on Justice Sandra Day O'Connor, who experienced many of the same gains and setbacks experienced by other women who sought a legal career (Figure 9.1). Although O'Connor graduated along with her peer, Justice William Rehnquist, among the top three students in her 1950 Stanford Law School class, unlike her male class mate(s) she was not offered an attorney's position in any California law firm. Rather, she was offered a job as a legal administrative assistant, a secretarial position (Kitzerow 2014). To counter such bias, she chose to open up a private practice and when her husband's legal career took him oversees she followed him there. Upon their return to the United States and their move to Phoenix, Arizona, she found legal work in public service, where she began to establish a strong record of success. After the birth of her second child, she stopped her legal practice for five years to be a full-time mother. Then, once again, she sought work in the public sector and was active in Arizonan party politics; this work included many community engagement activities and led to her notable career in the state senate. By the late 1970s, she was well regarded within the state and was appointed to the Arizona Court of Appeals.

A few years later, in 1981, when President Reagan sought to fulfill his election promise to appoint a woman to the nation's highest court he surprised many by selecting O'Connor because she had neither served on a state high court nor any of the federal courts. Her appointment was heavily criticized by both conservatives and liberals. Conservatives feared that, as a woman, she would support pro-choice positions and preserve *Roe v. Wade*, which provided women with the right to have an abortion without restriction in

Figure 9.1 Sandra Day O'Connor, c. 1981–1983. *Source:* Prints & Photographs Division, Library of Congress, LC-USZ62-86846.

the first trimester of pregnancy. Liberals feared that, as a Republican, she would strengthen the conservative voice among her brethren on the Court. Many persons on both sides thought that she was ill-prepared to serve on the Court because she was moving from an intermediate state appellate court and not competent; her gender was not publically mentioned as a reason to disqualify her, as both Republicans and Democrats were careful not to make overt discriminatory claims of non-competence on the basis of sex. Despite the concerns that were raised, her appointment was ratified and Justice O'Connor became the first woman to serve on this prestigious bench in 1981. Ultimately, time would show that she was a moderate and important swing voter on the Court. Her judicial opinions evidenced a balanced, pragmatic voice on the Court (see Oyez 2014). Justice O'Connor was a revered member of the Court, and is credited with opening the doors to other women to serve on high courts at the state and federal level. In 2005, Justice O'Connor resigned from the bench and formally retired from public service. Her resignation letter to President Bush was concise and allowed him the opportunity to appoint a successor prior to the end of his term in office (CNN 2005):

Dear President Bush:

This is to inform you of my decision to retire from my position as Associate Justice of the Supreme Court of the United States, effective upon the nomination and confirmation of my successor.

It has been a great privilege, indeed, to have served as a member of the Court for 24 terms.

I will leave it with enormous respect for the integrity of the Court and its role under our constitutional structure.

Sincerely,

Sandra Day O'Connor

Family played a key part in her decision to retire, as she wished to spend time with her ailing husband and children in Arizona. She continues to make public appearances and it is quite fitting that Arizona State University has named its law school, Sandra Day O'Connor College of Law, in her honor.

How does Justice O'Connor's biography compare with those of other female attorneys and jurists? Is she exceptional because she was the first US Supreme Court female justice? Does her path in the practice of law evidence gains for other women in law? In the United States, four women have been appointed to the nation's high court: Justices O'Connor (1981–2005), Ruth Bader Ginsburg (1993–), Sonia Sotomayor (2009–) and Elena Kagan (2010–). Justice Ginsburg is the second woman to be appointed to the Court and presently serves along with Justice Sotomayor, the first female Hispanic jurist, and Justice Kagan, who was the first woman to be Dean of Harvard Law School before obtaining her appointment to the Court.

Women and their employment in the legal profession

Portrayals of women working in the legal profession on fictional television shows such as *Ally McBeal*, *Sex and the City*, *Judging Amy*, and *Parenthood* may skew your opinions about women working in these roles today, as well as the realities they face. Worldwide, today, women have seen some gains in legal employment as judges and lawyers, but these gains have been slowed by social and cultural views that women do not belong in a male-defined profession, a profession marked by tough competitiveness and highly intellectual analysis. Although women make up half of law school classes in the United States, they comprise about one-third of the practicing bar. Modern legal practice is divided into hierarchical structures: large prestigious law firms, medium-sized firms, small firms or solo practices, public service law, and so on. Persons working in large firms which represent corporate interests are paid more than persons working in the public sector; not surprisingly, more women are found working in the public sector upon graduation from law school than in prestigious law firms (Dinovitzer and Hagan 2014; Kaye and Gastwirth 2009). Dinovitzer and Hagan (2014), in analyzing gender and race segregation in the legal profession as lawyers move from one position upon law school graduation to other positions, found that, over time, salary inequity and employment segregation persists. A recent study of Utah female lawyers revealed pervasive sex bias whereby female lawyers reported experiencing sexual harassment and discrimination in pay, advancement, and work assignments (Weiss 2010). Weiss (2010) explains another bias that the study identified:

> a "maternal wall bias" in which mothers are perceived as less committed to work, subjected to heightened scrutiny and given less challenging assignments. One woman said she was told that women should not be attorneys because they always put their family first. Another said her boss treated women lawyers more like secretaries, and he "completely wrote me off" after she became pregnant.

One reason that women lawyers state for entering a lower paid, public sector position is to balance family interests (Brown and Mendoza 2010). Lawyers who work in public governmental positions may be able to count on standardized work hours and a salary that is not based upon **rainmaking**. Rainmaking is the ability of a lawyer to create billable hours and if a woman desires to balance work and family demands, then having to work long hours into the night as an associate or staff attorney in a firm to generate required billable hours is an employment option that some women attorneys choose not to take (Bernat 1992; Brown and Mendoza 2010; Kitzerow 2014). Problematically, for both men and women, legal practice in a law firm structured on the billable hour system provides little concern about individual lives and family. However, it should be mentioned that women working in the public sector do not necessarily have it easier in regard to the delicate balance between work and family responsibilities. During the high profile O. J. Simpson trial, Marcia Clark found herself in a custody battle with her soon to be ex-husband, who cited that because of her work, she hardly saw or spent time with her sons (Boxall 1995). Because of this, he was seeking primary custody of the children.

Kitzerow (2014) re-interviewed women in 2010; she had previously interviewed these women in 1975 when law school doors were being opened to female students. She discussed with these women the various stages of their long careers in law and compared them to contemporary, recent female law students. The established women had been lawyers who had gained admission to the bar in three distinct time periods: the pioneer group graduated from law school prior to 1963, the transition group graduated between 1964 and 1972, and the third group graduated from law school between 1973 and 1975. By 1975 about one-third of law school classes were comprised of women, as law schools were required to eliminate gender bias in admission decisions. Kitzerow discovered that these women faced challenges in legal practice: that certain legal jobs were not open to them, that they needed to balance being a wife and mother or forego having children altogether, and that women did not make as much money or get the same respect as their male colleagues received. One interviewee said:

> I think it depends on what type of law firm and what type of law you are going to practice. I know with family law, that's not necessarily an issue because actually women attorneys outnumber male attorneys. Some of the other fields, maybe intellectual property or corporate law or some of those that are male-oriented or male-dominated, it [one's gender] might be more of an issue. (Kitzerow 2014, 189)

The women in the pioneer group tended to forego motherhood, whereas the women in the modern group believed that they could balance family life. These women all worked hard, they found that it was difficult to balance long hours at work with family responsibilities, and they experienced a lot of stress. The women felt that their law school and first employment experience was fine but, over time, gender stereotypes and gender differences in treatment and pay made legal practice difficult.

The percentage of women attending law schools in the United States reflects the numbers of women in society and graduating from universities. The American Bar Association (ABA 2014) reports that in the 2012–2013 academic year, 48% of first year law students were female and 47% of law school graduates were female. Many women did well in law school as evidenced by their position as an editor on a law review; of the top 50 ranked schools, women comprised 38% of editors-in-chief of a law review; at all other law schools in the United States 51% of editors-in-chief were women (ABA 2014). However, women still lag behind men in legal employment and earnings. The American Bar Association (2014) reports that the legal profession is comprised of 66% men and 34% women. Of the women practicing law, only 20% are partners in private practice, 17% are equity partners, 4% manage large firms, and 45% are associates in a private firm. If prestigious private practice is considered, women comprise only 21% of general counsel positions for a Fortune 500 company. If prestigious judicial clerkships are considered, then women are well represented in these public sector jobs: women hold 51% of all judicial clerkships, with 46% of federal clerkships and 55% of state clerkships held by women. Nonetheless, as of 2012, about a third of women serve as judges: three women justices on the US Supreme Court (33%), 56 judges serve on the federal Circuit Courts (33%), and 451 women are federal District Court judges (24%) and, at the state level, 116 women serve on state high courts (32%), 316 serve on state intermediate courts of appeal (32%), and 11,059 serve as judges on courts of general jurisdiction (25%) (ABA 2014).

The salaries earned by women in the law are less than those earned by men. In 2013, the US Bureau of Labor reported salary levels for women lawyers to be about $500 per week less than men; from 2004 through 2013, the labor reports show that women lawyers earned 73% to 79% on the dollar what male lawyers earned (ABA 2014). Women law partners' salaries average about $200,000 less per year than those of male law partners (see http://www.americanbar.org/content/dam/aba/images/young_lawyers/gender_compensation_chart.PNG).

Part of the continued gendered nature of legal practice is that women still earn lower salaries than men in law firms and also face a **glass ceiling**. A glass ceiling is the barrier that women face for vertical mobility, a gender barrier that does not appear immediately but, over time, it becomes evident that women's advancement in law firms has been modest (Wallace and Kay 2012). Women who work part time on a "mommy track" may end up removing themselves from legal practice altogether. If they return, once their children are teenagers, the women lag behind other lawyers in terms of salary and career advancement opportunities (Jacobs 2014). However, in general, when men take family leave, their leave requests are viewed favorably, the men are viewed as exceptional fathers, but women who engage in child-rearing responsibilities are viewed as not taking their legal careers seriously (Wallace and Kay 2012). Law firms which have a better gender balance among their partners and staff are more likely to be supportive of women attorneys who attempt to balance family life and work. Because women are still not fully represented in the top tiers of a law firm hierarchy, glass ceilings remain (Jacobs 2014; Wallace and Kay 2012).

Research has shown that women's salaries are depressed across all forms of legal practice, particularly when women are stratified to fill primarily public sector legal positions (Dinovitzer and Hagan 2014; Dinovitzer, Reichman, and Sterling 2009). Cabraser (2014), a female tort litigator in California, has attended hearings before a multijurisdictional judicial panel that determines whether actions can be combined from across the United States into a central lawsuit. She states that during one day of hearings only 10% of the lawyers were female and only a few of these actually argued the matter before the judicial panel. Thus, **gender segregation in the legal profession** creates a persistence of inequity throughout the legal job market.

Gender, race and ethnicity of attorneys

Women in every nation experience **gender discrimination** and gendered lives. This means that on the basis of their sex, females have clearly circumscribed roles and responsibilities which hinder their full participation in the legal profession. In some nations the level and intensity of the discrimination are tempered and not always obvious; in other nations, however, the discrimination is overt. One of the reasons that women have sought positions as lawyers and judges is to eliminate barriers to the full participation of women in society. In Western nations, as women entered the legal profession they were able to help promote legal and social changes in the status of women, but some barriers to equality remain (Clay-Warner and McMahon 2007; Leiper 2006; Wallace and Kay 2012). In common law nations, law had been legally classified as an exclusive male domain until the twentieth century, and in many third world nations, today, women are still legally barred from participation in society through barriers to education, voting, and work, and such cultural barriers affect women's ability to practice law (Cardinal 2010; Guyard-Nedelec 2007; Leiper 2006; Mossman 2003; Norgren 2013; Scales-Trent 2010; Włodek-Biernat 2010).

The first African-American federal judge was Constance Baker Motley in 1966. Still, the legal profession is primarily comprised of White attorneys. If you consider Fortune 500 general counsel positions in the United States, 92% of attorneys are White and male, 7% are African-American and, 1% are Hispanic (ABA 2014). A low percentage of women lawyers are partners in a law firm (2%) and only 11% are associates in a firm or serve as staff attorneys (14%) (NALP 2014) (Table 9.1).

Table 9.1 Women and minorities at law firms – (US) nationwide by type of attorney. Figures are based on 1,209 offices/firms covering a total of 117,934 lawyers.

	Total #	OVERALL		ASIAN		BLACK/ AFRICAN-AMERICAN		HISPANIC	
		% Minority	% Minority Women	Total %	% Women	Total %	% Women	Total %	% Women
Partners	53,725	6.71%	2.16%	2.48%	0.89%	1.73%	0.60%	1.91%	0.48%
Associates	49,190	20.32	11.06	10.01	5.40	4.19	2.55	3.90	1.95
Counsel	10,619	8.04	3.52	3.22	1.49	1.92	0.81	2.18	0.94
Staff Attorneys	2,358	22.77	14.21	8.82	5.05	7.85	5.43	4.24	2.71
Other Attorneys	2,042	11.21	6.56	4.06	2.15	3.13	2.25	3.19	1.57

Source: © National Association for Law Placement and reproduced with permission.

In Europe, the right of women to vote was slowly provided between 1915 (Denmark) and 1984 (Lichtenstein), with many nations extending suffrage to women between 1918 and 1947. As in the United States, the right to vote did not eliminate all gender barriers in employment or salary inequities for women in law. Women who seem to experience the most success in legal practice are persons who are able to work in balanced firms and come to the firm with a clear status of respect. For example, Ballakrishnen (2013) analyzed the global influence of emerging markets and women in the Indian legal profession. These law firms represent global clients and her preliminary interviews of women attorneys found that the high-status women lawyers did not experience gender discrimination. She posits that the very high status of these Indian women lawyers in the global firms mediated their mistreatment; they were not viewed or treated as a secretary, they did not experience pay inequity, but instead they experienced a gender-blind practice. As one female lawyer explained (Ballakrishnen 2013, 1275):

> I think we are probably – most of the people who come here would never be mistaken for anything but a lawyer because we come from a certain strata of society … But I don't know about other professions – my brother is a doctor with the armed forces and there you can see the distinction between the ranks – and it is something that he told me about. Women, for example, don't get promotions and if you have kids, then the penalty is obvious. [It is a] very hierarchical organization and my sister in law – who is also a doctor – tells me stories about how she is not at all taken seriously … and this is different from anything that I have experienced.

These successful women lawyers are connected on teams, come from high social elite families, and have a strong educational background. In addition, these women work hard, and are viewed by their male peers as dedicated and careful in their dealings in the workforce. According to Ballakrishnen, since the Indian legal profession is generally hostile to women, the fact that women in large firms can negotiate a gender neutral workplace and thrive is an important lesson to learn for the future of the profession.

Not all women in firms fare as well as the high-status women lawyers in India. Women lawyers in Iran, Canada, and Senegal have found gender, cultural, and societal restrictions that might make legal practice difficult (Kaheny, Szmer and Sarver 2011; Scales-Trent 2010; Włodek-Biernat 2010). In Senegal, for example, legal work to change laws that discriminate against women is difficult because of the socio-religious context that provides men with an elevated status over women. However, women lawyers who work within a Senegalese women's association for the advancement of women and children do find some respect from high-ranking leaders in the nation. It might be that both the government and the women's lawyers association are looking to benefit from collaborating with each other. However, religious forces are still aimed at keeping women in the home and veiled. According to Scales-Trent (2010, 143), "Social change is hard. It takes a long time. It is often not even possible. And the Association of Senegalese Women Lawyers is only one actor in the very complicated fabric of Senegalese society."

Women lawyers have connected worldwide in European, Asian, and African women's lawyer conferences and bar associations in order to provide each other with shared experiences and support. In Africa, for example, the Southern African feminist and human rights organization sets its mission at supporting evidenced-based reforms to support women in society. In 2013, the Second Annual Europe Regional Conference was held on the theme of "Gender Equality & International Protection of Human Rights," and in Asia a conference was held on the "Pacific Regional Feminist Legal Theory and Practice Training of Trainers." These conferences discussed continued problems for equal opportunities in employment, child-rearing, and human rights for women. The conference themes evidence the need for women to connect with each other and with supportive men. It will take a concerted effort of every person to work together to combat barriers to women in the law.

 SPECIAL LEGAL ISSUES: Discrimination in Iran

On the International Women's Day in March 2010 Zahra Rahnavard published a very bold statement, published on many websites which support the opposition against the Iranian regime.

On that occasion Rahnavard wrote: 'We want deceit and darkness to end, we want an end to discrimination, be it class discrimination, financial, cultural or discrimination against women. We want respect for personal freedoms, and this does not mean we do not pay heed to the collective or its concerns, but we believe the individual too has a right. And usually, in highly ideological systems, the individual is not allowed to have an opinion or desire of his own. But this is what the green movement is asking for.'

She continued: 'I would also like to talk about women. The highest ideals for women are freedom and putting an end to discrimination. This is not only specific to women of Iran, it is an ideal women across the world struggle for. In certain countries women have had more success in removing discrimination but we have not been successful. This is a reality. I have always said that the Islamic Revolution is an incomplete project. We were hopeful that the great ideals of Islamic Revolution and its great leader Imam Khomeini would substantiate in the Islamic Republic. Since the revolution succeeded very quickly we expected ideals such as freedom, rule of law, equality, public welfare, eliminating class discrimination and others will be realized in Islamic republic. But it did not happen. Pursuing these very same ideals particularly women issues is the goal of green movement.'

Source: Włodek-Biernat (2010, 507).

How do women jurists fare?

Female judge television programs, such as Judge Judith Sheindlin's *Judge Judy*, may make it appear that there are large numbers of women judges across the nation. This is not the case. Women judges make up a small percentage of jurists, and are more likely to preside over the lower courts than serve in appellate courts. Judgeships hold an attraction for lawyers because they offer some security and independence; however, gender disparities still occur. Despite the popularity of *Judge Judy*, the judge, who is very assertive, is often criticized for being abrasive or displaying qualities of bullying (Barnes 2014; Rhode 2001). Berson (2010) found that, in 1964, there were only two female judges. Since that time, female judges have grown to about a third of the federal judiciary. Judge Tacha, a federal judge serving on the Tenth Circuit, says, "If anyone pursues a legal career, especially a judgeship, with the sole motivation of monetary gain, I would never encourage it. It's the wrong reason to become a lawyer and especially a judge" (Berson 2010, 29). Judge Tacha notes that while changes in federal laws have enabled women judges to receive the same salary as their male colleagues, females have not achieved true equality in the workplace.

To become a judge/justice on the United States federal bench, candidates must be nominated by the president and confirmed by the senate. To help facilitate the selection process, the American Bar Association will screen potential candidates and rank them for consideration by the president; in addition, the state senator from a candidate's home state will be contacted and asked for his/her preliminary support. Sen (2014) analyzed how American Bar Association rankings can disadvantage women candidates for judicial appointments. Sen found that even if various reasons that affect the nomination of a candidate for a federal court judgeship are controlled for, women and minority nominees consistently receive low ABA ratings. Sen also found that if a female or minority judge is appointed to a federal court, those with low ratings do not have significantly more decisions overturned by a higher court. Thus, Sen (2014) comments that ABA ratings are important in securing a positive appointment to a federal court but do not ultimately affect judicial performance. Sen argues that the low ratings of female and minority judicial candidates are a reflection of bias that systematically disadvantages these nominees.

TEXT BOX: Women in the federal judiciary: Still a long way to go

Over the past three decades, an increasing number of women have joined the legal profession. Since 1992, women's representation in law school classes has approached 50%. Despite record numbers of female judicial nominees, the percentage of female federal judges, however, is far lower. It is of critical importance to increase the representation of women on the federal bench.

When women are fairly represented on our federal courts, those courts are more reflective of the diverse population of this nation. When women are fairly represented on the federal bench, women, and men, may have more confidence that the court understands the real-world implications of its rulings. For both, the increased presence of women on the bench improves the quality of justice: women judges can bring an understanding of the impact of the law on the lives of women and girls to the bench, and enrich courts' understanding of how best to realize the intended purpose and effect of the law that the courts are charged with applying. For example, one recent study demonstrated that male federal appellate court judges are less likely to rule against plaintiffs bringing claims of sex discrimination, if a female judge is on the panel.

But to obtain true gender diversity, the number of women in the federal judiciary, including the Supreme Court, must be increased.

- Upon the confirmation of Associate Justice Elena Kagan, the Supreme Court counts three women among its nine Justices for the first time in history, still only one-third of the members of that Court. Only four of the 112 Justices ever to serve on the highest court in the land have been women.
- Fifty-nine of the 171 active judges currently sitting on the thirteen federal courts of appeal are female (almost 35%). When broken down by circuit, women's representation on several of these individual courts is even lower than on the courts of appeals overall:

- In particular, women are underrepresented on the Third Circuit (where they make up about 23% of judges) and the Eighth Circuit (18%).
- Thirty-two percent of active United States district (or trial) court judges are women.
  - But there are still nine district courts around the country where there has never been a female judge.
- For women of color, the numbers are even smaller.
  - There are 77 women of color serving as active federal judges across the country, including 39 African-American women, 25 Hispanic women, 10 Asian-American women, one Native American woman, one woman of Hispanic and Asian descent, and one women of Hispanic and African-American descent.
  - There are only 11 women of color on the U.S. courts of appeals. Five of those women sit on the Ninth Circuit Court of Appeals, two sit on the DC Circuit, and one woman of color sits on each of the First, Fourth, Sixth and Seventh Circuits. Therefore, there are seven federal courts of appeals without a single active minority woman judge.
- If currently pending judicial nominees are confirmed, the number of women in the federal judiciary would increase.
  - Of President Obama's 318 judicial nominees to date (including his nominees to the Supreme Court), 132 are women. Forty-eight of these nominees have been women of color (26 African-American women, 10 Hispanic women, eight Asian-American women, one Native American woman, one woman of Hispanic and Asian descent, and one woman of African-American and Hispanic descent).
  - About 42 percent of President Obama's confirmed nominees have been women. This has increased the number of women on the First, Second, Third, Fourth, Sixth, Eighth, Ninth, Tenth, Eleventh, D.C., and Federal Circuits as well as on a number of district courts. Fourteen judges have been confirmed as the first woman judge in their district; seven more as the first woman circuit court judge in their state.
  - The number of women of color on the federal bench has increased dramatically as well. The number of Asian-American women judges has tripled, and includes the first Asian-American circuit court judge. Eight states have their first African-American female judges, and three states have their first Hispanic female judge.
  - With the confirmation of the 10 currently pending female nominees, women's representation on a number of other courts will improve – including the Eleventh Circuit.

By the nominations he has made to date, President Obama has taken an important step towards increasing the representation of women, including women of color, on the federal bench. Now it is up to the Senate to do its part, to improve access to, and the quality of, justice for all Americans.

Source: Reproduced with permission of National Women's Law Center. Accessed August 14, 2014, http://www.nwlc.org/resource/women-federal-judiciary-still-long-way-go-1

Women, the international bench, and legal practice

Legal analysts agree that professionalism in the judiciary requires judges to put aside their political and personal bias and decide cases based upon the law and legal processes. Such professionalism is tied to judicial accountability and ensures that the judiciary remains a distinct branch of government with independence. Judicial independence is associated with judicial decision making that promotes the highest principles of law to flourish even during tense political times or in rigid regimes.

However, race and gender of a judge may still affect how lawyers view a judge's competence. Gill, Lazos, and Waters (2011) found that gender and racial bias persists when lawyers evaluated judicial performance in Nevada. Gender and racial bias existed even when controlling for prestige of the judge's law school and whether the judge had a record of being overturned on appeal. In short, their study showed that White, male judges were evaluated more highly than female and minority judges.

 GLOBAL PERSPECTIVES: Female judges in Syria

When women became judges and lawyers, questions about qualifications and capabilities were not the only queries raised; some people wondered whether the gender of the judge (lawyer) would make a difference in case outcomes. In Syria, women are not appointed to **sharia courts**, sharia is the Muslim law that comes from core principles in the Koran and governs the law in many Muslim nations. In sharia courts, men and women are not viewed equally as witnesses in a proceeding and female judges are therefore also viewed as unqualified to oversee the proceeding (Cardinal 2010). The gender distinction is based on classical thought; as one judge maintained, "A judge deals with an assembly of litigants and men, and is required to exert his independent opinion, rationality and intelligence … [A] woman is less rational and rarely has an opinion … [S]he is not qualified to attend an assembly of men" (Cardinal 2010, 199). To contest these views, women judges and lawyers find it necessary to challenge the interpretation of religious texts which view women as incompetent on the basis of their sex. Because women make up 14% of the Assembly in Syria and hold 12% of judgeships (non-sharia courts), women argue that sharia law does not apply in modern times. The exclusion of women from the sharia judiciary is not necessarily viewed by women judges and lawyers in Syria to be discrimination because the religious text is viewed as an important part of the social and cultural context of the society (Cardinal 2010).

Yet, women lawyers can make a difference in the acceptance of women in the legal profession. As one judge said, "I was approached by the senior partner for litigation. In a not so very enthusiastic voice, he said, 'Toal, we're putting you in the courtroom. We've got to have somebody that can talk to these women.' And I never looked back. I became a litigator and had the privilege of litigating for many different interests, including the interests of women" (Toal 2010, 1588). As Miller and Meloy (2007) found, women jurists can help frame issues affecting women in the law from divorce and child custody issues to gender discrimination and employee pay equity. The female judges interviewed by Miller and Meloy indicated that their gender can be a positive factor in their judicial temperament because they are patient, admit that they do not have all the answers, and bring this temperament to their decision making. In this regard, the female jurists are sensitive to cases in which women are victims, and do not start with the stereotypical notion that women are to be blamed for their victimization (Miller and Meloy 2007). One female judge remarked about her views on domestic violence, for example:

> I have for years felt that it was important that victims of those kinds of crime be treated like victims of other crimes. I don't think just because it's between people who know one another that the option shouldn't be available … But I think that the option of an arrest and a trial and a conviction is one that ought to be accessible to victims of domestic violence. And it ought to be used. (Miller and Meloy, 2007, 716)

Having women on the judiciary, then, helps courts to achieve a wide diversity of views that might otherwise be missing if the courts are staffed with only males. Judicial legitimacy requires courts to consider pluralistic contexts of human rights in a changing world. Grossman (2011) found that international courts of justice that include female jurists have social legitimacy. Although international studies on the impact of women in the judiciary are rare, Grossman (2011, 454) states that male and female judges may decide cases differently and therefore having an overrepresentation of one gender will result in biased outcomes that are "incompatible with normative legitimacy" of the courts.

Necessary legal system policy responses

By the end of the twentieth century, legal practice in the United States was highly stratified and law firms based productivity on the billable hour. The profession, in the first two decades of the twenty-first century, is undergoing further change and transformation. The American Bar Association and State Bar Associations have continued to analyze the impact of various admission and employment practices on women and minorities in an attempt to eliminate overt and tacit discrimination. Gender equity committees are discussing how to eliminate the view that women with children should be paid less or are not effective attorneys. The notion that part-time attorneys are not committed to their firms or clients continues to hold women back. In addition, equity committees are re-examining the billable hour system. Brown and Mendoza (2010, 68) argue that the "billable hour system is not only corrosive to long-term relationships with clients but it has hurt the legal profession as a whole." Indeed, the notion that work is more effective when done over long days and hours hinders the ability of women who work part-time in order to raise children to be fully appreciated for their dedication to their profession and family. Consequently, just as Justice O'Connor took time off from her practice, some women fall out of the profession altogether. In Massachusetts, for example, 60% of the inactive bar is comprised of women. Brown and Mendoza (2010) maintain that the legal profession is not about preserving a "profession" at all costs but about finding, in this new millennium, how legal practice can provide the best for clients, firms, and attorneys.

Alternatives to the billing system are proposed because they could enable women to seek law firm practice, and extend their proficiencies into a broader array of legal practice (not just governmental work, education, or family law). These alternatives could end up maximizing a firm's profitability because the flexibility serves client and attorney needs (Brown and Mendoza 2010). When law firms have a more balanced representation of women and men, then the firms are able to attract and keep clients and attorneys. Women and men attorneys want to reduce the stress that they feel in legal practice and be able to enjoy their family life. Any barriers to women's legal practice also impact men; if the profession works to accommodate the changing needs of a community by eliminating gendered hierarchies in the practice of law, then another social transformation in the law will occur.

Conclusion

Women's formal entrance into the legal profession began in the United States in the late nineteenth century. It was not until laws that discriminated against women in the United States, and in every other nation, were rescinded that women were able to attend law schools and gain entrance into the profession. Despite the accolades that some women have received for their ability to achieve high positions in the practice of law or on high courts of justice, most women find barriers to legal practice. These barriers continue to stress that the legal field exemplifies male attributes of aggression, shrewdness, and superiority. Although women may show that they can be aggressive and have the intellectual capacity to be excellent lawyers, they are paid less and promoted less. Rather than fight the system, women have opened up new legal practices and sought to modify the way in which legal practice occurs. Women, worldwide, have coped by forming female legal associations, continuing to strive for equality in all laws that disadvantage women, and attempting to provide a balanced life for themselves and their family.

Can women lawyers have it all, a family and a successful practice? Only time will tell if true equality and equity will be achieved in the twenty-first century. Such equality and equity must be done at a worldwide level to eliminate social, cultural, and political disadvantages associated with being a female in society. Until women are accepted as a heterogeneous group, not all the same and not all wanting the same form of legal successes, then women will continue to be viewed as an anomaly in the law.

Suggested readings

Kitzerow, Phyllis. 2014. *Women Attorneys and the Changing Workplace: High Hopes, Mixed Outcomes.* Boulder, CO: Lynne Rienner Publishers.
Smith, J. Clay, Jr (ed.). 2000. *Rebels in Law: Voices in History of Black Women Lawyers.* Ann Arbor, MI: University of Michigan Press.
Sotomayor, Sonia. 2013. *Mi Mundo Adorado.* New York: Vintage Books.

Student engagement activities

1 Determine how many female judges are serving on courts in your community; where did they go to law school and what led them to the bench?
2 Discuss the practice of law with several female and male attorneys in order to determine how, or if, they balance family life with legal practice.
3 Compare the percentage of women in law schools in your community with the percentage of female attorneys in public practice, family practice, or working in large law firms.

Discussion questions

1 What are the critical responsibilities of legal counsel and does gender of the attorney matter in the performance of these duties?
2 What are social, legal, political, and cultural dimensions that hinder women's entrance into international courts as attorneys and judges?
3 Explain how the legal system is, or is not, gender neutral.

Key terms

Disenfranchisement
Doctrine of coverture
Enlightenment
Equal Pay Act of 1963
Gender discrimination
Gender segregation in the legal profession

Glass ceiling
"Mommy track"
Natural law
Sharia courts
Title VII of the Civil Rights Act of 1964

References

ABA (American Bar Association). 2014. "A Current Glance at Women in the Law, July 2014." *American Bar Association*. Accessed August 8, 2014, http://www.americanbar.org/content/dam/aba/marketing/women/current_glance_statistics_july2014.authcheckdam.pdf

Baksi, Catherine. August 27, 2013. "Solicitor 'Told to Stay Single' Settles Discrimination Claim." *The Law Society Gazette*. Accessed August 25, 2014, http://www.lawgazette.co.uk/practice/solicitor-told-to-stay-single-settles-discrimination-claim/5037152.article

Ballakrishnen, Swethaa. 2013. "Why Is Gender a Form of Diversity? Rising Advantages for Women in Global Indian Law Firms." *Indiana Journal of Global Legal Studies*, 20: 1261–1289.

Barnes, Brooks. May 23, 2014. "Others Fade, But Judge Judy Is Forever: At 71, She Still Presides." *New York Times*. Accessed August 20, 2014, http://www.nytimes.com/2014/05/24/business/media/others-fade-but-judge-judy-is-forever-at-71-she-still-presides.html?_r=1

BBC (British Broadcasting Corporation). 1997. "UK 75 Years of Women Solicitors." *BBC News*. Accessed August 8, 2014, http://news.bbc.co.uk/2/hi/uk_news/40448.stm

Bernat, Frances P. 1992. "Women in the Legal Profession." In *The Changing Roles of Women in the Criminal Justice System*, 2nd edn, edited by Imogene Moyer, 307–321. Prospect Heights, IL: Waveland Press.

Berson, Susan A. 2010. "Women in Law: Making Herstory: U.S. Circuit Judge Encourages the Next Steps Toward Equality." *ABA Journal*, 96(3): 28–29.

Boxall, Bettina. March 2, 1995. "Marcia Clark's Husband Cites Trial in Custody Fight." *Los Angeles Times*. Accessed August 26, 2014, http://articles.latimes.com/1995-03-02/news/mn-37861_1_marcia-clark

Bradwell v. State of Illinois, 83 U.S. 130 (Wall., 1872).

Brinkmann, Paul. December 3, 2012. "'Tall, Male and Jewish?' Greenberg Traurig Denies New Discrimination Allegations." *South Florida Business Journal*. Accessed August 25, 2014, http://www.bizjournals.com/southflorida/blog/2012/12/tall-male-and-jewish-greenberg.html?page=all

Brown, Katherine L., and Kristin A. Mendoza. 2010. "Ending the Tyranny of the Billable Hour: A Mandate for Change for the 21st Century Law Firm." *New Hampshire Bar Journal*, 51: 66–69.

Brundige, Elizabeth. November 25, 2012. *Memorandum: Exclusion of Women from the Legal Profession in the United States of America, the United Kingdom, and South Africa*. Avon Global Center for Women and Justice. Cornell, NY: Cornell Law School.

CNN (Cable News Network). 2005. "O'Connor Resignation Letter." *CNN*. Accessed August 4, 2014, http://www.cnn.com/2005/LAW/07/01/oconnor.letter.nobanner/

Cabraser, Elizabeth. 2014. "Where Are All the Women in the Courtroom?" *Lieff, Cabraser, and Heimann & Bernstein*. Accessed July 24, 2014, http://www.lieffcabraser.com/blog/2014/02/where-are-all-the-women-in-the-courtroom.shtml

Campos, Paul. 2013. "Legal Academia and the Blindness of the Elites." *Harvard Journal of Law and Public Policy*, 37: 179–186.

Cardinal, Monique C. 2010. "Why Aren't Women Sharia Court Judges? The Case of Syria." *Islamic Law and Society*, 17: 185–214.

Clay-Warner, Jody, and Jennifer McMahon. 2007. "From the Bassinet to the Bar: The Effect of Motherhood on Women's Advancement in the Legal Profession." In *It's a Crime: Women and Justice*, 4th edn, edited by Roslyn Muraskin, 679–688. Upper Saddle River, NJ: Pearson.

Dinovitzer, Ronit, and John Hagan. 2014. "Hierarchical Structure and Gender Dissimilarity in American Legal Labor Markets." *Social Forces*, 92(3): 929–955.

Dinovitzer, Ronit, Reichman, Nancy, and Joyce Sterling. 2009. "The Differential Valuation of Women's Work: A New Look at the Gender Gap in Lawyers' Incomes." *Social Forces*, 88(2): 819–864.

Egelko, Bob. March 5, 2011. "Mary Morgan, 1st Openly Lesbian Judge, Retires." *SF Gate*. Accessed August 27, 2014, http://www.sfgate.com/bayarea/article/Mary-Morgan-1st-openly-lesbian-judge-retires-2528208.php

Farmer, Ann. 2010. "Order in the Closet: Why Attire for Women Is Still an Issue." *Perspectives*, 19(2): 4–7.

Gershman, Jacob. March 26, 2014. "Judge Kopf Causes a Stir with Blog Post about Female Lawyers." *Wall Street Journal*. Accessed August 20, 2014, http://blogs.wsj.com/law/2014/03/26/judge-kopf-causes-a-stir-with-blog-post-about-female-lawyers/

Gill, Rebecca D., Lazos, Sylvia R., and Mallory M. Waters. 2011. "Are Judicial Performance Evaluations Fair to Women and Minorities? A Cautionary Tale from Clark County, Nevada." *Law & Society Review*, 45(3): 731–759.

Grossman, Nienke. 2011. "The Effect of the Participation of Women Judges on the Legitimacy of International Courts and Tribunals." *American Society of International Law*, 105: 452–455.

Guyard-Nedelec, Alexandrine. 2007. "Discrimination Against Women in England and Wales: An Overview." *Gender Forum: An Internet Journal for Gender Studies*, 17: 1–6. Accessed August 8, 2014, http://www.genderforum.org/issues/working-out-gender/discrimination-against-women-lawyers-in-england-and-wales/

Hall, Carla. January 25, 1995. "The O.J. Simpson Murder Trial: Court Costumes: The Way They Dress Is One Way Attorneys Can Manipulate the Show, Experts Say." *Los Angeles Times*. Accessed August 20, 2014, http://articles.latimes.com/1995-01-25/news/mn-24228_1_court-costumes

Jacobs, Deborah L. August 5, 2014. "At Law Firms, Mommy Track Still Holds Women Back." Forbes/Personal Finance. Accessed February 19, 2016, http://www.forbes.com/sites/deborahljacobs/2014/08/05/at-law-firms-mommy-track-still-holds-women-back/#30503ef2259f

Jordan, Gwen H. 2009. "Agents of (Incremental) Change: From Myra Bradwell to Hillary Clinton. *Nevada Law Journal*, 9: 580–645.

Kaheny, Erin B., Szmer, John J., and Tammy A. Sarver. 2011. "Women Lawyers Before the Supreme Court of Canada." *Canadian Journal of Political Science/Revue Canadienne de Science Politique*, 44 (1): 83–109.

Kaye, David H., and Joseph L. Gastwirth. 2009. "Where Have All the Women Gone? The Gender Gap in Supreme Court Clerkships." *American Bar Association*, 49(4): 411–437.

Kitzerow, Phyllis. 2014. *Women Attorneys and the Changing Workplace: High Hopes, Mixed Outcomes*. Boulder, CO: Lynne Rienner Publishers.

Leiper, Jean McKenzie. 2006. *Bar Codes: Women in the Legal Profession*. Vancouver, Canada: UBC Press.

McAfee, David. 2014. "Greenberg Traurig Settles Atty's $200M Gender Bias Action." *Law 360*. Accessed August 25, 2014, http://www.law360.com/articles/445037/greenberg-traurig-settles-atty-s-200m-gender-bias-action

Miller, Susan L., and Michelle L. Meloy. 2007. "Women on the Bench: Mavericks, Peacemakers, or Something Else?" In *It's a Crime: Women and Justice*, 4th edn, edited by Roslyn Muraskin, 707–722. Upper Saddle River, NJ: Pearson.

Morello, Karen Berger. 1986. *The Invisible Bar: The Woman Lawyer in America 1638–the Present*. New York: Random House.

Mossman, Mary Jane. 2003. "Legal Education as a Strategy for Change in the Legal Profession." *International Journal of the Legal Profession*, 10(2): 149–165.

Mossman, Mary Jane. 2008. "'New Questions' about Women's Access to the Legal Professions." *Otago Law Review*, 11(4): 585–601.

Mullarkey, Mary J. 2004. "Two Harvard Women: 1965 to Today." *Harvard Women's Law Journal*, 27: 367–379.

NALP. 2014. "2012–2013 NALP Directory of Legal Employers." *NALP Bulletin.* Accessed August 1, 2014, http://www.nalp.org/0413research

Norgren, Jill. 2013. *Rebels at the Bar: The Fascinating, Forgotten Stories of America's First Women Lawyers.* New York: New York University Press.

Oyez. 2014. "Sandra Day O'Connor, Biography." *U.S. Supreme Court Media.* Accessed July 30, 2014, http://www.oyez.org/justices/sandra_day_oconnor

Reynolds, Emma. January 9, 2013. "'Stay Single – and Don't Have Babies!' What Solicitor Claims She Was Told by Boss Who Wanted to 'Control' Her." *Daily Mail.* Accessed August 25, 2014, http://www.dailymail.co.uk/news/article-2259474/Stay-single–dont-babies-What-solicitor-claims-told-boss-wanted-control-her.html#ixzz3BTCpHEpy

Rhode, Deborah L. 2001. *The Unfinished Agenda: Women and the Legal Profession.* Chicago, IL: American Bar Association.

Roe v. Wade, 410 U.S. 113 (1973).

Scales-Trent, Judy. 2010. "Women Lawyers, Women's Rights in Senegal: The Association of Senegalese Women Lawyers." *Human Rights Quarterly*, 32(1): 115–143.

Sen, Maya. 2014. "How Judicial Qualification Ratings May Disadvantage Minority and Female Candidates." *Journal of Law and Courts*, 2(1): 33–65.

Tani, Karen M. 2012. "Portia's Deal." *Chicago-Kent Law Review*, 87: 549–570.

Toal, Chief Justice Jean H. 2010. "Symposium: Great Women, Great Chiefs: Remarks." *Albany Law Review*, 74, 1583–1589.

Wallace, Jean E., and Fiona M. Kay. 2012. "Tokenism, Organizational Segregation, and Coworker Relations in Law Firms. *Social Problems*, 59(3): 389–410.

Weiss, Debra C. November 2, 2010. "'Maternal Wall,' Sex Bias Block Advancement for Women Lawyers, Utah Study Finds." *ABA Journal.* Accessed August 25, 2014, http://www.abajournal.com/news/article/maternal_wall_sex_bias_block_advancement_for_women_lawyers_utah_study_finds/

Włodek-Biernat, Ludwika. 2010. "Iranian Women, Quest for Freedom and Equality." *Polish Sociological Review*, 172: 503–509.

Zaretsky, Staci. December 3, 2012. "This $200 Million Class Action Case Claims Women Are Being Elbowed Out by the Greenberg Traurig 'Boys Club.'" *Above the Law.* Accessed August 25, 2014, http://abovethelaw.com/2012/12/this-200m-class-action-case-claims-women-are-being-elbowed-out-by-the-greenberg-traurig-boys-club/

CHAPTER 10

Women working with post-conviction offenders

Student learning outcomes

After reading this chapter, you should be able to:
- Describe the history of women entering the corrections profession.
- Summarize the nature of corrections work for women today.
- Describe the issues that female corrections workers encounter on the job.

Introduction

In January of 2011, 34-year-old corrections officer Jayme Biendl was working her normal shift at Monroe Correctional Complex in Monroe, Washington, a prison compound holding inmates ranging from minimum, medium, and maximum custody levels. She had been working as a corrections officer since 2002 and received the "Officer of the Year Award" at the facility in 2008 (Chan and Ostrom 2011). Overall Biendl enjoyed her job as a corrections officer, but on numerous occasions she had expressed concerns about her safety to her supervisors. Specifically, she had concerns about the lack of video surveillance in the prison chapel, because she often worked in that area alone (Chan and Ostrom 2011). Unfortunately, on January 29, 2011, her worst fears came to fruition. Biendl was strangled to death by an amplifier cord in the prison chapel by Byron Sherf, a 52-year-old prisoner serving life without the possibility of parole for previous rape convictions. Sherf was later found guilty of the death of Biendl and sentenced to death (Miletich 2013). How could this tragedy have been prevented? Why weren't Biendl's concerns heard?

While the majority of corrections officers, female or male, abide by the rules and protocols of the institutions they work in, there are still times when professional boundaries are crossed. One egregious case of female correctional officer misconduct surfaced in 2013 in Baltimore, Maryland. Apparently, 13 female corrections officers were involved in a conspiracy to help members of the gang Black Guerilla Family, incarcerated at the Baltimore City Detention Center, a jail, to smuggle cells phones, marijuana, cigarettes, and prescription pills in exchange for money and gifts (Winter 2013). In addition to the smuggling of items, several female corrections officers were having sexual relations with one incarcerated inmate, Tavon White, the purported ring leader of the Black Guerilla Family gang. He impregnated four female officers, and one female officer was impregnated by White

---

Women, Crime, and Justice, First Edition. By Elaine Gunnison, Frances P. Bernat, and Lynne Goodstein.
© 2017 John Wiley & Sons, Ltd. Published 2017 by John Wiley & Sons, Ltd.

on two separate occasions (Winter 2013). A few of the female officers even had White's name tattooed on their bodies as well. The officers have since been convicted in federal court (Zoukis 2015). How could this have happened? Could such activities have been prevented? Are women working in correctional facilities somehow vulnerable to the manipulation of men?

 CASE STUDY: Claire Lewis

Female corrections officers face safety concerns regardless of which country they work in. In 2010, Claire Lewis, a female corrections officer in England, was attacked by an irate inmate in Frankland Prison – a high security prison (Armstrong 2012). When Lewis and one of her male colleagues opened the cell door holding an inmate, the inmate came blazing out of his cell with a broken chili sauce bottle. The inmate immediately slashed Lewis' colleague and began chasing Lewis through the high security wing. As he chased her, he screamed at her multiple times that he was going to kill her (Armstrong 2012). Eventually, the inmate caught up to Lewis and plunged the broken bottle into her back (Chorley 2013). Fortunately, Lewis survived the horrific attack. Following the attack, Lewis was unable to return to work due to experiencing depression and pain from the injuries she sustained (Hutchinson 2011). She cannot return to work due to medical reasons, as she can no longer perform the work she once did or even lift anything heavy – so even reassignment to another staff position such as gardening is no longer an option for her as she cannot lift a shovel (Hutchinson 2011). Additionally, Lewis has reported that she suffers from post-traumatic stress disorder (Hutchinson 2011). The inmate who initiated the attack was later acquitted of the attempted homicide charges against her and her colleague (Hutchinson 2011). This brutal attack might have been thwarted or less serious injuries might have been sustained by the victims had the corrections officers been issued stab-proof vests. Since this incident garnered national attention in England, the government finally decided in 2013 to issue stab-proof vests to corrections workers – two years earlier the government had declared that such vests were unnecessary (Chorley 2013).

In this chapter, we provide a historical overview of women working in corrections and provide current statistics as to the number of women working in the profession today. We will also seek to explain how women working in corrections in the United States may be similar and/or different from women working in the corrections field around the world. Next, we will examine the many challenges that women in this profession encounter on the job and include discussion on the role that gender, race, and sexual orientation have in these challenges. Finally, we discuss the effectiveness of women working in this field both inside and outside the prison walls.

History of women working in jails and prisons

The journey for women working in the corrections field was fraught with similar obstacles experienced by women entering work in the policing profession. In 1822, the first entry point for women working in the correctional system occurred when Rachel Perijo was hired as jail matron in Baltimore, Maryland (Britton 2003). Approximately 10 years later, when separate living arrangements were established for females at Auburn Prison, New York, a female **prison matron** was hired to work there (Zupan 1992) (Figure 10.1). Despite this early progress, the acceptance and push for women to begin working in prisons did not burgeon until the 1870s. In 1870, the National Prison Association Meeting was held in Cincinnati, Ohio, whereby corrections officials from across the nation convened to discuss changes needed in the correctional system (Latessa and Smith 2011). At this meeting, it was decided that women offenders, who had been predominately housed in prisons with men, needed separate facilities due to the rampant abuse they were experiencing from both fellow male prisoners but also from male correctional officers (Rafter 1985). In addition to separate all-female facilities, it was deemed important that these new female institutions be staffed with a variety of only female workers, ranging from correctional staff to wardens. It was thought that by staffing female prisons with only women correction officers, it would eliminate or reduce sexual abuse of female prisoners by male correctional staff. Additionally, it was thought that women would know how best to treat, or reform, female prisoners. Early female prison reformers included Katharine Davis, Superintendent of the New York State Reform at Bedford Hills from 1901 to 1914, and Miriam Van Waters, Superintendent of the Massachusetts Reformatory for Women from 1932 to 1957 (Britton 2003; Freedman 1981). These early reformers were able to attract a higher number of educated women for employment into their institutions as well as make conditions more humane for confined women. Many of the early female correctional workers also were required to live at the institution where they were employed (Feinman 1994). While women were wanted for warden positions for female prisons, men still predominately held these positions in the 1930s (Root 1932).

Figure 10.1 Virginia Cayou, Matron of the Stillwater, Minnesota, Prison. Detail from a group photograph of all the guards and staff, c. 1890. *Source:* From the Collections of the Washington County (MN) Historical Society.

The idea that women could work as reformers for female criminals outside of the prison walls also extended to other areas of corrections, including probation. The National Prison Association Meeting in 1870 also expanded the use of **probation**, a punishment served in the community in lieu of a jail or prison sentence. Women were viewed as ideal probation officers to work with female offenders, particularly female juveniles, to help restore the "fallen" girls' morals and make them upstanding citizens (Miner 1910). Miner (1910, 36) explains the sentiment at the time as follows, "The work for girls and women must be done by women who bring to it intelligence, common sense, tact, skill, sympathy and enthusiasm, faith in human nature and in the task they are undertaking. They must be efficient and trained workers and women with personality." During this era, entry for women into employment in female prison institutions and other correctional agencies was more readily accepted than in other occupations such as policing.

While women did slowly enter the profession as prison matrons, they were paid less for their work than their male counterparts, worked long hours, and lacked the authority to make reforms for their clients (Britton 2003). Additionally, prison matrons worked in overcrowded conditions and were often untrained (Britton 2003). This resulted in most women matrons being unable to serve in other capacities besides in a supervisory role – a role at odds with the reformatory role that was the original motivation for their employment in the field. Upon further inspection, there was also a clear lack of diversity in females that were hired as prison matrons. The majority of the early prison matrons were Caucasian and it wouldn't be until 1919 that the first African-American women were hired as prison matrons (Smith 2012). In regard to other positions in the corrections field, such as probation and parole, Caucasian women were also favored for employment in these positions. When women of color were hired, they were typically designated to supervise other girls and women of color. One of the first African-American women hired as a parole officer in New York in 1950 was Cynthia Piggott (Miles 2013). Piggott recalls that "At first, I was assigned to parolees in African-American neighborhoods. After time, that changed" (Miles 2013). Along with recommendations by the National Prison Association to increase employment of women within the corrections profession, the Civil Rights movement, and subsequent movements by various organizations such as the Women's Prison Association, also advocated for the hiring of women in the corrections field (Nink 2008). Sadly, despite such strong support, the momentum to hire more women in the corrections field stalled over time. In a census of women working as correctional officers in 1978, it was found that only 6.6% of the staff, at that time, was female (Nink 2008).

Women wanting to work as officers in male prisons or with male prisoners experienced an exponential amount of resistance. More often than not, women working in male prisons found themselves removed from contact with the inmate population and relegated to working in administrative positions, control booths, or in a surveillance capacity (Britton 2003). In a survey of probation and parole agencies in all 50 US states and two US territories in 1970, Stout (1973) found that of the 53 agencies that were surveyed, only 28 of these allowed women to supervise men. There are a few reasons why women were not hired to work in prisons for men in greater numbers. One reason for their lack of entry or acceptance into working in male institutions can be attributed to discrimination (Britton 2003). It was argued that if women worked in these institutions they would risk undermining the security of the institution or be more likely to become victimized. For example, if a woman was unable to subdue a male inmate, she could become injured or put the life of her co-worker in danger. Further, if the women became emotionally attached to the confined men, administrators thought they might break prison rules (e.g., engage in sexual relations with inmates or smuggle contraband into the institution), thereby undermining the overall security of the correctional institution.

The feminist movement of the 1970s, as well as legislation and lawsuits, assisted women in breaking through the gender discrimination barrier. The entry of more women working in correctional institutions, particularly male institutions, was achieved with the passage of **Title VII of the Civil Rights Act of 1964** and the **Equal Employment Opportunity Act of 1972** (Britton 2003). While these legislative acts made it easier for women to be hired in correctional institutions for males, there was a loophole that correctional administrators could utilize to exclude women from certain positions. This loophole was known as the **bona fide occupational qualification (BFOQ)**. This exemption allowed employers to legally not hire a woman for a particular position if it was demonstrated that she could not perform the particular duties of the job (Britton 2003). Some employers, including correctional administrators, used this loophole as a means to discriminate against hiring women. For instance, correctional administrators established height or weight restrictions or "no contact" rules between officers and inmates of the opposite sex, which negatively impacted the ability of women to be hired for positions in male prisons. As a result of BFOQ, women began filing lawsuits to eliminate such barriers and further increase their access to working in male institutions. In 1977, the court case **Dothard v. Rawlinson** brought specific attention to this discrimination (Britton 2003). Rawlinson, a female college graduate, applied for a correctional counselor position in Alabama but was denied the position based on height and weight restrictions. She challenged this restriction as well as their policy banning contact between women and male inmates in maximum custody institutions. The Supreme Court ruled that height and weight restrictions were discriminatory; however, the court upheld that some positions in male institutions do qualify for a BFOQ (Britton 2003). That is, there may be some positions that women could hold in a male prison that may make them more vulnerable to a sexual attack by male inmates. For such a position, it is legally permissible for an institution to restrict a female for applying for the job.

Apart from overt and subtle gender discrimination by correctional administrators, another reason for excluding women from working with male inmates grew out of a concern to protect the privacy of male prisoners (Zimmer 1986). Should the rights of privacy for inmates be utilized as a factor for not hiring women *or* men to work in correctional facilities? Lawsuits were filed by inmates throughout the 1970s and 1980s, challenging their rights to privacy when being guarded, pat searched, strip searched, or body cavity searched by a staff member of the opposite sex. The lawsuits filed by male inmates cited the violation of their **Fourth Amendment** rights (i.e., unreasonable searches) or **Eighth Amendment** rights (i.e., cruel and unusual punishments). However, the courts have ruled that male prisoners can be guarded or searched by female staff (Flesher 2007; Martin and Jurik 1996). For instance, the courts ruled in *Smith v. Fairman* **(1982)** that pat searches of male inmates by female guards did not violate their constitutional rights. Additionally, the courts ruled in *Somers v. Thurman* **(1983)** that male inmates could not claim that body cavity searches by female guards violated their right to privacy (Flesher 2007). Thus, while concerns over inmate privacy have arisen with increasing female employment in prisons for men, the courts have ruled that such concerns do not supersede the ability of women to work in such institutions. Rather, female correctional officers are not only permitted to guard males, but they are also allowed to carry out their specific duties regardless of whether the inmate does not prefer to be searched, observed, or supervised by female officers.

 GLOBAL PERSPECTIVES: Entry into corrections for women across the globe

For women pursuing corrections careers in other first world countries, their entry was very similar to that of their US colleagues. Women corrections workers found employment in working with female offenders rather easily, but their employment in prisons for men was fraught with resistance. Women working in prisons for men found themselves either working as volunteers or in clerical positions. While women were employed as correctional officers in prisons for men in the United Kingdom and Australia at about the same time as women in the United States, it took another decade before women were accepted as officers in prisons for men in other countries (Newbold 2005).

In New Zealand, for example, women were not employed to work in prisons for men until the mid-1980s. The push for changes in employment for women in corrections in New Zealand was in response to legislation mandating equal employment opportunities for women (Newbold 2005). The first female correctional officer hired to work in a minimum security male prison in New Zealand in 1985 was Celia Lashlie (Newbold 2005). After Lashlie started her position, the hiring of female corrections workers proliferated in New Zealand. However, initially, the hiring of women correctional officers to work in minimum security prisons for men was more readily accepted than hiring them to work in male maximum security institutions. Eventually, the resistance to their employment in male maximum security prisons broke down, and women increasingly began to find work as correctional officers in female *and* male institutions across New Zealand (Newbold 2005).

Despite some of the earlier setbacks that women faced working in the corrections field, from initially being hired to work in prisons to challenges regarding their employment within prisons for men, women have entered work in this field in greater numbers than in other criminal justice professions, such as policing. Obtaining accurate figures on the total number of women working in the field is difficult as it requires an inspection of multiple sources of publications on employment data in the field. Additionally, the most recent figures on the number of women working in the correctional field are a bit outdated. Despite the statistical shortcomings, we do know about their representation in the correctional workforce and their education backgrounds. In 2005, it was reported that women represented approximately 35% of all employees in state correctional facilities in the United States (Cook 2005). In contrast, in 2003, females represented approximately 30% of correctional staff in the Federal Bureau of Prisons (Federal Bureau of Prisons 2003). Most recently, it was reported that there were approximately 43,000 female corrections officers across the nation, a stark contrast to well over 100,000 employed male corrections officers (Elmore 2013). Of the females working in federal prisons in 2003, the majority were African-American, with Caucasians and Hispanic-Americans representing almost equal numbers of staff (Federal Bureau of Prisons 2003). According to the Bureau of Labor Statistics (2015), corrections officers are required to have at a minimum a high school education, and, in some cases, a bachelor's degree. Upon inspection of educational status of federal correctional staff in 2003, the majority of men and women have at least a high school degree or some college education (Federal Bureau of Prisons 2003). The employment outlook for corrections officers is on an upward trajectory, with growth in the field estimated to be 4% from 2014 to 2024 (Bureau of Labor Statistics 2015). In regard to statistics for women working in the corrections field outside of prison, in 2006, women and men represented almost equal numbers of full-time employees in state parole agencies (Bonczar 2008). The investigation into the number of parole employees was the first official census conducted by the Bureau of Justice Statistics to date (Bonczar 2008). While the agency launched its first census of probation employees in 2014 the findings of that investigation have not been released (Bureau of Justice Statistics 2014). Thus, at this time, the number of women employed in the probation sector is not yet known.

Today, career opportunities for women working in the corrections field have expanded beyond just working in jails and/or prisons. Increasingly, women are working in community corrections positions in roles such as probation and parole as officers or supervisors. Kim and colleagues (2003, 408) explain: "Currently, female correctional professionals work as consultants, commissioners, or directors in departments of corrections, and presidents of national organizations, as well as wardens in prison." While women may have broken through barriers blocking their advancement to top positions in the corrections field, the success should be interpreted with caution. As is the case for female police officers, women are still underrepresented at the top administrative posts in the corrections field (Martin and Jurik 1996). For instance, women have increasingly become employed as wardens in both female and male prison facilities, but they are not employed as wardens at equal rates to men (Kim et al. 2003). Currently, women are still being hailed as the "first" wardens hired at various correctional institutions across the nation (Cornejo 2010). In 2014, Kim Butler became the first female warden of Menard Correctional Center, an all-male, maximum security prison in Illinois (Hahn 2014). She is only the second female in the state of Illinois appointed to be a warden of such a facility (Hahn 2014). For women of color, the journey to top-tiered correctional positions is also difficult to obtain due to discrimination; thus, they are still unrepresented in these positions.

⚖️ SPECIAL LEGAL ISSUES: Prison law of China

In 1994, the Prison Law of China was passed and stipulated many procedures to be implemented within prisons in China to combat problems (e.g., abuse, coercion) in the handling of both male and female prisoners (Yang 2012). While the law mostly focused on issues pertaining to prisoners, there was a section of the law that addressed prison administration (Yang 2012). Specifically, in regard to administration, the law promulgated the establishment of at least one warden at each prison and stated that "police of prison," or corrections workers, perform their duties with honesty and treat prisoners humanely. Article 40 of the law specified that female prisoners be supervised by female corrections workers (Figure 10.2). Since the law was passed, women have become incarcerated at increasing rates in China. According to the Dui Hua Foundation (2011), the Guandong Women's Prison can hold 5,000 offenders and is considered to be the largest prison for women in the world. With the burgeoning incarceration of female offenders in China, prisons for women have had difficulties in staffing females as corrections officers and wardens. It is not uncommon for there to be a shortage of corrections officers. In one study, a female corrections officer explains the frustration with staff shortages: "because supervisory female staff have a high-risk job and cannot leave work early, they must work continuously, and there is a lot of pressure. Once when I worked for more than 40 consecutive hours, my cellphone was left outside of the prison, and I could not contact family" (Lei, Lu, and Jianjun 2014, 28). These shortages in staff have resulted in some scholars calling for the hiring of more female corrections staff, including wardens (Yang 2012).

Figure 10.2 Police guards stand at a security gate inside the No. 1 Detention Center during a government guided tour in Beijing on October 25, 2012. The rare visit to the facility, which has capacity for 1,000 inmates, was opened to the foreign media as Beijing prepares for the 18th Congress of the Communist Party of China. *Source:* Ed Jones/AFP/Getty Images.

Challenges to women in the field of corrections

The media has a tendency to distort the work that female corrections workers perform and the challenges they face. When reflecting on media portrayals of women corrections workers, perhaps classic movies such as *Caged Heat* (1974), in which Warden McQueen runs a female prison, or the popular Broadway production-turned-movie *Chicago* (2002), depicting the corrupt Matron "Momma" Morton, may come to mind. The recent Netflix hit *Orange is the New Black* may also shape the opinions of the public as to the role that male corrections officers have in female institutions. Other "reality" based shows, such as *Prison Women: Females on Guard,* airing on the National Geographic Channel, may also come to mind. Female correctional workers are employed in a number of positions both within prison and in the community working as probation and parole agents. As with any profession, the challenges and experiences that women working in the correctional field face are no different from other those of women working in the private sector. Additionally, the challenges that female correctional workers experience is often similar to the hardships that women employed as law enforcement officers experience. What are some examples of challenges that women face when working in the field of corrections?

Abuse

One clear challenge that women working as correctional officers face on the job is abuse from inmates or a general lack of respect for their authority by inmates. Female correctional officers may receive "cat calls" from male and female inmates as well as be on the receiving end of degrading comments and verbal abuse that are often geared towards their gender and/or sexuality. Crewe (2006), in a study of male prisoners in the United Kingdom who were interviewed about their female guards, indicated that some male prisoners often sexualized the female officers and were not afraid to make lewd comments to the officers. It is as if the men viewed the female officer more in terms of her gender than as an authority figure in the institution. One prisoner reported,

> I say things. "You've got a nice bum" or "you look nice." I don't know why I do it, it just comes out of my mouth automatically. I shouldn't be doing that, cos they can have you up for it, but I just do it like I'm on the out. I just look at them as women." (Crewe 2006, 404)

In another study of 132 female and male corrections officers in two prisons in the Province of Quebec, Canada, the officers also reported experiencing verbal abuse, or intimidation (Gomez del Prado 2012). While such experiences on the job are perhaps to be expected given the population, it might be surprising to learn that female correctional officers view women inmates as being more disrespectful than male inmates and even more emotionally taxing to guard. Britton (1999, 461), in an examination of female and male correctional officers working in a state prison, reports on this aspect of respect from the perspective of a female correctional officer:

> White female officer, women's prison: But as far as respect, the women that have gone from female units to the male units, I've known some that did quit because they were getting shipped back to a female unit. They will no longer work with females once they've been on a male unit. Because of the respect. They don't have to take the abuse they take from women. It's a completely different world on a male unit. The men will not and cannot argue with you, or talk back to you, where with the women, you just have to take it and take it and take it.

It may be that poor correctional administration and the lack of clear policies may contribute to and even exacerbate abuse, such as sexual harassment, by inmates against female guards. For instance, in Iowa, Kristine Sink, a female correctional officer, who supervises violent male offenders in a maximum security prison, filed a lawsuit against correctional administrators regarding repeated sexual harassment by inmates, which spiked after they had watched various movies and television shows such as *Delta of Venus*, *Coffey*, and *Cruel Intentions* (Associated Press 2013). Sink claimed that following the inmate consumption of the media, she experienced an increased level of harassment. She also claimed that she complained to her supervisors but was reprimanded when she did so and was further instructed to continue showing the media content (Associated Press 2013). Female probation and parole officers share some of the same experiences in their interactions with offenders. Community corrections officers may also experience challenges to their authority role, as well as be the recipients of comments about their gender. Petrillo (2007) interviewed female probation officers in London and discovered that power struggles sometimes emerged between the officers and their sex offender clients. One officer explains this struggle:

> When I first joined the team that was the hard thing, when I heard such anti-social views towards women and initially it provoked a very strong reaction inside me and then I've got to work very hard to maintain my empathy, my professionalism really ... I mean, I've got one very, very difficult ... the way he looks at me, he's very, very defensive and there's a real struggle with that relationship. I'm a woman in a position of power and so he really struggles with that dynamic and he acts out quite a lot in sessions with me. (Petrillo 2007, 398)

Thus, regardless of where women may be employed in the corrections field, they may experience some forms of abuse from their clients.

The verbal abuse, **stereotypes**, and harassment that female corrections workers experience from offenders is not limited to just this group – rather, female corrections workers can also experience such behaviors from their male or female colleagues (Britton 2003; Martin and Jurik 1996; Rader 1997). Women correctional workers may endure verbal abuse that is directed towards their gender and/or sexuality. That is, female guards, wardens, and probation and parole officers may experience comments regarding their abilities to perform their job or unprofessional comments that somehow intertwine their sexuality and race into the equation of whether they can perform their duties effectively (Britton 2003). In 2007, New York State Division of Human Rights awarded a lesbian prison guard, Alicia Humig, close to $1 million due to relentless verbal abuse and physical threats that she received from a male colleague (Feuer 2007). The abuse that she received was directed towards her sexuality, and, in many instances, the abuse occurred in front of the inmates she was guarding, which served to undermine her authority (Feuer 2007). Another case of gender and sexual-orientation discrimination occurred in Washington State in 2007. The female corrections worker reported:

> her co-worker told other staff that she was a lesbian who "hated men" and male members of her staff would not get ahead working for her. She further alleged that one supervisor suggested that she use the men's restroom instead of the women's, and another supervisor challenged her ability to manage her subordinates. The employee stated that when she complained about her co-worker's comments, she was told to "pick her battles wisely" and "take the high road." (Mallory, Hasenbush, and Sears 2013, 32)

Additionally, a transgender correctional officer in New Hampshire resigned following "three years of harassment and physical abuse based on her gender identity, including co-workers kicking her, snapping her in the breasts, threatening to handcuff her to a flagpole and take off her clothes, and slamming her into a concrete wall" (Mallory et al. 2013, 10).

Verbal abuse directed toward the officer's skin color has been endured by women of color, with the perpetrators of such offensive language being both Caucasian and African-American male colleagues, making the women's job even more hostile and stressful (Smith 2012). Why would male minority corrections workers engage in racial or gender slurs against their female minority colleagues? Such behaviors from male colleagues may stem from hostility or resentment of women competing with them for promotional opportunities (Rader 2007). Minority male corrections workers may already experience marginalization based on their race and participate in such behaviors towards their female colleagues as a way to become more accepted into the workplace culture. Also, in an effort to help ensure their advancement or secure a promotion, they may engage in such practices as a method to assert their position in the organization. In a study of over 2,000 corrections officers, Britton (1997) found that both male and female African-American officers were less satisfied with their job than White officers. This finding regarding satisfaction suggests that race and gender may contribute to perceptions of the work environment.

Apart from experiencing verbal abuse on the job, female corrections workers may experience physical and/or sexual assault as well. A female correctional officer in Arizona was brutally attacked in 2013 by two male inmates as she escorted 50 unrestrained prisoners across the prison complex by herself (Blair and Stout 2013). Prison officials surmise that the inmates were trying to kill the officer, as they later found her name along with several other names on a hit list (Blair and Stout 2013). In December of 2013, a female Miami-Dade corrections officer was sexually assaulted by 17 male inmates (Wagner 2014). Following the vicious attacks, she took 60 days off from work. When she returned, she was shocked to learn that her supervisors had failed to report the assault to law enforcement authorities. Only when the victim threatened to report the incident to police herself, did her supervisors finally officially report the attack to law enforcement – 73 days later (Wagner 2014)! There is limited research pinpointing the exact number of workplace violence incidents (e.g., rape, robbery, assault) experienced by corrections officers – especially as these incidents relate to gender. However, it is known that between 2005 and 2009, corrections officers (along with law enforcement officers and bartenders) experienced a higher rate of workplace violence incidents than others working in positions such as taxi drivers, convenience store clerks, or teachers (Harrell 2011). Additionally, during this same time period, males were more likely to experience such victimizations than females (Harrell 2011). Given the possibility of violence in their occupation, female correctional officers have reported fear of victimization from both inmates and staff. In a study of female and male corrections officers in the United States, researchers have found that female officers do perceive a risk of inmate violence at a greater rate than male officers (Gordon, Proulx, and Grant 2012). For parole officers, male or female, fear of victimization or even death is often at the forefront of their minds when they check up on their clients at their residences. Their fears are not unfounded as they are often entering dangerous situations – sometimes by themselves and perhaps unarmed. In 2006, Canadian female parole officer Louise Pargeter was killed, and sexually assaulted after her death, by one of her clients after she arrived at his residence to check on him (Aggrawal 2010).

Stereotypes

Female correctional officers working in prisons for men face negative stereotypes about their ability to work in these institutions. The stereotypes range from their physical ability, or use of aggression, to carry out their duties effectively to concerns about their likelihood of becoming sexually involved with inmates (Jenne and Kersting 1996; Peterson 1982; Zimmer 1986). In an examination of barriers experienced by 33 female and male correctional officers working in male prisons, Jurik (1985) reports on the opinions regarding women working in these institutions as well as some of the problems women face on the job. One example of a challenge that women face in these institutions are beliefs that women are just not suited for the job. One male officer explains, "This place works on your mind after a while. Women just can't take that kind of strain. Most of them will crack" (Jurik 1985, 379). Additionally, male officers in her study expressed concerns about the physical strength of women and how taller, presumably stronger male inmates could overpower them. The death of Biendl in Washington State in 2011 may serve to reinforce the concerns that male corrections workers have about their female colleagues. Yet, other male officers expressed concern about their female colleagues becoming too emotionally involved with male inmates. One male supervisor reported, "The first thing I always ask about an officer is 'Who owns him? – Me or the inmate?' Women sometimes go soft on the inmates. We had one who got involved. She started bringing stuff in to him. She got dirty [i.e., smuggled contraband to inmates]" (Jurik 1985, 379). In 2012, a female correctional officer in England, Zanib Khan, was convicted to a one-year prison term for exchanging love letters with and making sexual phone calls to several incarcerated inmates that she worked with (Alleyne 2012). Thus, female correctional officers are not only stereotyped on their abilities, but they are also met with malign suspicions about their abilities to carry out their duties effectively and ethically. When cases arise such as the female officers' sexual contact with incarcerated jail inmates in Baltimore, it further solidifies the stereotype that many have regarding women officers, their sexuality, and their close proximity to working with male offenders.

Sexual harassment

Apart from the stereotypes held about female officers' abilities, **sexual harassment** may also be encountered on the job from their co-workers. There are no official statistics that report the actual number of incidents experienced by female correctional workers. However, researchers have found that female corrections officers do perceive higher levels of harassment than their male colleagues (Savicki, Cooley, and Gjesvold 2003). Despite the lack of official data and the research that exists on perceptions of harassment, results from qualitative research have yielded many reports of such experiences. Pogrebin and Poole (1997), in an examination of the work environment for 108 female sheriff deputies working in local jails and adult detention centers, found that these officers experienced widespread sexual harassment from their male colleagues. One subject reported, "I have been touched, poked, brushed against – I've had a guy come up from behind me and lick the back of my neck and say, 'Real nice, Sweetheart. You smell good enough to eat'" (Pogrebin and Poole 1997, 50). Another female officer reported, "The sexual harassment thing – believe me – it's happening. It goes on constantly. I hear it and see it a lot … I get invitations to spend the night, 'the-wife-is-out-of-town' kind of crap – and this was from a supervisor. He was very skilled at harassing. He did it when no one else is around" (Pogrebin and Poole 1997, 50). More recently, in a study of 14 correctional officers, Matthews, Monk-Turner, and Sumter (2010) report that half of the officers in their sample had experienced sexual jokes or comments on a weekly basis and some officers experienced such behavior on a daily basis. One subject, when queried about whether she had experienced harassment replied, "Well, who hasn't?" (Matthews et al. 2010, 62). All too often, female corrections officers endure such harassment due to fear that harassment may worsen after reporting it or that by reporting it their careers may be harmed in some manner (Zimmer 1986). Women working in other areas of correctional work, such as probation and parole, have also encountered such harassment. In 2012, a female deputy probation officer filed a $1.5 million sexual harassment lawsuit against the Chief Probation Officer, David Muhammad, in California (Pearlman 2012). According to the lawsuit, the victim stated that her supervisor would summon her to his office under the guise of a work-related discussion and then touch her inappropriately. The relatively recent nature of such incidents should be a reminder that such behaviors are not a historical artifact, but rather that harassment is still a prominent issue facing many women correctional workers in the field today. Many female corrections officers who have been victims of sexual harassment often do not report it due to fear of retaliation from co-workers, or they are concerned that if they do report it their careers in corrections will essentially be over (Harrison and Kanoff 2010). These experiences often result in reports of lower overall job satisfaction by female corrections officers, or job burnout, or they may lead to the victims quitting work in the corrections field altogether (Harrison and Kanoff 2010; Savicki et al. 2003).

Blocked advancement

The stereotypes and harassment that women corrections workers experience on the job may inhibit their opportunities for career advancement in their profession. Jurik (1985) describes how women working in the corrections field may experience blocks to their career advancement due to their performance evaluations. All employees, regardless of profession, undergo some form of review, and those in the corrections field are no exception. As with any employee, performance evaluations become a part of an individual's permanent employment record. Thus, if standards for accessing the performance of employees are not clear or the evaluation itself is biased in some way, this can stymie the advancement of those working in the corrections field – particularly for women and minority corrections workers. As described by Jurik (1985, 385), "Despite formal attempts to substitute universalistic for particularistic criteria in these reviews, the ambiguous and discretionary nature of the guidelines lead to inconsistent evaluations of officers." Therefore, without specific criteria to evaluate employees, supervisors may be subjective, and even biased, in their evaluations. In Jurik's (1985, 385) study, one female officer reported, "My first time on yard duty, a resident came up and asked a question and I was written up. On my performance evaluation it said: 'Over-familiar with residents.'" Since performance evaluations are scrutinized by corrections administrators making promotion decisions, then clearly if such evaluations are skewed in a negative direction for a worker, advancement is less likely to be obtained.

Perhaps their limited advancement is not due to poor performance evaluations, but rather the structure and culture of correctional organizations in general. That is, since correctional organizations were initially formed by men and for male employees, this has created a history of gender division, whereby men hold positions higher in the organization than women (Acker 1992; Britton 2003). Thus, women working in corrections tend to have a much more difficult time not only moving up the ranks in an organization that was never created for them, but also breaking past beliefs that work in corrections, particularly in prisons, is a job best carried out by men (Cheeseman 2012). In a qualitative study of women who were working or had worked in institutions or community corrections positions, Matthews and colleagues (2010) stated that the majority of women in their sample reported that men had a better chance of obtaining promotions than women. Some of the women in the study stated that promotions that went to male colleagues may have been "political" decisions or because women were perceived as not being as capable as their male colleagues in performing the duties of the new position. One subject recounted, "From my experience I've seen more men be promoted than women but I don't think that necessarily means that men have more chances than women, I think they might fill the shoes a little better" (Matthews et al. 2010, 58). This statement is profound in that men may be selected for positions over women as they "fit in" more than women. Scholars may indeed be correct in that correctional organizations have not been and are not currently structured to support female and male employment roles. For women who are able to obtain promotions in their careers, their advancement may be perceived by their male colleagues as tokenism or some form of sexual favoritism (Cheeseman 2012; Jurik 1985).

Stress

Working in the criminal justice system in any capacity can be stressful. Wells, Colbert, and Slate (2006, 63) explain that stress experienced by corrections workers can be categorized as follows: "internal to the organization; external to the organization; the job or task itself; or personal in nature." Given the work environment that correctional officers encounter on a daily basis, it is understandable why both male and female officers experience high levels of stress. The stress experienced by correctional officers on the job may impact not only their perceptions of inmates, but also their interactions with them. Misis and colleagues (2013, 1), in an examination of job stress experienced by male and female corrections officers, found that officers who reported higher levels of stress tended to interpret inmates as "being unfriendly, antisocial, and cold." The stress that the job elicits can impact not only job performance, but it also may permeate into their home lives (i.e., external stress). In a study of correctional officers working in prisons for men, Jurik (1988) reported stress experienced by female correctional officers. One officer in the study expressed stress over her job performance, stating, "I feel pressured at work – to prove myself when my co-workers and supervisors are sure I can't do it" (Jurik 1988, 303). Other officers described how the stress of the job seeped into their personal lives. For example, one reported: "It's a macho environment, and I have to act aggressively to succeed. I work here all day, talk loud, act tough. I go home at night and find myself talking in a deep, loud voice to my kids" (Jurik 1988, 303). Another female officer explained how the constant barrage of sexual remarks by inmates in the course of her job impacted her relationship with her husband, stating, "Sometimes, I can't even relate to my husband … I hear sexual remarks all day. I come home and he makes a loving joke or innuendo, and I jump down his throat" (Jurik 1988, 303).

For other corrections workers, the harassment experienced on the job may create internal and personal stress that impacts their physical and/or psychological health (Wells et al. 2006; Pogrebin and Poole 1997). The stress of their work experiences, for instance, may result in feelings of anxiety, fear, anger, and depression, thereby impacting the psychological well-being of the female officers. One officer describes the psychological problems that she experienced due to the sexual harassment she was encountering on the job: "I just stayed mad. I had a big chip on my shoulder. I hated the constant abuse and kept thinking that one day I would just kill someone" (Pogrebin and Poole 1997, 52). Unfortunately, for some corrections workers, the stress turns inward and results in the taking of their lives. In 2008, a New York female rookie probation officer committed suicide in her office cubicle (Sederstrom 2008). African-American correctional officers experience additional types of stressors, such as the strain of supervising an increasing number of African-American prisoners (Maghan and McLeish-Blackwell 1991). That is, they may bear an additional emotional burden of supervising prisoners who have been ensnared by the criminal justice system due to discrimination in society and the system. Additionally, African-American correctional officers have reported that it is often stressful when they are supervising persons that they may have known or that may have been from their neighborhood (Maghan and McLeish-Blackwell 1991). Cheeseman and Goodlin-Fahncke (2011), in an examination of work stress among those employed in correctional institutions, found that female corrections workers reported higher levels of work stress than their male colleagues. Wells et al. (2006) examined stress experienced by female and male probation officers. The researchers uncovered that female probation officers experienced elevated levels of physical stress but lower levels of occupational stress in the course of their jobs compared to male probation officers. However, these results should be interpreted with caution as more male probation officers were serving in supervisory roles, which arguably exert more occupational demands and stressors on whomever serves in that capacity. Despite this caveat, the stress experienced by female correctional and probation workers may manifest into detriments to their physical and psychological health over time.

Imbalance between work and home life

Other challenges expressed by female officers are the difficulties in juggling work and personal responsibilities at home. Matthews et al. (2010) reported that female correctional officers in their study expressed the nature of the shift work and schedule irregularities as problematic. With the constant fluctuation and long duration of shifts, typically lasting approximately 10 hours, female officers, especially those who were single mothers, reported difficulties in making childcare arrangements (Matthew et al. 2010). The sexist environments that female corrections workers may be exposed to sometimes exacerbated these scheduling difficulties. A female parole officer reported, "[Once I] was propositioned by my supervisor. I was a single mom; my boss knew one particular shift would be extremely convenient for me. He would give me the shift if I would sleep with him. I declined … However, many other women who were 'successful' in parole were successful because they accepted those propositions" (Ireland and Berg 2006, 145–146). The challenges that female correctional officers face in regard to scheduling are similar to such concerns raised by their colleagues in law enforcement positions.

For some female correctional officers, there really is no balance between work and family – rather, one tends to supersede the other. If the officer wants to be promoted, then she may need to place work before family. One correctional officer explains:

> I tended to put work before everything else even when I know I shouldn't of. That's probably why balancing a family and work and everything would be so hard at times. But I would say that it was probably the dedication that helped me be promoted. I'd have to say with promotions come sacrifice. (Matthews et al. 2010, 63)

For this officer, to demonstrate dedication to her job and subsequently earn a promotion, she may have needed to forego time with her family to put significant hours into her work. Female corrections officers have higher levels of work–family conflict than their male colleagues (Griffin 2006). With such role conflicts, it may not be surprising to learn that the divorce rates are high for those working as corrections officers (Pollock 2004). The inability to balance work and family due to occupational demands may be one factor as to why more women are not represented at higher-level positions in the corrections field. It may also be that women are choosing to "opt out" of applying for higher-level positions in an effort to "opt in" to making their families a priority. However, is there a better way? Should women working in the field have to make a choice?

 GLOBAL PERSPECTIVES: Women in corrections across the border

While female corrections workers in the United States experience challenges on the job, how their struggles are similar or different from the struggles experienced by female officers located in other countries is difficult to ascertain. The absence in knowledge is due to the fact that, unfortunately, very little research has been conducted on corrections workers across the globe. However, research conducted by Walters and Lagace (1999) adds some understanding to this gap in knowledge through its examination of 866 female and male corrections officers in Canada. The researchers found that female corrections officers were more likely to accept other females as their colleagues and reported higher levels of job satisfaction than their male colleagues. These findings regarding female officers in Canada are distinct from female officers in the United States, who may not be as satisfied with their jobs due to various forms of harassment by inmates and colleagues as well as blocked opportunities. The researchers also found that female Canadian officers were less likely to be interested in custodial prison orientations but rather more interested in rehabilitative orientations. While not the same comparison group, this finding is very similar to differences found in the philosophical orientations of female wardens in the United States (Kim et al. 2013).

Effectiveness of women correctional workers

While many in the corrections field may not have valued or currently value female correctional workers, women do indeed play an important and valuable role in the profession. Concerns have arisen about whether corrections officers would become sexually involved and/or manipulated by their clients, whether they could work effectively with *both* male and female offenders, whether their physical security could be compromised, and whether they could refrain from being emotional. Why have concerns arisen about their sexuality and their ability to carry out their duties effectively? What is known about their effectiveness on the job? Despite such concerns, female corrections workers are competent and capable in carrying out their job duties and possess many qualities that contribute to their effectiveness in their jobs. Interestingly, research has revealed, for instance, that inmates actually do perceive female corrections officers to be effective in their job. In a British study that examined perceptions that inmates held regarding female and male corrections officers, Boyd and Grant (2005) stated that offenders did not rate female and male corrections officers differently in terms of their competence or use of discipline and control. The only difference that the researchers found in regard to inmate perceptions was that the offenders rated female corrections officers higher on professionalism than their male colleagues. Additional research has revealed that women corrections workers are just as capable as their male counterparts – particularly in violent or aggressive situations (Jenne and Kersting 1996). However, it just may be the case that female corrections workers do not get sufficient opportunities to demonstrate their physical prowess, as their male colleagues may instinctively intercede in such situations as a means of "protecting" them. When such instances arise, female corrections workers may need to be assertive toward their colleagues to let them know that they are capable of getting the job done. One female correctional officer explained, "The man will try to take control of the situation unless a female deputy is very verbal. I'm not a person who pushes, but I've had to literally turn around and say to a deputy, 'I will handle it,' and show him that I am in control" (Pogrebin and Poole 1997, 46). Additionally, the stereotype that women corrections workers may not be as aggressive in subduing male inmates or that their lack of aggression may place harm on their male colleagues has not been substantiated in the literature. In fact, research has revealed that women correctional officers utilize similar levels of aggression, and in some instances perhaps more, in particular hostile or violent situations (Jenne and Kersting 1996). The finding that women may be more aggressive in some instances substantiates some claims made by researchers that women working in the corrections field may overcompensate in some manner (e.g., aggression or pursuit of education), as a means to assert their competence and foster their acceptance or as a method of adapting to their work roles in the face of gender discrimination and stereotypes (Ireland and Berg 2006; Jenne and Kersting 1996). One female parole officer explains how she overcompensated during her parole career: "There were a number of times when I did find myself making efforts above and beyond the norm in order to prove myself [because I am a woman]" (Ireland and Berg 2006, 144). For instance, female corrections workers may feel compelled to not only work harder but perhaps pursue higher education as a means of "proving" their authority and intellect to those male colleagues who not only think otherwise but also verbalize their thoughts to their female co-workers (Ireland and Berg 2006). Another female parole officer was told by personnel that she "would not be promoted because only men get promoted" (Ireland and Berg 2006, 143). Armed with that information, the parole officer vigorously pursued higher education and completed her bachelor's degree, thereby opening up promotion doors that were previously closed to her. While she was still female, she now had the necessary credentials to "prove" to upper administrators that she was more than capable of performing her job.

Like female law enforcement officers, female corrections workers rely on their communication skills not only to perform their duties but also to ensure their safety on the job. The utilization of verbal skills is an inherent feature of all correctional employment positions in the field, from corrections officer to parole officer (Pogrebin and Poole 1997). In a qualitative study of 12 female parole officers, Ireland and Berg (2008) report that verbal communication is a critical component of the officers' jobs and that effective communication is a key to their personal security. One subject, who supervised high-risk sex offenders on parole, explains:

> During the entire time I was a parole agent, I never had a situation when a parolee put his hands on me. Never. We had to have good communication skills; we have to be able to recognize volatile situations; and you have to be able to know how to handle those situations by using your communication skills. I have been involved in situations that could have easily turned volatile, but my manner, my demeanor, my communication skills, and the manner in which I dealt with these individuals has made a very big difference in the way that they have responded to me. (Ireland and Berg 2008, 483)

More often than not, female corrections workers utilize their verbal skills when interacting with offenders, whereas male corrections workers may tend to use a more confrontational style in their interactions. In fact, many community corrections counselors and officers utilize a restorative justice approach when working with their clients. **Restorative justice** refers to "a process of conflict resolution that brings together all parties affected by the harm or wrongdoing (e.g., offenders and their families, victims and their families, other members of the community, and professionals)" (Sun 2013, 16). With this approach, corrections workers can help offenders express their apologies to their victims and assist offenders in learning how to better problem solve and cope with their problems in the process as well. Since female corrections workers tend to be rather skilled in their communication, the restorative justice approach is well suited to their style in helping them work with their clients. Additionally, with successful offender reentry becoming a greater focus in the corrections field, their use of verbal skills may become especially important in helping ex-offenders reintegrate effectively into society (Gunnison and Helfgott 2013). That is, while communication skills may be useful to de-escalate confrontation situations with offenders both inside and outside the prison walls, these skills can be particularly useful in assisting ex-offenders in their reintegration. For many community corrections officers, their ability to establish a rapport with their clients and help guide them to make better choices may be one element that aids in successful ex-offender reentry. Gunnison and Helfgott (2013, 159–160), who examined successful ex-offender reentry from the perspectives of ex-offenders and community corrections officers, noted the following account by one female corrections officer in their sample:

> Everybody in my unit calls me "the mother," so I go in there and I guess I mother people. I don't want to excuse their bad behavior and I want to hold them accountable, but at the same time, I want them to feel that they can come and talk to me. I want you to call me and I want to talk to you about drug use before you start using again. I want a chance to intervene. I want a chance to teach you the different things you can do, show you different behaviors. Refer you to different counselors, or if it's an NA meeting or whatever it is. Sit down with you and have an opportunity to find out what your individual specific needs are, maybe get some background on where things come from, although I'm not certain if it's important enough if you were abused as a child. It's kind of where are you today and where can we go from here to shift your thinking one degree in a positive direction and get you going in a different direction.

Therefore, effective communication skills by corrections officers, male or female, may be pivotal in helping ex-offenders successfully navigate back into society after serving incarceration terms.

Research on the effectiveness of female wardens on the job is scant. However, the little research that has been conducted on female wardens has indicated that there are few differences between female and male wardens (Kim et al. 2003). In a national survey of 641 female and male state prison wardens, Kim and colleagues (2003) found that all wardens, regardless of gender, believed incapacitation was a chief goal of prisons. However, the researchers also found that a greater percentage of female wardens believed that rehabilitation played an important role in their institution. All in all, in terms of how wardens carried out their duties, the researchers did not discover any significant differences. When Kim et al. (2003) further probed wardens about various aspects of their job, a few gender differences emerged. For example, the researchers found that female wardens were more likely than male wardens to seek input from line staff in regard to policy recommendations, but, on the other hand, female wardens were less likely than male wardens to reach out to colleagues for support to cope with stress (Kim et al. 2003). Thus, from the little research we can uncover, female wardens are indeed effective in their positions, but there may be some subtle differences between female and male wardens in regard to their philosophies and how they may carry out their duties or cope with stress.

Women corrections workers are *indeed* effective in their jobs whether working behind bars or out in the community – even if their styles of carrying out their duties tend to be a bit different from those of male officers. While the presence of women in the corrections field has been met with resistance, it is clear that their entry into the profession has resulted in not only an overall improved image of corrections, but they have also assisted offenders in their reentry process. Current research has revealed that women working in the field are met with less resistance today in their jobs than they historically have experienced (Carlson, Thomas, and Anson 2004). Despite the knowledge that has been gained about females employed in the corrections system, there is still much more that we need to learn about their experiences both in the United States and abroad. The increased use of **qualitative** research methodologies should assist researchers in learning more about women employed in the corrections field, but there needs to be support from correctional administrators at all levels to allow researchers to enter their facilities and permit the stories of women to be recorded (Patenaude 2004).

Conclusion

In this chapter, we provided a historical overview of women working in the corrections field. In the past, it was difficult for women to enter the corrections profession – particularly for women of color. Today, however, the role of women in corrections has improved due to the feminist movement, legislation, and lawsuits. Despite these advances, the culture within corrections may stymie the experiences of women working in the profession today and, in many departments, contributes to continued harassment and discrimination of female corrections officers. Female corrections workers have unique skills, such as solid communication skills, that are both an asset for their male colleagues and for helping those in their communities. With better training in correctional training academies and removal of any corrections worker, male or female, that may be engaging in harassment and discriminatory practices, and creating shift schedules that help to balance work and life for all corrections workers regardless of the position that they hold, the corrections profession may become a better place for women to work in.

Suggested readings

Lambert, Eric G., Hogan, Nancy L., Altheimer, Irshad, and Jennifer Wareham. 2010. "The Effects of Different Aspects of Supervision Among Female and Male Correctional Staff: A Preliminary Study." *Criminal Justice Review*, 35: 492–513. DOI: 10.1177/0734016810372068

Leibling, Alison. 2011. *The Prison Officer*. New York, NY: Willian Publishing.

Lunsford, Sara. 2012. *Sweet Hell on Fire: A Memoir of the Prison I Worked In and the Prison I Lived In*. Naperville, IL: Sourcebooks.

Student engagement activities

1   Research the history of entry for women into prisons and community corrections agencies in the state/county/province in which you reside. Be sure to search for newspaper articles that may have reported on it. Write a one-page summary of the history of women entering corrections and critically analyze their entry into the field by examining not only the number of women entering the field but also the race and educational backgrounds of those women entering the professions. If possible, describe how women were portrayed at this time in the newspaper reports.

2   Watch two episodes of *Prison Women: Females on Guard* (National Geographic Channel). Record how women working in the Miami-Dade jail are portrayed in terms of their duties and roles within the profession. What do you notice in terms of how they carry out their duties? Do they voice any concerns about their jobs? What do you notice in regard to their interactions between one another and the inmates? Write a one-page summary of your observations.

3   Research a country (besides the United Kingdom) where women work in the field of corrections. Write a five-page essay covering the history of women entering the field in your selected country, provide the current number of women working in the field, and describe any challenges that they may face on the job. Within your essay, compare the similarities and differences between female police officers in the United States with female corrections workers in your chosen country.

Discussion questions

1   Why have women been welcomed into working in the corrections field more than in law enforcement? What have been some barricades for their entry into working in men's prisons?

2   What types of abuse do female corrections workers face on the job? How do their colleagues sometimes contribute to the abuse?

3   Given the challenges that many female corrections workers face in juggling family and their careers, what do you think could/should be done to assist women (or even men) working in this profession? What policies would you recommend? Why?

Key terms

Bona fide occupational qualification (BFOQ)

Dothard v. Rawlinson (1977)

Eighth Amendment

Equal Employment Opportunity Act of 1972

Fourth Amendment

Prison matron

Probation

Qualitative

Restorative justice

Sexual harassment

Smith v. Fairman (1982)

Somers v. Thurman (1983)

Stereotypes

Title VII of the Civil Rights Act of 1964

References

Acker, Joan. 1992. *Gendered Organizational Analysis*. Thousand Oaks, CA: Sage.

Aggrawal, Anil. 2010. *Necrophilia: Forensic and Medico-legal Aspects*. New York, NY: CRC Press.

Alleyne, Richard. June 8, 2012. "Prison Guards Caught Having 'Inappropriate Relationships' with Inmates." *Telegraph*. Accessed August 11, 2014, http://www.telegraph.co.uk/news/uknews/9318554/Prison-guards-caught-having-inappropriate-relationships-with-inmates.html

Armstrong, Jeremy. January 7, 2012. "Prisoner Who Stabbed Warden with Broken Bottle Let Off After Claiming 'Stress.'" *Daily Mirror*. Accessed August 11, 2014, http://www.mirror.co.uk/news/uk-news/prisoner-who-stabbed-warden-broken-157418#ixzz3A6f24zdm

Associated Press. January 7, 2013. "At Iowa Prison, Female Officer Says Inmates Harassed Her After Watching Violent & Sexually Graphic Movies. *New York Daily News*. Accessed October 2, 2013, http://www.nydailynews.com/news/national/prison-inmates-watched-violent-sexually-explicit-movies-article-1.1234724#ixzz2hXcrViyu

Blair, Allyson, and Steve Stout. August 8, 2013. "Arizona Corrections Officer Brutally Beaten by Inmates." *CBS 5, KPHO*. Accessed August 13, 2014, http://www.kpho.com/story/22926300/az-female-corrections-officer-nearly-beaten-to-death-by-inmates

Bonczar, Thomas P. 2008. "Characteristics of State Parole Supervising Agencies, 2006." Washington, DC: US Department of Justice. Accessed November 5, 2013, http://www.bjs.gov/content/pub/pdf/cspsa06.pdf

Boyd, Elizabeth, and Tim Grant. 2005. "Is Gender a Factor in Perceived Prison Officer Competence? Male Prisoners' Perceptions in an English Dispersal Prison." *Criminal Behaviour and Mental Health*, 15(1): 65–74.

Britton, Dana M. 1997. "Perceptions of the Work Environment Among Correctional Officers: Do Race and Sex Matter?" *Criminology*, 35(1): 85–105.

Britton, Dana M. 1999. "Cat Fights and Gang Fights: Preference for Work in a Male-Dominated Organization." *The Sociological Quarterly*, 40 (3): 455–474.

Britton, Dana M. 2003. *At Work in the Iron Cage: The Prison as Gendered Organization*. New York, NY: New York University Press.

Bureau of Justice Statistics. 2014. *Census of Adult Probation Supervising Agencies, 2014*. Washington, DC. Acccessed on February 11, 2016, www.bjs.gov/content/capsa.cfm#publication

Bureau of Labor Statistics. 2015. *Occupational Handbook, 2016–2017 Edition: Correctional Officers and Bailiffs*. Accessed February 10, 2016, http://www.bls.gov/ooh/protective-service/correctional-officers.htm

Carlson, Joseph R., Thomas, George, and Richard H. Anson. 2004. "Cross-Gender Perceptions of Corrections Officers in Gender-Segregated Prisons." *Journal of Offender Rehabilitation*, 39(1): 83–103. DOI: 10.1300/J076v39n01_05

Chan, Sharon Pian, and Carol M. Ostrom. January 30, 2011. "Monroe Guard Complained bout Working Solo Before Inmate Killed Her." *Seattle Times*. Accessed October 1, 2013, http://seattletimes.com/html/localnews/2014082475_guard31.html

Cheeseman, Kelly Ann. 2012. "Women Working in Corrections: Where Have We Been and Where Are We Going?" *Research Notes, American Correctional Association*. Accessed October 22, 2013, https://www.aca.org/research/pdf/ResearchNotes_December2012.pdf

Cheeseman, K. A., and W. Goodlin-Fahncke. 2011. "Women Working Within the Walls: The Effect of Gender on Correctional Employee Perceptions of Work Stress." *Corrections Compendium*, 35(2): 1–7, 18–19.

Chorley, Matt. October 18, 2013. "'I Almost Died': Prison Officer Stabbed in the Back by Inmate with Broken Chili Sauce Bottle on Why Ministers Are Right Finally to Issue Stab Proof Vests to All Jail Staff." *Daily Mail*. Accessed August 11, 2014, http://www.dailymail.co.uk/news/

article-2465793/I-died-Prison-officer-stabbed-killer-broken-chilli-sauce-bottle-ministers-right-FINALLY-issue-stab-proof-vests-jail-staff.html

Cook, Nancy. 2005. "Women in Corrections: An Essential Asset." *Corrections Today*, 67(6), 8.

Cornejo, AnnMarie. May 2, 2010. "First Female Warden in Charge at California Men's Colony." *Tribune*. Accessed November 15, 2013, http://www.sanluisobispo.com/2010/05/02/1125046/first-female-warden-in-charge.html

Crewe, Ben. 2006. "Male Prisoners' Orientations Towards Female Officers in an English Prison." *Punishment and Society*, 8(4): 395–421. DOI: 10.1177/1462474506067565

Dothard v. Rawlinson. 1977.

Dui Hua Foundation. August 28, 2011. "Surging Numbers of Women in Prison Present Unique Challenges." *Human Rights Journal Blog*. Accessed August 13, 2014, http://www.duihuahrjournal.org/2011/08/surging-numbers-of-women-in-prison.html

Elmore, Christina. September 22, 2013. "Guarding Prisoners: Women Tackle One of the Toughest Jobs on Earth." *Post and Courier*. Accessed November 15, 2013, http://www.postandcourier.com/article/20130922/PC16/130929892

Federal Bureau of Prisons. 2003. *Sourcebook of Criminal Justice Statistics, 2003*. Accessed October 17, 2013, http://www.albany.edu/sourcebook/pdf/t1107.pdf

Feinman, Clarice. 1994. *Women in the Criminal Justice System*, 3rd edn. Westport, CT: Praeger.

Feuer, Alan. October 7, 2007. "Guard Awarded $850,000 Over Sexual Harassment." *New York Times*. Accessed August 13, 2014, http://www.nytimes.com/2007/10/12/nyregion/12harass.html?_r=0

Flesher, Flyn. 2007. "Cross-Gender Supervision in Prison and the Constitutional Right of Prisoners to Remain Free from Rape." *William & Mary Journal of Women and the Law*, 13(3): 841–866.

Freedman, Estelle. 1981. *Their Sister's Keepers: Women's Prison Reform in America, 1830–1930*. Ann Arbor, MI: University of Michigan Press.

Gomez del Prado, Gregory. 2012. "Intimidation in Prison: Effect on the Professional Practices of Correctional Officers from Québec." *Criminology*, 45(2): 301–322.

Gordon, Jill A., Proulx, Blythe, and Patricia H. Grant. 2012. "Trepidation Among the 'Keepers': Gendered Perceptions of Fear and Risk of Victimization Among Corrections Officers." *American Journal of Criminal Justice*, 38: 245–265. DOI 10.1007/s12103-012-9167-1

Griffin, Marie L. 2006. "Gender and Stress: A Comparative Assessment of Sources of Stress Among Correctional Officers." *Journal of Contemporary Criminal Justice*, 22(5): 4–25. DOI: 10.1177/1043986205285054

Gunnison, Elaine, and Jacqueline B. Helfgott. 2013. *Offender Reentry: Beyond Crime and Punishment*. Boulder, CO: Lynne Rienner.

Hahn, Valerie Schremp. May 28, 2014. "First Female Warden of Maximum Security Menard Prison Worked Way Up in System." *St. Louis Post-Dispatch*. Accessed August 13, 2014, http://www.stltoday.com/news/local/illinois/first-female-warden-of-maximum-security-menard-prison-worked-way/article_191939d0-a181-544f-99f4-f5848608f7d8.html

Harrell, Erika. 2011. *Workplace Violence, 1993–2009*. Washington, DC: Bureau of Justice Statistics. Accessed August 11, 2014, http://www.bjs.gov/content/pub/pdf/wv09.pdf

Harrison, Jill, and Kelsey A. Kanoff. 2010. "Perceptions of Sexual Harassment on the Inside." *Corrections Compendium*, 35(1): 8–15.

Hutchinson, Lisa. November 13, 2011. "Frankland Prison Guard Speaks of Attack by Killer." *Chronicle*. Accessed August 11, 2014, http://www.chroniclelive.co.uk/news/north-east-news/frankland-prison-guard-speaks-attack-1407014

Ireland, Connie, and Bruce Berg. 2006. "Women in Parole: Gendered Adaptations of Female Parole Agents in California." *Women & Criminal Justice*, 18(1/2): 131–150. DOI: 10.1300/J012v18n01_05

Ireland, Connie, and Bruce Berg. 2008. "Women in Parole: Respect and Rapport." *International Journal of Offender Therapy and Comparative Criminology*, 52(4): 474–491. DOI: 10.1177/0306624X07307782

Jenne, Denise L., and Robert C. Kersting. 1996. "Aggression and Women Correctional Officers in Male Prisons." *The Prison Journal*, 76(4): 442–460. DOI: 10.1177/0032855596076004005

Jurik, Nancy. 1985. "An Officer and a Lady: Organizational Barriers to Women Working as Correctional Officers in Men's Prisons." *Social Problems*, 32(4): 375–388.

Jurik, Nancy. 1988. "Striking a Balance: Female Correctional Officers, Gender Role Stereotypes, and Male Prisons." *Sociological Inquiry*, 58(3): 291–305. DOI: 10.1111/j.1475-682X.1988.tb01063.x

Kim, Ann-Shik, Devalve, Michael, Devalve, Elizabeth Q., and W. Wesley Johnson. 2003. "Female Wardens: Results from a National Survey of State Correctional Executives." *The Prison Journal*, 83: 406–425. DOI: 10.1177/0032885503260176

Latessa, Edward J., and Paula Smith. 2011. *Corrections in the Community*, 4th edn. Cincinnati, OH: Anderson.

Lei, Cheng, Lu, Xiaogang, and Chen Jianjun. February 26, 2014. "Research Report on the Treatment of Women Detainees in China – Using the Bangkok Rules as the Starting Point of Analysis." Paper presented at Women in Prison: An International Symposium on the Bangkok Rules. Accessed August 13, 2014, http://www.duihua.org/wipconference/cheng_en.pdf

Maghan, Jess, and Leasa McLeish-Blackwell. 1991. "Black Women in Correctional Employment." In *Change, Challenge, and Choices: Women's Role in Modern Corrections*, edited by Joann B. Morton, 82–99. Laurel, MD: American Correctional Association.

Mallory, Christy, Hasenbush, A., and Brad Sears. 2013. *Discrimination Against Law Enforcement Officers on the Basis of Sexual Orientation and Gender Identity: 2000 to 2013*. University of California, Williams Institute. Accessed August 14, 2014, http://williamsinstitute.law.ucla.edu/wp-content/uploads/Law-Enforcement-Discrim-Report-Nov-2013.pdf

Martin, Susan E., and Nancy C. Jurik. 1996. *Doing Justice, Doing Gender: Women in Law and Criminal Justice Occupations*. Thousand Oaks, CA: Sage.

Matthews, Cassandra, Monk-Turner, Elizabeth, and Melvina Sumter. 2010. "Promotional Opportunities: How Women in Corrections Perceive Their Chances for Advancement at Work." *Gender Issues*, 27(1–2): 53–66. DOI: 10.1007/s12147-010-9089-5

Miles, Deborah E. March 2013. "First Female, African-American Parole Officer in NY Remains an Inspiration. *The Communicator*. Accessed November 7, 2013, http://www.thecommunicator.org/032013/paroleafricanamericanwomen.htm

Miletich, Steve. May 15, 2013. "State Prison Inmate Sentenced to Death in Murder of Guard." *Seattle Times*. Accessed October 2, 2013, http://seattletimes.com/html/localnews/2020993936_scherfverdictxml.html

Miner, Maude E. 1910. "Probation Work for Women." *Annals of the American Academy of Political and Social Science*, 36(1): 27–36.

Misis, Marcos, Binta, Kim, Cheeseman, Kelly, Hogan, Nancy L., and Eric G. Lambert. 2013. "The Impact of Correctional Officer Perceptions of Inmates on Job Stress." *Sage Open*, 3: 1–13. DOI: 10.1177/2158244013489695

Newbold, Greg. 2005. "Women Officers Working in Men's Prisons." *Social Policy Journal of New Zealand*, 25: 105–117.

Nink, Carl. 2008. *Women Professionals in Corrections: A Growing Asset*. Centerville, UT: MTC Institute. Accessed November 11, 2013, http://www.mtctrains.com/public/uploads/1/2010/10/Women-ProfessionalsInCorrections-Aug08.pdf

Patenaude, Allan L. 2004. "No Promises, But I'm Willing to Listen and Tell What I Hear: Conducting Qualitative Research Among Prison Inmates and Staff." *The Prison Journal*, 84(4): 69S–91S. DOI: 10.1177/0032885504269898

Pearlman, Eve. March 20, 2012. "Deputy Files Sexual Harassment Lawsuit Against Chief Probation Officer." *Alameda Patch*. Accessed October 15, 2013, http://alameda.patch.com/groups/politics-and-elections/p/deputy-files-sexual-harassment-lawsuit-against-chief-3677a5ded6

Peterson, Cheryl B. 1982. "Doing Time with the Boys: An Analysis of Women Correctional Officers in All Male Facilities. In *The Criminal Justice System and Women*, edited by Barbara R. Price and Natalie J. Sokloff, 399–412. New York, NY: Clark Boardman.

Petrillo, Madeline. 2007. "Power Struggle: Gender Issues for Female Probation Officers in the Supervision of High Risk Offenders." *Probation Journal*, 54: 394–406. DOI: 10.1177/0264550507083538

Pogrebin, Mark R., and Eric D. Poole. 1997. "The Sexualized Work Environment: A Look at Women Jail Officers." *Prison Journal*, 77: 41–57. DOI: 10.1177/0032855597077001004

Pollock, Joyceln M. 2004. *Prisons and Prison Life: Costs and Consequences*. Los Angeles, CA: Roxbury Publishing Company.

Rader, Nicole E. 2007. "Surrendering Solidarity: Considering the Relationships Among Female Correctional Officers." *Women and Criminal Justice*, 16(3): 27–42. DOI: 10.1300/J012v16n03_02

Rafter, Nicole H. 1985. "Gender, Prisons, and Prison History." *Social Science History*, 9(3): 233–247.

Root, William T. 1932. "The Prison Warden of the Future." *The Prison Journal*, 12: 3–7.

Savicki, Victor, Cooley, Eric, and Jennider Gjesvold. 2003. "Harassment as a Predictor of Job Burnout in Correctional Officers." *Criminal Justice and Behavior*, 30(5): 602–619.

Sederstrom, Jotham. October 15, 2008. "Probation Officer Kills Self in Office." *New York Daily News*. Accessed August 13, 2014, http://www.nydailynews.com/news/probation-officer-kills-office-article-1.298748

Smith v. Fairman. 1982.

Smith, Brenda V. 2012. "Uncomfortable Places, Close Spaces: Female Correctional Workers' Sexual Interactions with Men and Boys in Custody." *UCLA Law Review*, 59: 1690–1745.

Somers v. Thurman. 1983.

Stout, Ellis. 1973. "Women in Probation and Parole: Should Female Officers Supervise Male Offenders?" *Crime & Delinquency*, 19: 61–71. DOI: 10.1177/001112877301900108

Sun, Key. 2013. *Correctional Counseling: A Cognitive Growth Perspective*. Burlington, MA: Jones & Barlett.

Wagner, Meg. May 13, 2014. "Florida Prison Guard Says 17 Inmates Assaulted Her; Supervisors Took 73 Days to Report Attack." *New York Daily News*. Accessed August 11, 2014, http://www.nydailynews.com/news/crime/jail-73-days-report-sexual-attack-officer-report-article-1.1790323#ixzz3A6lU9OLH

Walters, Stephen, and David Lagace. 1999. "Gender Differences in Occupational Characteristics of Canadian Correctional Officers." *International Journal of Comparative and Applied Criminal Justice*, 23(1): 45–53. DOI: 10.1080/01924036.1999.9678632

Wells, Terry, Colbert, Sharla, and Risdon N. Slate. 2006. "Gender Matters: Differences in State Probation Officer Stress." *Journal of Contemporary Criminal Justice*, 22: 63–79. DOI: 10.1177/1043986205285381

Winter, Michael. April 23, 2013. "Baltimore Guards, Inmates Indicted for Gang Corruption." *USA Today*. Accessed October 16, 2013, http://www.usatoday.com/story/news/nation/2013/04/23/baltimore-plot-smuggle-contraband-jail/2107523/

Yang, Mugao. 2012. *Chinese Female Offenders: Corrections System Research*. Nanjing, China: Nanjing University Press.

Zimmer, Lynn. 1986. *Women Guarding Men*. Chicago, IL: University of Chicago Press.

Zoukis, Christopher. April 9, 2015. "Forty Defendants, Including 24 Guards, Convicted in Widespread Corruption Scandal at Baltimore City Jail." *Prison Legal News*. Accessed March 27, 2016, https://www.prisonlegalnews.org/news/2015/apr/9/forty-defendants-including-24-guards-convicted-widespread-corruption-scandal-baltimore-city-jail/

Zupan, Linda Z. 1992. "The Progress of Women Correctional Officers in All-Male Prisons." In *The Changing Roles of Women in the Criminal Justice System*, edited by Imogene L. Moyer, 232–244. Prospect Heights, IL: Waveland Press.

CHAPTER 11

Conclusion

Student learning outcomes

After reading this chapter, you should be able to:
- Discuss issues pertaining to women offenders.
- Discuss issues pertaining to women as victims of crime.
- Discuss issues pertaining to women professionals in the criminal justice system.

Introduction

Ray Rice, a National Football League (NFL) player for the Baltimore Ravens, was arrested on February 15, 2014. Since his arrest, the relationship between Ray Rice and his fiancée at the time, Janay Palmer, and the relationship among the news media, the public, and law enforcement have come under scrutiny. His arrest brought public attention to the issue of domestic violence when the public saw for themselves in September of 2014 a recorded video of the incident. The slowly rolled-out information and video called into question whether policies and laws can abate domestic violence or if social media and community commentary must occur before something is done about violence against women and children.

The NFL is a league that made over $9 billion in 2013 (Burke 2013), and football stars can earn a tremendous amount of money during the time that they play on professional teams. Among the top three 2014 salaried players were Jay Cutler (Chicago, $17,500,000 base), Eli Manning (New York, $15,150,000 base) and, Peyton Manning (Denver, $15,000,000 base). If Rice had been able to play in 2014, his base salary would have been $3,529,412 (Sportrac 2014). Because NFL stars also get endorsement deals with companies to promote their products, the amount of revenue earned by players can be staggeringly high. Consequently, it is in the League's interest to respond to public concerns about players on and off the field. Companies that contract with the NFL and its players want to secure a strong image when their products are advertised. Since half of the fans of the game are women, the image that women have of the NFL is also important to the League because it does not want to lose revenue if players are viewed as violent off the field.

In 2006, the NFL elected Roger Goodell to be its commissioner and since that time the League has had 57 players accused of domestic violence. While the League's policies aim to punish players who commit offenses, including domestic violence, the League has handled domestic violence by players inconsistently over the years (Keneally 2014). Keneally reports that 10 players were cut from their teams, 12 were suspended, and 34 cases of domestic violence went without any punishment

Women, Crime, and Justice, First Edition. By Elaine Gunnison, Frances P. Bernat, and Lynne Goodstein.
© 2017 John Wiley & Sons, Ltd. Published 2017 by John Wiley & Sons, Ltd.

from the League after Goodell became commissioner. In the first eight months of 2014, four players were charged with a domestic violence crime; as the public became captivated by NFL player violence, more players came under scrutiny in September 2014. Adrian Peterson, for example, was suspended indefinitely when allegations of child abuse arose (McLaughlin and Payne 2014). Peterson was indicted on September 12, 2014, for felonious injury to his child; he hit his 4-year-old son with a tree branch, which caused broken skin and other injuries in June of 2014 (Good 2014; Rosenthal 2014). Eventually, he pled no contest to a misdemeanor offense (ESPN, NFL 2014). Jonathan Dwyer was arrested on September 18, 2014, for aggravated assault on a woman and her toddler in his home in July; the team response to the arrest was to immediately deactivate him (Weinfuss 2014). On the heels of the public attention to and condemnation of NFL player violence and the League's vacillating response to arrests of players, Goodell decided to have four female experts in the field of violence against women review NFL policies and practices. Goodell said, "Because domestic violence and sexual assault are broad societal issues, we have engaged leading experts to provide specialized advice and guidance in ensuring that the NFL's programs reflect the most current and effective approaches" (Breech 2014).

So why now? What has happened since February 2014 to bring attention to the NFL and how it responds to family violence? On Valentine's Day, 2014, Rice and his then fiancée, Janay, were in Atlantic City. While in a hotel elevator, a fight occurred. Elevator video footage that was released in September of 2014 showed Janay slapping Rice. Rice responded to the slaps with a quick blow to Janay's head. She fell down, unconscious. After the serious blow to Janay, Rice was heard telling hotel staff that she was drunk and needed to be brought to her room. The staffers said that they did not see any injuries to her because her hair covered much of her face; however, upon awaking she reportedly said, "how can you do this to me" and Rice called someone to let them know that he was going to be arrested by the police (McIntyre 2014). The hotel staff called the police, saying a domestic dispute had happened. After she was taken to a hospital, both Rice and Janay told similar stories about the injury. Because Rice is a football star – he ranks third on the team's all-time rushing list and ranks fifth for all-time touchdowns – his arrest made news media take notice (*TMZ* 2014). A few days after the incident, a criminal complaint was filed and a video of Rice dragging a woman from a hotel elevator was released to the public by *TMZ* (Duggan 2014; *TMZ* 2014). *TMZ* is a television show devoted to rooting out scandals and showing the public juicy news footage of stars and celebrities in compromising situations. *TMZ* is credited with keeping the story in the news while reporters sought video footage about what had happened inside the elevator. A month after the assault, Rice and Janay were married.

Rice and his wife have presented a solid front to the public and say that they are a loving couple. Janay Palmer Rice wants to put the assault behind her and does not understand why the public will not let the incident be put to rest (Fowler and Keating 2014). Initially, Rice and Janay were both arrested because she admitted to slapping him, but this was before a video from inside the elevator was made public. *TMZ*, realizing that there was a story to be told because the initial video showed Janay to be passed out cold when Rice pulled her from the elevator, kept digging for video from inside the elevator. During the summer months, as *TMZ* kept the public informed about the arrest of Rice, the NFL responded by suspending Rice for two games. The NFL has a policy regarding player behavior and against domestic violence to make sure that players have high standards of personal conduct, both on the field and off (Edelman 2014). The policy, however, had been inconsistently applied (Table 11.1).

When the video footage from inside the elevator was finally aired on television, the public saw Rice deliver a very strong blow to a woman's head, knocking her out cold; the public demanded action. The public also demanded answers as to how much information the NFL had prior to its two-day suspension of Rice. The two-day suspension seemed like a minor penalty for such a serious

Table 11.1 NFL arrests database: *San Diego Union-Tribune*, September 16, 2014. Adapted from a compilation by Brent Schrotenboer and Merrie Monteagudo – it only shows DV arrests between January 1 and August 31, 2014.

Date	Team	Name	Incident	Resolution
8/31/2014	NY Jets	Quincy Enunwa	Arrested and charged with domestic violence and simple assault after an incident with a woman in a New Jersey hotel room.	
8/31/2014	San Francisco	Ray McDonald	Arrested on suspicion of felony domestic violence in San Jose.	
5/13/2014	Carolina	Greg Hardy	Arrested on two misdemeanor charges after he allegedly assaulted and threatened his ex-girlfriend.	Convicted July 16. Given 18 months' probation and 60-day jail sentence (suspended). Sentence on hold pending Nov. 17 jury trial.
2/15/2014	Baltimore	Ray Rice	Arrested and charged with simple assault after he allegedly struck fiancée Janay Palmer in an Atlantic City casino elevator. A grand jury indicted him on a more serious count of aggravated assault in March.	Ravens cut Rice; NFL suspended him indefinitely after a video of the incident was made public in Sept.

Source: Reproduced with permission of San Diego Union-Tribune.

violent offense. Consequently, the NFL imposed another sanction that indefinitely suspended Rice from the League and he was released by his team. To respond to media coverage on the incident and public pressure, the NFL commissioner also formed a group of experts, under the leadership of the company's vice president of community affairs and philanthropy, to advise the agency on policies and programs to respond to domestic violence and sexual assault (Sifferlin 2014). But the public, during the Fall, 2014, consistently demanded answers by the NFL about how much information they had prior to the initial suspension of Rice, how much violence is perpetrated off field by players, and why the NFL was not taking violence against women seriously. The NFL's public admission in September, 2014, that they made a mistake in not suspending Rice indefinitely earlier in the summer was meant to appease the public and business sponsors. Some reports show that the League had learned that Rice was charged with a felonious assault in violation of its policy and had seen the video from inside the elevator prior to the two-day suspension (McManus 2014). However, the League maintained that it was only after the elevator video came to light that the two-day ban was changed to an indefinite suspension of Rice from the League. Upon appeal of his indefinite ban, Rice won reinstatement and began seeking to be picked up as a free agent by another team (Busbee 2014).

Crime is ubiquitous and every day you see reports in the news about crime somewhere in your community or around the world. Crime stories sell papers, and attract our attention on social media sites and in television news shows. Headlines that particularly attract our attention deal with violence or children. One such report was entitled "Three Italian Nuns Found Murdered in Burundi Parish, Authorities Say" (*New York Daily News* 2014). Another report mentions that video of an assault on shoppers by teenagers in the United States can be seen by clicking on a video taken by a cell phone (Caulfield 2014). What is not surprising is that the offenders of these violent crimes are predominately male and that the victims in these stories are male or female, child or adult.

In the United States, professional athletes have been provided social prestige and social status. With their athletic prowess comes fame, money, and an avenue into the social elite. Many of these professional athletes come from poor and working-class families. They competed in college sports on athletic scholarships and are thrust into a limelight because they evidence the best of the best in athletic skill. Devoted fans love their professional and college teams and star athletes. However, these athletes, like the rest of society, are subject to the same laws, same social views and same social pressures as everyone else. They can commit crime and they can be victims of crime. As heroes, they have fans who detest them when they do wrong and fans who will love and support them even if they commit violent crimes. It is time to analyze how society is going to handle crimes against women and children. It is time to stop blaming victims, even if they do not wish to prosecute offenders. It is time for each of us to know more about the context of women and crime and respond with informed analysis of what works and what does not.

 CASE STUDY: The Australian rugby team and group sex session

US football players are not the only famous athletes who perpetrate crimes against women. In 2002, allegations of a group sexual assault surfaced by a 19-year-old New Zealand woman against 11 members of an Australian rugby football team, the Cronulla Sharks (Nurka 2013). The players were on a pre-season tour in New Zealand when the incident occurred at a hotel. The victim was invited to the hotel room by two players. Over the next two hours, she was sexually assaulted by 12 members of the team (players and staff), many of them apparently presuming she was consenting to the "group sex session" (Nurka 2013). While the sexual assault was investigated in both New Zealand and Australia, no charges were filed against any of the perpetrators (Nurka 2013). Given the celebrity status of the rugby players, their cases made national and international headlines.

The depictions of crime and victimization presented in this and the foregoing chapters help to highlight what we know about gender and crime. They also help to bring to light the neglected analysis of women and crime from both a domestic and international point of view.

Purpose of this text

There are over 7 billion people in the world; most of the population growth occurred after 1800 when the world's population was estimated to be 1 billion. In 10 years, by 2024, the world population is expected to reach 8 billion people (US Census Bureau 2014; Worldometers 2014). Internationally, there are approximately 100 girls for every 101 boys, or, stated another way, about half the world's population is female (US Census Bureau 2014). As the world population grows and the nexus among nations and economies becomes intertwined, we need to consider what to do about vulnerable populations; among these vulnerable people are females whose victimizations may be discounted because they are female. Such a dismissal of female victimization occurs when social and cultural norms discount the lives of people that they consider to be inferior or that they consider should be blamed for what happens to them. Victim blaming is reinforced by laws that create gender inequalities. Looking at crime and victimization from a male perspective of crime prevents nuanced understanding of the cultural and social limitations placed on females as offenders, victims, and workers in the criminal justice system (Figure 11.1).

Figure 11.1 International Women's Day logo used in 2011 for global UNHCR operations. *Source:* Prawny Clipart Cartoons and Vintage Illustrations.

In some countries, gender inequality exists because of policies or laws that impact childbirth and child-rearing. For example, China's one-child policy negatively impacts girl births and results in more female baby deaths and the sale of females into sexual slavery. In other nations, a gender imbalance may occur during times of war, in which case there may be more males killed than females, but females may be kidnapped, raped, and sold. If you consider specific forms of crime and victimization that pertain to gendered power imbalances, females tend to be negatively impacted more than males for certain offenses regardless of country of origin (e.g., sex trafficking, prostitution, and domestic violence). To address issues of gender, crime, and justice, this text looked at three salient criminal justice concerns: women as offenders, women as victims, and women as professionals in the criminal justice system. We aimed to provide a cross-cultural perspective and to include previously neglected areas of inquiry (e.g., bullying and cybercrime, and international perspectives on criminal justice).

Women, feminist criminology, and criminal justice

We used a feminist lens to analyze the most salient issues facing women and girls and analyzed cultural similarities and differences in our understanding of crime and victimization. We also addressed issues of cross-cultural perspectives of crime and victimization and analyzed criminal justice agency and policy responses to female offenders and victims. On September 20, 2014, actress Emma Watson addressed the United Nations to launch a *He for She* campaign (Watson 2014). The campaign is to acknowledge that feminism is not about hating men, but about female equality and human rights. Men and women are important in the pursuit of justice for victims of crime and oppression; when particular victimizations impact half the world's population, then it is time to stop wondering if it occurs and start eradicating it. Our aim is not to cast blame on any one agency, person, or community; rather, by using a feminist perspective we are able to view the macro-level factors that affect crime and victimization while understanding the localized responses to it at the micro level of analysis. As the saying goes, "think globally and act locally."

 GLOBAL PERSPECTIVES: Islamic feminism in the Middle East

Muslim women in the Middle East still struggle with how to unite to achieve gender equality (Wagner 2012). On the one hand, some Muslim women prefer to adopt a secular feminist approach – the attainment of rights through the lens of Western liberal ideals (Wagner 2012). However, this approach has not been particularly appealing to many Muslim women, given the patriarchal society in which they reside (Wagner 2012). Many in Muslim society, male and female, view secular feminism as a threat to family values and social morals. On the other hand, other Muslim women prefer to utilize an Islamic feminist approach – the attainment of rights in the context of their religion (Wagner 2012). By utilizing an Islamic feminist approach, Muslim women may place themselves in a better position to obtain some sought-after rights, as they can rally both female and male supporters who support equality measures but also want traditional cultural values to be maintained. Regardless of what approach Muslim women may adopt in their quest for equality, they are at grave risk of victimization for pursuing their ideals. It has been reported that in countries such as Egypt, feminists have experienced sexual harassment and sexual violence from the military and media (Wagner 2012). For instance, a campaign of sexual violence was unleashed by the Egyptian government on women activists in 2005 (Wagner 2012). By 2011, the military had implemented virginity tests for female protestors. Egyptian-American Mona Eltahawy, a secular feminist, describes the tests as "nothing more than rape with a foreign object" (Wagner 2012). The media has also been unkind to women activists. It is not uncommon that women activists' names have surfaced in media reports which question their morality or accuse them of some immoral behavior (Wagner 2012). These smear campaigns by the media appear to be pretty successful in causing many Muslim women to shy away from any form of feminist movement.

Concern about women as offenders, victims, and practitioners in the criminal justice system has been growing since the mid-twentieth century. Western nations modified laws to eliminate gender bias and respond to the specific needs of females. In the twenty-first century, many of these legal modifications have been adopted in virtually every nation, as third world nations attempt to gain economic and political support from Western nation partners. The issues that nations have been responding to include how to handle rape and sexual assault, how to reduce domestic violence, how to provide services to poor women and children who are victims of crime, how to assist female offenders and female prison inmates, how to assist women transition out of prison and assist their children while they are incarcerated, and how to adapt traditionally male criminal justice agencies and professions to include women workers. Women, as half the world's population, cannot be ignored and their concerns and experiences must be addressed for social and political justice to be achieved. For hundreds of years, women's stories were muted as the socio-cultural, political, and legal milieu of nations focused on male power and privilege.

⚖️ **SPECIAL LEGAL ISSUES: UN *Bangkok Rules***

To address the significant gaps in the existing international standards for the processing of and treatment of women offenders and prisoners, in 2010, the United Nations passed a resolution called the *United Nations Rules for the Treatment of Female Prisoners and Non-Custodial Measures for Women Offenders* – also known as the *Bangkok Rules* (Penal Reform International 2013). The *Bangkok Rules* are comprised of 70 rules that serve as a guideline for the treatment and care of incarcerated women and include recommendations such as alternatives to the use of incarceration for women; gender-specific programming; provision of adequate health care; humane treatment; and protection from violence (Penal Reform International 2013). The adoption of a global policy sends a powerful message that women matter, no matter who they are or where they reside, and allows for a united effort to achieve reforms for *all* women.

During times of war and political unrest, women's victimization (rape, sexual slavery, and murder) have been easily overlooked as inconsequential. When over 200 girls were kidnapped from their school in Nigeria in 2014 because they wanted an education, their plight was condemned worldwide, but the investigation was delayed and then quietly went cold within three months' time. Only the few girls who escaped at the time of the kidnapping are home safe, the rest are still unaccounted for (Onuah 2014). In November, 2014, the leader of the anti-Western group that kidnapped the girls said that the girls would not be returned to their families and that they had been married off to Islamic militant fighters (*ABC News* 2014). Presumably, the marriages are to enable fighters to have children with the girls and build militant communities; additionally, the kidnapping of school girls provides the militant group with an outlet to terrorize girls who seek to become educated.

To address gender inequality and the unique life experiences of women and girls, criminology must examine gender as an important factor that impacts individuals, families, communities, nations, and international neighbors. When considered as a whole, the experiences of women and girls, men and boys, and the GLBTQ community occur in a gendered context of discrimination, neglect, and ignorance around the world. This text attempted to heighten your awareness of the gendered nature of crime and victimization in order to provide an understanding about why the needs of women and girls cannot be dismissed any more. The Nigerian school girls cannot be dismissed or forgotten because it seems impossibly difficult to infiltrate political militant groups who abuse girls for power and their own ill. Until the gendered nature of female and male offending patterns is understood and how these patterns feed into victimization, then legal and political policies and changes will not be enough to respond to the cries of help from women and their families around the globe.

TEXT BOX: International Women's Day 2015 Theme: MAKE IT HAPPEN

Each year International Women's Day (IWD) is celebrated on March 8. The first International Women's Day was held in 1911. Thousands of events occur to mark the economic, political and social achievements of women. Organisations, governments, charities, educational institutions, women's groups, corporations and the media celebrate the day.

(continued)

Various organisations identify their own International Women's Day theme, specific to their local context and interests. Many charities, NGOs and Governments also adopt a relevant theme or campaign to mark the day. For example, organisations like the UN, Oxfam, Women for Women, Care International, Plan, World Association of Girl Guides & Girl Scouts (WAGGGS) and more – run exciting and powerful campaigns that raise awareness and encourage donations for good causes. The UN has been declaring an annual equality theme for many years.

Source: http://www.internationalwomensday.com/theme.asp. Accessed June 2, 2015.

Filling the gaps and suggestions for change

In the twentieth century, there was concern that women were becoming more aggressive and that the women's movement was responsible for female crime and victimization. Indeed, it was posited that if women became more "male-like" through the female liberation movement, then women would behave more like men and engage in similar patterns of crime. That is, women would become more aggressive and violent (e.g., Adler 1975; Pollock 1950), or become more available to committing property crime if they were no longer bound to the home environment (e.g., Simon 1975). Women were blamed for hiding their violence, because they were thought to be biologically predisposed from an early age to be devious – they could, after all, as Pollock (1950) claimed, hide their periods and so, too, women could cunningly hide their criminality. Without contrary views of women, early criminological theorists were able to frame a view of women which was based on the lack of scientific knowledge about the nature and context of crime and gender.

Those early theories which blamed women's biology or attributed female crime to the women's liberation movement were not substantiated by academic inquiry. Pollock, Adler, and Simon's works challenged the field of criminal justice to examine more closely the issue of gender and crime. A seminal piece of writing, and one that inspired feminist criminology, was "The Etiology of Female Crime: A Review of the Literature," by Dorie Klein (1973). Klein exposed sexism (and racism) as the root of discriminatory theories and treatment of women offenders. She argued that the female offender is not physically or psychologically different than other females and that to analyze female crime will require criminologists to pay attention to the socio-legal and economic factors that impact a person's relation to the state: the need to survive, to eat, to be human. Crime should neither be analyzed in terms of what is evil or good, nor what is appropriate for one's gender; rather, criminology needs to break away from the traditional view of females and understand the context of crime when addressing issues of class, gender, and race (Klein 1973; Klein and Kress 2014).

Contrary to Adler and Simon's claims, criminologists studying female offenders and female victims have found that women are neither as violent as men nor commit the same forms of property crime as men. Crime statistics show that women commit less crime than men and comprise less than one-tenth of the world's prison population (Austin, Bloom, and Donahue 1992; Covington 2004; Klein and Kress 2014; UK Aid and Penal Reform International 2013). However, for particular types of crime, females are more likely to be offenders (shoplifting, prostitution, and check fraud) or the recipients of violence (family homicide, domestic abuse, rape and sexual assault, cyberstalking and stalking, and sexual harassment). Women's poverty and need for money are associated with offending patterns. Convicted women are primarily single heads of households responsible for the care of their children; they are poor and undereducated. They are not feminists who are challenging political and economic inequities; rather, these women are tied to their neighborhoods and families and seeking to get by on a day-to-day basis. If imprisoned, the women worry about their children and how they will manage upon release; they may have drug and alcohol dependencies and suffer from emotional abuse and depression. Research, as discussed in earlier chapters, shows that there is a strong connection between female offending and female victimization. Many women in prison have histories of family violence and were victims of sexual assault. Female victims may experience depression, suicidal tendencies, and become reclusive, and the impact of domestic violence can be felt from one generation to another. When rape and battering offenses are accompanied by global atrocities, the impact can be felt internationally through forced migrations, sexual and labor trafficking, the spread of infections and disease, increased poverty, and illiteracy (see Bedont and Martinez 1999).

If we look at the collective work of Joanne Belknap, Meda Chesney-Lind, Kathleen Daly, Jeanne Flavin, Lorraine Gelsthorpe, Nancy Jurik, Barbara Koons-Witt, Catherine MacKinnon, James Messerschmidt, Jody Miller, Merry Morash, Joycelyn Pollock, Nicole Hahn Rafter, Claire Renzetti, Darrell Steffensmeier, amongst many other feminist criminologists and scholars,[1] we understand that crime and victimization are not distinct categories. We also begin to understand that a feminist lens helps to explain how these categories intersect when females are oppressed by social, cultural, and legal institutions. The response to these issues requires us to challenge oppression by integrating our knowledge about gender, crime, and victimization. Mainstream criminology has limited our understanding of women and crime because it has not provided a bridge to understand the nexus between crime and victimization, and regards sex and gender as a singular unit by applying what is known about male criminality to females (Britton 2000; Flavin 2001).

To address gender differences requires criminologists to create sophisticated models of crime, gender, race, and victimization (see Britton 2000). Stephanie Fohring (2015), for example, developed an integrated model of victimization to bridge the fields of psychology and criminal justice. She utilized both qualitative and quantitative data to assess a victimization program in Scotland and found that multiple theories and models are needed to develop models of crime and victimization reporting patterns. She found that victims may use a variety of cognitive tools to prevent having a victim label. Many of the respondents, for example, downplayed the victimization incident by saying that it was trivial; other respondents said that the incident was less serious than what might have happened to other victims of crime. These cognitive defensive tools to minimize a victimization experience result in the victims also avoiding making a report to the police. If community agencies are to help victims, then simplistic models will fail to address the needs of violent crime victims and fail to understand the needs of individual victims. Integrated models which utilize multiple theoretical frames, address the policies and political power structures, address the individual pre- and post-crime needs of victims, and include gender as a social and cultural construct that is different from sex can help provide much needed answers to what social and legal changes must occur when responding to women in the criminal justice system. As Flavin (2001, 276–277) asserts, "overcoming androcentric theorizing involves more than simply extending theories designed to explain male criminality to women or presenting theories in gender-neutral terms. It requires recognizing gender as a social process relevant to the actions of men as well as women." The point is that women are not a singular unit and should not be viewed and treated as "males" in the criminal justice system.

Legal changes

One method of remedying gender disparity, gender inequity, and gender discrimination in the legal system is to modify laws. At the international level, a major change occurred when in 2002 the Rome Statute became effective. The **Rome Statute** is a treaty that was created by signatory state parties in 1998 and formed the **International Criminal Court (ICC)** (see Rome Statute 2002). The ICC handles major criminal violations when states (nations) are unable or unwilling to prosecute offenses. Among the offenses that are prosecutable in the ICC are the crimes of genocide, crimes against humanity, and war crimes (Article 5). In Articles 7 and 8, the Rome Statute specifies that crimes of rape, sexual slavery, enforced sterilization, forced pregnancy, forced prostitution, and other gender-specific offenses are crimes against humanity (Rome Statute 2002 with amendments). To ensure that the legal system is responsive to women victims, the Rome Statute also provides that judges include male and female jurists, that prosecutors have experience with female victimization, and that staff have an understanding of victim trauma (Bedont and Martinez 1999; Rome Statute 2002, Article 68). Presently, 122 states are parties to the treaty, although several other states (including the United States and Russia) have signed the treaty but have not ratified it (see United Nations, Treaty Collection 2014). To be a party to the treaty means that a state can be brought before the ICC for prosecution of crimes against humanity, war crimes, or genocide. Being a signatory to the treaty indicates that the nation agrees with the ideas of the treaty, but has not agreed to the jurisdiction of the court.

However, legal changes cannot remedy all inequities. The ICC handles major state violations and actions during times of war or when nations are unable or unwilling to prosecute major injustices (crimes against humanity or genocide). Additionally, the ICC cannot force a party to bring an action and cannot force all nations to ratify the treaty. The reach of that law can only go so far as to handle offenses to which signatory parties wish to avail themselves to it and the jurisdiction of the ICC. Such limits are also found within nations. In the United States, for example, if a victim of a crime refuses to report his/her victimization, for whatever reason, then the legal system cannot begin to process the crime. If a crime is reported to the police, the police will need to collect physical and/or testimonial evidence which will enable them to have probable cause to arrest a person. If arrested, the state has to prove criminal responsibility of the accused beyond a reasonable doubt. At each stage in the criminal justice process, evidence may be lost, witnesses may no longer wish to participate in a prosecution, or the trier of fact (e.g., a jury) may not find that the evidence is enough to convict a defendant.

In the criminal prosecution of crimes against women (whether the female is the offender or victim or both), perceptions about the offense and the characterization of the female can impact the outcome of a trial. The law may make a particular activity a crime, but in the prosecution of the offense many extra-legal factors affect the ultimate decision. Among the extra-legal factors that can impact the outcome, as this text has shown, are the race, age, class, and gender of the accused and of the victim. As seen in the Rice situation, as time progresses, the legal and social view of the incident changes. On May 21, 2015, the charges of domestic violence against Ray Rice were dismissed by a judge because Rice completed a pretrial diversion intervention program (Wilson 2014). What happens in the legal system might be based on how the public and media present Rice as the time to make decisions about the criminal charges nears. Perceptions about incidents are not just about the legal rules which define crime but the social and cultural context in which the behavior occurs. Criminal justice policies and laws that aim to be "gender-neutral" end up having a net-widening effect that takes transgressions that were previously viewed as minor and characterizes them as criminal.

While the law might eliminate some injustices, it can create other inequities of scale – it can create or entrench disparity. Research on girls in the juvenile justice system has consistently found that despite gender-neutral language, girls are prosecuted for status offenses (truancy, incorrigibility, being a runaway) and housed in detention facilities more than boys. To remedy such disparity, criminal justice professionals (the police and prosecuting attorneys) sought to proscribe behaviors for boys and girls in similar ways. The result has been an apparent increase in the arrests of girls for minor assaults, although girls are not as violent as boys; the increase in arrests is due to police "boosting" the transgression of minor assault from a status offense to a minor criminal offense (Steffensmeier et al. 2005). Gelsthorpe (2012) points out that the treatment of female offenders must take into account their race, immigration status, and needs. The community and criminal justice system have to work together to be responsive to gender offending patterns and causes and to make appropriate decisions about the suitability of imprisonment for female offenders who are "vulnerable" and/or have been crime victims (Gelsthorpe 2012).

In short, the law can help change inequalities and inequities but it cannot do it alone. People matter. It matters how crime and victimization are conceived, presented, and analyzed. It matters how offenders and victims are viewed, presented, and analyzed. The context of crime, victimization, and people may vary from community to community and nation to nation; but, the view of inequities of scale when gender enters the dialog has had a consistent refrain despite legal changes. Women are demanding that the law and its application respect their humanity, hear their cries for justice, and eliminate barriers to their full participation in their nation states.

Socio-cultural and political change

To begin to achieve legal equality and equity, discriminatory laws should be eliminated. To remedy gender inequality and inequity, the cultural and political norms of a society should be ameliorated to accommodate both females and males. Cultural and political norms that solidify a view of females as inferior to males, that disregard injustices that harm females, and that reinforce patterns of victimization which impact women and children must be changed. Each individual, each societal unit and each governmental entity will need to reframe policies and practices that would otherwise make legal changes insignificant. Change cannot be done solely on legal paper; it has to become tangible and real.

It is fitting that the 2014 International Women's Day Celebration focused on inspiring change. While past themes focused on the ravages of war, rape, female exploitation, and social inequities which disempowered women and girls, the 2014 theme recognized that action requires both a positive world view and an ability to act. The theme for International Women's Day 2015 was "Make It Happen." Changing laws helps to set a base for challenging unfair and discriminatory conditions, always a good place to start to remedy inequities. Changing social norms can be forced when laws and policies no longer support such conditions and inequities. In looking at the NFL and the media coverage on domestic violence during September of 2014 it becomes clear that, but for the *TMZ* footage of Rice hitting a woman in an elevator, the public would not have asked what can be done to abate violence against women and children by our heroes.

Conclusion

A feminist approach to crime and victimization is not about touting women over men, girls over boys. A feminist approach to crime and victimization is about addressing socio-legal-cultural and historical inequities which facilitate violence, poverty, and social injustice. By examining how female offenders and victims are viewed and treated, we can see how societies and cultures maintain or refute gender inequality and inhumanity at the local and global levels.

This text challenges the reader to understand the context of gender, crime, and law. Law cannot be the only answer to addressing gender inequality. As the history of women has shown, changing the law may not change the behavior; as the history of women in the criminal justice system has shown, women may be blamed for their sexual victimization or abuse, women may be blamed for a child's wayward behavior, women may be blamed for not performing at a higher level of work productivity than men if they have children, women may be blamed … To counter these views of females, the challenge is for criminologists to develop internationally appropriate lenses. These lenses must accept that women are not as violent as men, that women are not to be blamed for their victimization, that women offenders are looking to survive, and that women professionals must be incorporated into the fabric of our social and legal institutions.

There is much scholarship that can and should be required reading for persons addressing issues of female crime, female victimization, and female contributions to the criminal justice profession. This text has provided many suggestions to further the discourse. Continued analysis of the intersection of race, class, gender, and crime at the international and domestic levels must occur to redress hundreds of years of misconceptions about women and the inequity that political and social inequality has wrought on half the world's population.

Suggested readings

Feminist Criminology (journal published by Sage Publications).
International Feminist Journal of Politics (journal published by Taylor & Francis).
International Review of Victimology (journal published by Sage Publications).
Women & Criminal Justice (journal published by Taylor & Francis).

Student engagement activities

1 Develop a theme for International Women's Day for your local community.
2 Explain how the intersection of race, class, and gender impacts crime and victimization in your community or nation.
3 Develop a YouTube video that can help explain how women and girls are impacted by crime, as either offenders or victims.
4 Develop a policy for a professional workplace that provides clear consequences for persons who are arrested for domestic violence. Will they be suspended with or without pay? Will they be fired? Will they have a right to appeal the disciplinary decision?
5 Read the recent issues of *Women & Criminal Justice* or *Feminist Criminology*; discuss what the articles are about and how they compare and contrast to the materials found in this text.

Discussion questions

1 How can the media be leveraged to educate society about all acts of violence that impact women – not just those involving celebrities or famous athletes?
2 What is the direction of feminist work currently? What do you think the next step of feminists should be?
3 Can you think of laws, policies, and/or programs that need to be implemented or expanded to assist women as offenders, victims, or working professionals?

Key term

Rome Statute of the International Criminal Court (ICC)

Note

1 We do not wish to diminish any scholar not on the listing provided here. We wish to acknowledge the many contributions to the study of women and crime that many scholars have made by citing various references throughout this text.

References

ABC News. November 1, 2014. "Boko Haram Leader Says Kidnapped Nigerian School Girls Have Been 'Married Off' to Fighters." *ABC News*. Accessed December 3, 2014, http://www.abc.net.au/news/2014-11-02/boko-haram-leader-claims-kidnapped-girls-have-been-married-off/5860332

Adler, Freda. 1975. *Sisters in Crime: The Rise of the New Female Criminal*. New York, NY: McGraw-Hill.

Austin, James, Bloom, Barbara, and Trish Donahue. 1992. *Female Offenders in the Community: An Analysis of Innovative Strategies and Programs*. San Francisco, CA: National Council on Crime and Delinquency.

Bedont, Barbara, and Katherine Hall Martinez. 1999. "Ending Impunity for Gender Crimes Under the International Criminal Court." *The Brown Journal of World Affairs*, VI(1): 65–85.

Breech, John. September 17, 2014. "Cardinals RB Jonathan Dwyer Arrested on Domestic Violence Charge." *CBS Sports*. Accessed September 18, 2014, http://www.cbssports.com/nfl/eye-on-football/24713531/cardinals-rb-jonathan-dwyer-arrested-on-domestic-violence-charge

Britton, Dana M. 2000. "Feminism in Criminology: Engendering the Outlaw." *American Academy of Political and Social Science*, 571(1): 57–76. DOI: 10.1177/000271620057100105

Burke, Monte. August 17, 2013. "How the National Football League Can Reach $25 billion in Annual Revenues." *Forbes*. Accessed September 17, 2014, http://www.forbes.com/sites/monteburke/2013/08/17/how-the-national-football-league-can-reach-25-billion-in-annual-revenues/

Busbee, Jay. November 28, 2014. "Ray Rice Wins Appeal, Eligible to Play." *Yahoo! Sports*. Accessed December 3, 2014, http://sports.yahoo.com/blogs/nfl-shutdown-corner/ray-rice-wins-appeal–eligible-to-play-200153633.html

Caulfield, Philip. September 8, 2014. "Shocking Footage Shows Violent Teen Mob Attacking Shoppers, Workers at Tennessee Grocery Parking Lot (VIDEO). " *New York Daily News*. Accessed September 8, 2014, http://www.nydailynews.com/news/national/violent-teen-mob-attacks-shoppers-workers-tenn-grocery-store-video-article-1.1931987

Covington, Stephanie. S. 2004. "A Woman's Journey Home: Challenges for Female Offenders." In *Prisoners Once Removed: The Impact of Incarceration and Reentry on Children, Families, and Communities*, edited by Jeremy Travis and Michelle Waul, 67–104. Washington, DC: The Urban Institute Press.

Duggan, Dan. February 19, 2014. "Ray Rice Arrest: Police Say Ravens RB Knocked Fiancée Janay Palmer Unconscious in Atlantic City." *NJ.com*. Accessed September 17, 2014, http://www.nj.com/rutgersfootball/index.ssf/2014/02/ray_rice_arrest_police_say_ravens_running_back_knocked_fiancee_janay_palmer_unconscious.html

Edelman, Marc. September 16, 2014. "Why the NFL's Indefinite Ban of Ray Rice Won't Stand." *Forbes*. Accessed September 16, 2014, http://www.forbes.com/sites/marcedelman/2014/09/16/why-the-nfls-indefinite-ban-of-ray-rice-wont-stand/

ESPN, NFL. November 5, 2014. "Peterson Enters No Contest Plea." *ESPN, NFL*. Accessed December 3, 2014, http://espn.go.com/nfl/story/_/id/11819670/adrian-peterson-minnesota-vikings-enter-plea-lesser-charge-felony-child-abuse-charge-avoid-jail

Flavin, Jeanne. 2001. "Feminism for the Mainstream Criminologist: An Invitation." *Journal of Criminal Justice*, 29(4): 271–285. DOI: 10.1016/S0047-2352(01)00093-9

Fohring, Stephanie. 2015. "An Integrated Model of Victimization as an Explanation of Non-involvement with the Criminal Justice System." *International Review of Victimology*, 21(1): 45–70.

Fowler, Tara, and Caitlin Keating. September 14, 2014. "Ray Rice and Wife Step Out Together as Friends Defend Their Marriage." *People*. Accessed September 16, 2014, http://www.people.com/article/ray-rice-janay-rice-friend-loving-couple

Gelsthorpe, Loriane. 2012. "Justice Committee: Written Evidence from Professor Loraine R Gelsthorpe, University of Cambridge." *United Kingdom Parliament*. Accessed December 3, 2014, http://www.publications.parliament.uk/pa/cm201314/cmselect/cmjust/92/92vw42.htm

Good, Dan. September 17, 2014. "Minnesota Vikings Reverse Course, Suspend Adrian Peterson." *ABC News*. Accessed September 17, 2014, http://abcnews.go.com/Sports/minnesota-vikings-reverse-suspend-adrian-peterson/story?id=25557213

Keneally, Meghan. September 19, 2014. "How the NFL Has Punished Players Arrested for Domestic Violence." *ABS News*. Accessed September 19, 2014, https://abcnews.go.com/US/nfl-punished-players-arrested-domestic-violence-goodell-era/story?id=25534452

Klein, Dorie. 1973. "The Etiology of Female Crime: A Review of the Literature." *Crime and Social Justice: Issues in Criminology*, 8(2):3–30.

Klein, Dorie, and June Kress. 2014. "Any Woman's Blues: A Critical Overview of Women, Crime, and the Criminal Justice System." *Social Justice*, 40(1/2): 162–191.

McIntyre, Jason. September 10, 2014. "Janay Rice Told Ray Rice: 'How Could You Do this to Me? I'm the Mother of Your Kid' After She Regained Consciousness." *USA Today Sports*. Accessed September 17, 2014, http://thebiglead.com/2014/09/10/janay-rice-told-ray-rice-how-could-you-do-this-to-me-im-the-mother-of-your-kid-after-she-regained-consciousness/

McLaughlin, Eliott C., and Ed Payne. September 18, 2014. "Vikings: Adrian Peterson Won't Play Until Legal Issues Are Resolved." *CNN*. Accessed September 18, 2014, http://www.cnn.com/2014/09/17/us/adrian-peterson-child-abuse-charges/

McManus, Jane. August 29, 2014. "Severe Penalties for Domestic Violence." *ESPN*. Accessed September 16, 2014, http://espn.go.com/espnw/news-commentary/article/11425377/nfl-implements-domestic-violence-penalties

New York Daily News. September 8, 2014. "Three Italian Nuns Found Murdered in Burundi Parish, Authorities Say." *New York Daily News*. Accessed September 8, 2014, http://www.nydailynews.com/news/world/italian-nuns-found-murdered-parish-article-1.1932004

Nurka, Camille. 2013. "Shame and Disgrace in Australian Football Culture: Rape Claims and Public Affect." *Women's Studies International Forum*, 38: 43–51. DOI: 10.1016/j.wsif.2013.02.003

Onuah, Felix. June 20, 2014. "Nigeria Wraps Up Kidnap Investigation with 200 Girls Still Missing." *Reuters*. Accessed 8, 2014, http://af.reuters.com/article/worldNews/idAFKBN0EV1C420140620

Penal Reform International. 2013. "UN Bangkok Rules on Women Offenders and Prisoners: Short Guide." *UK Aid*. Accessed December 4, 2014, http://www.penalreform.org/wp-content/uploads/2013/07/PRI-Short-Guide-Bangkok-Rules-2013-Web-Final.pdf

Pollock, Otto. 1950. *The Criminality of Women*. Philadelphia, PA: University of Pennsylvania Press.

Rome Statute. 2002. *Rome Statute with Amendments*. Accessed September 15, 2014, http://www.icc-cpi.int/iccdocs/asp_docs/Publications/Compendium/Compendium.3rd.01.ENG.pdf

Rosenthal, Gregg. September 12, 2014. "Vikings' Adrian Peterson Indicted in Child Injury Case." *Around the NFL*. Accessed September 18, 2014, http://www.nfl.com/news/story/0ap3000000393519/article/vikings-adrian-peterson-indicted-in-child-injury-case

Sifferlin, Alexandra. September 15, 2014. "NFL Recruits 4 Women to Advise on Domestic Violence and Sex Assault Policy." *Time*. Accessed September 16, 2014, http://time.com/3378819/nfl-recruits-4-women-to-advise-on-domestic-violence-and-sex-assault-policy/

Simon, Rita. 1975. *Women and Crime*. Lexington, MA: Lexington Books.

Sportrac. 2014. "Top Salary Rankings." *Sportrac*. Accessed September 17, 2014, http://www.sportrac.com/rankings/nfl/

Steffensmeier, Darrell, Schwartz, Jennifer, Zhong, Hua, and Jeff Ackerman. 2005. "An Assessment of Recent Trends in Girls' Violence Using Diverse Longitudinal Sources: Is the Gender Gap Closing?" *Criminology*, 43(2): 355–405. DOI: 10.1111/j.0011-1348.2005.00011.x

TMZ. 2014. "Ray Rice." *TMZ*. Accessed September 16, 2014, http://www.tmz.com/person/ray-rice/

UK Aid and Penal Reform International. 2013. *UN Bangkok Rules on Women Offenders and Prisoners, Short Guide*. Accessed September 15, 2014, http://www.penalreform.org/wp-content/uploads/2013/07/PRI-Short-Guide-Bangkok-Rules-2013-Web-Final.pdf

United Nations, Treaty Collection. 2014. *CHAPTER XVIII Penal Matters; 10. Rome Statute of the International Criminal Court*. Accessed September 15, 2014, https://treaties.un.org/pages/ViewDetails.aspx?src=TREATY&mtdsg_no=XVIII-10&chapter=18&lang=en

US Census Bureau. 2014. *International Data Base World Population by Age and Sex*. Accessed September 4, 2014, https://www.census.gov/population/international/data/idb/worldpop.php

Wagner, Rob L. February 2, 2012. "Islamic Feminism in the Middle East." *International Policy Digest*. Accessed December 4, 2014, http://www.internationalpolicydigest.org/2012/02/02/islamic-feminism-in-the-middle-east/

Watson, Emma. September 22, 2014. "Emma Watson Speaks at UN Women He for She Launch." *YouTube*. Accessed December 3, 2014, https://www.youtube.com/watch?v=v6XTx2Rg04g

Weinfuss, Josh. September 18, 2014. "Jonathan Dwyer Arrested, Deactivated." September 18, 2014. *ESPN NFL*. Accessed September 18, 2014, http://espn.go.com/nfl/story/_/id/11544985/jonathan-dwyer-arizona-cardinals-arrested-two-counts-suspicion-aggravated-assault

Wilson, Aaron. May 21, 2015. "Ray Rice's Domestic Violence Charges Dismissed by New Jersey Judge." *Baltimore Sun*. Accessed February 19, 2016, http://www.baltimoresun.com/sports/ravens/ravens-insider/bal-ray-rice-completes-pretrial-intervention-in-domestic-violence-case-in-new-jersey-charges-being-dismi-20150521-story.html

Worldometers. 2014. *Current World Population*. Accessed September 4, 2014, http://www.worldometers.info/world-population/

Glossary

Abortion – The intentional termination of a pregnancy through medical or surgical means, resulting in the death of the fetus.

Acquaintance rape – Sexual assault where the victim is somehow acquainted with the perpetrator.

Acute crisis phase – A phase that occurs immediately after the rape and can last for a few hours to a few weeks.

Administrative disciplinary procedures – When university campuses seek to determine whether conduct codes were violated.

Adoption and Safe Families Act (1997) – Requires termination of parental rights for children who have been in foster care for at least 15 months.

Age–crime curve – Those who commit crimes are more likely to be between the ages of 16 and 24, with criminal involvement tapering off thereafter over the life course.

Age-graded Theory of Crime – Theory put forth by Sampson and Laub in 1993 stating that when individuals establish quality bonds to employment or marriage that these bonds can foster desistance from crime.

Alcohol – A substance that can affect one's behavior; in the criminal justice system it can be associated with violent behavior or victimization.

Anti-abortion activism – Collective action by a group of individuals who challenged and attempted to overturn damage at the *Roe v. Wade* (1972) decision.

***Barefield v. Leach* (1974)** – Required institutions to provide equal opportunities for women who are incarcerated in regard to programming.

Bash boards – Online bulletin boards that demean a person or peer group with hateful comments.

Battered women defense – A defense used in court when a person is accused of a violent crime, particularly if the person killed a domestic partner or intimate who the defendant claims abused them physically, sexually, and/or emotionally. This defense's viability depends on the state's criminal law and legal defenses.

Battered women syndrome – Refers to when a woman is repeatedly physically, sexually, and/or emotionally abused by a spouse, and, due to fear for her life, kills her batterer.

Battered women syndrome defense – A defense used in court that the person accused of an assault or homicide was suffering from this syndrome at the material time. This defense's viability depends on the state's criminal law and legal defenses.

Battered women's shelters – Shelters that provide safe housing for women who were victims of domestic violence.

Biology theoretical perspective – The theory that biology has a direct role in contributing to criminal behavior.

Biosocial criminology – The theoretical traditions that both biology and environmental factors have a role in contributing to criminal behavior. Biosocial Theory of Sexual Victimization – Reflects on the interrelationships between macro- and micro-oriented theory and stems from the disciplines of biology and anthropology.

Bona fide occupational qualification (BFOQ) – Allowed employers to legally not hire a woman for a particular position if it was demonstrated they could not perform the particular duties of the job.

"Born criminal" – The idea that criminals are born, not made.

Buck v. Bell **(1927)** – The Supreme Court upheld the use of sterilization in Virginia, leading to a 17-year-old girl, Carrie Buck, being the first person in Virginia to be sterilized due to her alleged mental deficiencies and parental incapability.

Bystander intervention – A promising rape prevention strategy on college campuses that approaches women and men as potential witnesses to sexual violence and teaches them to intervene safely and effectively before, during, and after incidents of sexual victimization.

"Cautionary instruction" – Given by judges to sensitize jurors to the assumption that accusations of rape were easy to fabricate.

Center for Disease Control (CDC) – A federal agency that conducts and supports health promotion, prevention, and preparedness activities in the United States with the goal of improving overall public health.

Chicanery – A victim is tricked into divulging private secrets and publishing them online.

Chivalry thesis – A perspective that female offenders are treated more leniently in the criminal justice system due to chivalrous attitudes held by law enforcement and court officials.

Classical school of crime – Perspective put forth in the late 1700s that crime is deemed to be a rational choice and, thus, punishment for committing crimes should be swift and should be proportionate to the crime committed.

Clery Act – A law that requires all two-year and four-year colleges and universities to file annual reports with the federal government on campus crime, to make information available to prospect students and to develop prevention programs. Together, these regulations are also known as the Jeanne Clery Disclosure of Campus Security Policy and Campus Crime Statistics Act.

Co-correctional facilities – Institutions that house both women and men together in one facility.

Cognitive behavioral therapy – Identified as an effective treatment at reducing recidivism for offenders. This therapy seeks to change the cognition patterns of offenders, or "thinking errors" and alter negative behavioral patterns.

Commonwealth Franchise Act – An Act passed in 1901 in Australia that provided all women in Australia (except for some Aboriginal women) the right to vote.

Community corrections – Sentences that are served in the community.

Compulsory sterilization – Programs allowed by government policies that force people to undergo surgical sterilization.

Contemporary definition of rape – The unlawful penetration of a person against her/his will, by the use or threatened use of psychological coercion and/or physical force; forced sexual intercourse means vaginal, anal, or oral penetration by the offender. Rape also includes incidents where penetration is from a foreign object (e.g., a bottle), victimizations against male and female victims, and both heterosexual and homosexual rape. Attempted rape includes verbal threats of rape.

Cooper v. Morin **(1980)** – Prison administrators could no longer treat female prison inmates differently, thereby eliminating a tendency to treat female inmates in a disparate manner from male inmates.

Correctional programming – Established programs in prisons for women, also known as treatment programs.

Corroboration requirement – Requirement that additional evidence is needed besides victim testimony.

"Crack mothers" – Mothers who use cocaine or crack during their pregnancy.

Crime – An intentional act in violation of the criminal law committed without defense or excuse, and penalized by the state.

Criminal law – Laws that define particular acts as illegal.

Criminal sexual conduct – The elimination of the term "rape" by some states from their books to create a new crime category called sexual assault. Some states utilize language such as "criminal sexual conduct" and divide it into degrees of seriousness.

Criminology – The study of the causes of crime and criminal behavior.

Custodial – Women who committed felony violent and property crimes were sentenced to this type of institution. Custodial institutions housed offenders, required women to work on prison farms, and offered women inmates little to no rehabilitation programming.

Cyber drama – Spreading gossip online about a victim that is spread to a few persons and then stops.

Cybercrime forensic specialists – Experts who use computer and digital forensics to help fight cybercrime and can investigate allegations and collect evidence.

Cyberharassment – Repeated offensive messages.

Cyberstalking – Use of a personal online environment to repeatedly threaten the victim with harm and intimidation; the victim feels tremendously fearful and unsafe.

Cycle Theory of Violence – A theory that consists of three phases (tension building, explosion, and love contrition) to help explain violence within domestic relationships.

Declaration of Sentiments – An outline of the disenfranchisement of women in society by men through the articulation of 18 points, or sentiments.

Denigration – Putting the victim down and sending or posting untrue rumors and gossip.

Differential associations – The theory put forth by Sutherland that criminal behavior is learned and is learned from intimate personal groups in a process of communication.

Direct controls – Parental supervision of children (e.g., exerting discipline) while they are in their presence.

Disenfranchisement – To deprive someone of a right or privilege or to strip a person of his/her power.

Doctrine of coverture – A legal doctrine that stated that, when married, a woman's legal rights and obligations were absorbed by those of her husband.

Domestic violence – Involves violent, aggressive, or extremely controlling behavior perpetrated within a domestic relationship against any partner, whether gay or straight, and regardless of marital status, age, socio-economic status, or gender.

Dothard v. Rawlinson **(1977)** – Brought specific attention to job discrimination. The Supreme Court ruled that height and weight restrictions were discriminatory. However, the court upheld that some positions in male institutions do qualify for bona fide occupational qualification.

Double discrimination – Discrimination against both gender and race or gender and sexual orientation.

Economic abuse – The abusive control over another person's finances and not allowing a person to work to earn a living or get an education. It can also include the withholding of a person's work visa or passport.

Eighth Amendment – Prohibits excessive bail, excessive imposed fines, and infliction of cruel and unusual punishment.

Eligibility of Women Act – Passed in 1918, this act permitted women to be elected to Parliament in the United Kingdom.

Email and cell phone image dissemination – Sending a pornographic or sexual image to a victim and then resending it to others within a social network.

Email threats and dissemination – Posting a message to a victim and spreading it to others.

Embezzlement – Stealing of funds from an account that a person has been entrusted to oversee, such as a financial account for a school, business, or the government.

Emotional abuse – Psychological and verbal abuse displayed by intimidation and threats.

England v. Dallas **(1990)** – Brought attention to the plight of lesbian applicants and paved the way for lesbians to be hired by police departments.

Enlightenment – A philosophy based on the belief that "all" people were born with inalienable rights to life, liberty, and property/happiness.

Equal Employment Opportunity Act of 1972 – Sought to strengthen Title VII of the Civil Rights Act of 1964 by again asserting that those seeking employment should be treated fairly and should not be discriminated against based on their race, sex, religion, color, or national origin.

Equal Employment Opportunity Program – Instituted policies such as affirmative action and offered assistance to those who may have been discriminated against.

Equal Pay Act of 1963 – Required that men and women be given equal pay for equal work.

Ethnocentric – Pride in one's race/ethnicity.

Eugenics – Efforts to use science to improve the characteristics of a population.

Evidentiary rules – Rules of evidence to provide guidance of what is or is not admissible in a court of law.

Exclusion – Keeping a person out of an online group.

Exposure – Posting or sending material about a person that was meant to be kept private, including images that are sexual.

Family and Medical Leave Act of 1993 – Requires that employers provide 12 weeks of leave to new mothers and also requires employers to hold the position for the woman upon her return from leave.

Federal government – A union of states under a central government distinct from the individual governments of the separate states.

Federal prisons – These house women convicted of crimes that violate federal laws, such as bank fraud, embezzlement, extortion, or drug trafficking.

Federal Welfare Law (1996) – Prohibits states from allowing ex-offenders with drug-related felony convictions to receive any form of welfare benefits, including food stamps for a lifetime.

Feminist criminology – A branch of study within the field of criminology that seeks to understand women who offend, victimization that impacts women, and women who work in the criminal justice system.

Feminist theory – Specific theories or perspectives that offer explanations for female offending, victimization, or gender inequality.

Feminist Theory/Theories of Rape and Sexual Victimization – Centered on sexual victimization from a feminist perspective, it is one of the most significant theories that has driven much of the research and anti-rape activism that has flourished over the past several decades.

Flaming – Angry, rude, or vulgar text or email message.

Focal Concerns Theory – Holds that judges, who are often backlogged with cases, are under pressure to resolve cases as quickly as possible to avoid further delay in the court system.

Fourteenth Amendment – The right to privacy.

Fourth Amendment – Protects the right of people to be secure in their persons, houses, papers, and effects, as well as against unreasonable searches, seizures, and warrants that are not based on probable cause.

Gang – A group of three or more individuals that share an identity and often engage in criminal activity.

Gender – Not biologically based, but culturally based. A product of social interactions and factors, such as the role or position a person has in society, as well as the identity that he/she has formed.

Gender discrimination – A prejudice or discrimination that is based on a person's sex.

Gender disparity – Differences in criminal sentencing due to gender.

Gender neutral – Something that is applied to both male and female genders.

Gender-responsive programming – Programming that meets the specific needs of women.

Gender segregation in the legal profession – Inequity in the legal profession; women lawyers are relegated to less prestigious and less profitable positions.

General Theory of Crime (GTC) – The theory put forth by Gottfredson and Hirschi that crime will occur when an individual with low self-control is exposed to a criminal opportunity.

Glass ceiling – The invisible barrier that blocks working women from advancing into senior positions in the workplace.

Glover v. Johnson **(1979)** – Ruling that the lack of programming (e.g., vocational, education, and rehabilitation) that women inmates were receiving was inadequate. It required that state prisons provide equal programming opportunities for incarcerated females and males.

Grand jury – A selected group of citizens who have been summoned and assigned to examine and inquire on criminal complaints and decide if a trial is warranted. If a trial is found warranted, an indictment is issued.

Griefing – Cyberbullying that is intended to cause the victim or the victim's peers to feel grief, or to keep a victim out of an interactive game.

Griggs v. Duke Power Company **(1971)** – The court ruled that businesses, including the police profession, cannot establish a policy that has a detrimental impact on the hiring of a particular group in society.

Group battering programs – Treatment programs for men and women who have abused their partners, be it physically, verbally, sexually, psychologically, or by another form of abuse.

Group therapy – Under the supervision of a therapist, patients meet in a group to describe and discuss their problems together.

Happy slapping – Posting of an embarrassing video or a video of a physical assault of a victim in an online or social network site.

Hate crimes – Crimes directed at another person based on his/her race, color, religion, national origin, gender, sexual orientation, gender orientation, and/or disability.

"Hidden rape victim" – Refers to circumstances of victimization that would meet the legal definition of rape, but where victims would respond "no" to questions about whether they had been raped.

Image and video – Posting videos and images of a victim on YouTube or other public web space.

Immunity – The act of being granted legal protection or exemption from legal liability.

Impersonation – Pretending to be a victim and posting materials which make that person look bad.

Impunity – Exemption from punishment or freedom from the injurious consequences of an action.

Incidence of rape – A way of thinking about victimization by estimating the percentage of people who are sexually victimized during a specified time period.

Index 1 crimes – The FBI reports on an annual basis the number of arrests for eight index crimes (homicide, burglary, robbery, rape, aggravated assault, larceny-theft, arson, motor vehicle theft).

Indiana Women's Prison – Opened in 1873, this prison was the first female-only institution.

Indict – To issue a formal charge for a felony offense.

Indirect controls – The control that parents have over their children while they are not in their presence (e.g., the children desist from certain behaviors due to fear of punishment or parental disapproval).

Individual therapy – A process in which clients work one-on-one with a trained therapist.

Inmate code – The system of norms, values, language, and attitudes all prisoners are expected to follow.

Instant messaging – Using IM to send harassing messages or messages filled with hate towards a targeted victim.

Institutionalization – The process whereby the prisoner learns the formal rules of the correctional institution.

Institutionalized persons – Prison and mental hospital inmates.

Interactive game harassment – The use of profane and harassing language to persons playing interactive games over the internet.

Intergenerational Transmission of Violence Theory – Theory that focuses on the influence that their environments, especially childhood environments, have on men who become rapists.

Intersectionality – The interconnected nature of social categorizations such as race, class, and gender as they apply to a given individual or group, regarded as creating overlapping and interdependent systems of discrimination or disadvantage.

Intimate partner violence (IPV) – Physical, sexual, or psychological harm by a current or former partner or spouse.

Involuntary sterilization – A procedure that both men and women have been forced to undergo without their consent that makes them unable to conceive children.

Jim Crow laws – Laws from 1876 to 1965 that resulted in racial segregation of African-Americans and in discriminatory practices against African-Americans.

Jurisdiction – The official power to make legal decisions and judgments.

Labeling Theory – This perspective holds that labels are stigmatizing – particularly deviant or criminal labels. These labels may affect self-concept and result in individuals engaging in crime.

Lawrence v. Texas **(2003)** – A ruling by the US Supreme Court that declared that state statutes criminalizing sodomy were unconstitutional.

Laws – Recognized by a particular country, county, or community as a system of rules that regulate or control particular actions of its members by enforcing consequences or penalties if broken.

Liberation hypothesis – The suggestion by Freda Adler in the mid-1970s that the liberation of women in US society would allow women to enter the workforce in greater numbers and, hence, these women would now have more opportunities to engage in crime.

Life course – This perspective holds that researchers should examine offending patterns over the life span of an individual.

Macro-oriented theories – Theories that look at societies or cultures as the entities that set the stage for sexual violence.

Male Peer Support Theory – A theory which posits that social support from peers is instrumental in perpetuating woman abuse.

Manifeste des 10 – An Act passed in 1996 in France that required equal representation of women in politics.

Marital exemption – Based on the definition of rape, this implied that a man could not be arrested for raping his wife.

Marital rape – Any unwanted intercourse or sexual penetration obtained by force, the threat of force, or the lack of consent between a marital couple.

Marital rape exemption – A law that permitted a man to rape his wife.

Marriage restriction laws – Laws that restricted two parties from marrying if they were not "healthy" or "intelligent."

Maximum classified prisons – Prison system classification whereby security is the chief concern and inmate movement is restricted.

Medium classified prisons – Prison classification whereby security is a concern, inmate movement is less restricted, and rehabilitations programs can be found.

"Men Against Women" – An organization created by several men in the Los Angeles Police Department in the 1980s to harass and intidimate their female colleagues in an attempt to compel them to quit.

Mental health – The mental state of an individual. Many incarcerated women and those in the community corrections sector suffer from mental health issues and are in need of help.

Micro-oriented theories – These seek to differentiate – at the individual level – between those who would be prone to commit an act of sexual violence from those who would not.

Minimum classified prisons – Prison classification whereby security is less of a concern, inmate movement is less restricted, and rehabilitations programs can be found.

Misdemeanors – Less serious crimes that carry lower levels of punishment.

"Mommy track" – Mothers who work part-time to raise a family are believed to remove themselves from vertical mobility within a business, firm, or company.

Mules – Those who carry/smuggle drugs.

National Crime Victimization Survey (NCVS) – Administered by the Bureau of Justice Statistics, this survey collects information from victims on non-fatal violent and property crimes, reported and not reported to the police, against persons aged 12 or older from a nationally representative sample of US households.

National Incidence Based Reporting System – An incident-based reporting system for crimes known to the police.

National Violence Against Women Survey (NVAWS) – A survey that examines the safety of women both inside and outside of the home, such as perceptions of fear of sexual harassment, sexual violence, physical violence, and threats by strangers, dates/boyfriends, other known men, husbands, and common-law partners.

Natural law – A body of unchanging moral principles regarded as a basis for all human conduct.

Newgate Prison – A prison in London featured in Elizabeth Fry's book in 1827, highlighting the atrocities experienced by incarcerated women at this prison.

Offender reentry – The process of ex-offenders' reentry and reintegration into society after incarceration.

Order of protection – A civil, not criminal, proceeding that generally results in the perpetrator being restricted from seeing, calling, texting, or emailing the victim for a brief period of time.

Parenting programs – Programs offered at various female prison institutions whereby the female is allowed to keep her child with her while she is incarcerated and she takes part in intensive parenting activities to assist her in parenting effectively.

Password theft lockout – Stealing the victim's password and pretending to be the victim while sending provocative messages or images.

Pathways – These refer to the life-course trajectories that individuals follow across their life span.

Patriarchal – It is argued by feminists that most societies are male dominated and that most social institutions within societies are designed to perpetuate and maintain this male dominance.

Permeable – The barrier between the pregnant woman and developing fetus, but it is susceptible to substances that the pregnant woman consumes, inhales, or injects. A membrane or material that allows liquids, gases, or other substances to pass through it.

Phishing – Tricking a victim to reveal information about himself/herself and then disseminating it online, or using the victim's password to engage in unauthorized postings or purchases.

Phobias – Intense fears, including fear of objects or settings that victims associate with the rape, such as a weapon or the location where the rape occurred.

Physical abuse – This ranges from mild forms of physical force (e.g., pushing, shoving, pinching, excessive tickling, throwing objects at a person) to serious forms of force (e.g., use of a weapon, stalking, choking, punching) that can result in serious bodily injury or the death of the victim.

Police culture – Attitudes and values within the policing profession that officers internalize in the police socialization process, which begins in the training academy.

Police matrons – Women hired to handle and oversee women and girls held in custody in either jails or prisons.

Policy implications – Policies that can be implemented to combat a social problem.

Pornography and marketing list inclusion – Signing a child victim up to receive numerous emails and instant messages from pornographic websites and marketing lists.

Positivist school of crime – Crime thought to be due to some individual difference such as biology or intelligence.

Post-traumatic stress disorder (PTSD) – A disorder that can develop after a person is exposed to one or several traumatic events (e.g., serious injury, sexual assault, or warfare).

Power-control Theory – Explicitly focuses on the criminality of women and is a theory that contributes to better understanding why men commit more crime than women.

Prevalence of rape victimization – A way to look at the scale of rape by estimating the total number of individuals who have been victims at some point in their lives.

Primary deviance – Norm violations or crimes that an individual commits are quickly forgotten and do not affect their self-concept.

Primary prevention – Refers to working to reduce the incidence of a problem within the entire population.

Prison matron – The name given to early female workers who worked in jails and prisons.

Prisonization – The process of inmates adjusting to prison and their eventual acceptance of both the formal and informal rules.

Probation – A punishment served in the community in lieu of a jail or prison sentence.

Projet de loi du 15 mars 1983 – An Act passed in France that prohibits discrimination based on sex.

Protocol to Prevent, Suppress and Punish Trafficking in Persons, especially Women and Children (2003) – An Act passed to address trafficking by seeking punishment for perpetrators and protecting victims.

Pseudo-families – Female cliques formed in female correctional institutions. Members of the family network adopt roles such as the mother figure or sister figure and provide female inmates with protection from other inmates.

Pseudonym – A false name – for example, used online to hide a person's identity from his/her victim.

Psychopathological explanation – An approach to thinking of rapists as having inherited or developed one or more forms of mental illness or psychological pathology. This explanation focuses on what personality factors or mental illness would make individuals possessing these traits more likely to commit violence.

Qualitative – The purpose of this type of research is to accomplish a more detailed understanding of a specific organization or event, rather than a generalized description of a large sample of population.

Rape of children – Both boys and girls are victimized by sexual assault, virtually always by individuals known to them and often in situations in which both the children and family members view the adult as trustworthy.

Rape crisis centers – Centers that offer rape victims support regarding medical and legal systems, trained and knowledgeable advocates to accompany victims to medical and legal appointments or court appearances, and group counseling to assist victims with their emotional distress.

"Rape culture" – A culture that leads rape victims to be treated differently from victims of other crimes and characterized as supporting rape myths.

Rape kit – In order to collect evidence after a rape has occurred, this kit includes materials and instructions to help nurses and doctors handle physical evidence in the course of performing an extremely invasive physical examination.

Rape laws – State and federal laws that apply to acts of sexual assault.

Rape in the military – Sexual victimization that happens in the armed forces and military institutions. Victims are frequently penalized, ostracized, and prompted to terminate their military careers while their assailants remain.

Rape myths – False beliefs about rape.

Rape shield laws – Laws that protect rape victims from being identified in the media, but also from having to undergo a form of sexual interrogation by defense attorneys when testifying in court.

"Rape trauma syndrome" – The combination of symptoms that can develop in the aftermath of rape, such as extensive adverse cognitive, affective, behavioral, and physiological effects.

Rape among vulnerable populations – Rape occurring to vulnerable women in society, such as street prostitutes, incarcerated women, elderly women, and poor immigrant women.

Reformatory – Women who had committed public order offenses such as prostitution, premarital sex, and adultery were sentenced to reformatories. At reformatories, women would participate in rehabilitation programming and were trained in domestic skills.

Reorganization or recoil phase – Victims may experience guilt or self-blame, a phase that can last for months or even years.

Representation of the People Act – Passed in 1928, this Act permitted all women the right to vote.

Restorative justice – A process of conflict resolution that brings together all parties, such as offenders and their families, victims and their families, other members of the community, and professionals, affected by harm or wrongdoing.

Restorative justice programs – This approach views community members' participation in coping with the fallout from the criminal act as critical and stresses the importance of dialogue between offenders and community members about the harm caused by the crime and what can be done to repair the damage.

Right of privacy – A person's right not to be the subject of a search or seizure without probable cause or a warrant.

Roe v. Wade **(1973)** – A landmark decision that underscored women's rights regarding matters of their reproduction, while continuing to consider the issue of the fetus' potential for human life.

Rome Statute of the International Criminal Court (ICC) – A treaty that established the International Criminal Court and created four international crimes: genocide, crimes against humanity, war crimes, and crimes of aggression.

Safer Internet Day – A day that encourages an international activity to bring awareness to cyberbullying.

Screen name mirroring – Creating a screen name that is similar to a victim's screen name so as to create confusion.

"Second assault" – Victims can be reluctant to report rape to authorities to avoid resistance, skepticism, or rudeness and feeling as if they have been assaulted again.

"Second rape" – Victims of rape might experience this feeling if a case went to court and the victim experienced aggressive questioning by the defense or was forced to reveal his/her prior sexual history.

Secondary deviance – A deviant and/or criminal act comes to the attention of significant others such as friends or family members or formal social control agents, such as police, who then apply a negative label.

Secondary prevention – A prevention process whereby professionals attempt to identify individuals or organizations at high risk of the problem and then develop strategies to reduce these factors.

Self-control – A key component of Gottfredson and Hirschi's General Theory of Crime whereby individuals possess behaviors such as impulsivity, risk taking, and the need for immediate gratification.

Self-report surveys – Administered by researchers, respondents are asked about the number of crimes that they committed over a specific time period.

Sending malicious code – Sending malware or viruses to a victim; usually perpetrators are skilled in advanced computing technology.

Seneca Falls Convention – The first women's rights convention, held in New York in 1848.

Serious crimes – These are crimes that have a significant impact on the victim – that is, loss of life or severe physical and/or emotional trauma.

Sex – A determination made through the application of socially agreed-upon biological criteria for classifying males and females.

Sex crimes – These crimes refer to crimes that are sexual in nature in terms of motivation or victimization.

Sex Discrimination Act – An Act passed in 1975 in the United Kingdom that prohibited sex discrimination in employment and education.

Sex role socialization – It is argued by feminists that the mechanisms of teaching boys and girls from the youngest age to confirm to appropriate sex roles results in males and females having very different perspectives on sex, love, and affection.

Sex-segregated prisons – Prisons that may house both men and women, but they are kept separate from one another.

Sex trafficking – Girls and women forced into prostitution.

Sexting – Inducing a person to send sexual pictures which can then be distributed to others.

Sexual abuse – The forced sexual assault or rape of a person, including pressure to have sexual relations when a partner does not want to consent.

Sexual assault nurse examiners (SANE) – Individuals who provide emotional support and compassionate medical care to rape victims while keeping in mind the legal requirements to retain the necessary chain of evidence.

Sexual harassment – Unwelcome sexual advances, requests for sexual favors, and other verbal or physical harassment of a sexual nature.

Sexual objects in the mass media – In media outlets, the presentation or depiction of women as sexual objects to be desired and conquered; this has been identified by scholars as a contributor to rape.

Sexual selection – Part of the Biosocial Theory of Sexual Victimization and a process whereby human females and males have evolved different physiological and psychological attributes.

Shackling – The use of metal and plastic devices to restrict an inmate's ability to move freely.

Sharia courts – Based on Muslim law that comes from core principles in the Koran and governs the law in many Muslim cultures.

Situational factors – When examining a female intimate partner homicide in which a male is the victim, factors surrounding the event emerge that may explain the woman's use of lethal force.

Skinner v. Oklahoma **(1942)** – The Supreme Court ruled against the compulsory sterilization law, resulting in sterilization laws being repealed in most states.

Smith v. Fairman **(1982)** – The courts ruled that searches of male inmates by female guards did not violate their constitutional rights.

Social control theoretical perspective – This perspective refers to the various social control perspectives that view criminal behavior to be the result of the absence of bonds or due to a latent trait.

Social Feminist Theory – The theory that examines the gendered social organizations of men and women within the context of capitalism in the United States.

Sodomy laws – These stem from a religious foundation, prohibiting deviant sexual acts such as anal intercourse.

***Somers v. Thurman* (1983)** – The courts ruled that male inmates could not claim that body cavity searches by female guards violated their right to privacy.

State prisons – Institutions that hold convicted felons.

Statutory rape – Sexual contact between an adult and another person, or a minor, who is below a required legal age to consent to the sexual contact.

Stereotype – A thought or belief that does not reflect reality, but is a widely held, fixed, and oversimplified image or idea of a particular type of person.

Stigmatizes – Regards or describes in a strongly disapproving manner.

Strain theoretical perspectives – These perspectives refer to the various strain theories that posit that individuals may commit crime due to inability to achieve goals.

Suffrage movement – An organized movement established to advocate the right for women to vote.

Surgical-center standards – Abortion clinics are required to meet these standards, meaning that all abortions, including nonsurgical procedures, are required to be performed in hospital-style operating rooms.

Tertiary prevention – Relapse prevention in an effort to prevent a problem behavior from recurring once it has taken place.

Text wars and text attacks – Group of bullies gang up on a victim by sending hundreds of emails or text messages to the victim.

Therapeutic programming – Used for helping drug offenders both within and outside of prison, it has been shown by research to lower rates of drug relapse and criminal recidivism.

Title VII of the Civil Rights Act of 1964 – Prohibits employer discrimination on the bases of race and color, as well as national origin, sex, and religion.

Title IX – Title IX of the Education Amendments of 1972 states that no person shall "on the basis of sex, be excluded from participation in, be denied the benefits of, or be subjected to discrimination" in an educational program supported by the federal government. The Clery Act is enforced through this Act.

Tokenism – A minimal gesture made by a policy or practice toward the inclusion of members of minority groups.

Trafficking Victims Protection Act (2000) – Passed in an effort to combat the human trafficking around the world.

Transgender inmates – Inmates who may biologically belong to one sex but identify as the other.

Transgendered – Those who identify as a member of the opposite sex.

Turf protection – Establishing neighborhood boundaries and protecting those established boundaries.

"Unborn victims of violence act" – Laws in which fetuses at any state of development may be treated as legal victims if they are harmed or killed during the commission of certain state or federal crimes.

Uniform Crime Reports – Published each year by the Federal Bureau of Investigation and report on the number of arrests, as reported to police.

"Utmost resistance" – Stipulated by the legal system that a woman must exhibit this type of resistance in order to be believed as a credible victim.

U-Visa – A visa for immigrant victims of violence to stay in the United States.

Violence Against Women Act (VAWA) – An Act that was passed in 1994 that allocated federal funding to the investigation and prosecution of violent crimes against women and protects victims of domestic violence.

Voting/polling booths – Online polls created to embarrass persons by allowing others to vote on derogatory titles such as "ugliest" or "most promiscuous."

Waiting periods – As legislated by 26 states, there is generally a 24-hour waiting period between the time that women receive pre-abortion counseling and when they may receive the procedure.

Warning wars – Making a false allegation against a victim that she/he is posting illicit information so that an internet provider will issue a warning or suspend the victim from service.

Website creation – Creating a website that is designed to demean and belittle a victim or a peer group.

White-collar crimes – Crimes committed within the workplace including occupations such as banking.

World Health Organization – A specialized agency of the United Nations concerned with international public health.

Index

Note: Bold page numbers refer to the glossary.

Women, Crime, and Justice, First Edition. By Elaine Gunnison, Frances P. Bernat, and Lynne Goodstein.
© 2017 John Wiley & Sons, Ltd. Published 2017 by John Wiley & Sons, Ltd.

Indexer: Dr Laurence Errington